CW01465586

THE PERFECT PREY

Translated by Donald Gardner, Sam Herman, Richard Jurgens
and Annie Wright

Jeroen Smit

THE PERFECT PREY

2009 Prometheus Amsterdam

Original title *De prooi. Blinde trots breekt* ABN *Amro*
© 2008 Jeroen Smit
© 2009 Translation Uitgeverij Prometheus, Donald Gardner, Sam Herman,
Richard Jurgens and Annie Wright
Cover design Mart Boudestein and Robbie Smits
Cover illustration Sylvia Weve
Author's photo Bob Bronshoff
www.uitgeverijprometheus.nl
ISBN 978 90 446 1293 6

Contents

Foreword

Why has Holland's leading international bank been reduced to a mere shadow? For 183 years, ABN Amro and its predecessors were the driving force of the Dutch economy. The nation's flagship. This was where the best bankers were trained; ABN Amro carved out new terrain for Dutch companies abroad. Its green and yellow logo gave Dutch travellers a sense of pride in cities around the world.

Until recently, ABN Amro catered to millions of private customers and hundreds of thousands of companies. It was at the heart of financial networks in the Netherlands and, to a lesser extent, United States, Brazil and Asia.

ABN Amro made huge profits. In 2006, it cleared 4.7 billion euros. In the seventeen years after ABN and Amro merged, profits rose by an average of 16 per cent a year. Turnover grew from five to almost 23 billion euros. Its workforce practically doubled to 108,000.

Yet despite its size and growth, in recent years the bank had lost its sense of direction. Analysts, shareholders, customers and later even its own employees voiced a deafening chorus of doubt regarding the bank's leadership and policy; hardly anyone believed in its strategy any more.

In the spring of 2007, I set out with a completely open mind to find out why it was that ABN Amro had foundered. As in my previous book about another Dutch corporate giant, Ahold, I wanted to create an accurate and accessible reconstruction. One based around the stories of those directly involved.

This reconstruction begins in 1990, when two bitter rivals, ABN and Amro, the two Dutch banks with the biggest high-street profile, merged. They joined forces because both banks burned with ambition to be global leaders. For years, ABN Amro was one of the predators in a banking world that was consolidating, in which efficiency and economy of scale went hand in hand.

But then the predator became the prey. ABN Amro was now fair game. After a vicious struggle, in October 2007 a consortium comprising Royal Bank of Scotland, Fortis and Banco Santander paid 71 billion euros to split the bank into three. No bank had ever cost that much money.

Why had the predator become the prey? Over the last eighteen months I asked that question to 12 (former) governors, 17 (former) members of the managing board, 43 (former) general managers and department managers and a handful of ABN Amro's consultants. With some, I spoke more than once. I also spoke to over 30 managing directors and (president) governors of other banks (including various members of the managing boards and supervisory boards of Fortis and ING), politicians, supervisors and one or two civil servants.

In all, I conducted 133 off-the-record interviews with people who had played key roles between 1990 and 2007. Managing directors who had taken important decisions, or should have done. Off-the-record means that no one is quoted directly. This reconstruction is written from the perspective of the omniscient author.

Almost without exception, the demise of ABN Amro had left these men angry, sad, disappointed and frustrated. The interviews resulted in over 900 pages of personal reconstructions and subjective truths. As Douwe Draaisma, professor of history of psychology in Groningen, points out, 'Memory helps us safely through time'.

Each conversation began with the same question. Why has the bank disappeared? And ended with the same question. What should I not leave out of this reconstruction at any cost? In the end, it was ABN Amro's defective management and flawed governors that drew the spotlight in almost every conversation. Many of those I spoke to admitted their own share of the blame, however cautiously. This story is therefore about the bankers who ran ABN Amro, most particularly about Rijkman Groenink, the man who sat on the managing board for almost twenty years, the last seven as its chairman.

More than anything, this book reflects those interviews. By comparing the various personal observations and interpretations, and placing them in chronological context, I have tried to make this reconstruction as accurate as possible. It is a version of the truth that most of those involved will, I hope, be able to recognise and acknowledge.

I have done my best to avoid mistakes. As many of the facts as possible were checked and all kinds of situations and opinions were referred in dozens of interviews to the people involved. In these conversions I often disclosed parts of my reconstruction and asked those involved to point out anything they might consider incorrect.

There were a few instances in which key players blatantly contradicted one another. In most cases I have left it that way. In one case I had to decide which truth to follow. I chose the truth that seemed most likely in the overall context.

As the conversations continued and heads nodded, I became increasingly confident about committing the story to print. I apologise if, despite all this, there are any factual or other errors in the book.

ABN Amro, or what remains of it, never opposed my attempts to speak to the principal players in this drama at any time. In one of two instances (former) employees of the bank even helped me contact people I wanted to interview.

I would like to thank everyone I spoke to for their time, their honesty, the piles of confidential material that they gave me and above all the trust they have shown. For many it was the need to draw lessons from the collapse of this financial institution that prompted their candour. Lessons about how managing directors, governors, supervisors and politicians do their work. Lessons that apply across the board in corporate Holland.

I would also like to thank advertising designer and friend Eugène Roorda, who convinced me that the cover could be much better, and his colleague and art director Mart Boudestein for the design. My gratitude also to Peter Boer for sifting through the photos.

My thanks to my good friend and specialist on financial matters Hans Horn for his pointed and constructive criticism. And my thanks to one of the best sparring partners around, who prefers to remain anonymous, for his support from the sidelines. This wise man, an expert on ABN Amro, helped me correct and put situations and sketches of individuals into perspective.

Above all, I would like to thank my wife Doret and my breathtaking sons Jack and Rover for the patience they showed to their husband and father, who spent far too little time with them while engaged in this project.

This book is dedicated to Johan and Sarah; they taught me that the most important thing is to become who you are.

From Predator to Prey

24 October 1987–5 September 2007

Rijkman Groenink was a hunter. That bright Saturday morning in October, the Amro banker decided to go duck shooting. Together with his hunting companion, he was bobbing gently on the water, close to the Wieringermeer polder, in North Holland. His loaded rifle was pointing down.

Groenink enjoyed the excitement of hunting. The risks and the result, the intense flavour of the meat that you've shot yourself. He couldn't stand not shooting if he went hunting; he hated coming home empty-handed. The 38-year-old banker only played games he could win. Whatever he did, he had to excel.

His bank had experienced some major difficulties that past week. On the nineteenth of October bourses around the world had collapsed. Share prices had fallen so fast, analysts were describing it as the worst financial crisis since 1929. On Black Monday, Amro's drop of 28 per cent had been over twice as bad as the rest of the shares on Amsterdam's stock exchange. The explanation was simple. Amro had invested almost twice as much in securities as ABN, its nearest rival.

Groenink remained unaffected by the panic that engulfed his fellow managing directors. The world of shares and bourses was not his immediate concern. It didn't really interest him. Yet the longer the problems persisted, the more chance they'd eventually land on his desk. As general manager of corporate business he was answerable to the managing board and responsible for the department of special credit.

For years, Groenink had been in charge of the bank's high-risk credit department; assessing what chance Amro's chronically sick clients had of actually staying alive. And whether they were sufficiently reliable to be given one last opportunity. His interest, the bank's interest, had been his criterion.

As a lawyer, he enjoyed this game. He was extremely good at judging how far to humour a client's often desperate reasoning, balancing on the edge of bankruptcy. As a specialist, he could analyse the various positions precisely and test the boundaries of the possible. He loved to explore areas that others never dared enter, or were incapable of entering. That's where he found his inspiration to attack, often in surprising ways.

The two hunting companions hardly talked. Silent and concentrated, they scoured the mist, searching for the scout. Once they saw that first duck fly overhead they knew the rest would follow. That's when they'd strike. In a split second they would have to load, aim and fire.

Groenink liked it here. This confrontation with the elements was how he recharged his batteries. He needed this, because he worked long weeks. Very long; a hundred hours a week was no exception. Here, far away from his complex dossiers, he could relax in absolute calm. Surrounded by people, he was always on his guard.

He resented owing his successes to other people's unpredictable talents. When out hunting, his success depended solely on his own powers of concentration and response. Groenink was a loner. He preferred the outdoors to people.

That day the hunters had no luck. By the time the sun rose, not a shot had been fired. There were ducks. Plenty in fact. But they made off before a rifle could be raised. The men decided to call it a day. They unloaded their guns. Slowly, they chugged to shore.

On their way back they saw a group of ducks lying on the water. His companion motioned to Groenink to try just one more time. He loaded the shot back into his rifle. But once again, the birds flew off before he could shoot.

As his companion returned the boat, Rijkman Groenink went over to his van. Opening the door, he placed the rifle on the ground. That's when it happened. With a single crack the rifle let off two shots: hundreds of lead pellets fired from below straight through his arm, just above the elbow.

Groenink screamed. Blood spurted through the sleeve of his wax coat. The hunter knew that his artery had been cut: a huge piece of his right arm must have been torn apart. He cried out with pain, but understood immediately that if he didn't keep a cool head he might not survive this accident.

He ran to a nearby farmhouse and rang the bell. A woman answered, taken aback by the man at the door, screaming and gushing blood. But she acted fast. Grabbing a tea towel and a coat hanger, she tied off Groenink's arm. She bound the tea towel with the coat hanger tight enough to stem the blood.

The woman took Groenink to a doctor, who quickly sent him on to the nearest hospital in the town of Hoorn. All the while, the young banker remained fully conscious. Gingerly, he tried to feel into the sleeve of his coat. Where was his arm? How much of it was left?! Without the coat, the shot would have severed his entire arm. He realised that he still ran the risk of losing it, the arm that did everything. He wasn't going to let that happen.

At the hospital, Groenink warned the doctors as they rushed to examine him. "Whatever you do, the arm stays." And with that, he collapsed.

Rijkman Willem Johan Groenink was born on 25 August 1949 in Den Helder, to a Protestant family. He was the eldest of three. His unusual first name – literally Richman – was a Groenink tradition; his grandfather had also been called Rijkman.

He enjoyed a happy childhood in Hilversum. His father was a schoolteacher and came from respectable Frisian middle-class stock. Groenink Senior's passions were intellectual debate and chess. Mother came from Amsterdam; she ran the household. She was a strong woman; decisive. Her son used to call her an adoring tigress. It was his mother who encouraged him to achieve, and she would often tell him: get busy. He was never as close to his father who took little interest in the ups and downs of family life. It irritated Groenink that his father showed little ambition in his career, hardly seemed to care. He couldn't understand that.

At school, he made a handful of friends. These were to be lifelong friendships. They listened to Bob Dylan, Eric Clapton and Crosby, Stills, Nash & Young. Groenink could often be found on the tennis court and developed into a proficient tennis player. He played football occasionally, but found it too rough, too physical. Then the young Groenink took up volleyball.

In the third form at Christian Lyceum, he started going out with Lucia Rodenburg. Her father was on the Philips board; in the 1970s he became the first from outside the Philips family to lead the company. His career intrigued the young Groenink.

After failing his final exams, Groenink switched to the municipal college, passing gymnasium alfa – languages and humanities. There was no chance he could study medicine; he considered law, history and literature. He kept his options open and enrolled at Utrecht University. There he joined the Utrecht student fraternity.

Inspired by his girlfriend's father, Groenink decided to follow his law degree by taking a business administration course at Manchester Business School. There he acquired a fascination for complex financial questions. He enjoyed figuring out the best ways for companies to finance their activities. He turned out to be good at it.

In 1974, he decided to look for a job in the corporate sector. But after a couple of interviews he was so disappointed by the mediocrity of the people he met that he reset his sights to two specific banks. He applied to both; the two banks with the highest profile in the country: ABN and Amro. His conversation with the Amro recruiter went better than the rather distant impression he received from the ABN representative.

Both banks made him an offer. Groenink was disappointed that ABN wanted him for their domestic division; he had wanted to be a part of their famous overseas operation. Yet ABN was the bank with which he and his family had banked for years. He wavered, tossed a coin and was happy when fate chose Amro. At 25, Groenink was grateful that the coin hadn't sent him to ABN. At Amro it soon became obvious that the new trainee was going places.

At the end of the compulsory Working as a Team course, the new trainees were asked what their dream was. One described a nice house, the other mentioned a caravan, a third talked about living a happy family life. Finally, Groenink, unable to contain his irritation, dismissed the answers of the other trainees as either false or hypocritical. If you came to work at Amro, he said, your ambition had to be to reach the top of the company. That's what he wanted: to be the boss.

Trainees who started working for the bank around the same time soon realised that Groenink's career would not be an average career. Towards the end of his first year, the managing board invited him to defend a report which he had helped write. Board member Henk Talma Stheeman was impressed and asked him to become his personal assistant. All the managing directors had a PA to do various kinds of jobs. Groenink enjoyed being able to look behind the scenes and see how the board worked, the board on which he aimed to be sitting in the shortest possible time.

Thirteen years later he was well on his way. Groenink loved the bank; the bank loved him. In the intervening years he had been deployed in the field that had fascinated him from the start: finance. More specifically, and almost exclusively, financing companies in trouble. And Amro had plenty of those.

His first major assignment came in 1979, from board member Hans Foppe. He asked him to refloat a loan of 500 million dollars to a Norwegian shipping company, Havtor, that had stranded. He succeeded. Credit specialist Foppe was delighted by his keen analytical mind and noticed that Groenink could quickly grasp the essence of extremely complex issues. Moreover, he was a tough opponent when negotiating.

That was just what Amro needed in the years that followed; these were the hardest years in the bank's history. The Dutch economy was going through a difficult period, with many on the brink of defaulting. And it was noticeable that these credits were often loans that Amro had provided. At ABN, they were enjoying their arch rival's predicament. Every time they had been beaten to a client, they had complained that Amro's cowboys took far too many risks. This was payback.

Groenink was deployed to limit the damage as far as possible. When companies found themselves in trouble, it was his job to make sure the bank didn't lose out. He did his work well. Groenink won most of his fights.

People who sat at the negotiating table with Groenink in those years learned to fear him. His boyish appearance often caught his protagonists off guard. Few could match his ability to listen and sympathise as the clients told their story, and then suddenly twist round to focus on the bank's interest. It left the client stunned.

In the early 1980s, he began looking at around 2 billion guilders in credits that the bank had lent to diamond traders in Antwerp, who were now increasingly defaulting. This was a difficult area, since the bank had to allow the client to retain the collateral: dealers had to be able to show a diamond in order to sell it. Since the bank was unable to hold the diamond, the bank loan was in effect unsecured. This was a dangerous situation. Eventually, so many diamonds and dealers had gone missing that the bank started to worry.

Foppe asked Groenink to draw up an inventory. Of the 2 billion guilders, the bank had to write off one billion. Where possible, Groenink impounded the diamonds, then he liquidated the whole portfolio. In the end, Amro's losses came to around 500 million guilders.

The bank was forced to dig so deep into its reserves in those difficult years, that its rivals were convinced it was about to go bankrupt. But Foppe was happy. Things could have been much worse.

At the bank, stories abounded about the battles Groenink had fought and the triumphs he had scored. They called him the Terminator.

All this didn't go unrewarded. In 1982, Foppe promoted Groenink to manager of special credit, known familiarly at the bank as the wreck office. Suddenly, the 33-year-old banker was one of Amro's top fifty. He saw himself, ironically, as "a professional doom merchant who uses all his ingenuity to figure out where things could go wrong".

Now any credit problem that arose would see Groenink in charge. As he handled the complex financial problems of these bankruptcies and the incalculable chaos that engulfed them, he learned. He organised countless so-called hospice structures in which a company's terminal parts would be allowed to die and its healthy elements would continue further in a new company. Groenink enjoyed testing the boundaries and, if possible, shifting them.

Some cases received a high media profile. Like Amro's allegedly questionable role in the Masson affair. ABP investment manager Masson felt that Groenink had not informed him properly or on time regarding the property transaction that finally caused his downfall. His name was also mentioned in connection with the Voskamp affair, when a greenhouse builder went bust in 1985. Not only had Amro restructured his loans, it turned out that the bank was a shareholder. Groenink had sat on both sides of the negotiating table.

Groenink continued to rise even further following his decisive action in the Boskalis question. In 1984, the dredging company found itself in serious problems due in large part to the refusal by Argentina's government to pay for work on a 1,800-kilometre gas pipeline: the Cogasco project. Boskalis incurred a loss of almost half a billion as a result. Knowing that the export risk was covered for 95 per cent by the Dutch state, a consortium of 52 banks took over all the dredger's risks and debts. The banks restructured the company, trimming it down to its viable elements. Groenink led the consortium. Much of the creative thinking was done by a 34-year-old Amro colleague: Wilco Jiskoot.

During the negotiations, Groenink met ABN banker Harry Langman. The rival's board member had been present when Groenink had dressed down one of his own bosses, Amro managing director Rob Koole. When Roelof Nelissen, Amro's chairman, called Langman a few days later and asked him what he thought of Groenink, his advice had been unequivocal: either you fire a man like Groenink before he's forty or you promote him to your managing board; he clearly doesn't like answering to superiors.

Langman's advice seems to have been taken seriously. On 1 January 1986, Groenink was appointed general manager of corporate business, the last step before the board.

Groenink earned the bank lots of money. Some even saw him as the bank's saviour after the extreme difficulties of the early 1980s. His boss, Hans Foppe, kept a watchful eye on him. He admired Groenink's creativity; he noticed how he managed to turn situations from essentially hopeless to feasible. Groenink would add new demands to the terms of a loan, for example, which some colleagues considered legally doubtful. In cases like that, Foppe generally tended towards caution, although he would compliment his junior colleague's inventive approach.

Groenink's boundless ambition provided fertile ground for all kinds of whole and half truths. A juicy story that circulated at the bank was Groenink's supposed remark to a secretary who had worked for him in the 1970s, that if she stuck by him she would soon be the secretary of the chairman of the board. There were all kinds of anecdotes about Groenink and money. It wasn't his driving passion, yet it was obvious Groenink wanted to be rich. His reasoning was simple: being rich is how you show that you're successful.

Groenink knew one thing for certain: he wanted to be more successful than his father. A father who still banked at ABN and who, whenever he discussed work with his son, would invariably mention the rival bank. It irritated

Rijkman that he had to correct his father each time and explain that he worked for Amro.

As Rijkman Groenink came round from the anaesthetic at Hoorn hospital he noted with satisfaction that his arm was still where it should be. However, the doctors informed him that a transplant of a vein from his lower leg had failed. They had been shocked by the continued bleeding and feared that the arm might yet have to be amputated. Once again, Groenink insisted that this was unacceptable.

They decided to move the banker to Amsterdam's Free University (vu) hospital. There they had the expertise to save the arm. That evening, when his boss Hans Foppe visited him at vu's medical clinic, he was impressed by his young colleague's stubborn resolve.

A second operation followed at vu hospital. The doctors consulted for hours; could they leave the arm in place or not? They tried a new vein one more time. But again the blood began to clot. Finally, at the third attempt, it took. They had saved Groenink's arm.

Meanwhile, all those operations had left him vulnerable. Groenink caught a serious bacterial poisoning of the blood. It struck hard. It seemed to develop into a general internal infection: a sepsis. That Sunday night he fell into a coma. Desperately, the doctors searched for an antibiotic to effectively counter the bacterial infection. On Monday night, his wife Lucia was informed that her husband might not make it to the next day.

In a final attempt to avert the worst, the doctors injected the dying patient with a full range of antibiotics. It worked. Rijkman Groenink had survived his self-inflicted wound.

Lying in hospital, he realised what had gone wrong that morning at the lake. After they had decided to abandon the hunt, he had removed his shot from the rifle, as you're supposed to. Presumably, that decision and the act of removing the ammunition had imprinted itself in his mind to such an extent that it never struck him to remove the shot a second time after he had picked up his rifle to have another go at a pair of ducks.

He had paid a high price. The pain was terrible. His physicians had told him that it would remain, more or less, for the rest of his life. He would require considerable rehabilitation and would have to see a physiotherapist regularly for many years to come.

The doctors warned him: with a prognosis like that, nine out of ten people spend the rest of their life sitting beside a window under a cloud. But Groenink wasn't worried: he wasn't going let that happen. It wasn't in his nature. Nothing would stop him realising his dream. Nothing!

Groenink's colleagues were impressed by his tremendous resilience. Within a couple of weeks of his accident he was sending them handwritten cards. Groenink had learned to write with his left hand. People began making bets at the bank: would he be back by Christmas, or would it be New Year? Groenink gathered his strength and made his first appearance at the bank between Christmas and New Year.

He could hardly do anything due to the pain in his arm. But Groenink refused to accept it. Tennis was his sport, and he kept it up. With his left arm. He couldn't serve any more, the power with which he now played was nothing like before. But he persisted, although he felt frustrated that he could no longer do the things that he used to do. Being a bad loser, he decided to stop playing competitive games.

He had also been a reasonable golfer. That too was history. He trained intensively to learn to play with one arm. Groenink was proud when his handicap dropped to 30 following an intensive training course. And he started shooting again. He had an extension fixed to his rifle to enable him to lift with his bad right arm and shoot with his left. To the chagrin of his wife.

In the hunting world, people had placed the blame for the accident squarely on his shoulders. A hunter should never walk around with a loaded gun. Never. It's unforgivable. No one should ever take that kind of risk. An accident like that would turn public opinion against hunting, and give the impression that people who hunt are cowboys. For a while, Groenink stopped receiving invitations to hunting events. He was unconcerned.

In the spring of 1988, Amro's managing board discussed whether or not to appoint Rijkman Groenink to the bank's highest executive organ. The job would entail considerable travel. The managing directors wondered whether he would be up to it physically.

Yet the tremendous discipline with which he focused on recovering, earned him respect. He was there all the time, and he worked hard. Harder than ever. Groenink always read all the documents. Moreover, he had made a personal commitment never to complain about the accident. He wanted to prove to those around him that it hadn't upset his plans. For his colleagues it was clear: Rijkman Groenink had shown that he wasn't going to fall. And if he did fall, he would get back up, wipe the dust from his coat and carry straight on.

Board chairman Nelissen, another keen analyst, was impressed. He considered Groenink a brilliant banker, although he disliked his swagger. For Nelissen it seemed as if Groenink enjoyed trumping his colleagues a little too much. Whenever that happened, the tough board chairman would cut him short. He put it down to his youth and forgave him.

When in late May 1988, the sudden departure of managing director George Ernest Loudon left a vacancy in the boardroom, Nelissen hesitated. Two general managers presented possible candidates: Rijnhard van Tets and Rijkman Groenink. If he appointed one, he ran the risk of forcing the other to leave. He decided to take on both. From the outset it was clear that the two new managing directors would not be friends.

Groenink adapted quickly to his new status. The people who reported to him respected his intelligence and persistence. He was a strict boss for those who worked under him. He never tired of explaining to them that the game isn't lost until the final whistle. Groenink was only interested in colleagues who ranked among the world's best in their profession, or at least showed that they were aiming for the top. They had to have ambition. Otherwise he didn't even listen to them.

Groenink had no time for half-baked ideas. He couldn't stand it when they were considered out of respect for the person who had proposed them. It didn't matter what their job was at the bank. Their ideas were stupid and he had no qualms saying it.

That others found his tough approach too confrontational left him unaffected. He stood for struggle, debate, combat. When he fought he showed his best qualities, and the same applied to everyone else. That's why he encouraged others at the bank to confront each other. Some called it a Darwinist management style.

Many colleagues dreaded meetings with Groenink. He was constantly testing people, asking unpredictable questions or making strange jokes.

Meetings with Groenink were never boring. One-on-one conversations would often go reasonably well. As soon as Groenink found himself surrounded by more than one colleague he had to show who was boss. His appearance confused people. Though he was almost 39, he still looked like a student. He got on well with the couple of women at the bank's top level. They had to be able take a knock or two, but once he was sure they were tough enough Groenink tended to become protective and shield his female colleagues. It wasn't done to fight with women.

People were in constant danger of becoming the butt of his extraordinarily clumsy sense of humour. Groenink enjoyed disorienting those around him with his puerile jokes and asides. Once, when visiting a colleague proudly showing off his renovated house, Groenink pointed to the brand new floor tiles and noted that they, apparently, still had to be removed.

It's hard to know how to respond to that kind of humour, because it's never quite clear whether it's actually meant as a joke or not. Especially since his colleagues knew that he rarely said anything without some purpose. He always had an agenda whenever he spoke to anyone. He never relaxed with his colleagues, for a drink at a café for example. No one had ever seen him even slightly tipsy. Which disappointed people who worked for him. It made him somehow inhuman – never one drink too many, never a moment to let off steam together. Groenink was always in control.

A favourite subject for jokes was the competition. At Amro they tended to look down on relatively boring banks like Postbank and NMB. It was the chic, old-fashioned ABN – the bank that imagined itself superior to everything and everyone, Amro's arch-rival – that they laughed at most. Not least Groenink, who felt that ABN had little sense of discipline. He was astonished at their gigantic overseas network, which seemed to be earning nothing at all.

The rivals knew each other well; in a small country like the Netherlands directors of the two largest banks would often meet, both professionally and privately. Almost all of them lived in the wealthy Gooi region east of Amsterdam. In the spring of 1989, Rijkman Groenink had lunch with Jaap Kamp. As general manager of personnel, Kamp was one rung below managing board level. They met through their wives, who played tennis together.

Groenink told Kamp in confidence that the merger with Belgium's Generale Bank looked set to fail. He suggested enthusiastically that Amro and ABN should merge instead. With a huge grin, he proposed that he and Kamp should lead the new super-bank together.

5 September 2007

Twenty years later, Rijkman Groenink welcomed his one-time bosses and former colleagues to ABN Amro's head office. He had been chairman for over seven years. He had wanted to go down in history as the man who had led ABN Amro in consolidating the European banking sector. It was to have been his legacy. By now he knew that he had failed; ABN Amro no longer decided its own fate. Like its chairman, the 183-year-old bank was on its last legs.

Theoretically there had been three options. Following the collapse of the merger with ING in March, Groenink had set his sights on joining forces with Barclays. But the price the British were prepared to pay fell short.

Some ABN Amro bankers had felt that turning ABN Amro into a purely European, regional bank would have been a healthy option. It was a scenario that few at the bank, which had seen the world as its oyster, had ever really wanted to think about. A scenario that had come too late anyway. No one was listening to the bank's people any more.

Now the shareholders were in charge and all indicators suggested that they would accept the highest bidder. In April, they had demanded that the management focus on one interest only: the bank's owners, its shareholders. The board's task was to ensure that the sale of the bank raised the most money possible.

The highest offer had come from a consortium of three banks. They were willing to pay 71 billion euros. It was the largest takeover in the financial sector ever. Royal Bank of Scotland (RBS), Fortis and Santander had been stalking ABN Amro for the past five months. The Scots, Belgians and Spanish wanted only one thing: to tear the bank into three, for profit.

There had been only one way to prevent this: if the Dutch finance minister Wouter Bos refused to give the consortium the required declaration that the government didn't object to the takeover. It was a slim chance. The Hague's love affair with the bank had evaporated over the past few years.

In recent months, Groenink had done all he could to forestall the bank's break-up. He had spoken on the phone to the minister several times, practically ordering him not to let it happen, telling him to inform the consortium that they shouldn't count on getting his permission. He realised that he had insulted the minister.

He had appealed to Nout Wellink of De Nederlandsche Bank (DNB) – the president of Dutch Central Bank, the man responsible for providing the minister with binding advice – to take the initiative and oppose the merger. He had asked Wellink to tell the three consortium banks that they couldn't be sure of receiving his permission, that breaking up this important bank presented too great a risk. But Wellink had made it clear that he wouldn't be able to do so without political cover.

Now Groenink knew that he had failed. A merger with Barclays might have represented an acceptable failure. At least the bank would have continued in its present form, though in other hands. But this was unacceptable. He would much rather have had shares in Barclays in exchange for his ABN Amro shares and options, than the approximately 24 million euros that the consortium would soon be transferring to his account.

The restaurant on the 22nd floor of the bank's head office gradually filled with retired managing directors. These were the bankers that had built ABN Amro over the last forty years. The nineteen-year-old merger between ABN and Amro, the creation of *the* bank, had been their life's work.

Groenink saw their sombre, angry faces. They held him responsible. The ABN bankers in particular: they felt he had squandered their legacy. One or two had already criticised him in the press. Groenink realised that this would be the hardest audience to persuade to sympathise with the bank's current plight.

The former managing directors feared that the bank would be broken apart. The bank's core, its domestic operation, would be absorbed by Fortis. Fortis! The country's fourth bank, the least important, the one that had never mattered at all. A disgrace. Their bank, the eighth in Europe, thirteenth in the world, would cease to exist. How could such a huge, profitable bank with such a magnificent history, one which had played such a crucial role in the country's economy, be ignominiously torn to shreds?

ABN Amro seemed to have been abandoned on all sides. Rumours had circulated about a meeting at Catshuis the previous week. Prime minister Balkenende and finance minister Bos, had asked leaders of the major Dutch investment funds on the AEX stock exchange whether the sale of ABN Amro would trigger a selling spree of Dutch companies. Companies that were clients or used to be clients, companies that had received help from ABN Amro in the past were among those represented. Yet no one in the political world had stepped up to throw ABN Amro a lifeline. There had been little sympathy for the bank.

Groenink looked round the room. He was clearly tense. The board chairman knew the forty faces seated at the five round tables well. They had been members of the managing board, or one rung lower: general manager. Over the last 33 years, he had worked closely with all of them. He recognised his former boss, Roelof Nelissen. The man who had promoted him in 1988 at the age of 39 to Amro's managing board. On the next table, Rob Hazelhoff, then still chairman of the ABN board. They were the two bankers who had combined ABN and Amro in 1990. The merger had created Holland's biggest bank.

This was the eighth time Groenink had stood here in front of the same group of peers. It was an old tradition: every September, when the half-yearly figures were released, the former leaders met to hear the chairman's plans. Groenink never enjoyed these gatherings. He knew their aversion, the doubts they had about him. Especially the former ABN leaders: they considered him arrogant, macho, a power broker.

Of course, he had never really cared what they thought about him. If these people had done their work better in the 1990s, had made the bank more efficient and had taken clearer choices then he wouldn't have had so many problems and the bank would now have stood tall. He hoped that they would understand that he found the current solution just as unacceptable. That he loved the bank as much as they did. That he was losing too.

Beside Groenink sat Jan Kalff, his haughty, erudite predecessor. The two men despised each other. Groenink felt that Kalff had stalled for too long in the 1990s, pretending all was well. Six months after taking over in late 2000, Groenink had informed the bank's president Aarnout Loudon that the bank was run-down and in desperate need of repair.

Kalff had been livid. The very idea was ridiculous. ABN Amro had been in perfect shape when he handed over the chairmanship. And if there was anything wrong, then Groenink was equally responsible. At least under his leadership the board had worked in consort. Groenink had destroyed all sense of team spirit.

Kalff and Groenink had never openly acknowledged their differences. Bankers don't talk about that sort of thing. They tend to be discreet. They prefer to focus on business rather than people. In previous years, these meetings had generally been dominated by a sense of pride in the bank's joint past. That made for a far lighter atmosphere.

While analysts and shareholders were asking increasingly searching questions about what ABN Amro was up to, here gentlemen wondered whether the bank was going in the right direction. Whether profits were continuing to rise and if the bank was still hunting. Hunting to win, to conquer and grow even bigger. That the outside world had been questioning ABN Amro's future these last nine years had created a sense of camaraderie.

Moreover, they were convinced that political, administrative and corporate Holland would collectively ensure that their institution, the court purveyors of banking in the Netherlands, remained. That the leading players in the Dutch economy more or less owed it to the bank that had given so much over the last two centuries. It might take a little longer, and Groenink might not be the right man for the job, but one day the bank's magnificent history would ensure that its potential would be realised. It had to.

It was not until the previous September that some of the former managing directors had begun to entertain doubts. Groenink had given a sombre speech. He had talked of vigilance and advised the bank to look to its future. And that it was not entirely certain that the bank would be able to determine its own future. They didn't know at the time that the managing board and supervisory board had already decided on a merger, as the junior partner.

Now it was clear that even that humbling prospect had failed. Since the letter from that aggressive hedge fund with the strange name, the Children's Investment Fund (TCI), which owned just one per cent of ABN Amro's shares, the bank had lost control of its own future. Rijkman Groenink, chosen to lead the bank because of his fighting spirit and courage, had been unable to regain the initiative. It wasn't easy for the forty bankers, but if they were honest they would have realised that the merger of ABN and Amro, the combination of forces that would grow into a truly global player, had failed.

Groenink stood up and cleared his throat. As they watched him, a couple of former Amro colleagues noticed that the chairman was standing with his back to the light. They remembered that invaluable lesson which Roelof Nelissen had taught them: always make sure that the light shines in your opponent's eyes; it gives you a natural advantage.

It grew quiet. Rijkman Groenink welcomed everyone and began his story, without notes. He outlined the need to establish a market value of at least 100 billion for the bank as the consolidation within the sector reached its endgame. Only then would ABN Amro remain a global player. He described his numerous attempts in recent years to take over other banks, or to merge. He explained how the bank's share price had begun to slide once it became obvious that the stated ambition of reaching the world's top five had not been reached. Which led to the bank's value falling beneath the 40 billion mark.

Groenink hoped that his audience would understand that this had turned the balance of power around completely. Now he, Rijkman Groenink, was the junior and could no longer set the pace at the negotiating table.

Groenink told how he had been surprised in February by TCI's letter. The letter in which TCI declared it had lost confidence in the bank's management and demanded that an opportunity be made for the sale and possible division of the bank. Almost immediately the bank's shares had begun to rise. The increasingly expensive shares had brought an end to the delicate merger negotiations with ING.

He explained that earlier in January he had had an excellent discussion with the people who had sent the letter. They had promised to give the bank six months to improve its results. Results which Groenink had been confident the bank would deliver: in 2007 the many reorganisations and strategy adjustments would at last begin to bear fruit.

With a sigh, he declared that an unfortunate combination of circumstances had meant that the bank didn't get those six months. Groenink talked about Davide Serra. The man behind Algebris hedge fund, which had already calculated in the summer of 2006 that ABN Amro would be worth twice as much sliced in pieces. He revealed that Serra and TCI founder Chris Hohn had formulated a plan to force the bank to split.

Groenink described the relationship between Serra and Matteo Arpe, chairman of the board of the Italian bank Capitalia. ABN Amro had owned an 8 per cent stake in that bank for years. After taking over Antonveneta, ABN Amro had envisioned establishing a second European domestic market in Italy. But Arpe wanted to keep Capitalia out of Dutch hands, and had apparently convinced Serra in February that ABN Amro was preparing to take over Capitalia in the near future. Serra and Hohn were dead set against this, and decided not to wait for events to unfold but to apply pressure. Which is when they sent their letter to the board – and to the media – demanding either the sale or the division of ABN Amro.

Groenink sighed. He assured his audience that the bank had not been planning to take over Capitalia at that time. Arpe, Serra and Hohn had no grounds for suspicion. ABN Amro had been negotiating with ING and – in the background – with Barclays. The chairman concluded that what the bank had suffered more than anything was bad luck.

Serra, Arpe, Hohn, Algebris, TCI; the audience was stunned. And irritated. What did he mean by bad luck? How could bad luck bring about the collapse of an institution like ABN Amro? Why didn't he take the blame himself? It was under his watch that the bank had switched strategy so often no one understood which direction it was headed. Moreover, despite his promises, Groenink still hadn't succeeded in making the bank cost-conscious and customer-focused. Why didn't Groenink talk about that?

From their colleagues and successors they had heard how the bank had practically fallen to pieces in recent years. How the top had failed. They had heard about the endless paralysing feuds in the boardroom. About Groenink's absence of leadership and the total lack of confidence among the general managers under him and the governors above him. In the end, he had alienated everyone. In their view, it was Rijkman Groenink who had gambled away the bank's trust, inside and out. In effect, he had gambled away ABN Amro.

Groenink sat down and the man beside him prepared to rise. As he got up, Jan Kalff felt a tremendous sense of loss engulf him. The grim atmosphere of contained anger weighed him down. He sympathised with his colleagues. It was only natural that they should find it unacceptable that their bank was being carved up. He more than any understood that.

Kalff was furious with Groenink. He should never have been made chairman. Kalff had argued passionately for Jan Maarten de Jong when he stepped down. As had Hazelhoff in fact, then on the supervisory board. The two former chairmen, both of ABN stock, had warned specifically in 1999 against appointing the macho Groenink.

They were not the only ones to have disapproved. Financial director Tom de Swaan had opposed the appointment. Kalff knew that his friend and colleague, managing director Rijnhard van Tets had actually threatened to resign if Groenink were made chairman.

Tears welled in his eyes. He held the back of his chair. He hadn't expected that. This was the turning point, this very moment. His colleagues could see his emotion. The invariably impeccable Kalff tried to focus on his choice of words and referred to the consequences of the situation Groenink had sketched as "extremely unsatisfactory".

Kalff declared that he had lost confidence in the current board. A board that had put the bank up for sale. This was the worst possible situation that a company could face. And that in a year in which the bank was about to make record profits. Kalff was not talking about the shareholders, he had never given much attention to them anyway. He was worried about the staff, and above all the customers. He had received numerous letters and phone calls during the past months from former clients: clients who were becoming concerned.

With his voice shaking, he wondered what this collapse would mean for the really big clients. They would have to bring their holdings in Brazil and Italy to Santander. Their private affairs and their Dutch activities would go through Fortis. For everything else they would need Royal Bank of Scotland. Would they do that? Could the bank do that to them? Kalff was searching for words... for heaven's sake, it was as if the customer no longer even mattered.

The tension in the room was rising. Retired managing director Dolf van den Brink tapped on the table and asked for attention. He wanted to stop the afternoon becoming too sombre.

Listening to Kalff, the old ABN hand had recalled the almost wild euphoria that had gripped the bank after Rijkman Groenink's appointment. Everything would be different. And everything was different. While Kalff was chairman no one had ever spoken out of turn; from the moment Groenink took over there was fighting, incessant fighting. The board had become an arena in which each managing director fought his own corner. As the investment bankers began to dominate the bank, ABN Amro had succumbed to greed. Absence of coordination and cooperation had ensured that Van den Brink's cherished ideal of a universal bank was consigned to the bin. In 2002, aged just 54, he had been forced by Groenink to retire.

As Van den Brink watched those sad and angry faces, he felt he had to say something to raise morale. He pointed out that while the bank could boast an impressive history, the future would last even longer. That it was the board's responsibility to start working seriously on a scenario in which the consortium would take over the bank. He called on everyone in the room to recognise the reality and to accept the partnership with Fortis.

All around heads nodded sympathetically. Of course Van den Brink was right. They had to ask the current board how the bank proposed to fulfil its responsibility. In recent months, the press had reported that Groenink had no love for the consortium. But then, was Van den Brink the right man to make such an appeal? Everyone knew that Van den Brink had been invited to join Fortis's supervisory board. That he had declined. It would hardly have been right as a consultant to the bank and formally still on the payroll. Yet they also knew that since then he had regularly met and advised Jean-Paul Votron, Fortis's CEO.

To answer the question about how the negotiations with the consortium were progressing, Groenink handed over to fellow managing director Wilco Jiskoot. Since the supervisory board's failed attempt some three months earlier to remove Groenink, Jiskoot had been in charge of the bank's talks with the consortium; the talks about the bank's future.

Jiskoot was sorry that he hadn't been given the appointment earlier. Not as chairman, for he had never sought the limelight. But as negotiator. All those years under Groenink had been a huge frustration for him. He was the bank's best deal maker, but in those seven years Groenink had preferred to negotiate the bank's takeovers and mergers alone. He was grateful that the governors had finally decided to listen to him.

Jiskoot was deeply disappointed in Groenink. He thought him a weak leader, forever trying to divide and conquer. He disapproved of Groenink's indecision. The bank should have sold its subsidiary in the United States earlier and focused emphatically on its corporate division. That kind of thing takes time. Jiskoot couldn't understand why the original decision in 2000 to focus on investment banking had been reversed eighteen months later.

He felt that all the decisions in recent years under Groenink's regime had only been half taken. There had always been room for manoeuvre. The board could never tell exactly where Groenink stood, what he really wanted for the bank. That left them feeling uncertain. He too. Like his colleagues, eventually he was no longer prepared to keep silent. For years the board had been paralysed, now it was every man for himself.

Rijkman Groenink watched Wilco Jiskoot. They had known each other thirty years. Never as friends though. If anyone had disappointed Groenink, it was this man. For years, Jiskoot had promised that his corporate business division would be hugely profitable. That this was where ABN Amro's future lay. But Jiskoot had only lashed out more money. Time and again he had shown himself incapable of managing his division. Incapable of making choices, or of cutting products and services. A couple of times Groenink had told Jiskoot privately that he was a bad manager. Jiskoot had been livid.

Groenink would have loved to have fired Jiskoot. Years ago. But president Aarnout Loudon had held him back; it would have been irresponsible. Jiskoot, who was in touch with all the country's captains of industry, was simply too powerful.

For years, Groenink had done everything he could to contain Jiskoot's ambition of turning ABN Amro into a major investment bank. They had been in a constant conflict. Right to the end: Jiskoot had spared no effort to ensure that the Barclays deal failed.

It was a battle that had lasted years. Eventually, they both lost. Jiskoot's vision of ABN Amro hadn't materialised either. Not by a long chalk.

Jiskoot recognised everyone there too – he had been with Amro since 1976. He knew that these men believed that a Barclays deal would have been the bank's best option. Nonsense, reasoned Jiskoot. He explained that under Barclays, little would have remained of ABN Amro. The British would have taken all the top jobs. It would have been a coup.

Jiskoot told his audience that there was nothing wrong with the consortium taking over the bank. Over the past few years ABN Amro had unwittingly prepared itself for just such a takeover. Every bank is always looking to be among the five largest in a country or market. ABN Amro realised this in the American Midwest, in Brazil, the Netherlands and eventually even Italy. These had all been gigantic retail operations with no prospect of synergy. He had been warning about this for years. He had never believed that owning a string of retail banks would make ABN Amro a successful global bank.

Just then, his phone rang. Jiskoot apologised and asked fellow managing director Piero Overmars to round off. Many in the audience couldn't help smiling. He was always doing that. Every time they had been in a meeting with Jiskoot he invariably walked off at some point. Jiskoot was the only person who could get away with it: they all knew that those calls often led to commissions for the bank for advice on share issues or mergers or takeovers.

When Overmars finished, Rob Hazelhoff stood up. ABN Amro was his baby. Everyone knew that the bank's death sentence had affected him deeply. Hazelhoff had intimated that he wouldn't be joining next month's tour of De Bazel, ABN's former head office on Amsterdam's Vijzelstraat, organised for the present audience. Feelings had run so high, he no longer drove down Vijzelstraat.

Jan Maarten de Jong held his breath as his former boss rose. Three months earlier he had been with Hazelhoff at a meeting of (former) Heineken directors where the topic of ABN Amro had come up. The former chairman had been so upset, he had become unwell. They had even admitted him to hospital for observation.

Hazelhoff had found the whole train of events revolting. He was angry at Groenink. He had never understood that he was running a universal bank. A bank with a place for a corporate business division, but not a dominant place. Making deals for personal profit had become more important than serving customers. Hazelhoff blamed Groenink for firing ABN managing directors such as Jan Maarten de Jong, Dolf Collee and Dolf van den Brink. They might have applied the brakes to the Amro ambition of creating a major investment bank.

Hazelhoff had watched as ABN Amro bankers had increasingly worked for their own benefit. Opportunism, focusing on bonuses and short-term results had been the cause of the credit crisis that had erupted a month earlier, according to the *éminence grise*. Because of that opportunism, banks no longer trusted each other – the problem at the heart of the crisis. Consequently no one trusted the banks to shepherd the economy any more. It was a disaster, felt Hazelhoff. In his day, the bank had taken a share of the responsibility for the stability of the country's economy. There was no sign of that now.

As the 77-year-old Hazelhoff cleared his throat, silence descended. Many smiled as they heard that familiar gravel voice: they knew that Hazelhoff was always the last to speak at these gatherings: the final say.

Hazelhoff noted that the bank's strategy had changed far too often under Groenink. That this had left customers, staff and shareholders with a profound sense of uncertainty. Uncertainty is the last thing a bank needs. If there's one thing a bank depends on, it's reliability. Groenink had gambled away people's trust in the bank.

And that insane focus on creating value for shareholders. Clients, account holders had more money in the bank than shareholders. That was why he had always opposed rewarding managing directors with share options. Some former managing directors shifted nervously on their chairs at these words. If the consortium were to pay out their options at the current rate of over 38 euros a share, they, like the bank's top, would earn a lot of money from any options they still owned. For some of them, it would mean millions.

Hazelhoff couldn't understand that the shareholders had managed to gain control over the bank. Helped by a chairman who had led the way in dismantling the protective measures which had been so carefully constructed in 1990. In his day, contact with clients had been paramount, as long as that went well, the bank had nothing to worry about.

Above all, he wondered why Groenink had never fought to defend the bank. He was a fighter, wasn't he? Why hadn't Groenink replied immediately to those people at TCI? He should have responded within the hour: Thank you very much, we always welcome new shareholders. But according to our rules, the managing board manages the bank, and the board's policy is presented to the annual general meeting of shareholders for approval. We shall therefore not be placing your proposals for policy changes on the agenda. Just when he should have fought, he didn't.

Roelof Nelissen was listening intently to Rob Hazelhoff. He wondered whether he should say something too. Whether there was anything to add. Groenink, Kalff, Jiskoot and Hazelhoff had said a lot already.

Anyway, it wasn't that bad. If it's your own suggestion to allow yourself to be taken over by Barclays, you can hardly blame other banks for showing an interest. In Nelissen's view, the bank's problems lay far deeper. Things had gone wrong at ABN Amro long before the takeover struggle had started.

Nelissen would have liked to say a few words about the supervisory board and especially about Aarnout Loudon, the man who had led the governors for ten years, the man who had been responsible for appointing Groenink.

Where had the supervisory board been all these years? He and Hazelhoff had been governors until 2001. He had seen how Loudon and Groenink had acted in consort, always keeping in close touch. Hadn't Loudon realised that you have to be able to hold a man like Groenink back, with a heavy hand if necessary, if only to rein in his ambition? He had done precisely that when Groenink had sat on his managing board. But if he had said that now it would have looked as if he were protecting Groenink. No. Not that.

As Nelissen listened to Hazelhoff he realised that the latter had allowed the loss of his beloved bank to affect him far more than it had affected himself. He decided not to speak.

I

PREDATOR

I

Compromise

1990–1994

When they saw each other they had to laugh. ABN chairman Rob Hazelhoff waved to the man he had got to know so well over the previous weeks. Roelof Nelissen, chairman of Amro Bank, was also looking forward to the meeting. The staff at DNB, the Dutch Central Bank, were flustered; in the reception hall they had placed Holland's two premier bankers as far away from each other as possible.

The two bankers had decided to play a practical joke. Nelissen had known that Hazelhoff was due to be there and had made an appointment with DNB president Wim Duisenberg at the same time. He had added that he would be bringing a friend.

A friend? They would once have considered it unlikely they would ever be friends. Of course they respected one another. But Hazelhoff found Amro's short frontman rather cold and hard. He thought Nelissen a good manager, but felt himself a better banker. Nelissen respected Hazelhoff as a banker, but he exaggerated and embroidered too much. Amro's chairman distrusted friendship in business dealings. It was better not to become friends.

They also had their reservations about each other's banks. Hazelhoff considered Amro anything but solid as a lender of credit. He was particularly concerned about the lack of diligence shown by his bank's rival. In the early 1980s, Amro had been forced to dig deep into its reserves to avoid collapse. His own people thought that Amro bankers were cowboys, sometimes irresponsible even.

Nelissen acknowledged that ABN had come through the 1980s unscathed, but felt that his own bank had made major strides by confronting those problems and was now being managed on modern and efficient lines, compared to the old-fashioned ABN. He considered ABN a "bank for today and yesterday," while Amro was a "bank for today and tomorrow".

Despite the doubts and contradictions the two bankers were convinced that their banks could no longer ignore each other. In 1992, people, products, services and capital would be moving around Europe without any restrictions. Directors of all the comparatively small Dutch banks – in a European context – were struggling to find a way of staying alive in the European single market. Two other rivals: NMB and Postbank, had already merged six months earlier.

European unification also went hand in hand with another concept that no board agenda could ignore: globalisation. Globalisation would divide the world into three markets: United States, Asia and Europe. New information technology would soon create a 24-hour economy in which everything connected to everything else. Banks that wanted to be part of this needed to be big. Only a bank that processed huge numbers of transactions could afford the necessary investment.

ABN and Amro both operated in the relatively small domestic market of the Netherlands. They would have to take over foreign banks in order to be among the world's leaders. If they combined forces, they would be able to afford large, expensive takeovers.

Earlier attempts to merge had all failed. ABN would have preferred to join up with Nationale Nederlanden, an insurance company whose corporate culture was far closer to ABN's. However, since banks and insurers are not allowed to merge under United States law, and since they both had major interests in the United States, the match came to nothing.

Six months earlier, Amro had been forced to pull the plug on merger talks with Belgium's Generale Bank which had already reached an advanced stage. The combination would have created the fourth largest bank in Europe and the fifteenth in the world. Amro had hoped to be a global player by now. But a change at the top at Generale had led to increasing friction and misunderstanding. The Belgians and the Dutch drifted apart. Frustration at this turn of events reached such a pitch at Amro that Nelissen forbade any mention of the matter.

Like ABN, Amro longed to be a global player. Like ABN, they seemed further from their goal than ever. While they had both been among the world's top twenty banks in 1980, ten years on, Amro had dropped to 46th and ABN to 48th. If they were to do anything about this, they would have to talk to each other.

Five weeks before, on 15 February, they had begun talking. Hazelhoff and Nelissen had met in Utrecht, following an invitation from Herman Wijffels, chairman of Rabobank, to discuss the costs of financial traffic in the Netherlands. Neither ABN nor Amro had been able to cover these costs, as a result of which their market share of 7 (ABN) and 9 per cent (Amro) had been far too small.

The two men had driven back to Amsterdam together. Nelissen invited Hazelhoff for coffee at his head office on Foppingadreef. They exchanged confidences. Hazelhoff revealed that ABN had been talking to Nationale Nederlanden. Nelissen mentioned that Amro had been in touch with an insurance company, Aegon. And they each admitted to the other that neither of their banks would survive the coming years alone. And that they were both stuck.

Nelissen then revealed that he had commissioned an internal study – based on the available annual reports – to determine which Dutch bank would be the best candidate for a merger. The conclusion had been ABN.

ABN had commissioned a similar investigation and had come up with NMB Postbank as the most logical partner, although they had quickly concluded that this would not be a particularly rational move. Apart from anything, the cultural gap with the chic ABN was huge. And so it was Hazelhoff's turn to intimate that a similar study at ABN had pointed in the direction of Amro. With combined assets of 400 billion guilders, the two banks together would rank 16th in the world, which wasn't bad.

Their respective investigations had also shown that the two banks were at that time roughly similar in size. They were making comparable profits, even their shares were then more or less at the same level. If they joined forces it would be as equal partners. No premiums would have to be paid. It was a unique opportunity. So the two men agreed to meet at one another's homes and continue their discussion.

In four conversations of a couple of hours each they hammered out the contours of a merger between ABN and Amro. Without having asked a single investment banker, consultant or lawyer to sit in. No one knew about it. Fearing that a chauffeur might let something slip, the two times Hazelhoff had visited Nelissen at his home in Laren, he had driven from Huizen in his wife's Volkswagen.

The chain-smoking chairmen had agreed two points in advance. They would only talk to each other; if anyone else became involved they would immediately start worrying about their own career. Moreover, they would only discuss matters in broad outline, otherwise the discussion would become bogged down in detail.

They had satisfied themselves that on paper at least the two banks were compatible. Nelissen eyed ABN's extensive network of overseas offices; he particularly admired the bank's growing position in the United States. Hazelhoff realised that Amro had clearly advanced further as an investment bank. In the 1980s Amro had issued shares for major companies such as DSM and DAF.

Even before their first conversation, Rob Hazelhoff had already made a crucial decision. He had often noticed that mergers failed to materialise when domineering personalities refused to give way to each other. It had always annoyed him. After all, even a company chairman is an employee. When companies join forces it should never be about the personal glory of their directors. He had resolved to clear up this question as quickly as possible. There was another point too. Hazelhoff, childless, an ABN banker of 36 years standing, had no wish to retire. The bank was his life. He wanted to stay as long as he was able. So he made a proposal: for the first two years, Nelissen would be chairman and the president of ABN, Shell man Dirk de Bruyne, would head the supervisory board. After two years, they would switch roles. Hazelhoff would take over the chairman's gavel and Amro president Frans van den Hoven would lead the governors.

When Hazelhoff laid his plan on the table at their first meeting, Nelissen objected. Hazelhoff, his senior by six months and far longer a banker, would be a more appropriate choice for the first term. Yet when Nelissen realised that the ABN chief really wanted it this way, he conceded. Nelissen, who had spent much of his working life in politics (as minister of finance and minister of economic affairs in the 1970s) had cherished the hope of retiring at 60; now he would be staying on until 1992 when he reached 61.

Hazelhoff had a persuasive argument: Nelissen was better at personnel and organisation. This merger would require close attention in the initial period. Hazelhoff would take charge of risk management at the new bank for the first two years. That would allow him to focus on an aspect of Amro that caused him serious concern: the quality of the credit department.

They also agreed that Jan Kalff, the senior banker at ABN after Harry Langman, who would shortly be retiring, should succeed Hazelhoff in 1994. For four years. Nelissen didn't consider his right-hand man Dick Meys would be ready to take up the chairmanship after Hazelhoff. Meys would have to internalise the business of the bank, its primary processes, more thoroughly. First Kalff, then Meys. They mapped out their successors into the next century.

When the two bankers walked into his office, DNB president Wim Duisenberg was surprised. When he heard their plan he was immediately enthusiastic. At DNB they had also been discussing the inevitability of Dutch banks consolidating. To facilitate this, DNB had recently been relaxing the structural regime and creating space for the big banks to be able to merge. This was not for altruistic reasons: supervising a smaller number of banks that carry weight in Europe would be good for the Dutch president's career.

Wim Duisenberg and his right-hand man Nout Wellink had often imagined that these two major banks might merge. They had discussed the enormous differences between their respective corporate cultures. Amro had been something of a worry in the early 1980s, while at DNB they used to call ABN the model farm. Duisenberg was glad the two men had managed to bridge their differences. But he warned them: the finance minister would have to issue a declaration of no objection. Duisenberg promised to do his best in The Hague.

Six days later, on a Saturday morning, Nelissen and Hazelhoff were sitting round the table in Duisenberg's office once again. The day before they had been given the go-ahead by their supervisory boards. Now they were sitting opposite finance minister Wim Kok and the ministry's treasurer general, Cees Maas. The bankers made it clear that they planned to announce their plan 48 hours later, on Monday morning. They wished to avoid foreign buyers becoming involved.

Kok and Maas immediately realised the significance of the merger for the Dutch economy. It was a sober business meeting. That Sunday morning the leaders of the main political parties met in The Hague. The message was clear: act fast. Kok and Maas asked the party leaders to communicate any objections they might have against the merger that very evening. None dissented.

On Sunday night, Nelissen and Hazelhoff received the green light to hold their press conference on the Monday morning. They were also told that Kok would simultaneously announce his intention to issue a declaration of no objection.

At the Amstel Hotel the two chairmen explained to the assembled press on 26 March 1990 why ABN and Amro had decided to merge. As Nelissen said, "Like in 1964 [the year both ABN and Amro were formed in previous mergers] when the Dutch economy began to internationalise, and banks started to grow in scale, the time has come to take another step." Asked how the new bank would deal with the enormous differences between their cultures, the Amro chairman replied, "There are similarities, and there are differences. That's what makes life interesting. But in some areas both will have to make changes." In barely six weeks, a handful of men had brought the country's two largest banks together.

This was not the only joining of forces in the financial sector that week. On Sunday, 1 April Hans Bartelds and Maurice Lippens embraced. The chairmen of Holland's Amev and Belgium's AG managed their merger rather differently.

They knew that the cultural differences between their organisations were huge. So they decided to go into Europe together, but to leave their local structures intact. Each would be able to make their own decisions more or less independently in their own national domain. Dutch insurer Amev became Fortis Amev and Belgian insurer AG became Fortis AG.

They had seen how suspicion and lack of communication had frustrated the planned merger of Amro and Generale Bank. The phlegmatic Dutch and the exuberant Belgians realised that the merger had fallen through due to the change of leadership in the Belgian bank. The 43-year-old Bartelds and 46-year-old Lippens were happy in the knowledge that they would steer the merger gradually, step by step, over the next twenty years.

At ABN and Amro, the news about the far smaller Fortis hardly registered. Personnel were still trying to get used to the idea of a merger with their principal rival. They would be joining the other bank, the bank they had been cracking jokes about for years. The other bank, where they had not applied for a job (or had been turned down). Everyone was naturally programmed to fight the other.

Directly after the announcement the same message went out in both banks: we had to, we needed scale. Scale, scale, scale. That engendered a sense of urgency. Both banks would have lost their independence if they hadn't merged. And no one would need to worry, since the two banks were the same size, and the marriage was one of equals.

Some Amro bankers were reminded of managing director Michael Drabbe's answer six months earlier, after the failure of the merger with Generale. Asked why Amro didn't join up with ABN, he had been adamant. "ABN works the way it worked yesterday and the way it has worked for the past hundred years. No. That's not for us. We're not like that."

At Amro's capital markets department, the pulsating heart of the corporate business division, the consternation was probably highest of all. Their head of department, Wilco Jiskoot, was astonished. His colleagues laughed when he told them. "Wilco, it's not April Fool's Day." When Jiskoot confirmed that it wasn't a joke, they soon went quiet. It couldn't be true, they simply couldn't take their colleagues at ABN seriously. Which made them realise that they had won without even having to fight: from DAF to DSM, Amro had beaten ABN in every major transaction in recent years. Amro would be the dominant partner.

At ABN they were equally surprised. They had counted on merging with the genteel Nationale Nederlanden. Everyone, high and low, felt a certain distaste at the thought of having to work with those aggressive, greedy Amro people. And here too, they felt confident. They were proud of their enormous network of overseas offices at ABN. They knew they would dominate that area of business: Amro's attempts to set up offices abroad had consistently failed. Of ABN's staff of 32,792, 12,563 were abroad. Of Amro's 24,033 staff, a mere 2,315 worked outside the country.

The tremendous sense of confidence in the corporate business department at Amro and the overseas network at ABN stood in sharp contrast with the huge doubts that weighed down on the two domestic networks. They experienced the differences between the banks every day. They were in constant contact. Moreover, the branch network was now suddenly duplicate. Every village had an ABN and an Amro, and both had their own business manager and private account manager, and so forth.

Higher up the hierarchy, the duplication continued. And even though the members of the respective boards knew each other and often met, they too were worried. About their own jobs, and about the different cultures. At ABN rumours abounded about the cut and thrust of discussions on the Amro board.

Nelissen and Hazelhoff were concerned about these differences. They knew that a tribal division had to be avoided at all costs. They made a deal, never to complain about each other. Hazelhoff told his staff that from now on he and Nelissen were the best of friends. The two men had overcome their incompatibility; they demanded the same from their subordinates. Nelissen warned his Amro colleagues time and again. "Be careful. You're carrying this merger."

Nelissen and Hazelhoff were aware of the problems that had plagued the merger of NMB and Postbank six months earlier. The Postbank staff felt as if they were being treated as second rate. The entire organisation had been consumed by a struggle that was causing damage to the bank. The union leaders signalled to the ABN Amro leaders: not like that.

Although they knew that computerisation at both banks would leave thousands redundant, they announced that there would be no compulsory dismissals. Hazelhoff had experienced the merger between Nederlandsche Handel-Maatschappij and Twentsche Bank in 1963. The rule then had been: it's not right to dismiss staff as a consequence of a merger. No, it's more than that, it's unethical.

To emphasise the principle of harmony, the two managing boards were combined. The merged bank would be led by fourteen men: twenty-eight hands on the wheel. That meant that many responsibilities would be shared. Some of the managing directors were a quarter of a team. Protocol was suddenly important again: people left the meeting in order of seniority. The youngest members of the board waited until last.

ABN managing director Heiko Geertsema and Ruud van Ommeren of Amro warned that there would be problems adjusting and a lack of flexibility. They felt that the top should set the right example and that the board should be radically trimmed. They were backed in the supervisory board by DSM chief Hans van Liemt.

But Hazelhoff opposed this. He had no desire to start the merger with smouldering resentment. Nelissen feared that keeping such a large pack of managing directors might turn them into poachers, but he also opposed downsizing. It would create unrest. Natural causes would shrink the board over five years to normal proportions. Some of their colleagues suspected that the two initiators of the merger actually preferred a large board. It allowed them to lord it over the crowd.

To sweeten the pill, Nelissen and Hazelhoff decided that the managing directors should receive a raise. They enjoyed an average salary of 600,000 guilders and a bonus of 400,000 guilders. Immediately a debate opened up about whether or not to offer share options. At Amro, managing directors had already been receiving options as part of their pay. Some ABN colleagues, especially the younger set, wanted options too. Hazelhoff was not in favour, he felt that a banker can't help but have inside information, so that it's never possible to cash in options in an honest way. Anyway, he thought it odd that a banker should wish to earn lots of money. He had been raised by his former boss and predecessor André Batenburg with the view that "You have a good salary. If you want to be rich, start your own business."

But Hazelhoff was on his own on that score. Options had arrived. In fact there was even a discussion whether the bank might not lend the tax due on options received. But that was beyond the pale for Hazelhoff and Nelissen: everyone should pay their own way.

When the fourteen managing directors met to celebrate the merger at a meal in a Thai restaurant, it became apparent that even when they weren't talking about business, they still weren't speaking the same language. Hazelhoff wanted to know in advance whether his Amro colleagues might be bringing gifts and if so, how much they were planning to spend. He received a reply that the Amro contingent were thinking in the region of "twelve fifty". So Hazelhoff asked his secretary to order some chocolates for the wives of the Amro managing directors. He got a shock when he arrived that night and found that his Amro friends had bought each of their ABN colleagues a set of cufflinks for 1,250 guilders.

It was taken in good spirit and the atmosphere was positive. They knew each other, they had studied together, almost all of them had been in the same student fraternities, mainly in Leiden, Utrecht and Rotterdam. Yet small things showed that they worked in different ways.

For example an Amro managing director's chauffeur would always be waiting, even if the managing director spent all day at the office. At ABN, a designated chauffeur who wasn't working could be used by someone else. The debate was brief. ABN got their way. They were astonished when they saw their new colleagues' cars. At ABN most managing directors drove a BMW, and no particular model. A modest car. Amro managing directors splashed out. For example, Dick Meys drove a Jaguar and Michael Drabbe had a Lincoln Continental.

There were other small things like that. At any major function ABN managing directors liked to toast the queen. At Amro they would ask for a moment's silence. The ABN people noticed that the requests for silence were beginning to dominate.

The fourteen men were convinced that in a merger based on equality, the board had to set the example. They discussed this and resolved among themselves: as long as we hold on tight to each other. Yet behind that resolve lay a mutual arrogance. Both sides were convinced that the other should be grateful they had agreed to merge. The ABN men believed it was time they taught their Amro colleagues how to provide credit in a responsible manner. Amro bankers felt it was their task to show their ABN friends how to run a bank the modern way.

These feelings were not spoken about directly; that was taboo. From the outset, staff were told never to talk in terms of ABN or Amro. Statements and agreements were made at the highest level: the ABN people would help the Amro people realise their dream: together they would expand the corporate business division. The Amro bankers would support their ABN colleagues in building up their international network. It would be a universal bank.

The managing directors understood that a merger of equals carried a price tag. Compromises had to be made. To preserve harmony, certain inefficiencies had to be tolerated, and sometimes new inefficiencies would be created.

To create a group elan, the bank sent its senior executives in successive groups of thirty – always half and half – for two-week courses at Insead business school in France. There they discussed the current state of banking by examining all kinds of case studies. The idea was to discover those aspects of their profession that connected them.

The board wanted to show that for the top it was about similarities, not differences. They held seances at which managing directors introduced themselves to the rest of the company. A standard question was always about their ambitions.

ABN people were especially shocked by the new man with the boyish face and the broad grin when he said quite openly that what he wanted was to be chairman of the bank. They couldn't have known that this extraordinary successful credit manager had already been approached by a number of American banks with offers of three or four times his present salary. Rijkman Groenink had turned them all down: this was his bank, this was where he wanted to be at the top.

In the supervisory board they wondered about the ambitious Groenink too. Albert Heijn, a victim of polio as a child, had tremendous respect for the way Groenink had pulled through after his hunting accident. He knew how hard it could be to fight through pain day in, day out. Yet Heijn was less enamoured by Groenink's familiarity and refusal to observe the social formalities.

From the first day of the merger, over 40,000 ABN Amro personnel in the Netherlands had been learning to work together. No one ever considered asking whether the shareholders of the two banks thought it was a good idea. Hazelhoff thought the question unimportant, a bank share was in his view "a bond with a bonus".

A suggestion was made that the bank might join forces with one of its main shareholders: Aegon insurance company. Jaap Peters, chairman of Aegon, was keen. There was even a plan, with ABN Amro and Aegon each taking a 20 per cent preferential stake in the other company, providing mutual cover in the event of a hostile takeover bid.

Nelissen and Meys were in favour, but not Hazelhoff. His right-hand man, Harry Langman, arranged a formula to exchange the shares in a way that protected the new bank against hostile takeover bids. The bank was willing to eat, but not to be eaten.

Shareholders in ABN and Amro received shares in ABN Amro Holding. At the same time, a new issue was announced of 260 million new preferential shares at a nominal value of 5 guilders. These preferential shares were like bonds: they provided an annual dividend of 9.5 per cent, but they had no voting rights. The shares were share certificates and the voting rights were retained by Stichting Administratiekantoor ABN Amro Holding. It held over half the voting rights in the bank and would be able to brush aside any interference from outside.

Aegon and Nationale Nederlanden, together representing a quarter of the bank's stock, protested. Directors Jaap Peters and Jaap van Rijn (Nationale Nederlanden) eventually reached an agreement. At the shareholders meeting of 31 July 1990, Rob de Haze Winkelman, chairman of the shareholders association (Vereniging van Effectenbezitters) complained, "I'm for the merger of ABN and Amro, but I'm against certificating." To which Nelissen responded curtly, "ABN and Amro are key elements in the Netherlands' economy that should not be allowed to come under foreign control." ABN Amro was now completely protected against hostile takeover bids, and at the same time had amassed a war chest of 1.3 billion guilders.

On 22 August 1990, the shareholders voted *en masse* for the merger. A week later ABN Amro shares were quoted on the Amsterdam exchange. The bank's shares immediately topped the AEX scoreboard.

That was a position they aimed to keep. Yet there were doubts about the name. Various opinions were aired: perhaps it would be better to stick to one of the names? No agreement could be found; neither side gave way. So for the while the bank remained ABN Amro, until something more suitable came along.

A few agencies were invited to submit ideas. Suggestions were made, such as AA Bank, or AB Bank, but there was little enthusiasm for these ideas. Among the ABN contingent it seemed a fruitless exercise, they knew that ABN Amro would eventually become ABN on the street. To the disappointment of their Amro colleagues the debate evaporated. A few months later, the bank decided to stick with ABN Amro.

Another discussion erupted over the location of the bank's head office. For over seventy years, De Bazel, the colossus on Vijzelstraat, had been the head office of ABN and its immediate predecessor, Nederlandsche Handel-Maatschappij. Nelissen considered De Bazel an impractical building. It was a historical monument: they couldn't change the structure so it would be impossible to work on one floor with fourteen board members.

For ABN's people, Amro's alternative on Foppingadreef was too ugly: the swimming pool, they called it. They would only agree to move if plans for a new, prestigious head office were agreed. Nelissen opposed this vigorously – it was a waste of money. But the former Amro managing director eventually conceded. A new home would be built on Amsterdam's Zuidas.

What really divided the ABN managing directors from the Amro managing directors was the way they approached credit. At heart, the ABN bankers didn't really trust their Amro colleagues. The ABN crowd felt that at Amro they considered commercial interests more important than risk assessment. For ABN it was always the risk that had priority. If it was deemed a bad risk, there was nothing the person in charge of the loan could do to make it happen.

It was an axiom at ABN that one bad credit decision could break a bank. That's why the ABN board met twice a week, every Tuesday and Friday morning, to review the latest credit applications. It might take a half hour; it might take much longer. Every credit application over 100 million guilders was referred to the complete managing board. Everyone would be expected to have read all the documents and to have an opinion. That way, the decision would be the whole board's responsibility.

The Amro top considered this hopelessly outdated; the experts were the bankers, not the board. They believed that far more attention should be paid to the commercial side. At Amro, the risk assessor might have the power to say no, but only in exceptional cases. It was the commercial judgment that carried the most weight. For the Amro people, the exaggerated concern exhibited by

ABN's board was totally unsophisticated and untenable when dealing with large numbers of credit applications. It slowed down the whole process. At Amro they felt that all credits under 1 billion guilders should be delegated.

Rijkman Groenink joked that ABN seemed to think there were only seven real bankers at the bank and that they were all on the board. It was incredible: the bankers below the managing directors were the experts. It was the board's job to manage that expertise, at a distance.

The discussion became heated. ABN managing directors complained that Nelissen reserved too little time at meetings for credit applications, mainly because he didn't really understand them. In the end they agreed once again to compromise: credits over 500 million guilders would be discussed by the new board. The frequency and required attendance of the entire board were based on ABN norms.

In practice, where smaller credits were concerned, Amro seemed to be tougher than ABN. An ABN regional manager had been able to sign for credits up to 5 million guilders. Once a person had reached the ABN's upper echelons it was all about trust and informal contacts. At Amro, after the problems of the 1980s, they had introduced the 'four eyes' principle. Two signatures were needed for every credit. To the frustration of the ABN contingent, the new bank adopted the Amro system. Loans became slower, for large clients and small alike, and more bureaucratic. And that was not something customers welcomed.

To ensure that all the senior executives knew one another, and where to find each other, it was decided to gather the top hundred together to spend 5 and 6 September 1990 in the country. The top fifty executives from each bank were invited. Members of the board, general managers and one rank below, department managers. If it had been an ABN party, country managers would also have been invited; but they weren't required for this exercise.

They met in a hotel near Aachen. Hazelhoff opened the first plenary session with a joke: "On an expedition to Mars, the astronauts meet some Martians who ask them ... how we do it. 'Well,' says the expedition leader to his female assistant, 'shall we show them?' So they do, and as they reach the end they start to go faster, as you do. When they finished, the Martians were impressed, but immediately wanted to know, 'So where's the baby then?' 'That takes another nine months,' the leader replied. To which the Martians respond 'So why were you in such a hurry towards the end?!'" The audience erupted in laughter. And relief among the Amro participants: so the ABN crowd weren't as prim and proper as they made out after all.

But Hazelhoff wondered whether his message had come across. He wanted his listeners to understand that the merger needed time.

The purpose of the Aachen gathering was for the hundred bankers to get to know each other. They were each given a dance card with a hundred empty squares and a hundred stickers with their name. Their assignment was to fill their card with the names of the 99 colleagues that mattered most at the bank. They could all speak Dutch to each other, unless they met Joachim Bähr, the only foreigner in the international bank's top hundred. One or two people wondered if that wasn't a little disproportionate for a bank with global ambitions.

The guest speaker, invited by Nelissen, was Aegon chairman Jaap Peters. Peters had been through three mergers. He warned them: mind the costs. Aegon's success was based primarily on a 30 per cent improvement in productivity per employee over three years. Peters reminded them of the importance of close involvement by management, "The top, especially the very top, has to set the example in these all-embracing processes. It's up to the top to ensure that decision-making is smooth and transparent, that the organisation's strategy is clear and that it's supported. The top has to communicate down to every level of the organisation. The employees want to know what the organisation's vision is, and they want to see the people behind the vision."

Regarding differences of culture Peters noted, "One of the courses for young academics joining ABN was a course on wines and etiquette; there was no such course at Amro. There were plenty of similar examples, many simply reflected different traditions and habits. This isn't a subject that ever bothered me. Everyone can do their work in their own way as far as I'm concerned. Although I thought things had gone too far when separate ties were introduced. I had those confiscated."

Peters closed with a warning. "It's clear that everyone in the organisation has to prove their worth again. So give people assignments they can manage. For us, the merger meant saying goodbye to many of our staff. In the first years after the merger, 40 per cent of the sub-top left, only two of those had jobs elsewhere. It was generally understood that a new organisation required new, relatively small leading teams." Peters received loud applause, and a week later, he also received a bill for a pair of swimming trunks he had rented at the pool where he swam a couple of lengths before giving his speech.

It was in the autumn of 1990 that the real work began. Hazelhoff focused on risk management. Nelissen concentrated on personnel and organisation in the new combination. The board was supported by a so-called merger secretariate. This was supported by a team from McKinsey under Buford Alexander.

The consultants presented a report entitled *Building a World Class Bank*, a technical plan to achieve complete integration by 1993. The word culture wasn't mentioned once. Some managing directors wondered whether Mc-Kinsey might not have been a little too statistical, too cold. But the board preferred it that way. They considered the soft side of the merger a danger. The word culture was taboo, precisely since the cultural differences were so great. To prevent customers experiencing problems as a result of the merger, the board informed the lower echelons that work on the merger would proceed in the evenings.

ABN general manager of credits Willem Brounts was put in charge of the merger secretariate. On the Amro side, the main man was commercial director and arithmetic genius Gerhard Zeilmaker (the man whose report, commissioned by Nelissen, had shown that ABN was Amro's best merger option). They would meet once a week with Nelissen and Hazelhoff to iron out targets and time lines.

In November, a set of targets for the next year were formulated. An increase in profit per share of an average 6 per cent. A higher average return on capital than 'concerns in the same sector and of a similar size'. It was agreed that the bank should focus on achieving greater efficiency. The cost and profit ratio would have to improve. The aim was to cut the efficiency ratio from 63.9 per cent to 62.5: for each guilder of turnover, costs should not be allowed to rise above 62.5 cents. Moreover, with a view to growing globalisation and the single European market, 50 per cent of the bank's profits should be made abroad.

It was agreed on paper that a situation should not be allowed to develop in which Amro ran the domestic operation and ABN took charge of all foreign business. Jan Kalff (ABN) and Rijnhard van Tets (Amro) joined forces to integrate the international networks. Kalff realised that many Amro people felt threatened and organised meetings at his home to try to calm their fears about ABN domination.

ABN's dominant position was obvious. ABN had 269 offices in 48 countries. Amro had a presence in 15 of those countries, with just 106 offices. In many countries, ABN was active in the local market and operated commercially; ABN had delegated far-reaching authority to these local banks. Amro's overseas offices were principally concerned with the interests of major Dutch clients doing business abroad, and their operation was directed from Holland. It was not long before the entire Amro structure was absorbed into the ABN organisation. For many Amro people working abroad, it meant their job.

Henceforth, the network was run by ABN people, practically all of them Dutch. Outsiders didn't understand the bank's informal network, and for the ABN contingent that informal element was their strength. They kept a map of the world on which they charted their growing number of offices in ever more countries and cities. "Another world tour," Amro colleagues would laugh whenever the ABN people presented their latest additions.

ABN bankers were proud of their global network and that it attracted medium and large companies. They would be able to say: I've got a friend there. If a client went on safari in Africa, the bank would make sure there were flowers in the hotel room. If one of their children was wandering around the world, they could always find help at a local ABN office. A little colonial perhaps, but it worked.

ABN people warned their Amro colleagues against trying to find out whether some little office in Quito was actually contributing to profits or not. After all, it wasn't fair to foist the costs of the couple of hundred people at head office who supported the international network and provided its work onto these local banks. A local office might make a loss for years, until it suddenly acquired importance for a major client and made up that loss.

Many Amro bankers had little time for this nostalgic, romantic image. But they kept quiet; the agreement at head office was clear: to support one another in their ambitions.

There was particular respect for the retail bank that Rob Hazelhoff (who had worked in New York for years) and Jan Kalff had built up in the United States over the past eleven years. This really took off in 1979, when ABN acquired LaSalle in Chicago. In the United States, banks could only take over companies in their own home state. Many major American and international banks were based in New York, and competed there. By choosing Chicago, ABN had the field to itself in Illinois. The American subsidiary's 65 branches provided 20 per cent of ABN Amro's profit. It performed a lot more efficiently than the Dutch organisation.

The speed and relative efficiency with which the overseas and commercial operations were integrated contrasted sharply with the rest of the bank. Two years were set aside to integrate the two head offices; four years to integrate the domestic branch network. Four years to ensure that tens of thousands of employees would all find their proper place. Without problems or argument.

A cautious recognition emerged among the ABN contingent, including Jan Kalff, that Amro's domestic organisation was after all slightly better. It was logical that an Amro man be given the reins: Michael Drabbe. He was a warm, charismatic man with a gift for speaking and for taking the long view. He used to say things such as: A reorganisation like this isn't such a big deal. It's like a tree full of birds. You shout boo loudly ... all the birds fly off ... before you know it, they're back in the tree ... only this time they're on different branches.

Drabbe believed in matrix organisation. An organisational model in which everyone had two bosses. There was room for lots of people. Which was good, because there could be no compulsory redundancies. The matrix would enable both the Amro and ABN manager in a village or town to be happy in their new job. One would become manager of the local ABN Amro branch; for the other a solution would be found that would also seem like a promotion.

The merger secretariate decided that the new organisation should mirror the old system. A crucial point for the unions. It was agreed that around 6,000 (out of 40,000) jobs would gradually disappear. Many would be gently encouraged to take early retirement at 58.

During those first years, the introduction of computers actually hindered integration. It was obvious to everyone at the bank that the success of the merger depended on the success of the computerisation. Both banks were using their own outdated IBM systems. Everyone realised that they had to choose one system for the whole bank.

It was an endless process of stalling, with no sign of a decision being made. Not least because there were not many people at the highest level who understood the bank's IT processes. All kinds of consultants were hired to draw up inventories. Both banks wanted to keep their own system. The result was stalemate.

ABN Amro bankers were flooded with questionnaires and inquiries to establish the requirements of the system. Different consultants all came back with the same advice: before deciding how to computerise, the organisation had to be brought into shape. They said it was impossible to create a functioning model based on the matrix organisation. No one listened. A cynical managing director noted one advantage: the longer the discussion continued, the less chance the employees' councils would interfere; procrastination would gain their support.

After two years discussing the matter, the Amro system was selected as the basis: the backbone. For ABN bankers it was a major defeat; they demanded that they should at least be able to recognise their old system in the new model. Hazelhoff agreed, he felt it would discourage ABN people if the system they had worked on were simply discarded. So the decision was made to couple the Amro product system with the ABN office interface. This so-called Openbank project was general manager Gerard Kalff's baby, another ABN figure and Jan Kalff's elder brother. It took a year to combine the two systems. It was only then that the two sides of the bank could be integrated.

Little attention was paid to the appeal by the board to senior executives to devote their evenings to merger questions and the daytime to clients. It took a long time to get used to each other. ABN bankers were used to rigid conventions. Once a person had risen to the bank's establishment, they were trusted. The top was an informal club with a powerful camaraderie. What ABN bankers noticed above all was that their new colleagues were well organised and well versed in numbers and details. They had everything mapped out, largely a result of the preparations for the proposed Belgian merger. Amro people suspected that the lack of preparation among ABN bankers was slowing the pace of change. So Amro bankers proposed leaving the integration process to them. Having prepared for Generale Bank, they had their system ready. Moreover, they felt that ABN had let its domestic operation run down, focusing its energy on foreign adventures.

This was a disappointment for Amro bankers. Many of the ABN managers had remained in their jobs for rather too long and had built up personal empires. ABN's structure lacked transparency. It seemed as if a person could have a career at the bank simply by getting through the entrance exam at the ABN debating club.

ABN employees were expected to do a three-day course to learn etiquette – how to eat, how to behave – when joining the bank. ABN people tended to look down on their Amro colleagues. They were known, with a smile, as the white-sock brigade. ABN people noticed that at Amro they all used familiar forms of address. At ABN you had to earn that. People in the top fifty used the familiar *je* instead of *u*. But only among themselves; if two managing directors were in a meeting with subordinates, everyone used the formal *u*.

New jobs had been created for thousands of employees as the sluggish matrix organisation took shape. The bureaucracy at head office was huge, there was a regional administration too, with a commercial manager and a manager for private customers. Below this, three district departments (with their own commercial and private managers) and then the branches (with at least one commercial and one private accounts manager). The bank had chosen not to make economies or synergise. Harmony was the key word.

So-called function columns were steered by head office. The board was convinced that final responsibility should lie with people who knew most about the bank's products and services. These worked at head office. Thus the executive in charge of private customer accounts imagined he had 13,000 people and fifteen regions under him.

In the regions, the people at head office were perceived as bureaucrats. A powerful staff that remained close to the final decision-making core, yet a staff that understood little about what moved the region and its clients. Almost every head office ukase was met by resistance from 'the people who actually earned the money'. The inevitable conflicts resulted in piles of reports, consultations, steering committees and the like.

ABN Amro's domestic branch network was like an arena – in its structure and its culture. Many bankers spent half their time fending off colleagues with conflicting interests.

At least two men were not fighting, and if they did then no one saw it. The consensus with which Nelissen and Hazelhoff led the merger earned grudging respect throughout the organisation. There was never a hint of dissatisfaction. The duo inspired many colleagues to make an extra effort, to bridge the massive gap.

Kalff worshipped Hazelhoff, called him a mythical seer, a true banker. Nelissen, who exhibited rather less empathy, was not quite as popular. He was more a successful cabinet minister than a successful banker. If he had to choose among the Amro managing directors, he would have chosen warmer personalities, such as Drabbe or Van Tets.

When Nelissen and Hazelhoff told Jan Kalff in mid-1991 that he would be Hazelhoff's successor in May 1994, he wasn't surprised. He was Hazelhoff's right-hand man, the senior banker and so, by ABN rules, the natural heir. Nelissen and Hazelhoff explained to Kalff that their plan was for Dick Meys to succeed him after four years. But Kalff wanted more time to put his stamp on the organisation, and explained that in writing. No further agreements were made.

Towards the end of the summer of 1991, managing directors Ruud van Ommeren and Heiko Geertsema began discussing the organisational feasability of various targets with the two heads of personnel affairs who reported to them, Ron Toorenvliet and Rob Mommers. A sombre Toorenvliet concluded that the merger would never succeed, since the cultures of the two banks were so different. Ommeren (who had worked at IBM before joining Amro) was not convinced about the cultural differences. Nevertheless, Geertsema was worried and asked Toorenvliet to put a few things in writing and to discuss these with the board.

Toorenvliet presented his findings on 15 October in a report entitled *Integratie en onze bedrijfscultuur: hoe creëren we een nieuwe nestwarmte?* (Integration and our corporate culture: how to create a new warm nest). The former ABN man explained that the new bank was not doing well. 'While ABN and Amro both had a strong culture; today's ABN Amro culture is weak, especially because of the clash of cultures and particularly due to the formalistic approach to the merger process. If we are to achieve our targets, we need to create a new warm nest. It is time to jettison the merger secretariate syndrom and make way for people-oriented processes.'

He noted that the 'macho corporate culture at Amro, in which individual role patterns dominate', clashed with the more 'feminine ABN culture in which leaders place group interests above their own individuality in every way ... Many Amro heroes are automatically antiheroes at ABN, and vice versa.'

Cautiously yet inexorably, Toorenvliet spelled out that many colleagues had lost their sense of direction. 'The merger created considerable collective and individual unrest and uncertainty at the bank. To say that this is due to resistance to change would be a mistake. If we continue to insist merely that people have to change, that everything is wonderful and that our merger is the best and the finest thing that could have happened to us, then the resistence and aggression will increase, because the emotion of the shock is being denied.'

Toorenvliet explained that many ABN people were bitter, and could often be heard muttering "I used to be with ABN, but now I'm a credit analyst". He called on the board to tackle the problem and to lead the way. 'If the leadership wants to make cuts it should show the right example at the top ... If the bank is interested in focusing on results, the appointments and management should reflect that intention.'

ABN Amro's managing directors read the report. It was not received well. Toorenvliet had placed too much emphasis on the differences; that was dangerous. The accent should be on similarities, on what unites the two banks. They decided to do nothing.

The bank began expanding the corporate business division. Major companies such as Unilever, Shell and Ahold had been advising ABN and Amro bankers for years to step up the pace. Equity was becoming an increasingly important source of finance for activities. They had been telling bankers that the quality of their service would have to improve significantly. Otherwise the new bank would lose much of the Dutch client base that it had taken for granted. Major American investment banks such as Goldman Sachs, Morgan Stanley and Merrill Lynch had state-of-the-art expertise in house and were better at offering shares globally and for a better price.

ABN Amro managing directors Louis de Bièvre (ABN), Dick Meys (Amro), Heiko Geertsema (ABN) and Rijkman Groenink (Amro) were collectively responsible for the Investment Bank & Global Clients division. They concluded that it was crucial to acquire a subsidiary in London to shore up the bank's marginal role in the far more important London market. The corporate business division was a serious player in the Netherlands' market, but nowhere else.

To their internal audience they explained that they would first have to focus on increasing their capacity to sell shares for clients in as many markets as possible. After all, it was possible to take over stockbrokers. The other side of a successful investment bank, major commissions to offer shares or advise on mergers and takeovers, would be harder to expand. This was down to the personal qualities of particular individuals: their expertise and contacts. These so-called rainmakers worked for the banks that paid the most. Those were the banks that made the best and biggest deals.

Dolf van den Brink (ABN) and Wilco Jiskoot (Amro), two general managers, were responsible for the corporate business network. It was their job to ensure that the expertise of the Amro people combined with ABN's international network. To the Dutch financial daily *Het Financieele Dagblad* an optimistic Jiskoot remarked, "There are only fifteen players who can offer a global network. Of the general banks only the three Swiss banks, Deutsche Bank and us ... for the rest there are just a dozen specialised investment banks like Goldman Sachs or Salomon."

In February 1992, the bank bought the London stockbroking firm of Hoare Govett from Security Pacific. It was the first takeover since the announcement of the merger. The acquisition of this rather poor performer cost the bank a mere 30 million pounds. Since the deregulation of the City and the Big Bang, margins in share trading had shrunk, and this had begun to have an impact on Hoare Govett.

Some in the banking world were surprised that ABN Amro didn't rename Hoare Govett immediately. That was the surest way to draw their new colleagues directly into their own camp and to make them realise that they had a new owner.

The Dutch bankers who went out to work with their 375 new British colleagues were frustrated that ABN Amro hadn't shown who was boss straight away. They found the arrogant Brits irritating; they looked down on the Dutch and made the point each time that London was their city.

But the board had decided that the Hoare Govett brand should remain. It was a solid British name with a reputation in the market; the managing directors were afraid that the real top people, the best traders, would walk away and wouldn't want to work with the relatively obscure ABN Amro.

One man who did walk away, as agreed, was founding father Roelof Nelissen. *Het Financieele Dagblad* concluded, 'Following a Belgian hangover, the little man with the pugnacious quiff had unleashed a groundbreaking bank merger.' To ensure that there was sufficient banking expertise on the supervisory board, he took a position as governor.

Rob Hazelhoff took over the chairmanship on 15 May 1992. The atmosphere in the top echelon changed overnight. The sober Nelissen was never one for small talk and always wanted to know straight off why anyone wanted to speak to him. Hazelhoff took his time. Colleagues who arranged to see him knew it didn't matter if they came half an hour late. Everything always took longer.

One of the major problems he had to deal with almost immediately was the integration of two subsidiary banks: ABN's Mees & Hope, and Amro's Pierson, Heldring & Pierson. Some suggested selling the two banks separately. But

Hazelhoff, who had brought Mees & Hope into ABN years before, wanted to combine them. And he got his way. MeesPierson was to find its own place in Europe and become the second Dutch investment bank after parent bank ABN Amro.

This caused considerable confusion. In Holland people didn't understand that MeesPierson could be ABN Amro's competitor. MeesPierson bankers were often told by prospective clients that they were already doing business with the parent company. From the start speculation was rife about when ABN Amro would divest itself of its subsidiary.

As the European single market approached, a constant subject for debate in the board was the need to find a major international takeover or if necessary to merge. There was an urgent need for a second European domestic market in order to be able to compete in the long run. Everyone knew it. That was the deal.

Dozens of banks were reviewed, but no real possibilities emerged. Hazelhoff was cautious. With their high price tags, and poor debtor portfolios (Germany, for example) there were no suitable options. In March 1993, Hazelhoff told *Het Financieele Dagblad* that the bank was looking carefully at the latest French privatisations. They had money, he said combatively.

Meanwhile, Hazelhoff ensured that the bank invested heavily in its international network. As if making up for lost time, Hazelhoff announced in the in-house *Bankwereld* that the bank intended to open 34 new offices that year. In the two years under Nelissen the number hadn't exceeded 19. The total network would comprise 460 offices in 53 countries.

Hazelhoff predicted that 1993 would be a challenging year. 'That is a euphemism for a year in which we shall have to work even harder to make a success of it.' He was right. And in January the reason became obvious.

Truck manufacturers DAF, one of the giants of Dutch industry, was on the point of collapse. Feverish attempts were being made by the Dutch and Belgian governments together with the banks, led by ABN Amro, to devise a rescue plan. The concern owed the banks around 3 billion guilders. A rumour circulating in the media put ABN Amro's share of the debt at over 1 billion guilders. It was all the more painful because Amro had been the bank that had launched DAF on the stock exchange four years ago, selling 850 million worth of shares. 'DAF rescue depends on ABN Amro,' announced *Het Financieele Dagblad* in late January.

Hazelhoff asked 43-year-old managing director Rijkman Groenink to head the DAF negotiations. When the rescue plan failed to materialise at the end of January, ABN Amro and Groenink were held to blame. The Belgian government was livid. In a letter, the Flemish minister of economic affairs Luc van den Brande stated, 'The banking consortium under ABN Amro demands that the Flemish or Belgian government surrender its collateral on the previous loan of 1.6 billion Belgian franks. The banking consortium makes the approval of the new loan of 100 million guilders dependent on acquiescence by Flanders. An impossible demand, and not open to discussion.'

Het Financieele Dagblad noted that 'Either Groenink discovered too late that the Belgians would find it impossible to meet his demands, or – if one were to think the worst – Groenink consciously decided to place this point as late as possible on the table in the hope that the Belgians would cave.'

Rijkman Groenink was the best known ABN Amro man in the media after Hazelhoff. He was the bank's public image whenever something went wrong. He regularly arranged high profile hospice structures: rescue operations in which healthy parts of companies were severed from the rest and the sick parts were allowed to go bankrupt. Often, the bank did well out of this and the shareholders were left holding the baby. Whenever Groenink was quizzed about his methods he would always explain that it was for the greater good. Since the general public had its money in the bank, people had to be sure that the bank would remain healthy.

Groenink complained about his negative press. He often wondered why the bank held press conferences; journalists understood nothing and what they wrote was never accurate. Groenink avoided journalists as much as possible. To the internal periodical *De Young Banker* he remarked, 'I came into the public spotlight at a young age, to my great annoyance. I never had a problem with it until my personal integrity was questioned in the HCS affair. Some of the gentlemen of the press decided to connect me with certain criminal actions, suggesting that I should be prosecuted for misuse of inside information and that sort of thing. It hurt personally. If they had done it on purpose I might have said, well it's part of a strategy, but to destroy a person's reputation unintentionally and unconsciously ... After the first few months of actual physical pain, you learn to live with it. Like politicians, you develop a thick skin. Then in the end you shrug your shoulders and think, well yes.'

The HCS affair had been his biggest exposure in the media. In the summer of 1991, Groenink had persuaded the three principal shareholders in the ICT company to invest a further 50 million guilders. Of the three financiers, Léon Melchior, Eric Albada Jelgersma and Joep van den Nieuwenhuyzen, the latter was worried about the relatively high price of HCS shares. He wanted as many shares as possible for his financial injection. Groenink responded with the words, 'So Joep, why don't you sell a couple of million shares?' The next day, the three of them sold 4 million shares to reduce the price. This led to an accusation of insider dealing against Van den Nieuwenhuyzen. That case was still being heard in 1993. By then Groenink had explained that his remarks had been in jest.

The three financiers were angry with Groenink, since HCS did eventually go bust and they lost their money. They felt that Groenink had done too little to save HCS and had used their money to pay off the bank debts. In the end, the bank had done relatively well.

On 18 November 1993, Melchior complained to Rob Hazelhoff. Harry Langman, now retired and Melchior's private banker, arranged the meeting. Hazelhoff made it plain that he had no wish to sit round the table with all three investors. So Melchior had bought out Albada Jelgersma and Van den Nieuwenhuyzen's claim and had carried on the fight alone. But Hazelhoff refused to be drawn. Dutch weekly *Elsevier* reported that Melchior took his revenge by withdrawing part of his one billion guilder fortune from the bank. Langman warned his former colleagues: a man like Melchior never forgets.

The bank's supervisory board knew nothing about this affair. It was a cosy Dutch get-together, but with eighteen members there was little opportunity for detailed discussion. The much-vaunted reduction in the number of governors was taking forever. Managing directors kept coming up with new arguments for appointing yet another governor: it had been promised, or it was useful. Governors were regularly being promoted from the bank's advisory board. That body, which met twice a year, comprised another 22 almost exclusively Dutch directors of major companies. Many governors had a sense that they had been appointed largely because this was how the bank acquired its clients.

The chairman of the managing board was responsible for its composition, in consultation with the head of the supervisory board. For example, Hazelhoff invited KPN chairman Wim Dik to join the supervisory board. Dik understood why immediately. The state-run organisation was on the point of being privatised. With a smile he pointed out to Hazelhoff that it wasn't clear yet what would happen and that the choice of banks to offer the shares would naturally be made by the financial director, Cees Griffioen. Yet he accepted the position.

It was obvious at meetings that the governors were not taken seriously as supervisors by the bankers. ABN Amro managing directors could not imagine that non-bankers would be able to contribute meaningfully to their discussions.

Being a governor of ABN Amro was above all an honour. Sometimes the lines could be pragmatically short. A few weeks after the DAF debacle, Maarten van Veen, the new chairman of Hoogovens, asked Hazelhoff if he could count on a stand-by credit. The steel plant was in difficulties. A predecessor as chairman of Hoogovens, Jan Hooglandt, was then president of ABN Amro. The request was discussed by the managing board. Groenink was critical, but Hazelhoff argued that the bank couldn't let this Dutch concern down.

By now the merger was three years old. The 1993 annual report noted proudly that the bank had opened another twenty new offices and now operated in sixty countries. The corporate business division, though small, was beginning to grow. The domestic division was in trouble. Though the new advertising campaign profiled ABN Amro as *the* bank, its results were disappointing.

Some of the managing directors, including Jan Kalff, considered the campaign arrogant; they wondered whether people would understand that it was meant to be tongue in cheek. When they expressed their doubts, they were told that it was good for the personnel. It was time the ABN and Amro staff started believing that they were working for *the* bank.

That was long overdue; the consolidation of the branch networks in the Netherlands was not going well. The number of branches had been reduced from 1,441 to 1,252. The domestic division was struggling under the growing bureaucracy. Overheads had risen steeply; the organisation's flexibility had declined and – what caused especial irritation – the number of consultative bodies had increased enormously.

The domestic division had turned in on itself. Clients were complaining and leaving. At head office it was whispered that Holland, when the balance was drawn up, was actually losing money. In the annual report, the board accepted some of the blame. 'The integration of the branch network has led to some inconvenience for our clients in certain areas.'

Yet little attention was paid to cutting costs. Many of the managing directors assumed that a bank like ABN Amro had no cost problems, just a profit problem: once clients discovered what the bank could offer them, the cost and profit balance would adjust by itself.

There was no real sense of accountability either. The ABN and Amro contingent treated each other with kid gloves: the consequences of failure were minimal. When a target wasn't achieved, Hazelhoff had the tendency to ask whether the assumptions made when the target was set were really correct. So there was always an excuse to ensure that a manager who failed to achieve needn't suffer the consequences.

With twelve men still on the board, its effectiveness was not optimal. Long and frequent meetings were needed to get everyone's agreement for a decision. Sharing portfolios – spheres of interest – between managing directors resulted in time-consuming attempts at harmonisation. No one felt a one-on-one responsibility for a particular area of activity.

And there was another worry: which direction was the bank heading? Former Amro managing directors such as Meys and Van Tets were anxious to set strategic choices. Yet Hazelhoff felt that a couple of hours twice a year was plenty of time to talk about strategy, otherwise people would sit and day-dream. He avoided consultants; they didn't understand banking anyway. Hazelhoff believed that a bank with a history like theirs had no need to worry about the future. Just keep banking cautiously and concentrate on what the client wanted. That was enough.

On the insistence of the supervisory board, it was decided in the summer of 1993 to draw up a strategy memorandum. This was circulated in strict se-crecy to the general managers, one rank below the managing board. After reading, the document had to be returned. Amro managers were amused to see that the ABN people actually did so, without making copies.

In his introduction, Hazelhoff explained that the bank would have to ex-pand further abroad since the possibilities for growth in the saturated domes-tic market were limited. Since it had been agreed in 1990 that half the profit should come from abroad, more acquisitions would be needed. Yet Hazelhoff was concerned. 'With regard to acquisitions, these should not be too large since, despite due diligence, the possibility cannot be ruled out that the bank may find itself with a bad bargain.'

When the bank drew up a balance for the first two-and-a-half years, the re-sults were discouraging. Earnings per share had risen by just over 5 per cent, not 6. The return on capital had not been the required 12 per cent, but hovered around 10.5 per cent. The efficiency ratio was especially disappointing. The target had been 62.5 per cent; the result lay 5 per cent higher at 67.5 per cent and had improved only slightly since the bank had first merged. Once again, the report underscored that the targets had been guidelines.

A number of new targets were set for the coming five years, which the man-aging directors involved described as vague: more growth abroad, gradual ex-pansion in the United States, further integration of the branch network in the Netherlands, and so forth.

An announcement was made on 29 October 1993 that the 56-year-old Jan Kalff would succeed Hazelhoff as chairman of the bank on 6 May 1994. By now Kalff had been on the board for seventeen years. Amro managing direct-or Dick Meys resented the appointment. He sent Hazelhoff a letter giving his support for Kalff's appointment, but stating that he expected to replace him no later than 1999.

After 42 years with the bank, Hazelhoff retired as chairman. 'Sturdy ABN Amro loses familiar gravel voice,' headlined *Het Financieele Dagblad*. 'If there was a cultural conflict and a struggle between the ABN and Amro blood groups, then this ABN representative won hands down. He is passing the wheel to P.J. Kalff, a man like himself, cast in the same respectable ABN mould.' The paper continued, 'Hazelhoff has the ability to break the tension at a meeting or press conference with a joke. The bank has reaped the benefits. To the outside world, Hazelhoff has managed to a certain extent to hide the bank's ingrained inaccessibility. But he has not managed to achieve real change. ABN Amro remains a commercial bank that finds it difficult to communicate with the public at large and the media. The bank will now continue under Kalff. Competition in the markets in which the bank operates is increasing; the need for judgment and discernment is growing.'

Regarding Jan Kalff, the consensus in the outside world was that the bank had made a clear choice for its ABN culture: the chairman would be a *primus inter pares*, not an all-powerful United States-style chief executive officer. *Het Financieele Dagblad* noted that 'Hazelhoff has chosen someone with a similar character and career profile. Unlike his occasionally flamboyant predecessor, Kalff is rather stiff, formal and well-mannered, but also – and he shares that with Hazelhoff – conservative and prudent.'

In a farewell interview with *Bankwereld* Hazelhoff noted, 'It's about managing risk and spreading risk. That's why you have to avoid macho behaviour in a bank at all costs. What do I mean by that? Being so focused on spectacular results that you fail to judge the risks properly.' Asked whether he feared that, he replied, 'There are some banks in the world that clearly have a standing above all others. That's where you need to be. At the same time, the bigger the bank becomes, the more danger there is of becoming arrogant. I can't emphasise enough: clients may not need us; we need clients.'

Kalff saw his priority above all to preserve unity in the managing board. A board in which members had spheres of interest rather than individual responsibilities. They were collectively responsible for the bank, they led it together. In consensus and harmony, setting an example to the rest of the organisation. With the accent on a cautious supply of credit. For the new chairman, banking was more an art than a science. Colleagues from the Amro stable were not impressed. Working at a bank was about thinking seriously. In fact they couldn't identify with their former ABN colleagues' vision of banking as a way of life.

While Hazelhoff started with the DAF affair, at the start of Jan Kalff's tenure it was the bank's leading role in the largest privatisation in Dutch history that dominated: the launch of the state-run KPN. It earned the bank 60 million guilders and was a success which was watched and discussed around the world. ABN Amro received considerable media exposure.

In the rest of the bank, staff watched jealously as their colleagues in the corporate business division stole the show. These were performances that they didn't entirely understand; it seemed to be more about individual deal makers than about the bank. Apparently there was a sexy side to banking. The central figure was Wilco Jiskoot. He more than anyone was convinced that ABN Amro's future lay above all in investment banking.

At his first major press conference, the new chairman made something of a gaffe. Kalff reported an improvement in the bank's figures for the first half of 1994 of 14.3 per cent. In fact the improvement was entirely due to profits in the United States. The results for the domestic operation were 5.2 per cent lower (945 million guilders). Costs had risen by almost 3 per cent and profits by a bare 0.4 per cent. Kalff remarked cautiously that after four-and-a-half years, the benefits of the merger of ABN and Amro had 'still to be fully realised'. He explained that the loss of market share in the Netherlands was due to excessive internal focus. 'We are concentrating too much on how our offices are designed. Next year we shall have to be more active in the market again and make up the terrain we have lost.'

2

Bureaucracy

1995–1996

Dick Meys, Michael Drabbe and Rijkman Groenink were the bruisers on Jan Kalff's board. These were the no-holds-barred types that made the loudest noise. Drabbe had charisma, he was a *bon vivant*. Groenink was smart, he liked to show off his analytical skills.

The 51-year-old Meys combined nous and charisma. Two qualities the new chairman of the domestic division sorely needed. Costs were rising exponentially. Because the best pay package had become the standard with the merger, the bank was paying out an average of 15 to 20 per cent more than its rivals.

On 20 January 1995, at Leiden's Stadsgehoorzaal theatre, Meys explained his concerns to the top managers of his division. "We have experienced a lot of problems with integration. We've turned in on ourselves. More than anything, what we lack is quality. I'm looking at a hall in which 99 per cent of the people are overpaid. We need to take a tight grip on the reins so we can make good on the promises we're advertising: namely, that we're the best bank in the country. We need to move towards a fundamental, crucial change of attitude; in essence, we need to be focusing on the client."

Meys revealed a few points about the new distribution philosophy that the bank would have to embrace. Project Irene, he called it. The audience laughed; they knew the story. At a meeting in Eindhoven a while before someone had asked what name to give the project. Meys' eyes had rested on his personal assistant Irene Verboon (he liked to call her his *chef de cabinet*). After a pause he came up with "Project Irene of course."

But the laughter soon faded. Meys hadn't finished. "It's clear to me that poor communication is causing uncertainty at every level of our organisation. Many of our people are afraid of being trapped and give up because they are uncertain about the consequences for their own position. Our culture and mentality has to change, staff cuts are inevitable. It can never be an aim in itself, but the result of the need to reduce costs."

Almost five years after the merger, the results of the bank's biggest money-maker had deteriorated dramatically year by year. In all markets, commercial and private, the division's share was lagging far behind. The prognosis for 1995 was not good. Meys said it was time to abandon the paralysing timidity. People weren't being judged for their performance because everyone was afraid of that wretched blood-group thing. The bureaucracy in the domestic division had ballooned. The complex matrix structure made the gulf between bank and client ever wider. The branch network had become a monster.

It was only the massive growth of the market that hid the poor results from the outside world. The commercial market had expanded almost 30 per cent in five years; ABN Amro had only grown 6 per cent. The private banking market had also grown almost three times ABN Amro's results. In real terms, the bank's market share had shrunk by about 10 per cent.

Dick Meys made no bones about his frustration at meetings of the managing board. The former senior civil servant liked to joke that if it all got too much for him he could always get a position as minister of finance. But Meys knew that people were listening to what he said. Everyone in the higher echelons understood that he would be succeeding Jan Kalff.

One Friday morning before the board meeting started, Meys asked the coffee lady for her trolley. He placed a stack of files and dossiers on top and steered it into the boardroom telling everyone "This is the shit every local bank manager gets every day ... how can they possibly think about their clients?!" Everyone laughed. And moved on to the pile of credit applications on the table.

Because Kalff had continued Hazelhoff's system. Twice a week, every Tuesday and Friday morning, the meeting started with discussions of credit applications. Some of the managing directors found it irritating. They merely scanned through the documents. Rijkman Groenink wanted to speed up the process. He challenged the chairman; he asked him if he knew what percentage of applications actually went through the board. To Kalff's response that he estimated around 60 per cent of volume and 40 percent of quantity, Groenink laughed. He had calculated that it was just 2 per cent of the number, and 20 per cent of volume. Moreover, he told Kalff, the board only saw the big applications, and these were applications that major clients normally get anyway, loans with negligible risk.

Kalff was unimpressed. He couldn't emphasise enough: it only took one bad credit to ruin a bank. However, henceforth they would not only review major credit applications above 500 million guilders, he also asked the central credit committee to refer smaller, high-risk loans to the board.

Meys' concerns were backed by the board. The bank's domestic division had to get back to work. The results of the domestic operation were clearly disappointing. The bank seemed to have turned into a giant meeting in which everyone was constantly writing and receiving memos and watching each other.

At branch level, head office seemed to be one of the main problems. Everything was directed from the top. What people should earn. The rate on a deposit. There was no room for initiative in the region. A local manager was helpless if the neighbouring Rabobank dropped its rates and snatched away the bank's clients.

Another major headache was the absence of clear accountability. People who failed to reach their targets could still count on getting at least part of their bonus. There was no transparency about how people were judged. And this lack of transparency left a suspicion of favouritism when it came to bonuses.

On 20 April 1995, Meys once again gave vent to his frustration. It was the management development department's annual get-together. Around two-hundred and fifty potential high-flyers were gathered in the hall. On the stage sat the Ajax top management, the football club sponsored by ABN Amro. Manager Louis van Gaal, commercial director Uri Coronel and Co Adriaanse (Ajax-academy director) had been invited as challengers by the ABN Amro top management.

Meys had just finished presenting the 1994 annual report to the press. He was sombre and angry. "Our organisation is too nice, too obedient, it's becoming docile. We seem to think of the bank as a friendly place, but it isn't really. We let people who can't function properly muddle along. I don't call that being friendly. We're too nice to each other, and now it's mediocrity that dominates. It's time we stopped mollycoddling. We have to start playing the ball. We have to be correct, but tough. Keeping the fouls to a minimum, like Ajax. I want people to be aggressive, dynamic, flexible. Take it to the edge of the acceptable. And anyone who has no feeling for service should find something else to do." Meys wondered whether this would work. "It's like pushing against a rope. The Dutch think that it's demeaning to serve. It's no surprise that we have the worst taxi drivers in the world."

The chairman of the domestic division, the man ordained for the chairmanship of ABN Amro, would never know if his words had any effect. On Thursday, 20 July 1995, late in the morning, fate struck. A truck crashed into a traffic-jam on Utrechtsebaan in The Hague, crushing Dick Meys' Jaguar. He and his chauffeur Frans Härzer were consumed in the flames.

The next day, NRC *Handelsblad* commented 'Banker Dick Meys died at the height of his powers, at the summit of his career, at the peak of his social involvement.' A few pages further there were 33 death notices.

The bank was in shock. The flag stood at half mast. Dick Meys had been a popular figure on the board for twelve years. At the memorial service at Onze Lieve Vrouwe van de Rozenkrans church in Amsterdam, chairman Jan Kalff could not hide his emotion. "His tremendous involvement and willingness to tackle issues and to state his opinion clearly meant that Dick always made a major impact on the divisions that he led. On behalf of the managing board I offer my thanks to Dick Meys for everything he did for the bank. No one should be surprised, it seems to me, that it will take a long time before we get used to his absence. The bank carries on, but for many of us it will be quite different."

One or two people were thinking that the race to the top of the organisation was now starting to get exciting. The bank had clearly been primed for Amro man Meys to succeed ABN man Jan Kalff. Many had felt reassured by the knowledge. Especially among the Amro bankers at the top: they had trusted Meys to get the bank moving in time. That scenario was now history. The succession was wide open.

The day after Dick Meys' death, the bank announced that Rijkman Groenink would be the new chairman of the domestic division, starting 1 September. Formally, the division was – together with ABN managing director Paul Ribourdouille – his new sphere of interest, since the board was collectively responsible for everything. Jan Maarten de Jong, second-in-command of the domestic division under Meys, took over Groenink's portfolio.

Groenink was keen. After almost ten years in charge of (special) credits he would now control the bank's core business. His hard work over the last twenty years had been rewarded. And Groenink had worked very hard.

When asked in an interview whether he ever had any free time he replied, "No. Because you have to put in so many hours and actually all the evenings, there's little free time left during the week. And if there is any, you have to try to make time to talk to your children and late at night with your partner."

Groenink knew that if he succeeded in this job, his chances of becoming chairman of the board would rise enormously. This was a position in which he could score; he knew that the domestic division was underperforming dramatically. To the internal periodical *Bankwereld* Groenink remarked, "The domestic division is obsessed by its own problems instead of the problems of its clients. But the bank has plenty of good people, talent and ideas, years of experience and a huge name. My ambition is to ensure that in the 21st century our clients will call us the 'bank of the century'."

The regional managers were invited to meet the new boss. They were given half an hour at head office. Some recalled that when Jan Kalff became chairman a year before, he had gone to visit all the regional managers in person. And for each visit he had set aside a day.

After years in control of credits, with a technical focus on the bank, Groenink was now in charge of 25,000 people working at over 1,200 bank branches. He decided to keep Irene Verboon – the eyes and ears of the division as Meys had called her – as his personal assistant.

Groenink was determined to make an immediate impact. In his first analysis he decided that there were far too many people working at the bank, between a quarter and a third too many. He proposed to cut at least 5,000 jobs. Kalff was shocked; he feared a confrontation with the unions and government and asked for a new analysis. Groenink realised that the time was probably not ripe for mass redundancies and proposed a gradual reduction of 2,000 jobs in the coming years, 1,300 of these at head office.

To assess how the domestic division should start earning more from its services, Groenink called in a consultant. He asked the deputy head of the supervisory board, Frits Fentener van Vlissingen, which consultant SHV had used for strategic advice.

Fentener van Vlissingen had been a governor of Amro since 1973. The Fentener van Vlissingen family ran the country's largest and most powerful family company: SHV. Frits, who had studied physical chemistry at Delft, avoided the limelight. When his father fell seriously ill in 1975 and he as the eldest son was given control of SHV, he told the family that he would remain until he turned fifty. Since 1983, he had focused on leading Flint Holding investment company.

It was through Flint that the family invested in property and especially in industrial companies, as well as real estate. At the same time, Fentener van Vlissingen devoted considerable time to several positions as governor and similar posts, all of which he did to support the interests of his family and SHV. Fentener van Vlissingen enjoyed being the spider at the centre of the web, in the background. He selected his contacts carefully.

He felt that a good relationship with the bank was important for the family business, just as his father, who had served as governor of Amsterdamsche Bank decades earlier. He was impressed by Rijkman Groenink's accurate analyses and even more by his bravura. Fentener van Vlissingen had followed his career for years and had asked him to sit on Flint's supervisory board. Groenink had been surprised and honoured; this was one of the most influential and wealthiest families in the country. He had accepted.

When Groenink asked him to suggest a good consultant, Fentener van

Vlissingen had given him Martin Simon's name. He had been using him as an organisational consultant at SHV for years. Simon was director and owner of Ikon (Industriële Konsulenten) Beleidskonsulenten, a small consultancy specialising in marketing and strategy. In Fentener van Vlissingen's opinion, Simon was an original thinker. His daughter Annemiek had worked at the firm in the early 1990s, after graduating in business administration.

One Friday morning in the autumn of 1995, Rijkman Groenink phoned Simon. He asked him to come round the next morning. But Simon was cautious; he told the ABN Amro banker that he was currently working for another bank, VSB. Groenink explained that this would not be a problem, he would call VSB himself and counted on seeing Simon the following day.

The two men were instant friends. Simon was impressed by Groenink's intellectual capacities. The consultant had little patience with people who didn't understand what he meant immediately. Groenink was bright and enjoyed a heated discussion, just as he did. Simon also met Irene Verboon that morning. So ABN Amro joined forces with Ikon.

Senior Ikon consultant Peter Dudok van Heel began by making an inventory of the bank's problems. He spent months talking to people in the organisation. He kept getting the same message: we hardly have time to do anything because of the constant flood of paperwork from head office and the regulation of everything we're allowed and not allowed. Serving clients seemed to be secondary. They had to go to different branches for different services. The example often given was of a director and owner of a company who goes to his local branch for a new bank card, but has to go to a larger branch for a mortgage and an even larger branch for a major loan. Clients found it confusing. Especially these days when computerisation made it so much easier to exchange information between branches.

For several months they met every fortnight. Some noticed that Groenink would always look at Irene before taking a decision. Simon joked about it, especially since Irene rarely said anything. The consultants felt that Groenink was a fantastic actor. He had extremely sensitive antennae, but didn't use them since for him people were purely functional.

Ikon's advice was unambiguous: the bank had to abandon its functional column philosophy. Head office had to delegate responsibilities to the regions. The region had to be in charge; that would stimulate enterprise in the bank. The local branch had to be the bank's image, with maximum delegated authority.

Simon argued that the bank should trust in people's professional abilities and their contact with clients. Give them the space to cross-sell. Enable them to draw in clients by offering them a discount on one product, then earn more from them on others.

This was a sensitive issue for the bank's head office. That was where the qualified staff sat, who felt uneasy about delegating major responsibilities to people in the field. It was a matter of debate for them whether people at a local branch could be enterprising. Surely bank employees should be people who avoided risk?

But Groenink took on Ikon's recommendations. At the annual Jaardag meeting he imitated Martin Luther King. "I have a dream: that we're working in a bank that swings, with rising market shares and growing profits. That we go to work each day grinning with pride because our clients like banking with us, and the whole country wants to bank with us. That we enjoy going to birthday parties again, and don't dread facing the criticism that's been thrown at us these past years. I have a dream: and we're going to make that dream happen, all of us."

Groenink continued, "A change of culture will have to be forced through. Because we have to deal with certain contradictions that we've been carrying around with us. Enterprise doesn't go well with our hierarchical structure; it's inevitable, since we're a risk-taking business which needs to control that risk. Enterprise doesn't go well with the cost-efficiency that we try to achieve at the central level."

The financial targets he attached to the plan were ambitious. By 1999, four years on, the bank's operational results would have to have increased by 20 per cent. Moreover, the bank's share in the crowded domestic market would have to have improved by at least 10 per cent while the level of customer satisfaction would have to have risen dramatically.

The members of his workgroup realised that their main concern was to increase profits. Turnover and sales had to improve. As did the dramatically poor customer satisfaction levels. The Ikon consultants predicted that costs would rise in the initial years. That was almost always the case when authority was decentralised in any organisation.

Throughout the months of preparation, the chairman of the board took no part in the discussion. It was clear that Rijnhard van Tets and Louis de Bièvre, the two managing directors of the corporate business division, disapproved of the new philosophy. They feared that costs would rise and wondered whether there was sufficient enterprise at local level to make up the loss.

Groenink kept his distance from the investment bankers, the so-called fee earners. He and Van Tets didn't get on. They never had. Van Tets considered Groenink a show-off, a troublemaker. Groenink found Van Tets arrogant and snobbish. In an interview with *Bankwereld* he remarked, "I wouldn't like to work for a bank that depends for most of its income on fees. I would feel extremely uneasy. It would make the bank dependent on stock exchange sentiment." If he had to choose between taking over a major American investment bank, a large asset management group or a third domestic market, Groenink said, "I'll take the third domestic market."

Despite these reservations, no one stood in Groenink's way. After all, it was his sphere of interest. He got a green light: others tacitly agreed not to interfere in his business if he agreed not to interfere in theirs. For the supervisory board, Groenink left the theoretical part of his presentation of his *Visie 2000* plan to Martin Simon. He knew that the governors' vice-chairman admired his consultant. Groenink gave the second half of the presentation: what to do with the domestic division? The whole package was accepted integrally.

The supervisory board was still a large group; most were older men. The average age was over 65. Kalff was proud that since 1996 the governors included two foreigners (the American Silas Keehn and the Frenchman Jean Marie Messier). Meetings were henceforth held in English. The question now was who would lead them as a successor to Jan Hooglandt.

At the time of the merger it had been agreed that new governors would serve a maximum of twelve years (three terms) and would retire in the year in which they turned seventy. But this applied only to new governors. The two vice-chairmen, Floris Maljers (since 1984 governor of ABN) and Frits Fentener van Vlissingen could remain until they reached seventy. It was expected. One of the two would have to become president.

But Floris Maljers, who was asked first, was not enthusiastic. The former head of Unilever wanted out. He had been president of Philips for three years and had his hands full with their problems. He had also been asked to be president of KLM as well as to chaperone Prince Willem-Alexander through an introductory course on commerce and industry. His wife had begun to complain that he was working harder than ever since he retired from Unilever.

Maljers had to choose. He had been a governor for twelve years; he had had enough. Moreover, KLM seemed more attractive. His "No" when Hooglandt asked him to follow on as head of the supervisory board was emphatic. With Hooglandt's permission, Maljers asked Fentener van Vlissingen to take on the post. After first agreeing, he changed his mind at the last moment. Fentener van Vlissingen preferred to remain second in command; at the centre of power, but without the time-consuming obligations that went with the position. He had been president once, for a year, at AkzoNobel. And that was only because they didn't want to make the recently retired board chairman Aarnout Loudon head of the supervisory board.

Fentener van Vlissingen's choice precipitated a crisis. Time was pressing. A new president would have to remain in place for a while. Most of the governors were too old; they would only be able to serve a couple of years. Others were still active in their own company. Hooglandt and Kalff whittled down the choices and arrived at the 59-year-old Aarnout Loudon. Hooglandt knew Loudon well, since he had been a governor at Hoogovens, when he was board chairman.

A disadvantage in their view was that he had only been a governor for two years, and hardly knew the bank. On the other hand, Loudon had a good reputation and the right kind of administrative experience. He was a lawyer, and he knew what a balance sheet looked like; as chairman of the AkzoNobel board he had done the finances himself.

Loudon, a member of a family of diplomats and entrepreneurs, had been chairman of Akzo for twelve years. He had merged the company in 1994 with Nobel Industries to form AkzoNobel and handed the chairmanship to Cees van Lede that same year. Since then, he had remained among the country's ten most powerful governors. Loudon was a natural as a managing director. In the distant past he had actually worked for a bank and had made no secret of his ambition in his next life to be a banker.

On 3 May 1996, Aarnout Loudon, the bank's youngest governor, was handed the presidency. Some other governors had their doubts. How effective would this prim and friendly, yet mechanical meeting-man be?

Three weeks later, on 21 May, Rijkman Groenink presented his credentials. His report, *Visie en Strategie Divisie Nederland. Op weg naar 2000* (Vision and Strategy for the Domestic Division. The Way to 2000), hit them for six. It was sent by the division secretary, Irene Verboon. The report echoed the words of her previous boss, Dick Meys, and above all a shocking account of the bank's dramatic failure in the Netherlands. ABN Amro was losing its market share fast and was making far less profit. The organisation was an 'overweight matrix', a 'sluggish bureaucracy'. 'A relatively large number of managers leading relatively few bankers. There appears to be indecisiveness, an unacceptable sense of distance from the market, insufficient innovation, less than full effort by people and use of resources.'

According to the compilers, there was a clear 'alibi culture with a lack of defined categories and responsibilities'. An image poll showed that clients saw and experienced the bank as not modern, not active, insufficiently flexible when lending, not client-focused and not service minded. 'In many aspects Rabo, ING bank and Postbank scored better.'

Groenink gave the operational leadership of the domestic division to three general managers. The head of the branch network, Henk Rutgers, knew Rijkman Groenink well. They had worked together at the special credits department for ten years. Meys had put Rutgers in charge of the branch network a year previously. Without consulting Henk Rutgers, Groenink promoted two regional managers to general manager. Suddenly Rutgers found himself in the company of Hans ten Cate (Rotterdam) and Dolf Collee (Eindhoven), two men who had until then reported to him. Groenink wanted this troika to form the division's executive leadership. That would enable him to deal with strategic issues.

Groenink spread his message in the regions with panache. Ensure that the bank has one culture, make the best man boss. Look to the market, compete, show enterprise. The people in the branches responded well to the fresh breeze of ambition blowing through the country. They had huge respect for Groenink's enormous expertise and skill. For credit questions, he was one of the best in his profession.

His managers talked of his ingenuity and his tremendous drive. The story about the hunting incident still circulated. Everyone remembered to be careful with his right arm, even shaking hands hurt. Groenink was still going twice a week for physiotherapy to build up his strength. He never complained about the pain and that also earned respect.

As did his phenomenal memory. Whoever Groenink met, he always recollected precisely what they had been discussing at their previous meeting. He would ask about the health of a member of the family, or refer to some other aspect of a person's private life. If he had a mind to, which was not always the case.

They were less happy with Groenink's haste. He had little time for disciplined management of change. He had no patience. Regional managers complained that their new boss had 'no mud on his boots'; it seemed as if he had no idea how things worked on the shopfloor. That implementing change, especially at ABN Amro, took time. Three months after issuing his *Visie 2000* report he was asking regional managers whether they had finished implementing it. When one of them said they would be starting the next week, Groenink was astonished. It was never quick enough for him. Everything had to be ready the next day.

Many also found his sense of humour awkward. Or rather: what he thought of as humour. At a dinner at a regional branch, where the cook had evidently done his best for the boss, Groenink wondered as the food was served, "You thought I was going to like this?!" To a regional manager proudly presenting his improved results he noted drily that the extra profit would soon be washed away by the five new regional offices in Timbuktu. With a grin he promised to do something about that once he was boss. Before talks with the employee council, Groenink laughed that Henk Rutgers should wear his yellow shirt if he wanted to get the best result from the negotiations.

Rutgers and Ten Cate warned Groenink. They felt he had set the bar too high. They knew that the targets would never be met. They also knew that costs would rise considerably in the first period, to enable branches to offer the full range of services. Nothing ventured, nothing gained, Groenink would retort sardonically, noting that the targets might be ambitious, but at least people would be doing their best.

The troika that led the domestic division found itself in trouble from the start. Members of the managing board felt a certain sympathy for the three. They noticed that Groenink did little to encourage harmony in the collective leadership, in fact it seemed as if Groenink actually pitched his subordinates against each other. It was anything but a team. Ten Cate and Rutgers complained about it; it was Collee who supported Groenink at every turn. He was the loyal vassal.

Among the top three there was little cooperation and a lot of conflict. Rutgers and Ten Cate were never going to be friends. Ten Cate and Collee were also constantly fighting. Groenink was not concerned. He explained that the clash of characters was where things happened, conflict was good. The best ideas emerged under pressure and stress.

The general managers felt like pawns in a game of divide and conquer. Groenink tended to give his subordinates different pieces of the puzzle, sometimes contradictory. This often led to misunderstandings and increasing tension. Groenink's analytical acumen actually prevented his immediate colleagues from challenging him: they didn't dare contradict anything he said. Groenink always knew better.

What many experienced as his overwhelming intellect widened the gulf between him and those around him. A gulf that separated a boss who seemed to win every conflict and above all, wanted to win. Groenink's closest colleagues felt that he should have spent more time dealing with the emotional side of the business. He should have shown more empathy. He was too concerned with being right, rather than getting things right.

They felt frustrated that Groenink never relaxed. The people around him had no sense of belonging, of forming a team. A team in which Groenink felt secure enough to let off steam. He was clinging to his image as a winner, nurturing it and making sure never to lose control. In the end, Groenink was inaccessible, even for the people closest to him.

For one of his colleagues it was a different story entirely. Rijkman Groenink and Irene Verboon fell in love. Ten Cate was the first to realise. He kept quiet. His friendship with Fentener van Vlissingen came in handy when Groenink suddenly found himself without a roof over his head after the divorce with Lucia Rodenburg. He was able to rent Fentener van Vlissingen's Amsterdam house for a while. Which didn't mean that Fentener van Vlissingen approved of the divorce. To friends he remarked that it seemed strange for a man to marry a woman who looked exactly like his former wife, only twenty years younger.

The news gradually spread. Now colleagues recalled meetings that had carried on until late and how at the end, as they were leaving, Groenink would remark to Irene that there was something he wanted to discuss with her. They understood why now.

Jan Kalff had occasionally walked into Groenink's office to find Rijkman and Irene discussing something on the sofa. The chairman had wondered at the time that there seemed to be something in the air. Romance had never crossed Kalff's mind. At ABN, divorce was frowned on; it was not many years since a divorce could cause a serious dent in a person's career. Years before, his elder brother Gerard had married Louis de Bièvre's first wife. It had caused considerable upset.

But even Kalff knew that this kind of attitude had become outdated. Besides De Bièvre, the unfortunate Meys had been divorced, as well as Drabbe. But Kalff warned Groenink and Verboon: it should not be allowed to cause a problem. They should be cautious. As the endless rumour and speculation spiralled, Groenink sent an email to everyone in the organisation: he and Irene were indeed involved. He hoped that people would now be able to get back to work.

Groenink's colleagues on the board disapproved of his divorce. It would be awkward on occasions when they met accompanied by their partners. Spouses had known each other for years; some had become friends and would now have to get used to a new face. It would lead to tension and conflicts of loyalty.

Some colleagues simply didn't understand: Groenink had such a nice, warm relationship with Lucia. Irene was a smart woman, but extremely rational. She was a lot like Groenink. But the few who ventured a remark directly to Groenink were met with a curt response. "Sometimes it's just over."

3

Dream

1996–1997

Wilco Jiskoot believed in ABN Amro's future as an investment bank. That was a deeply held conviction. He had always known that successful bankers were above all advisors to big companies. For years his father had been an influential banker, the major deal maker in Dutch industry. Jiskoot Senior would rather have been a farmer, but his great-grandfather Jan Lodewijk Pierson had founded Pierson, Heldring & Pierson. Jiskoot's father had been chairman of this leading investment bank until 1981.

As a youngster, Jiskoot had watched his father prepare major deals. At night he would keep tabs on the Amsterdam stock exchange prices as they were reported to him by phone. Like his father, the young Wilco had for a while thought of steering his intellectual powers in a different direction; he had fantasised about studying chemistry. But once he realised that the only prospect it held was to teach, he chose business economics instead.

In 1976, he joined Amro: the previous year the almost one-hundred-year-old Pierson, Heldring & Pierson had been taken over by Amro.

It was Fop Hoogendijk, the key deal maker at Amro, who was his principal mentor. In 1986, Hoogendijk appointed Jiskoot to a central position in the bank's share department. With it he explained that on this side of the bank's business there were no limits. This was where the bank's future growth lay. Here it was possible to earn money.

By now 46, the general manager of equity and merchant banking was no less convinced of this. Jiskoot had doubted the long-term profitability of the bank's traditional operation. Especially the bank's involvement in the domestic market, with its wafer thin profit margins. The club that Groenink now headed. The success of ABN Amro would rest largely on the organisation's achievements as an investment bank.

Jiskoot also believed in the success of the Amro culture. At ABN, colleagues were supposed to be friends; the investment banker didn't believe in that. Colleagues were colleagues, you had to be able to hold them to account. Jiskoot was convinced that the businesslike Amro culture was bound eventually to overshadow the outdated ABN culture.

His bosses, managing directors Rijnhard van Tets and Louis de Bièvre, were forging ahead. At the Bank of the Year Award in London in January 1996, ABN Amro's corporate business division was singled out. Business weekly IFR, awarding the prize for the second time to a European bank, cited three reasons: the remarkable merger of ABN and Amro, the solid network of overseas offices and the promising investment bank. In the latter category, IFR noted in particular the successful floating of KPN shares under Jiskoot's guidance.

An investment bank depends on expertise and contacts. A person who can read the market and knows who use that knowledge and how, can make a lot of money. In the Netherlands, ABN Amro's position and especially that of its principal deal maker Wilco Jiskoot had been unchallenged for years. It was also clear that there were too few major companies in the domestic market to provide a solid base for the corporate business division's international ambitions. The scope and power of American business were the reason why the United States ruled the roost in investment banking.

In the bank, and outside, a discussion had raged for some time: what should be the position of the increasingly expensive corporate business division as its focus shifted towards London? Analysts were wondering what ABN Amro was planning to do with the securities firms the bank had been buying and allowing to operate under their old names.

De Bièvre and Van Tets were the main advocates on the board for substantial expansion. They pointed to the industry's enormous growth. It was a fact. And at its hub were the stock exchanges that were becoming increasingly important in Europe. Growing numbers of private individuals were investing, not least in the Netherlands. By now 1.3 million households (20 per cent) were actively investing, around a third of them had started after 1994. A couple of years ago the super-rich Dutch pension funds had also been given the go-ahead to place more of their capital in shares.

Growing numbers of companies were discovering that fresh capital was to be found on the stock exchange. At the same time, the need for financial advice was increasing. While there had been around 200 relatively large mergers and takeovers in 1980, 16 years later there were around 40,000. The sums involved rose each year. In the Dutch market, by far the biggest for ABN Amro, the value of new and reissued shares in the first four months of 1996 stood at 5 billion. Prices were sky-rocketing; 1994 and 1995 were record years for new issues. In both years the market had raised over 10 billion guilders, of which most was due to the launch of KPN (whose shares were issued in two instalments).

In the board it was often said: if any part of the bank is to grow, it would be the corporate business division. It was an ambition worth pouring money into. Kalff had no problem with the growing corporate business division costing a couple of hundred million guilders a year.

In 1996, there was no need to worry about results. With profits of 3.5 billion guilders for 1995, the corporate business division had been good for 21 per cent of the total; for 1996 it would be 25 per cent. Kalff noted when presenting the annual accounts that "the breakthrough in the bank's profitability lay in the corporate business division". He continued proudly, "We have been jointly responsible for 172 share issues and we have been involved in mergers and takeovers to a value of over eleven billion dollars."

The bank also invested heavily. In 1994, ABN Amro took over the Italian securities firm of Cimo (75 employees). In France, the bank already owned Massonaud Fontenay Kervern and with CME the bank also had a stockbroker in Spain since 1992. In 1995, the bank acquired the Swedish securities firm of Alfred Berg, with 400 staff – the second largest trader and issuer of Scandinavian shares. And in 1996 the bank gained a majority stake in HG Asia, with 21 offices and 13 stock exchange seats.

In February 1995, Rijnhard van Tets had attempted to buy up part of the collapsed British Barings bank. In the end the whole organisation was acquired by ING.

Aad Jacobs, ING chairman, remarked that it represented "an extremely attractive extension of ING activities". Including the enormous debt, ING payed over 1.7 billion guilders. Fearing that the biggest rainmakers at Barings would turn their backs on the new owner, Jacobs promised on the day of the takeover that the 100 million pounds in promised bonuses would be honoured. Except for Nick Leeson, the trader whose speculations in Singapore had caused the bank to fail. A few months later, ING transferred its securities operation to Barings and moved the bulk of the corporate business leadership to London. With the 4,000 staff from Barings, ING's investment bank was now at a stroke bigger than ABN Amro, with 3,500 employees. That hurt.

Meanwhile, in London ABN Amro started work on an impressive new office to house its various activities, currently spread across three London establishments. It would be ready in 1998. ABN Amro had become one of Europe's biggest securities companies. In the summer of 1996, Jiskoot explained to *Het Financieele Dagblad* why ABN Amro had chosen a series of small takeovers rather than one large. He explained that small takeovers were cheaper and easier to manage. This reduced the risks of failure and improved the bank's competitive position. He also explained why the bank had rejected the accepted synergy benefits of having one recognisable name for the corporate business division. "What you take over is actually people. You have to do all you can to ensure that they feel at home in your organisation in the ensuing months. You have to give people room to get used to the new situation."

Jiskoot explained that traditional banking was becoming less profitable so that it made sense to put more resources into investment banking. He said that ABN Amro was aiming to achieve 40 per cent of its profits from investment banking. That was good. "After all, what would be left of the universal bank if the corporate business division grew even bigger?'

ABN Amro's capacity to trade in shares was enormous. It was on a par with the major American investment banks. But that wasn't enough. The bank needed to fill the front of the pipeline with transactions. Successful large investment banks generated their own transactions. They advised big companies to merge, or take over other companies. Or they advised on financing. For each transaction the investment bankers received a fee, a percentage of the deal.

Companies needed consultants with a proven track record. To get commissions from companies to take on these activities, a bank had to be in the so-called league tables: the top-ten lists of investment banks based on participation in major deals. Clients also demanded a good equity research department and sufficient capacity to distribute shares.

Jiskoot was proud of his collaboration with Rothschild. He had invited Tony Alt of Rothschild to participate in the KPN launch. That had gone so well that the two banks had decided to continue working together. Rothschild wanted trading capacity. ABN Amro would be able to profit from the strong position that the chic British investment bank enjoyed advising governments on privatisation.

To win more contracts in other areas, the corporate business division needed to expand by taking on new rainmakers. Deal makers who, like Jiskoot, had direct access to directors of major companies in Europe. Bankers with the guts to tell a captain of industry that they'd find themselves in trouble if they didn't sell part of their company, buy another firm, or issue more shares.

It was a lot to ask from a banker. They had to know the client's market intimately, if possible even better than the directors themselves. The message had to be conveyed with such conviction and bravura that a company director would feel isolated and alone if they didn't hire the bankers concerned. In the Netherlands there were very few experienced investment bankers with that sort of aggression; the bank was forced to look overseas.

Jiskoot heard that 37-year-old Hugh Scott Barrett was available. Having steered the merger between his Swiss Bank Corporation and the larger

British investment bank SG Warburg, his career seemed to have slowed down. Jiskoot used headhunter Russell Reynolds to approach Scott Barrett. The Brit was interested. He was offered a position as head of corporate finance at ABN Amro/Hoare Govett and a mandate to bring the ABN Amro corporate finance department (mergers, takeovers, share issues) into shape.

Scott Barrett asked his colleague Arnold van Os to join him at the bank. He would work from London, while Van Os worked the markets from Amsterdam. They were astonished at what they found in their new bank. This was a major global institution, yet it still worked and thought like a local Dutch bank. They were amazed by the informality of the decision-making process. And the way the bank's top people would meet in their free time outside the office and discuss business in a vague, intangible manner.

When they discovered that the managing board, and indeed the supervisory board spent hours discussing bonuses for investment bankers, they were shocked. Any bonus over 500,000 guilders had to be approved by the board. Scott Barrett knew that the sums at which ABN Amro baulked were nothing compared to the payments that major American rivals made to their talent. If ABN Amro wanted to get the best people working at the bank, they would have to dig deeper into their pockets. At the same time they saw that Jiskoot and Van Tets were gradually acquiring the money and trust to expand the corporate business division.

ABN Amro's corporate ambitions were watched with envy at subsidiary MeesPierson. Parent and subsidiary sailed the same waters. Generally the subsidiary gave way to the parent. They had both been interested in acquiring Alfred Berg. It was ABN Amro that took up the chase. At MeesPierson there was constant conflict between the two sections of the merged bank: the Mezen and the Pieren. Pierson, Heldring & Pierson had blossomed as an Amro subsidiary in the late 1980s. Since the merger with what they considered the inferior ABN subsidiary Mees & Hope those days were over. Profits in the first year after the merger stood at a meagre 5.4 per cent. The cost-profit ratio was 74 per cent, even worse than the parent bank.

After a relatively good year (1993), things went wrong again in 1994; income rose by 4 per cent, but costs spiralled by 10 per cent. And in 1995, ABN Amro's return on its approximately 2 billion guilders of capital in MeesPierson was a poor 9 per cent. Analysts expected ABN Amro to sell off its subsidiary. They estimated the price at 2.6 billion.

In May 1996, a new managing director was appointed. 48-year-old Joost Kuiper had been director of Amsterdam's options exchange for three years. He had worked at Amro for fourteen years after graduating in law, mainly in investment banking, for a while under the legendary corporate banker Fop

Hoogendijk in New York, Brussels and London and later as a director in Rotterdam. That was when he got to know his friend and colleague Rijnhard van Tets. Kuiper, who liked to think of himself as a "a slogger who never stops working", was so frustrated by the lethargic decision-making process at the bank that he left in 1987 to become financial director of Granaria, a cattle-feed company.

It was Van Tets who suggested to Jan Kalff that Joost Kuiper should head MeesPierson. They asked Kuiper to offer his ideas about the bank's future, keeping in mind a possible sale at some stage. He agreed.

But Kuiper didn't get the time to make any plans. In October, ABN Amro confirmed they were talking to Fortis about selling their subsidiary. The Dutch-Belgian bank and insurance firm had knocked on Jan Kalff's door several times. Kalff had held off at first, but in August he called Fortis himself to find out if they were still interested.

They were. With VSB as a subsidiary, Fortis had part of the Dutch market for private customers covered, but the corporate market and the capital market were areas in which Fortis played no role whatsoever. That gap would be filled by acquiring MeesPierson.

Rijnhardt van Tets headed the sale; he put Hugh Scott Barrett in charge of the negotiations. With typical British understatement, Scott Barrett noted that MeesPierson was not exactly a jewel. Investigation showed that there were too many provisions on bad loans, that the bank's administration was a mess. The talks between ABN Amro and Fortis didn't go smoothly. Both sides were frustrated. It was clear to the Fortis negotiators that ABN Amro knew little about what sort of bank MeesPierson was.

Fortis director Joop Feilzer, who led their negotiation team, judged the subsidiary to have been the least successful merger in the banking world. The Mezen and Pieren had fought each other tooth and nail, just short of actual violence. Fortis was to discover that some parts of MeesPierson were under tight supervision by the Dutch Central Bank, due to bad loans. They were livid and considered taking ABN Amro to court. Yet in the end they didn't. Fortis realised the acquisition also offered opportunities. A major cause of MeesPierson's failure lay with the parent bank. For years, ABN Amro had been cherry picking.

The negotiations were tough. Every time Van Tets and Scott Barrett thought a deal had been reached, Joop Feilzer came with another message from the home front that the price was still too high. After several of these crises, they finally settled in late December for 2.5 billion guilders, around ten times the bank's profit. Fortis director Maurice Lippens still considered the price too high, but agreed nevertheless.

Jan Kalff thought ABN Amro had been underpaid, but realised that there had been no alternative. To *Het Financieele Dagblad* he remarked that "In the end we came to the conclusion that there was little hope for the bank under our regime, so we had to cut the knot. We couldn't let MeesPierson waste away."

Fortis director Hans Bartelds was happy with the acquisition. With MeesPierson, Fortis was now the fourth bank in the Netherlands. Bartelds was also pleased that the internal balance with the Belgian half of Fortis was now also restored. In Belgium Fortis had recently acquired two other banks: ASLK and NMKN.

Joost Kuiper, who noted that his role in the proceedings had been largely passive, saw advantages to the move. "We could always persuade clients that we were smarter than our parent bank, yet the parent would always have more muscle. Which is why we often lost out."

For the Mezen and Pieren, the move to Fortis was a mixed blessing. Fortis was a less prestigious bank. However much they had hated ABN Amro, it was the country's biggest bank. After it came ING and then at a distance Rabo perhaps. The thought of being part of a rather small half-Belgian bank and insurance company was painful. And yet there was a sense of relief. Fortis had promised to open the windows. There would be room for enterprise.

While the life's work of his ancestors passed into Belgian hands, Wilco Jiskoot decided he should focus more on ABN Amro's strategy. To steer the bank in the direction of investment banking. Moreover, Jiskoot considered that the board was too distanced from the bank's clients. He didn't have the status that went with membership of the board. His clients, directors of major companies, often asked him why he wasn't part of the bank's highest echelon. It was a question he occasionally passed on to chairman Jan Kalff.

In the board they had their doubts: Jiskoot was a fantastic deal maker, but he was no managing director, no manager in fact. Which was why Hazelhoff had blocked an earlier attempt to appoint him to the board. Jiskoot was no diplomat either. Some managing directors found him rather abrupt, too impatient, boorish even. And he had no idea how to present himself. Jiskoot never sat in a chair, he slouched. Invariably smoking. At the same time, Kalff knew well that many of the major companies hadn't chosen ABN Amro, they had chosen Wilco Jiskoot's professional skills. If they failed to appoint Jiskoot to the board, and he left the bank, he would probably take many of those major clients with him. And few would know why.

Jiskoot made by far the most deals. He was quick and smart, and a keen analyst. No one set an issue price as accurately as Jiskoot. It was an art to set the price of a share so that the company selling felt that it wasn't too low, while the buyers had the feeling that there was room for the price to rise, if possible on the first day of issue. This was one of Jiskoot's skills.

Clients loved him. If Jiskoot thought that a client should choose one option, but the client went for a different option, Jiskoot would carry on just as enthusiastically with the client's choice. Managing directors were aware that some of the bank's governors were also keen supporters of their star consultant. Many of them had personal experience of his client-focus. Whenever they tried to reach him, wherever he was, they would always get to speak to him within ten minutes. And whatever the question, Jiskoot always came up with an answer.

Among his staff he was popular too. He was always accessible. Wilco Jiskoot defended his people and did whatever was needed to ensure that their interests were properly supported in the bank. Colleagues who worked for him considered him a good listener.

Jiskoot dismissed the doubts about his eventual appointment to the board as nonsense. He believed that it was possible to be both a good deal maker and a good managing director. His father had been both.

So on 1 January 1997, Jiskoot was elevated to the managing board. He was soon in the thick of it. Two months after his appointment, stories about Louis de Bièvre began to circulate. On the afternoon of 25 February 1997, the chairman of ABN Amro's corporate business division confirmed that 'in 1992 his wife had traded shares in an equity fund while being aware as a result of statements made by him of certain details relating to that fund'.

The board met that evening in emergency session. Advice was sought on several fronts. Publicity experts Ruud Hoek and Jules Prast were called in. They had no idea of the finer points. They were given a dilemma to consider: what if the impression were created that a high-ranking person at the bank had been guilty of insider trading? After a short consultation the publicity team decided that it would be impossible to sell that to the public.

Some of the managing directors, including Jan Kalff, were surprised by Groenink's tough stance in the discussion. The next morning, the bank announced that De Bièvre had decided after 35 years at the bank and 12 on the board, to resign with immediate effect from all involvement in the bank. That same day, Rijkman Groenink walked over to Hoek and Prast. He told them that he had never given much credence to publicity, but that their persuasive contribution the previous evening had shown him how important it was.

Jan Kalff realised that there was no other option, but thought it terrible – for De Bièvre and especially for the bank's image. Rijnhard van Tets became the new chairman of the corporate business division.

The corporate business division flourished. In 1997, ABN Amro was one of the coordinators, together with Rothschild, of the privatisation of Telstra, the KPN of Australia as it was called. This was the largest share issue of the year and placed ABN Amro for the first five months among the world's ten largest investment banks.

It whetted the bank's appetite. Proudly, Jan Kalff announced that ABN Amro's corporate business division belonged among the world's five or seven largest investment banks. Kalff warned that the required growth could not come exclusively from acquisitions; the bank would have to build. And that would cost money.

Lots of money. Especially for a bank built on the philosophy that its staff worked for the collective good. Many of the Dutch investment bankers could only fantasise about huge bonuses for the moment. By way of compensation, on the final day of the KPN deal for example, Jan Kalff personally thanked each of the investment bankers involved, shook their hand and told them that the bank was proud of them.

Jan Kalff's focus was firmly on the United States. Standard Federal Bank Corporation was acquired for 1.9 billion dollars. Although only really active in the Midwest, ABN Amro, employing 16,000 staff, was now the largest foreign bank in the United States.

Some analysts and investment bankers wondered why ABN Amro had financed this takeover with borrowed money. The stock market was good, the share price was good. This would saddle the bank with a huge burden, while the money could easily have been raised through the shareholders.

In the board the matter was not a subject for discussion. The managing directors were agreed that the bank should focus on improving the return on shares. Issuing new shares would dilute their value and force the price down. The managing directors felt that ABN Amro was undervalued on the stock exchange, compared to other banks. First the share price would have to rise, only then would it be possible to issue new stock.

In May, the bank's shares were officially quoted on Wall Street. Jan Kalff flew to New York to sound the opening bell. He was proud that the bank was traded on Wall Street, and saw it as the crowning achievement of the bank's robust and growing presence in the United States. He explained that the bank wanted to be more tangible for American investors and would not exclude the possibility that in the event of another major takeover ABN Amro might tap the American capital market with a new share issue. "There are no plans on the table," Kalff said to *Het Financieele Dagblad*, "but you can't keep paying cash for takeovers *ad infinitum*. We see the Wall Street quotation as an opportunity for future sellers to choose between cash and shares."

Rijkman Groenink was away. From March to May, he and Irene had taken a jeep to travel the ancient Silk Road; for centuries, the main link and trade route connecting Europe and Asia. It was the first time anyone at the top of the bank had been absent for so long.

Endless jokes were made about the perilous journey that the macho Groenink had undertaken with his new young love. Respect dominated: for a person who could do almost nothing with his right arm, it was a dangerous adventure.

At the bank's domestic division they had trouble getting used to Groenink's absence. In theory, the arrangement was that the boss would be away for three months. But the jeep had an antenna for a satellite phone. Groenink was reachable. People were constantly calling him, to report that something was going wrong. After which Groenink, to their great annoyance, would phone one of his adjutants: Rutgers, Ten Cate or Collee.

The governors had to get used to the idea too. When a potential collaboration with insurance firm Delta Lloyd was proposed, Rob Hazelhoff could not contain his irritation. It was Groenink who had said a year earlier that insurance should be a core competence of the domestic division, yet it was still only good for 2 per cent of the bank's total profit. The aim was to raise this to 10 per cent; a combination of forces with Delta Lloyd would achieve that. Groenink sat in on the meeting by satellite. Hazelhoff couldn't understand it. The man should have been present.

After his return, Groenink's stalwart jeep could regularly be seen in the car park outside Foppingadreef head office. Colleagues would wonder over to admire and fantasise. Not without reason. When he returned, Groenink announced that the trip had done him so much good that he would make sure everyone who had put in five years of intensive work for the bank would have the right to a two-month sabbatical.

The couple were back in time for Jan Kalff's birthday. But only Rijkman was invited as he and Irene were not married. Several leading figures complained about the confusion that Rijkman and Irene's relationship was causing. It was complicated to deal with her as the secretary of the division. She was their secretary, but she was also Groenink's partner. They felt they could no longer talk freely. The couple understood. In the summer of 1997, Irene left ABN Amro and a while later began working at Randstad employment agency.

Seven years after the merger, there were still eight men on the board. The balance between ABN and Amro had been carefully maintained: four and four. Dolf van den Brink, of the ABN set, was now the youngest and left the boardroom last. He had replaced Ruud van Ommeren. The managing directors still started their meetings on Tuesdays and Fridays by sifting through a pile of credit applications. These stacks could be as thick as 30 or 40 centimetres.

Jan Kalff was the undisputed chairman. He was practically always there. And on the occasional absence for a holiday, they could still reach him: he was in touch every day. Kalff had a tremendous sense of duty and earned his colleagues' respect. They admired his sober attitude. His eye for detail. Kalff would fume if a managing director ordered an espresso machine for his office. What was wrong with ordinary coffee? He found the countless colour photocopies ridiculous. More and more presentations to the board were accompanied by colour powerpoints and full-colour documentation for everyone in the room. Kalff was so annoyed that he sent a memo asking people to reduce the number of colour copies they made.

A continual plague was the cost of plane travel. This was a constant subject for debate on the board. The bank spent around 300 million guilders a year on flights. There seemed no way to reduce these costs. They tried everything to make savings while keeping their employees happy. Middle-ranking bankers would henceforth fly out to the United States on economy class, and return business class, arriving home rested.

Staff often remarked that it would help if members of the board set an example by making savings. But that was not part of the deal. The managing board flew first class. Occasionally they discussed which first class provided better service.

The rank below managing board, the general managers, managed to negotiate that they would fly first class if the flight took more than eight hours.

In fact, general managers and department managers were constantly being reminded that they were a rung below board level. If the board was still discussing the previous matter at a meeting, the summoned general managers or department managers had to wait. It was not uncommon for ten expensive bankers to sit and stand around in the corridor for 45 minutes or an hour, waiting to be called in.

It was always polite in the boardroom. Although the managing directors had a love-hate relationship with Jan Kalff, they respected his integrity, his unreserved involvement. But managing directors such as Jiskoot, Van Tets and Groenink considered Kalff too predictable, too cautious. Groenink found the atmosphere lethargic.

Occasionally he would test the chairman. For example, when plans were prepared for computerising the mortgage department. After consulting with department manager Ron Toorenvliet, the enthusiastic Groenink proposed discussing the 260 million guilder investment with the board. He didn't expect any problems.

When Jan Kalff complimented the department manager at the meeting and proposed to proceed, Groenink suddenly raised a host of objections. The difficult discussion that followed lasted two hours; the project passed with the slimmest of margins. Toorenvliet, who was sitting beside Groenink, was in shock. He couldn't understand it: his boss had approved the plan. The next morning, Groenink explained to him that it was natural that he didn't understand. It was a kind of higher mathematics. What he was really doing, however, was checking that the chairman realised precisely what was at stake.

All the board members would visit between ten and as many as thirty clients a year: this was executive involvement. It built up goodwill. Kalff believed in it implicitly. Not because a managing director's contribution was essential to a client, the bank had specific people for all its tasks. It was that clients wanted to know that the concern for their welfare went up to the highest level. It engendered a sense of trust.

Moreover, managing directors would often learn from these visits. About investment opportunities in Vietnam, for example. Which might lead to the bank considering Vietnam as an area for possible expansion. Clients would often have comments or suggestions about ABN Amro products and services or those of rivals, which might lead managing directors to new ideas.

De Jong, Van Tets, Drabbe and Jiskoot were especially keen on visiting clients; they were good at it. Jiskoot encouraged his colleagues to conduct themselves a little less like distant ambassadors on these occasions.

Rijkman Groenink ignored that sort of thing. It was not one of his priorities. Which disappointed his regional managers. They complained about Groenink's lack of client-focus. They also complained that they saw too little of their boss in the field; Groenink seemed to prefer his own office. It was not uncommon for him to cancel a promised visit to a major client's gala dinner at the last moment.

Kalff was closely involved with a number of the bank's clients. It was a tradition that the bank's chairman served Koninklijke Olie, for example. When Hoogovens accepted an ING offer in the late 1990s, an angry Kalff phoned the chairman of the steel plant's board, Maarten van Veen. He felt that Van Veen, a governor of the bank, had committed a form of treason by not choosing his own bank. In Kalff's view, after years of contact, he had a moral obligation to put ABN Amro first. The bank should at least have been given an opportunity to offer a lower price than its rival.

Clients found this attitude puzzling. It was as if the bank were operating in a different century. Some called it laziness; others called it arrogance.

Sometimes clients visited the managing board: Léon Melchior paid a call on Jan Kalff. Once again he brought up the HCS business, and Rijkman Groenink's role in the affair. That he had a right to compensation for the loss he had suffered. Like his predecessor, Jan Kalff maintained his reserve under Melchior's blunt tirade. He knew that as the bank's senior figure he had to be careful not to make any concessions. Especially when dealing with a man like Melchior, whose reputation was far from blameless. Yet Kalff recognised that Melchior's claim was not totally without merit. He decided to set up an inquiry.

Harmonious leadership, that was what Kalff considered most important of all. Joint responsibility for the bank's collective welfare: team spirit. That was how to create a culture in which you worked for each other and for the bank, not for yourself. That's why he insisted that the whole managing board signed the annual report. They all earned the same salary, after all, only the chairman received 20 per cent more.

The 1996 annual report showed excellent figures. Measured by its total assets, the bank had risen from eighteenth to fourteenth in the world rankings since 1990. Kalff preferred to focus on a different list: measured by profit, the bank stood in eleventh place.

Media pundits felt that ABN had won the merger. Writing in HP/De Tijd in the summer of 1997, investigative journalist Marcel Metze noted that 'The merger of ABN and Amro was a success. But what seemed to be a merger was actually a takeover: ABN chief Hazelhoff's clever "After you," turned the ABN Amro combination into an expanded ABN.'

That pleased Jan Kalff, always an ABN man at heart. He had devoted over 35 years of his life to the bank. With his aristocratic manner, he was the figurehead of a bank with an impressive history. A history in which ABN bankers more than any were immensely proud.

One subject concerned Kalff especially. The bank had grown fast. What tied all these employees and clients together? It was vital that they felt some sort of bond. Did they know what ABN Amro stood for? If the bank were to continue successfully, it had to cultivate a sense of common values. It was nice that the bank's non-Dutch contingent was growing, and it was vital. But did they realise sufficiently in London, in Chicago, in Amsterdam, in the 72 countries in which the bank operated, that they were part of a single organisation?

The chairman was worried about the bonus culture that had taken hold of the bank. It was as if people were working for themselves, not for the bank. Surely his colleagues should realise that a bank needed to place the highest value on propriety, reliability for clients and meticulous caution when it came to providing credit.

Jan Kalff decided to devote time to formulating the bank's core values. Values that would give his personnel a sense of common purpose. He wanted these values to be a personal statement and made a video in which, standing in the old ABN (and Nederlandsche Handel-Maatschappij) head office on Amsterdam's Vijzelstraat, he held forth on the importance of clear values. He explained how those values were embedded in the walls, and showed that they were illustrated in the stained-glass windows of the historical building.

With the decoration of his knighthood in his lapel and his collar tied to the highest button, the chairman expressed his concern. "Unity is crucial for our bank and more important than ever, yet increasingly difficult to realise." Most important was integrity. "Because when this is missing the bank is cheapened." Then came respect, for each individual and every society. Then teamwork, "because that is the essence and enables us to succeed as a bank with a universal network. In the interests of our clients we have to learn from each other, and share our skills with each other."

The last value was professionalism. As the camera zoomed in on a bronze figure of William of Orange, Kalff continued solemnly, "Only by bringing these values into practice will we be able to continue our success." And then, "All our stakeholders are important. First and foremost our clients, then our staff, then the society in which we conduct ourselves as model citizens. And through all of this we can ensure a premium result for our shareholders. In that sense the motivation that drives us is to create shareholder value."

In the next shot Kalff appeared in his office at Foppingadreef. Seated on the corner of his desk he explained what these core values meant for him in his work. "In the board we discuss all the major credits. So I get to see them myself. Sometimes everything seems to be right, yet I'm still left wondering what the client actually needs the loan for.' Then, suddenly standing up and with a strict face, "If I can't find a good answer for that and I continue to feel uneasy I have to decide not to award the loan. It may be a painful decision, but that's what these values demand of me."

The chairman concluded with a call to all staff to discuss these values and to implement them. "Because these values are essential for us today, vital for our future and consistent with our history."

Response in the bank was lukewarm: why should we bother with all this, everyone knows this anyway? I learned that from my mother as a child. Why is head office interfering like this? Why don't they tell us about the direction the bank is going, the choices that this will entail? Isn't wanting to do everything everywhere a little overambitious?

The subject of strategy was still being ignored. Groenink and Van Tets were particularly concerned that Kalff focused far too much on the history of the bank. He seemed to be managing with a rearview mirror. Nevertheless, there were more strategy discussions under Kalff than under Hazelhoff. Around four times a year the board gathered for an afternoon at the bank's Duin & Kruidberg country estate to reflect on all manner of subjects. Strategy was one of the topics.

Various managing directors were concerned about the share price. It seemed to be floating about uncertainly. Didn't shareholders believe in the universal bank concept? In the board the feeling was that the interests of the shareholder should be central.

Once a year, a morning was set aside by the board to review the bank's entire top two hundred. Where they stood, how they were doing, whether it wasn't time for a change. This rarely involved any really harsh judgments. Kalff felt it was unnecessary to be overly tough. If you were too severe you made people unhappy, people who might be good at their job, just not good enough to push further. That was a pity. Intellectually he could understand the growing criticism of his colleagues. They wanted greater accountability. But they had no common ground. If someone failed to reach the top 100, when should they get rid of him ... at 92 or 50?

If a colleague failed in some way, they looked carefully at the cause. A client might have left the bank for reasons that the banker had no way of influencing. You could hardly blame a colleague for a choice that the client had made independently.

Moreover, the bank's management information system focused entirely on gaining insight into transactions. It was impossible to find out about the income that a client was generating. That annoyed people like Jiskoot and Groenink, but no action was taken to change the situation.

The bank's upper echelon knew that the worst that could happen if you failed repeatedly would be a transfer to another department. There were examples of senior executives who held barely any responsibility any more, yet retained their salary and perks, sat quietly in their office and did vague, indefinable stuff.

Lack of accountability resulted from the habit among the 'men from het Gooi', as the two layers below the board were called, of appointing people in informal ways, without any sense of transparency.

Where human resources were concerned, one subject had nagged at his mind since his assumption of the chairmanship: the succession. Jan Kalff talked about it at least once a year with the bank president. It was the bank's tradition for the chairman to propose a successor to the head of the supervisory board, who would then appoint the candidate.

It had been agreed that if Kalff were struck down in some way, Michael Drabbe would at least take over in a temporary capacity. Again in discussions about the planned handover in May 2000, Loudon and Kalff preferred in the first instance to go with Michael Drabbe. The former Amro man was the senior managing director. For Kalff and Loudon, Jan Maarten de Jong, Kalff's right-hand man, was the undisputed reserve choice.

Kalff was not particularly close with Aarnout Loudon. Naturally a man like Loudon was highly regarded and he had a fantastic network, but Kalff would rather have had Floris Maljers as his counterpart. He was far more enterprising. Loudon seemed overly conservative, he seemed to respond rather than act. And he appeared to know remarkably little about banking, never contributing anything substantial to any discussions about the bank. Their talks were therefore generally brief. Too brief, thought Kalff.

Kalff was not particularly impressed by the quality of the supervisory board. He felt that the governors needed an injection on modern leadership. The chairman wanted more give and take. With Loudon's agreement, the successful chairman of Ahold, Cees van der Hoeven, was invited to join the supervisory board. Antony Burgmans, CEO of Unilever, was also asked to become a governor.

Towards the end of 1997, at another meeting at Duin & Kruidberg, the composition of the managing board was once again brought under review. The immediate reason was the retirement of Paul Ribourdouille in 1998. Kalff wondered whether it might not be a good idea to bring in someone from outside. He was thinking of former ABN chairman André Batenburg, who had brought the ministry of finance's treasurer general Coen Oort onto the board in 1977. It had been a well-received fresh breeze.

They made up a spontaneous list of possible candidates. The minister of finance, Gerrit Zalm, was one of the names. Alongside the former minister of economic affairs Hans Wijers, then a consultant with Boston Consulting Group. Also Bert Heemskerk, a former Amro man, who had left the bank in 1991 to become chairman of Van Lanschot Bankers.

Jan Maarten de Jong suggested Tom de Swaan, the number two at DNB, the Dutch Central Bank. De Jong had known De Swaan for years. Tom de Swaan would have liked to have become president of DNB, but the previous summer Nout Wellink had been appointed Duisenberg's heir. And since Wellink was only two years De Swaan's senior, that position seemed now to have moved out of range. Moreover, De Swaan had mentioned to De Jong that a job with a commercial bank might be an intriguing prospect.

Kalff found the idea interesting. As a central banker, De Swaan had an impeccable record. He would immediately be in line as a possible candidate for the chairmanship. And if someone else got that post, the board would have truly heavyweight chief financial officer (CFO) in its midst. Kalff recognised another benefit: De Swaan was neither ABN or Amro. It was resolved that Jan Kalff would approach Tom de Swaan in the new year.

As the year drew to a close, the bank held its annual Christmas dinner for the upper echelon at Duin & Kruidberg. The entire board, general managers and department managers were expected, with partners. Kalff felt it important: this informal mix of investments bankers and senior executives would encourage the bank's team spirit. The wines were good. They came from the bank's cellars. Jazz pianist Tonny Eijk provided a perfect musical setting.

The chairman had devoted long hours to the guest list. He invited publicity man Ruud Hoek to do the invitations and reminded him that Groenink should receive a single invitation, since he was still 'not officially with' Irene. But that turned out to be untrue.

Rijkman Groenink and Irene Verboon married on 12 December 1997. Few at the bank knew about it. Hardly anyone from the bank was invited, not even Hans ten Cate. Indeed, it was only just before the wedding that Ten Cate heard about it from Henk Rutgers. Rutgers let fall that he had been invited, as had Dolf Collee.

When a ruffled Ten Cate came for an explanation, Groenink pointed out that the situation had been problematic. He hadn't wanted to invited the ABN Amro board to his wedding. It would have been too much trouble. Paul Ribourdouille, the managing director who helped run the bank's domestic division, had also not been invited.

But not to leave out Ribourdouille while inviting his other close colleagues would have been too painful. So he had decided to leave out one of his three general managers too. Since he regarded all three equally highly, he decided on the colleague who would be able to deal with the apparent snub best. The fact that Ten Cate hadn't been invited was in fact the best compliment he could have wished for.

Ten Cate considered it a strange and dangerous explanation. It stirred his suspicions. Behind everything that Rijkman Groenink did there seemed to be some incomprehensible calculation. Surely that was the proof that Groenink was unable to feel any sense of empathy?

At the Christmas dinner the newlyweds Rijkman Groenink and Irene Verboon welcomed the guests and accepted their best wishes. Jan Kalff ventured a joke in his speech. He congratulated his fellow managing director that Project Irene had now been successfully completed.

4

Setback

1998

Michael Drabbe was popular. He set the pace in the boardroom. He may not have been much of an intellectual banker, but he had a gift for bringing people together and enthusing them. Subordinates who accompanied him at meetings with clients would be questioned afterwards not about statistics but about "What did you see in his eyes?" Drabbe was a people person, everyone agreed. He was street wise.

There were countless anecdotes about the 56-year-old managing director. He led a flamboyant life. He had started out as an artist in Paris, until in the late 1960s his father more or less forced him to get a job as a desk clerk at ABN. In the 1970s, he worked for Chase Manhattan in the United States. In 1979, he became an Amro managing director; four years later he was appointed to the managing board. After the merger with ABN, Drabbe was put in charge of the sluggish domestic division.

Drabbe was from Amro stock, but ABN bankers respected him. Especially because he was able to put his aggressive Amro ambitions into perspective. Drabbe explained the tremendous desire among Amro managing directors to change the bank's strategy as a result simply of Amro not being best at anything. Of course it was precisely what the ABN set wanted to hear. Particularly the appended warning that Amro people tended to like change for its own sake. Drabbe seemed to be able to bridge the gap between the ABN and Amro cultures.

Since Dick Meys' death, he had the best chance of succeeding Kalff, even if only for a couple of years. He was the senior managing director, and came from the Amro stable. It was Amro's turn. He had seen every part of the bank. Moreover, Jan Kalff had handed him his favourite overseas division.

That network was the pride of many ABN people. But what did those 850 offices in 66 countries actually earn? The managing directors approached the sensitive subject with caution in the board. Numbers expert Zeilmaker occasionally threw the cat among the pigeons by demonstrating that the overseas offices barely paid their way. This would inevitably lead to a debate: ABN people questioned the way the costs and profits were calculated.

When the supervisory board dealt with the subject, Wim Dik would recall with a smile how, as secretary of state for economic affairs in the early 1980s, he would often be met on his travels abroad by a consul from the ABN fold. In grand style. Managers of national networks were encouraged to take the post of consul, to cultivate contacts and serve the Dutch national interest. The bank paid for the appropriate accommodation, where numerous gala dinners would be held.

In the overseas division most of the money was made in the Midwest of the United States. In 1997, the bank earned 2.7 billion guilders abroad; 600 million more than in the Netherlands. Almost 60 per cent of this was in the United States. Inspired by the *Visie 2000* report produced two years previously for the domestic division, Drabbe invited Ikon consultants Martin Simon and Peter Dudok van Heel to philosophise with him about foreign strategy. Especially about the importance of new domestic markets for the universal bank.

The consultants sketched a scenario in which the universal network bank rested on various columns. The massive stone on top was the retail operation, the corporate business division and capital management. These were supported by the two domestic markets: the Netherlands and the United States. While for the consultants it may have been a mere intellectual exercise, Drabbe began disseminating his column theory as if it were Gospel. Wherever he came, the managing director would draw a kind of megalithic tomb, his body vibrating enthusiastically as he explained to his colleagues the need to strengthen support for the roof. The bank needed more domestic markets, to energise the network.

That the bank needed more domestic markets was not disputed. A domestic market guaranteed a flow of new large and medium-sized clients. Clients interested in the services of investment bankers or in the global transaction service (GTS). The latter was designed for international clients. For a company doing business in 30 countries, for instance, ABN Amro would be able to combine the various accounts and show exactly what was being earned day by day. If the company were turning over 50 million and only 10 million was needed on a specific day for payments, the bank could keep the remainder elsewhere, earning interest.

To make GTS profitable, the bank needed large numbers of major clients. In recent years the bank had invested around 2 billion guilders in the system. It cost around 400 million a year. The governors were shocked by these sums, but understood that there were at most only four other network banks (HSBC, Citigroup, Deutsche and JP Morgan) with a comparable system. They also understood that those four banks had a far larger domestic market, with numerous major companies who would use their services. To create new domestic markets, ABN Amro would have to buy up large banks. Preferably in Europe. But there was not much on offer in Europe, and banking was dominated by national interest. A takeover would only make sense if it placed the bank among the five largest in the country and drew major clients as a result.

Drabbe believed that ABN Amro's answer lay in emerging markets. In Asia and in Eastern Europe. Markets in which a new middle class was developing. Asia seemed especially interesting; he had lived there for several years. Drabbe was disappointed that ING was doing far better in many Asian countries, acquiring more licenses to provide bank and insurance services. The indefatigable Drabbe flew round the world in search of opportunities to further the bank's overseas ambitions. He took the time to find out about countries in which the bank hoped to expand, devoting two weeks to sit with country managers and work out what the local problems were.

In Vietnam, for example, the bank had trouble getting a banking licence. It would be possible to obtain one for a bribe of around 35,000 dollars, but Kalff and Drabbe refused absolutely to travel down that road. Drabbe asked country manager Boudewijn Poldermans to find out a little more about the governor of Vietnam's Central Bank. It turned out that he played the violin. During a visit to the Netherlands, Drabbe organised a performance by violinist Emmy Verheij at a dinner at the Muiderslot castle. The governor was deeply moved. A few weeks later, the bank had its licence.

In November 1996, Drabbe bought the Hungarian Magyar Hitel Bank for the modest sum of 100 million dollars. A small bank, that the managing director hoped "would develop into a little ABN Amro in Hungary", as he told *Het Financieele Dagblad*. Drabbe knew that ABN Amro had a lot of time to make up in Eastern Europe. In fact there was another reason for his regular flights to Budapest. Drabbe had fallen in love with the Mexican ambassador to Hungary. In the board he called her jokingly, his lady-friend.

No one knew which came first, the lady-friend or the Hungarian bank. Kalff assumed that it had been a bit of both. It didn't matter. He agreed that ABN Amro needed to put more effort in the burgeoning Eastern European market. In the corridors of the bank the new overseas policy was pleasantly summarised: wherever Drabbe finds a girl, we buy a bank.

'ABN Amro closes in on global top ten,' headlined *de Volkskrant* on 27 February 1998. During the presentation of the annual accounts for 1997, board chairman Kalff glowed with confidence. He described the rising profits of almost 17 per cent to over 3.8 billion guilders as "splendid". And noted that since the merger, profits had almost tripled. With total assets of 836 billion guilders, the bank could soon lay claim to a place among the world's top ten. Pre-tax profits stood at 5.8 billion guilders, 2.1 billion earned in the Netherlands, almost 1 billion by the corporate business division and 2.7 billion by the overseas division.

A negative element was the continued increase in costs. Earnings had risen by 24.5 per cent, but costs had increased by 27 per cent. The efficiency ratio stood at 69.1 per cent, against 67.7 per cent the year before. Kalff emphasised once again that "every part of the bank has promised to watch its costs this year".

The corporate business division's earnings were another disappointment, falling 3 per cent compared to the previous year, to 930 million guilders. Kalff emphasised that the bank would invest more in this area in the coming years, in order to compete with the large American investment banks. He explained, "Extra high bonuses need to be paid to attract top people. And they won't earn that back immediately, in the first one or two years."

Kalff was rather less laconic on his trip to London where he tried to explain to the bank's staff that they really ought to try to do better. In fact Kalff found the enormous bonuses galling. Especially since these were the cause of the disappointing results: while earnings had risen by 30 per cent, costs had increased by 47 per cent. Kalff sermonised to the assembled investment bankers that they should work harder, that they were too expensive. Kalff tried to persuade them that they should work more closely with the rest of the bank. During his address the hall gradually began to empty. While the chairman spoke, the remaining audience heard the purr of the Ferrari in the car park below as they started up and roared off. Kalff was livid; they had behaved abominably.

Yet for the Anglo-Saxon investment bankers, it had been Kalff who had struck the wrong note. He should have been grateful they were working for ABN Amro at all. That they were willing to put their expertise and network at the disposal of the Dutch bank. For them, this was not a job, it was a collaboration. Kalff should have understood that they had only joined ABN Amro to earn as much as possible together. They weren't working for the bank, they were working for themselves. As long as both parties benefited, they would continue.

The market for investment bankers was booming. Banks were fighting for talent. ABN Amro was competing against specialised American investment banks such as Morgan Stanley, Merrill Lynch and Goldman Sachs. Each of the local European markets had its own local giant: Société Générale in France, Deutsche Bank in Germany, UBS in Switzerland.

ABN Amro's corporate business division was still only big in the Dutch domestic market. Even in the American Midwest, ABN Amro was making little headway in this area. In 1997, more than half the turnover was still in the Netherlands. If the bank wanted to be among the world's five or seven largest investment banks, it would need to raise its game in Britain and the United States.

Kalff supported the idea of creating a large investment bank based around the bank's clients in various countries. He was increasingly impressed by the opportunities sketched by Wilco Jiskoot for the corporate business division overseas. Yet Kalff warned him: we're a universal bank, we'll never be a Morgan Stanley.

Meanwhile Rijnhard van Tets in particular tried to push the bank further. He proposed acquiring the American PaineWebber. Kalff had no faith in such a risky billion-dollar takover. Rijkman Groenink and Michael Drabbe agreed, they had their doubts about the value of the corporate business division anyway. Would it ever achieve sufficient scale to make up for its stupendous costs?

The quantity and size of the fast increasing bonuses were a constant theme in the discussions of both the managing board and the supervisory board. The vast majority were paid out to the investment bankers. Dolf van den Brink, the managing director responsible for human resources, reviewed the lists with Van Tets and Jiskoot. Year after year they kept asking for more.

Each time they explained that the really good specialists, whether traders or merger experts, would only join ABN Amro if they received a large enough bonus. In the Anglo-Saxon world it was customary for around 15 per cent of the amount a group of investment bankers earned for a bank would be divided in bonuses among themselves. This could often amount to millions per banker. And regularly even more. For 1997 they shared out around 400 million guilders among two thousand staff at the investment banking division. By far the most went to the top two hundred. They received bonuses of over 1 million dollars each.

Kalff was annoyed that he didn't even know most of those two hundred people. It was appalling, but he had to concede and guarantee bonuses in order to win key bankers over from other banks. Other members of the board, such as Jan Maarten de Jong and Michael Drabbe, also found the annual debate about the size of these bonuses irritating. Hundreds of millions were being spent on people who earned comparatively little for the bank. De Jong felt that enough was enough, yet Jiskoot and Van Tets seemed to raise the stakes higher each time. They defended themselves laconically: so let them take 20 per cent of the proceeds home, the rest would still be for the bank.

The Brits at Hoare Govett and Rothschild, as well as the well-paid staff at Alfred Berg, laughed. This Calvinist debate meant little to them. If you played the game then large bonuses were part of the deal.

Van Tets found it frustrating to have to ask for more money each time. He and Jiskoot tried to circumvent the problem: they explained to new colleagues that ABN Amro didn't need to pay huge bonuses because the bank was such a good employer. They told the investment bankers that they had security of tenure and would not be held to account as severely. But it was naive. The bankers weren't interested. What they wanted was a large bonus, and if possible guaranteed for a couple of years.

Van Tets didn't enjoy paying out bonuses. Each of the investment bankers would come to his room in turn. Many of them earned more than he did. There were times when he handed over a cheque for 2 million dollars and it would be handed back with the words: I'm worth more. If Van Tets told him to take it or leave it, the cheque would be pocketed with an angry frown. That was part of the game; if you looked pleased with your bonus, the boss might think you'd be happy with the same amount next year.

Then there were the tiresome arguments about who actually earned the most for the bank. Everyone claimed as much as possible for themselves. The commercial staff, the people who networked, would constantly bicker with the so-called product people. These were the bankers who actually served the clients.

The network-oriented investment bankers tried to prevent clients accessing the product people; as long as contact went through them, it was clear that it was their client. Meanwhile, the product people argued that clients chose the bank because of their product expertise.

In 1998, Van Tets made one last effort to change the system, to make it more Dutch. In future bonuses would be calculated on achievements measured over three years. It lasted less than a week. As soon as the change was announced, the best people began leaving.

Top investment bankers would only stay if the bank's bonus pool promised good bonuses. What made it complicated was that the bonus pool only began to improve if there were enough people making major deals. That was why bonuses had to be guaranteed in advance, otherwise no one would join.

Van Tets and Jiskoot were increasingly inclined to shift the whole investment bank discussion to London. There at least they understood the bonus issue.

But this had the opposite effect: the Dutch investment bankers began demanding London rates. Colleagues who had moved to banks such as CSFB, Merrill Lynch, Morgan Stanley and Goldman Sachs explained that they were treated differently there. One anecdote circulated about a colleague who had expressed disappointment while negotiating his fee with a major American bank that there was no lease car in the package. They immediately gave him 50,000 dollars to buy a car.

ABN Amro bankers who moved to London asked to be excused from the bank's generous expat package. They didn't want the rent subsidy, the nice furniture and the free schools. They wanted to be paid by local standards: a salary of 120,000 dollars and the prospect of a bonus of a couple of million.

Van Tets and Jiskoot expressed their concern to the board of an imminent brain drain in the Netherlands. After much discussion the board agreed to start paying London-type bonuses in the Netherlands. It would cost the bank hundreds of millions. And it created new tensions: as more Dutch bankers started receiving major bonuses, discontent began to spread in other sections of the bank.

Van Tets and Jiskoot showed Jan Kalff adverts in the *Financial Times* and *Wall Street Journal* in which large investment banks congratulated promoted colleagues with the title of managing director, MD. Managing director didn't mean that they were in charge of a large department with lots of employees; it meant that they were entitled to a larger cut of the bonus pool. The two investment bankers urged Kalff to use the title more widely at ABN Amro. There were only ten managing directors. The bank had been avoiding this for years.

The heads of the corporate business division were afraid that without this title, many colleagues would leave the division to become an MD elsewhere. Kalff gave way. Large groups of investment bankers could henceforth call themselves managing directors. The title was on a par with executive vice-president (EVP), formerly department manager; one rung below senior executive vice-president (SEVP), formerly general managers. That the new MDS in the corporate business division used this title was fine by the department managers. At least there was a difference now. Like Kalff, they feared title inflation.

But the genuine department managers began comparing themselves to the new MD department managers. That hurt. A department manager in the domestic division had difficulty leasing a Volvo 850 with a three-litre engine. His colleague, an MD department manager, bought whatever car he chose, or two. The decision had another side-effect: the bank's top hundred – the general managers and department managers – practically doubled. The investment bankers, good for 20 per cent of the bank's profit, were a majority in the top two hundred.

The rewards would eventually come, Jiskoot and Van Tets promised. The bank had the talent, and once this was known and accepted the so-called elephant deals would start to arrive: the huge commissions for share issues and mergers.

But many of the bank's clients were unconvinced. They doubted whether ABN Amro would ever be able to offer the same expertise and know-how that the major American banks had in house. Even the big British investment banks lagged behind. Governors such as Wim Dik and Cees van der Hoeven, chairmen of major Dutch multinationals such as KPN and Ahold, warned against excessive optimism. It would be difficult for large international companies to imagine that an investment bank based in a domestic market with only one airline and one major telecom company would be able to build up truly meaningful expertise. And that was all they would be prepared to pay serious money for: state of the art expertise in their industry.

Hugh Scott Barrett had his doubts too; operating from London he realised that the bonus discussion was above all a cultural problem. In London it was accepted. In fact ABN Amro would have to double its bonuses if it wanted to attract the best people. Would the parsimonious Dutch be prepared to take the plunge?

At head office it was generally agreed that the time had come to put an end to the wave of opportunistic foreign acquisitions. Drawing on the column philosophy it was decided that the bank should concentrate of certain focus areas. Areas in which the bank recognised potential for growth; areas in which autonomous growth and acquisitions would lead to new domestic markets, new columns. A central supportive role was played by the planning and control department. Headed by general manager Wilco ten Berg, the department attempted to map out exactly where the bank was earning money.

One country that had been unambiguously declared a no-go area was Thailand; it was far too corrupt. It came as a surprise therefore, when Michael Drabbe proposed acquiring the Thai Bank of Asia. He pointed out that the Asian crisis, for which the bank had just put aside a reserve of half a billion guilders to cover possible losses, might also offer opportunities. To the press Drabbe announced, "The crisis will enable us to buy." In some countries, notably Thailand, foreign banks were now able to purchase majority stakes in local banks. The weaker banks were particularly susceptible to takeovers.

One of these weaker players was Bank of Asia. Eleventh largest in Thailand, the bank cost a mere 400 million guilders and was described by the enthusiastic Drabbe as a "small universal bank with lots of potential". He knew that poor credit portfolios (insufficient securities and collateral) were a major problem in Asian banks. The close, opaque ties between banks, politicians and commerce made a sober businesslike assessment difficult. But Drabbe wasn't worried. "This bank is managed according to Western corporate values."

Although the planning and control department issued a clear warning against the acquisition, Jan Kalff silenced the discussion and decided that if Drabbe recommended the purchase, it had to be good for the bank. Moreover, the *Asia 2000* plan, which had been drawn up in 1996, aimed at a doubling of the number of staff in Asia.

In the supervisory board it was noted, rather disparagingly, that the expansion of the bank in Europe had yet to be realised since the merger. Outside the Netherlands, only the United States was doing well. Some governors wondered whether it wasn't perhaps time for the bank to move its head office to the United States. To Chicago, for example, home of subsidiary LaSalle. The American contribution to the bank's earnings had begun to match its domestic earnings. In the United States it all seemed to go so much easier and faster. During a collective meeting of the board in Chicago the proposal was actually placed on the agenda.

But who were the men sitting round the table? Jan Kalff, Michael Drabbe, Rijkman Groenink, Rijnhard van Tets, Jan Maarten de Jong, Wilco Jiskoot and Dolf van den Brink: they had lived practically all their life within around forty kilometres of each other. Their life was in Holland, in het Gooi or Aerdenhout. Of the twenty general managers (all men) only one was not Dutch. No, moving to the United States was clearly a bridge too far.

On the board, Rijkman Groenink began to take a closer interest in the European discussion. Earnings in his domestic division had been disappointing. Though operating results had improved by some 20 per cent over the last three years, the principal target – an increase in market share of 10 per cent – had not been realised.

Most worrying of all were the rapidly rising costs. For 1998 they would be almost 18 per cent higher than the previous year, while profits would increase by only 10 per cent. The number of branches had been reduced, but the number of people working at the bank had increased dramatically in order to be able to provide a complete package of services. In two years, the bank's staff had expanded by almost 15 per cent to over 25,000.

Yet the integration of services to boost the sale of more products to the same clients had produced the desired effect. It irritated Groenink that many of the 220 regional managers were using the autonomy they had been given to do the opposite of what they we supposed to do. Instead of trying to earn more money from underdeveloped clients, they were paying even less attention to them.

He realised that *Visie 2000* had not succeeded. Groenink gave Henk Rutgers the task of reorganising. Yet there was no money for this. A major discussion ensued. The atmosphere soon became ugly. The managing directors noticed signs of exhaustion in the domestic division.

Disappointing earnings in the domestic market, still the market with the smallest margins in Europe, proved to Groenink the need to find a second European domestic market. He was not the only one. Europe was in turmoil. ING had bought Belgium's Bank Brussels Lambert. In Germany, Bayerische Vereinsbank and Bayerische Hypotheken und Wechselbank merged to form Bayerische Hypo und Vereinsbank. In Switzerland, SBC and UBS followed suit.

ABN Amro's board decided to ignore the British market since prices were too high. Anyway, the bank baulked at the galloping tempo in Britain. Germany was also ruled out. They had eyed Commerzbank a few years ago, but the problems this bank had experienced integrating with smaller German banks were discouraging. Moreover, Drabbe had insisted plainly that he didn't plan to sit in the boardroom with Germans. And since everyone on the board held a veto, Kalff had concluded that there was nothing more to discuss.

And so they arrived at what they termed the southern corridor. That was where the vital second European domestic market lay. In February 1998, things began to move. France's state-run CIC was being privatised. Credit Industriel et Commercial was a medium-sized bank employing over 21,000 staff. Belgium's Generale Bank appeared to be interested but had just announced they would not be making an offer. In the media speculation was rife about the possible takeover of Generale Bank by the Belgian-Dutch Fortis.

ABN Amro moved in on CIC. A takeover would make France the desired second European domestic market. On 20 February, *Het Financieele Dagblad* reported that the Dutch bank could count on 'considerable sympathy' among personnel, management and unions. Since ABN Amro had no network in France, the unions judged that its promises to not restructure the bank radically were reliable. Kalff was enthusiastic. "We would acquire a major position in France. With fourteen hundred branches and millions of clients, CIC is one of the big retail banks in France."

The deadline for the offer was the following Monday, 1800. The media assumed that apart from ABN Amro, bids would also be submitted by France's big four banks (BNP, Société Générale, Credit Mutuel and Credit Commercial de France). Analysts judged the price would be around 10 to 14 billion francs (around 3 to 4 billion guilders) for a 67 per cent stake. European commissioner Karel van Miert warned, "We cannot rule out a French solution, but French banks should not receive an advantage."

Kalff assured the media that ABN Amro's bid was proportionate: CIC would soon begin to earn its way. He expected ABN Amro to show a "psychological advantage over the French bidders" since there was little overlap and not many jobs would have to go. *Het Financieele Dagblad* concluded cautiously that ABN Amro's bid was evidently not a knock out offer.

It wasn't. Some managing directors were disappointed and thought Kalff was being too careful. Rijkman Groenink and Rijnhard van Tets wanted to hike up the offer, but no one supported them on the board. Once Drabbe, in charge of the overseas offices, came down in favour of Kalff's caution, they backed down. But the doubts remained. Would the bid be high enough?

Especially since commentators were wondering openly whether the French minister of finance Dominique Strauss Kahn would select yet another foreign buyer, following the sale of two major French insurance firms (AGF and Athena) to Germany's Allianz and Italy's Generali respectively. Strauss Kahn had let it be known that he would be looking for a national solution for CIC. The relatively weak French banking sector needed shoring up.

On the evening of 14 April, Kalff received a call from Strauss Kahn. It was a short message: CIC would be going to Credit Mutuel. From the French minister's words Kalff surmised that while ABN Amro had offered the highest bid, the preferred choice had been for a French bank. When Credit Mutuel's bid of 13.4 billion francs was announced the next day, Kalff knew that ABN Amro's bid had been around 5 per cent higher.

It was a major blow for the board. Some suggested appealing to Brussels. But that would have caused an unseemly fuss: the managing directors had been brought up not to argue with authority. Moreover, the board was worried that a complaint to the commissioner would place ABN Amro's French subsidiaries, which provided about a third of the bank's European profits, under pressure. A couple of managing directors noted that in future it might be better to leave purchases to local investment bankers who knew the market better.

Michael Drabbe was disappointed. At the presentation of the annual report he said, "The French have chosen to set CIC back in time." During the press conference one journalist suggested that Begium's Generale Bank might prove a potential second European domestic market. Kalff responded cautiously, "Belgium is certainly interesting and promising and would make a superb supporting element. But it seems to be holding up the Fortis house. Anyway, why disturb a brooding hen?"

Fortis, primarily in the person of its Belgian chairman Maurice Lippens, had been trying for almost a year to acquire Generale Bank, known in Belgium as G Bank. Lippens was getting there, slowly but surely. The realisation in the Belgian establishment that this might lead to the creation of a single giant Belgian bank was encouraging.

Maurice Lippens came from a well-known French-speaking aristocratic family living in Flanders which was one of the founders of AG insurers in the early nineteenth century. Although his father, mayor of the Belgian town of Knokke, considered the commercial world a nest of thieves and had warned his son against becoming involved, he had followed his legal studies by doing an MBA at Harvard. This was sufficient for his uncle to invite him in 1981 to join AG, then still dominated by the Lippens family.

The wealthy Lippens had ambition: he wanted Fortis to grow fast. Taking over Generale would fit in well with his plans.

Lippens had another reason for wanting this takeover. He wanted to speed up the merger between Amev and his AG. Too many conflicts remained; the Belgians and Dutch refused to meet halfway. The Dutch had been insisting for some time that the whole organisation should become a Dutch company, while Lippens wanted it to be a Belgian firm. This went deep.

A few weeks before, the tension between the Belgians and Dutch had surfaced in a painful way. In late March, the Fortis Amev supervisory board had fired 51-year-old Joost Kuiper, who had arrived at Fortis through the acquisition of MeesPierson. Kuiper had been appointed chairman of Fortis Nederland six months previously. In a euphoric mood, Kuiper had announced to Fortis Nederland's supervisory board that little would change for the better in the bank as long as founding father Hans Bartelds remained in place.

He had painted himself into a corner. The Dutch at Fortis believed that Kuiper was conspiring with the Belgians. They blamed him for trying to force an issue that the two merger partners were not yet ready to face. Kuiper saw it differently, but had lost hopelessly.

Maurice Lippens was totally surprised when he heard Kuiper had been fired. No one had consulted him, the Belgian half of the bank. Yet it had been explicitly agreed that appointments and dismissals at that level would be arranged jointly. Moreover, he liked Kuiper's regular demonstrations of disdain for Dutch and Belgian partisanship. Lippens was livid. He was convinced that the board needed to be united for Fortis to succeed. He had had enough of the tortuous discussions about parity and informed his Dutch colleagues that this had gone far enough.

Bartelds and his right-hand man Henjo Hielkema (a former ABN Amro banker) explained to Lippens that it was an exceptional situation, Kuiper had committed high treason. There had been no option. The argument escalated and led to both sides realising that Fortis would have to find a new organisational structure, and fast. They knew that this would not be simple. Weeks of meetings followed, with impassioned discussions but no results.

Lippens decided one way of breaking the deadlock would be to take over Generale Bank: Fortis would become a Belgian company, it was the only solution. He was glad when the Dutch contingent intimated that Generale would suit Fortis well.

But there was one major obstacle: the directors of Generale Bank, led by Fred Chaffart, chairman of the *directiecomité*, had no desire to be taken over by Fortis. Chaffart feared the inevitable rationalisation of the bank: the combination was far too Belgian. For a healthy future, his bank had to look beyond the frontiers. Journalists Stefaan Michielsen and Béatrice Delvaux have shown in detail in *Zes huwelijken en een begrafenis* how Generale Bank was being pushed to accept the Fortis deal by prime minister Jean Luc Dehaene, the president of Belgium's Central Bank Fons Verplaetse and even King Albert.

The supreme strategist played the lead in this Belgian drama. Lippens, ever smiling, had two basic principles: occupy the terrain and don't avoid an opponent but look him straight in the eye. Lippens wanted a major Belgian bank. The previous year he had tried to buy Bank Brussels Lambert behind ING's back. He only withdrew when he found out how badly BBL was doing. Taking over Generale was his last chance.

His opponent, Fred Chaffart, was increasingly nervous in early April when he discussed strategy with Paul-Emmanuel Janssen, head of his supervisory board (a powerful body in Belgium since it represents the principal shareholders). While they met, they were surprised by a phone call from King Albert. He advised Janssen to reach an arrangement with Fortis. In the national interest. Janssen was put out, but managed to respond, "Your Majesty, it's not that simple. We have nothing against Fortis. We feel that their proposal isn't good for our bank, because ..." The king didn't give him a chance to finish. "Pardon me, but I don't have much time. I'm calling by GSM. I'm on holiday. When I get back to Brussels, we should discuss the matter in more detail." The line went dead. Despite several requests to the palace to see the monarch, the promised conversation never happened.

On 19 April, Chaffart outlined the terms to Lippens under which the *directiecomité* would agree to cooperate. Generale Bank would form the foundation for the three Fortis banks (ASLK, VSB and MeesPierson) and Chaffart would remain in charge. Lippens protested, but gave ground. Once it was apparent that a majority of his shareholders supported the Fortis bid, Chaffart decided on 9 May, under pressure from the shareholder-governors, to agree to the merger. On 13 May, the Belgian newspapers headlined that there would be a Big Belgian Bank. Fortis would pay out 410 billion franks (around 22 billion guilders).

A few days later, Lippens's Dutch colleagues were forced to concede that the Belgian half of the bank would carry far more weight after the acquisition of Generale Bank. Co-chairman Hans Bartelds realised that the Belgian culture would now dominate. It had been agreed with Lippens that they would aim at creating an independent concern in Benelux in Europe; now he was playing second fiddle. If there were only seventy branches in the Netherlands and a couple of hundred in Belgium, the new head of retail could obviously not be a Dutchman.

On Sunday 17 May, an agreement of principles was signed regarding the new Fortis structure. The Dutch presented it as a choice for a European future. To the home front in the Netherlands they explained that business considerations had prevailed, and that was good.

Various former Amro bankers had remained in contact since the failed merger with Generale ten years earlier. Rijkman Groenink and the Generale *directiecomité*'s André Dirckx still spoke occasionally. Groenink knew from Dirckx that the *directiecomité* and the chairman were unhappy about the course of events.

An old dream was revived. The ABN Amro board decided to make an offer for Generale Bank. Rijkman Groenink was in the driving seat. He headed the domestic division: Generale Bank would fall under his supervision in a new European division. The American investment bank Merrill Lynch was hired as leading consultant.

Jan Kalff hesitated, but eventually agreed. The bank had led the way with the merger of ABN and Amro, had led the way with the early development of the American bank and would now lead the way in building up a European power base. Moreover, Kalff's aversion to hostile takeovers would not be compromised since the directors and the president of Generale Bank all supported the ABN Amro initiative.

A robust discussion erupted when the subject was broached in the ABN Amro supervisory board. This was the first meeting joined by Unilever managing director Antony Burgmans. Burgmans wondered whether the managing board could be certain of winning the battle for Generale. Groenink was irritated by Burgmans's remark and pointed out that it had been discussed with the Generale Bank management and that they were in favour. Surely it was impossible for the management to be in favour and for it not to happen?

Former chairman Hazelhoff also expressed his concern at the end of the discussion. He found the idea logical, but he was convinced ABN Amro would never succeed. He noted that the sale of BBL to the Dutch ING had caused pain in Belgium. The Belgian establishment had planned to create a Big Belgian Bank out of BBL and Generale. They would be unlikely to let their last major bank disappear.

On Sunday afternoon, 24 May, Jan Kalff phoned Fred Chaffart to announce that an offer would be made. Chaffart warned him, "You'll have all of Belgium against you." Yet he knew also that there would be no future for him in a Fortis-Generale combination. Moreover, Chaffart believed that ABN Amro offered his bank far more potential. It would be less Belgian and more European, and it would mean far fewer redundancies. The shareholders would also be better off with a higher bid. After all, the Fortis bid was a hostile bid.

On Monday morning, Jan Kalff called Hans Bartelds. "Hans, I've got some unpleasant news. We have to look into this, we can't just let it pass." Bartelds sensed through the phone that Kalff was embarrassed and grew angry when the ABN Amro chairman tried to explain that this was not a hostile bid. His emotions were getting the better of the generally phlegmatic Bartelds. He pointed out to Kalff that the Fortis offer had already been accepted, that an agreement had been reached. It had been announced ... if this wasn't a hostile bid, what was it then, he asked rhetorically with suppressed rage.

Lippens couldn't believe it either. It was an incredible sign of arrogance by the Dutch bank. To think you can be a player in the game at such a late stage, without even finding out what was really at stake. He was furious at Chaffart. He felt betrayed by the man whose hand he had shaken in front of the cameras just eight days earlier.

On Tuesday 26 May, Kalff and Groenink expanded on their plans to Generale Bank's *directiecomité*. Chaffart recalled how Rijkman Groenink had persuaded him ten years earlier, when he was director of Tiense Suiker, to transfer his accounts from ABN to Amro. The latter was then planning to merge with Generale Bank. There were other happy memories of that attempt to merge Amro and Generale and its dramatic collapse. Chaffart was positive.

That same Tuesday afternoon, the bank organised a press conference. Kalff and Groenink glowed with confidence. "Welcome to Brussels, the home base of our future European banking division. We offer Generale Bank a dowry: Europe. Under ABN Amro's wings, Generale can be the biggest bank in the European Union, with its head office in Brussels. Fortis offers Generale Bank market leadership in Benelux. That's a niche and you can be happy there. But we offer Generale Bank Europe. It is the best solution for the bank, its shareholders, staff and clients."

Kalff emphasised that the offer of 450 billion Belgian franks (9,000 franks cash per Generale Bank share and 19 ABN Amro shares) was not hostile. Wilco Jiskoot and the investment bankers of Merrill Lynch had done the maths. The offer (around 24.5 billion) was about 15 per cent higher than Fortis. "We are confident that Generale Banks' *directiecomité* will support our plan."

On the Radio 1 news programme, Kalff commented, "No, I wouldn't call it anything other than a friendly offer. It depends on what the management thinks. We have complete faith that the management supports us." In the interview, he reflected on the fact that this would represent a historic reunion. ABN Amro and Generale Bank had both been founded by King Willem 1, when Belgium and the Netherlands had still been one country. In fact Generale had been founded in 1822, two years earlier than ABN Amro's predecessor Nederlandsche Handel-Maatschappij. As Kalff remarked, "It's a coincidence, the path that history sometimes takes."

The Belgian monarch had little sympathy for his nostalgia. The same day he summoned the governor of Belgium's Central Bank, Fons Verplaetse, to explain his concern regarding the Dutch coup. Verplaetse assured the king that he would do everything he could to divert ABN Amro's attack. Verplaetse phoned his Dutch counterpart, DNB president Nout Wellink, to tell him that ABN Amro's offer was considered remarkably hostile in Belgium. Wellink was less theatrical. He tried to focus on their common interests. He appealed to their common Benelux identity in Europe. Wellink had already been in touch with an old friend, the king's cabinet representative. He had told him unambiguously: a takeover by ABN Amro simply wasn't going to happen. In his discussion with Verplaetse, Wellink made it plain that he found the way the Belgians were blocking the takeover out of national interest problematic. Verplaetse's conclusion left little to the imagination. "Then it'll be a fight to the death."

Belgian newspapers carried headlines such as 'Goliath ABN steals G Bank from David Fortis'. *Het Belang van Limburg* captioned a photo of Jan Kalff with 'Jack-in-the-box' – Jack being the devil. Pictures of Greek temples abounded. All with three columns: the Netherlands, America's Midwest and Belgium. At a meeting with Kalff and Groenink, Belgian prime minister Jean Luc Dehaene stated that "We share your analysis of the changes in the European financial sector. But we consider that the Fortis project is a better solution for Belgium than ABN Amro's offer. We have no legal instruments to prevent you making your offer, but we shan't make it easy for you."

Maurice Lippens was furious. Either way, it would cost him money. ABN Amro had far deeper pockets than Fortis. He might even lose the battle right at the last minute.

Eyebrows were raised again and again as his managing board reviewed the clumsy, direct, arrogant way the Dutch were attempting to entice Generale Bank. Had Kalff and Groenink no idea of where power lay in Belgian commercial structures? Surely they should have realised that the managing board chairman's power was limited in Belgium, more like the head of the supervisory board in the Netherlands, while actual decision-making power lay with the leading shareholders on the supervisory board?

Yet Lippens still didn't feel confident. He tried everything to shore up the Fortis offer. What if Generale Bank's supervisory board agreed to an issue of 10 per cent extra shares? With the extra 10 per cent, Fortis's stake in Generale would come to 43 per cent. Since ABN Amro had declared that its offer had to be supported by 60 per cent of the shareholders, this would decide the matter in Fortis's favour.

On Wednesday 30 May, Kalff and Groenink appeared before Generale Bank's supervisory board to state their case. It was plain to them that Generale would become an ABN Amro subsidiary. They found the Dutch tone arrogant. Generale Bank's managing directors noticed also that despite the warnings that the entire Belgian establishment opposed the ABN Amro takeover, the Dutch managing directors seemed to care little about the political ramifications. The decision to use the Brussels office of the Dutch legal firm of NautaDutilh was awkward. What was smarter was to use ABN Amro's Belgian director Jean-Paul Votron to calm the fears of the Belgian unions.

Meanwhile, reports of Rijkman Groenink's hamfisted humour had begun to surface. At a dinner, for which he arrived late, and where a fine Margaux stood open on the table, he apparently sat down and ordered a beer. Few people like that sort of joke, and Belgians least of all. Although Groenink had almost always travelled to Belgium by car, on one occasion he flew by private plane. The Belgians were shocked.

More importantly, Groenink failed to win over Daniel Janssen (chairman of Solvay chemicals). Daniel was a younger brother of Paul-Emmanuel Janssen, another shareholder-governor. The brothers had diametrically opposing views about the future of Generale Bank.

On 29 May, *de Volkskrant* published a portrait of the architect of the Generale Bank takeover. 'Groenink has a reputation for being hard and emotionless. But people who work closely with him consider that he has become much nicer recently, without losing any of his intellectual keenness. But watch out. Giving up is not a word that appears in Groenink's dictionary. "His will-power forces people to respect him," says a colleague. "In the late 1980s he was the victim of a hunting accident. As a result he has a problem with one of his hands. If it were anyone else you'd notice. Not Groenink though."'

When Maurice Lippens read this, he realised that this could have happened to him too. Lippens also hunted. He never forgot that 25 years before on the way home from a hunt he had left a loaded gun in the back of the car. The worst thing you can do. But he had been lucky. The story about the hunting accident and its consequences gave him a new respect for Groenink. This was a worthy opponent.

Meanwhile, Groenink was feeling more confident than ever. He told his colleagues in Amsterdam that he had already decided where he wanted to live with his young family in Brussels. He was looking forward to running the Europe division. One of his colleagues was surprised to hear this. On the way to Brussels, Groenink had talked endlessly on the phone about a plot of land on the banks of the river Vecht that he intended to buy.

Groenink had stumbled on it together with his pregnant wife Irene. They had peeked over the fence and told each other: this was it. They wanted to build a house together. They fantasised about owning their own modern country estate, like the merchants of Amsterdam's Golden Age, on some neglected piece of farmland near Loenen on the Vecht.

For Lippens it was clear that Fortis had to raise its bid above ABN Amro. That led to a tough discussion in his managing board. Increasing the offer would be dangerous. There were doubts about Generale Bank's structural profitability. In the end it was agreed to raise the bid once. The shareholders supported the board and gave Fortis until Friday morning, 5 June, to outbid ABN Amro. They specifically stipulated that no further increase would be made. Fortis would not be able to pay a higher price.

ABN Amro's bid had cost Fortis at least 3 billion guilders, but Generale Bank now seemed to be leaning back towards Lippens. Throughout that day, Lippens jumped every time the phone went; he was petrified that ABN Amro would increase their offer and knock Fortis out of the ring. Lippens knew that if ABN Amro raised its bid by 5 per cent he would lose Generale Bank.

A few hundred kilometres north, Rijkman Groenink was telling his colleagues to do precisely that. He wanted to make an offer that Fortis couldn't match. The statisticians on the board advised against it. They calculated that ABN Amro had already made a maximum offer. They were already paying 25 billion for a bank that made less than a billion guilders profit.

Wilco Jiskoot backed Groenink. He knew that Generale Bank would be ABN Amro's if they increased their bid by 5 per cent. Their Merrill Lynch consultants had reached the same conclusion. A lively discussion followed. Some managing directors were unconvinced, they didn't believe Fortis would match the present offer. The board was split. They decided to vote.

It was a dramatic moment; they had never voted before. Jan Kalff insisted that every decision by the board should be collective. Not in this case though. Groenink was sure of Van Tets and Jiskoot's support. He needed one more vote for his Belgian adventure.

Those in favour hoped to get the fourth Amro man on the board on their side: Michael Drabbe. But the overseas boss decided to back the man he hoped to succeed as chairman. The board remained split: three for and the rest against. Van den Brink, Drabbe and De Jong supported the cautious Kalff. A further increase to beat Fortis's offer was rejected. Groenink was deeply disappointed; he knew ABN Amro had lost the battle.

Aarnout Loudon was in London when he got the message. He was annoyed. The president considered it a huge strategic error. But he didn't believe there was anything he could do to change it. He couldn't be certain that raising the offer would deliver Generale Bank to ABN Amro. But even if that weren't the case, raising the offer would at least force Fortis to pay out more. It was the logical thing to do.

That Friday evening, Daniel Janssen called Generale's supervisory board in emergency session at the bank's head office on Warande in Brussels. Paul-Emmanuel Janssen, chairing the board, tried to persuade the bank's managing directors to postpone their meeting to Monday. But Daniel refused. "You'll be surprised when you see how many people turn up."

Twenty-four of the twenty-eight board members (including six members of the *directiecomité*) were present that evening. Journalists Michielsen and Delvaux describe the meeting hour by hour. The Janssen brothers exchanged words. Daniel Janssen wanted to know from Chaffart why he supported ABN Amro's proposal. When he answered that he had not had sufficient time to work out the details of the collaboration with the Dutch bank, Daniel Janssen grew angry.

Tensions rose further when Paul-Emmanuel Janssen circulated a letter from Jan Kalff in which he warned the bank not to vote for the poisoned chalice construction. Kalff anounced that the board members who voted in favour would be held personally responsible and if necessary would be taken to court. Some of those present resented the suggestion. They were told to call Maurice Lippens. He assured them that he would cover any legal costs or claims. Around midnight, with seventeen for and nine against, Generale decided to take the chalice.

Earlier, they had discussed whether ABN Amro's offer was hostile or not. Eighteen had voted that it was; seven against (the *directiecomité* with Paul-Emmanuel Janssen). And so the board accepted the Fortis offer, raised by 15 per cent to almost 26 billion guilders.

That Saturday morning, the despondency in the ABN Amro board was palpable. Dolf van den Brink felt this was the moment to throw in a higher bid, to trump Fortis. No one responded.

Kalff asked Groenink, whose baby it had been, whether he still wanted to increase the bank's offer. He shook his head. Twenty-four hours earlier a 5 per cent increase would have been sufficient. Now Generale had become too expensive. Irresponsibly expensive. ABN Amro's managing board decided to throw in the towel.

For the second time in two months, the crucial second European domestic market had slipped through their fingers. The governors, who Van Tets had asked on Friday to be ready to meet, were told that they would not be needed.

Shortly before the press release went out, Jan Kalff called Hans Bartelds. He informed him that ABN Amro was giving up and withdrawing from the race. It was a brief, businesslike call. In the press release, ABN Amro's frustration was palpable. 'ABN Amro has had to take account in its deliberations of the need to recognise certain factors which play a role in Belgium and which in this case have subverted the guarantee that all shareholders may exercise a free choice.'

The disappointment was huge. Some former Amro bankers relived the trauma of the failed merger of Amro and Generale. They thought Kalff had been too cautious. He should have pressed ahead. Merrill Lynch's investment bankers were also disappointed; they had missed out on a sizeable bonus.

By the time Fortis took over the running of Generale Bank, Fred Chaffart and Paul-Emmanuel Janssen had already resigned.

Lippens hailed his victory as a birthday gift to the king. Albert II showed his pleasure and gratitude by raising Baron Maurice Lippens to the title of count.

The brand new count celebrated his triumph shortly after the takeover with a hunting trip to Spain. The guest list included Rijkman Groenink. When he failed to show, his fellow hunters joked: naturally, he wouldn't dare now.

Across the way, on Amsterdam's Zuidas, the ING managing board had followed Kalff and Groenink's misfortunes in Belgium with a certain *schadenfreude*. They congratulated themselves on having done a far better job the year before. Some commentators seemed to relish ABN Amro's defeat. They should have learned from the way ING had appraoched Belgium's BBL. ING directors Aad Jacobs and Godfried van der Lugt had taken the time to visit the bank's leading shareholders. ING had invested four years in grooming crucial shareholder-governors and had discovered how business is done behind behind the scenes in Belgium. Step by step.

In the ABN Amro managing board the disappointment was soon overshadowed by the sad news that the jovial Michael Drabbe was gravely ill. He had skin cancer. It was unclear how serious. Drabbe intimated that he would continue working as long as possible.

Jan Kalff had troubles of his own, too. Besides the sadness at his colleague's illness, his wife Lydia had announced that she wanted a divorce. He was completely surprised and heartbroken. They had a good life together, after all. Lydia had also contributed enormously to the bank. He had always felt that they had done so together. Now, for the first time in his life, Jan Kalff began to doubt about his devotion to the bank. Had the price been too high?

Jan Kalff had to gather all his courage to tell the board. When he told Aarnout Loudon and Frits Fentener van Vlissingen that his marriage was on the rocks he noticed their shock. They were not pleased. First the business with Groenink and now this. It shouldn't happen at a bank, it made the wrong impression.

In a strategy discussion, Jan Maarten de Jong, responsible for risk management at the bank, proposed helping Drabbe lead the overseas division. De Jong was willing to combine the functions because he knew that Tom de Swaan would be taking over his risk management portfolio in six months time, as the bank's first genuine chief financial officer. It had been announced in early May.

The 52-year-old De Swaan, who had worked as a supervisor of financial institutions for over twenty years, and since 1992 as head of his department, began on 1 June. It was not a smooth transition. De Swaan had been glad to receive Kalff's offer to work at the bank, but had at first declined. De Swaan felt flattered and the possibility of earning serious money attracted him. But he had just been appointed chairman of the Basel Committee in September 1997, a prestigious position in the world of banking supervision. The committee set the financial conditions that banks had to meet. De Swaan was to oversee the reformulation of these terms, to be called Basel II. He decided he should finish what he had started.

Following De Swaan's refusal, ABN Amro's board had resolved to move on to the second name on their list: Bert Heemskerk: a former Amro banker, then chairman of Van Lanschot, a small bank for wealthy private clients.

But from a conversation with Nout Wellink, it was clear that De Swaan was unhappy at DNB. He had been on the board for twelve years, and could have continued another fourteen years: as number two. It was evident that a commercial bank would be an appropriate move for his career. De Swaan stemmed from an Amsterdam family traditionally involved in commerce: at DNB they saw him as their commercial man. Wellink encouraged De Swaan to take up ABN Amro's offer after all. De Swaan called Kalff just in time to let him know. He hadn't contacted Bert Heemskerk yet.

They expected big things from Turbo Tommy at ABN Amro. A man who had gained that nickname at the Dutch Central Bank because he thought fast, spoke fast and decided fast. De Swaan was to be the board's first real CFO.

But now that it was obvious Drabbe would not be succeeding Kalff, another scenario began to loom. The succession to Kalff had not been mentioned in discussion with De Swaan, but it had not been excluded either.

De Swaan considered a heavyweight CFO crucial for ABN Amro. Since the merger, the position of financial supervisor had been passed around with remarkable frequency. Hazelhoff, Geertsema, Groenink and now De Jong. They had all been responsible for a while for overseeing the bank's costs. Their tasks included mapping out the budgeting process, charting the consequences of failure to meet targets and so forth. A strict and conscientious approach soon made the managing director unpopular; no one wanted that. They tended instead to focus on the risks attached to credits.

De Swaan pointed to the growing importance of investor relations, the need for solid checks and balances at the top of an organisation. The bank was acquiring increasing numbers of active Anglo-Saxon shareholders who wanted to know what was happening at the bank. More openness would be needed, more information about what the bank did.

The governors were thrilled with the managing board's proposal. One governor suggested that De Swaan might be able to contribute in another way too. For years, DNB had been trying to persuade ABN Amro and ING to meet for a discussion about a possible combination of forces. These first appeals had fallen on deaf ears. A man like De Swaan, with a broad view and authority within the Dutch banking world, would be able to set a dialogue in motion. One of the governors wondered whether it wasn't problematic that De Swaan had never drawn up a profit and loss account, had never played that sort of role in a company. A role in which he had to hold people responsible.

In the summer of 1998, the Dutch were relishing their football team's success in the World Cup in France. Until they were eliminated in the semifinals by Brazil, on penalties. The following day, ABN Amro took revenge. To general consternation, Michael Drabbe presented a plan to take over Banco Real, Brazil's fourth largest bank. Together with Floris Deckers, ABN Amro's man in Brazil, and general manager of the overseas division Joost Oyevaar, a ready-made deal was laid out for the board.

Drabbe and Deckers had first discussed the matter eighteen months earlier. Deckers had been in Brazil for four years. The bank, which had begun as

Banco Holandes Unido (BHU), had operated there for over eighty years. Its 48 branches and 2,600 staff were above all active in selling loans for second-hand cars. Drabbe wanted to know from Deckers about the possibilities for expansion, serious expansion. Could Brazil become a domestic market?

Unibanco and Banco Real were mentioned. The latter had been offered in late 1997 more or less on a platter. The 78-year-old owner, Aloysio de Andrade Faria, had five daughters, none of whom wished to take over the family business. Drabbe set up a steering group, including the people he expected to be his main opponents, gradually massaging them towards a positive decision.

Brazil was now proudly presented as a genuine third column in the universal network bank. Kalff described the acquisition as an 'attractive yet unmarried woman' and promised that the bank would already be contributing to share profits in 1999. The controlling stake cost 2.1 billion dollars: it was the biggest takeover in the bank's history. The Brazilian bank would continue to be called Banco Real.

Far out of sight of the self-congratulating Dutch, one man was sore. Emilio Botin, chairman of the fast expanding Spanish Banco Santander, had also had an eye on Banco Real. Botin considered South America a logical area for his bank to spread its net. But the Dutch had snatched that interesting bait away before he could pounce.

To finance the acquisition, as with the funding of the takeover of the American bank Standard Federal and the Bank of Asia in Thailand, ABN Amro decided to raise money in the capital market. The opportunity to exploit the positive climate on the stock exchange to issue new shares was not considered.

For eighteen months the bank's share price had remained almost stationary at around 18 euros. Investment banking, Thailand, Brazil, the United States. Where was ABN Amro heading? Analysts wondered increasingly. And what about the synergy of the various sections of the universal bank? Why would anyone want to buy shares in ABN Amro? After all, the bank still hadn't managed to cap its costs. The efficiency ratio was rising inexorably. From 67.5 per cent in 1995 to 69.4 per cent in 1998. While levels in other banks were falling.

In August, a proud Michael Drabbe drew up the balance in the internal *Bankwereld*. In the space of a year, the number of overseas employees had risen from 27,000 to 64,000. The overseas network had expanded from 850 offices and branches to 2,570 in 1998 (1,586 in Brazil and 112 in Thailand); since the merger an average of three countries had been added each year. 'Countries such as Thailand, Hungary and Brazil have the potential to become major platforms alongside the Netherlands and the United States for investment banking and commercial banking activities around the world. Brazil is a splendid addition.' It was one of Michael Drabbe's last services to the bank. His illness was taking its toll. In November, Drabbe handed over his responsibilities.

With Drabbe's departure, Kalff lost his natural heir. When the chairman was absent from a board meeting, the member who had been on the board longest took his place. Kalff asked Rijkman Groenink, together with Van Tets one of the longest serving board members, to chair their meetings in his absence.

Rijnhard van Tets, who had been appointed to the Amro board in 1988 on the same day as Groenink and was two years his senior, was not pleased. Van Tets considered Groenink far too combative, always looking for conflicts instead of finding solutions. The idea that Groenink would be telling him what to do was anathema to Van Tets; he asked Kalff to appoint him and Groenink instead as alternating deputy chairmen. And so it was decided.

The 48-year-old Floris Deckers, a loyal servant of the bank (originally ABN) since 1981, was rewarded for his efforts in August with the post of general manager. He retained responsibility for South America, his base remained São Paulo. At the same time, it was announced that Joost Kuiper would be working for the bank, also as a general manager.

Kalff and Van Tets felt they owed him this, after Kuiper had been forced to leave Fortis. Six months after having asked him to head MeesPierson in early 1996, ABN Amro had sold the subsidiary to Fortis. Kuiper had been part of the deal. Suddenly the former Amro banker was out in the cold. It was only logical to ask him to return to the ABN Amro fold. During a dinner in Van Tets's garden, Kalff asked Kuiper, a huge smile playing across his face, whether he would consider returning to his original employer.

Kuiper was pleasantly surprised. He emphasised that Kalff should know that he had been fired by Fortis for a reason. He explained that in a sense he was grateful. He had learned a lot. And so Kuiper returned for a second stint at the bank in which he had started his career, 25 years earlier.

The annual Christmas dinner was nothing like the previous year's affair. It was a massive gathering. The room was no longer big enough. There had never been so many new, often foreign faces. Old hands were surprised by the many Anglo-Saxon colleagues; they felt a little out of their depth and wondered whether these investment bankers, who worked at their own risk and for their own profit, could appreciate a moment such as this.

Jan Kalff stood between two halls filled with colleagues as he gave his Christmas speech. Publicity consultants had advised him to explain why his wife wasn't present. To help him they had written a few lines on paper.

As he looked at the page, ABN Amro's chairman searched for words. His audience was hushed, this was not the proud, radiant chairman they knew. For a moment Jan Kalff didn't know what to say.

5

Appointment

1999

This was the thirty-sixth year with the only employer he had ever known: his bank. ABN Amro was his life. Jan Kalff would always feel that way about it. It went deep. Perhaps too deep. For twenty-two years he had been on the managing board. At thirty-nine, Jan Kalff had been its youngest member ever.

For five years he had been board chairman, but if he were honest, the joy had begun to fade. He didn't think that the bank was suffering as a result, but his thoughts were elsewhere. Kalff missed his wife. Their divorce had forced him to look critically at himself. He had been chairman since 1994. He wouldn't have minded if someone else had taken on the task instead. But from the moment he had been asked to do the job he had never considered not doing it. It was only now that he realised that he had actually devoted all his time to the bank. He had let the bank dominate his life. And once again his sense of duty took command. This year he would have to nominate a successor.

As he grew older he thought increasingly about his father. It had been his bank once. For years, Kalff Senior had been Nederlandsche Handel Maatschappij's in-house lawyer. His father wanted his second son to become a lawyer too. Jan had been sent to Leiden to study law in 1955. But he had been fascinated by the banking profession since childhood. When Jan had told him in 1964 that he had been offered a good position at Nederlandsche Handel-Maatschappij (NHM), his father had asked him why he hadn't looked for a job with Amsterdamsche Bank. That was a good bank as well.

Kalff had good reason to steer his son in a different direction. He was not just NHM's lawyer; he was also lawyer to Twentsche Bank. He acted for two rival banks. It was still possible at that time. If you had integrity, you had trust. So Kalff Senior was one of the few to know that the two banks were on the point of merging.

His eldest son Gerard had already been working for two years at Twentsche Bank. He was uneasy with the thought that both his sons would be working at the same bank. But it was impossible for him to tell his children about the merger. So when Jan informed him he would be taking up the job offer at NHM, he could do nothing but accept it. He had to trust his sons to find a way of working together.

It was inevitable that banks would merge. NHM had to find a domestic partner in which to inject the huge capital it had acquired abroad. Twentsche Bank was the natural counterpart. The bank had expanded fast in the Netherlands but ran into trouble following a string of bankruptcies in the textile industry. The powerful NHM would in effect be taking over and dominating Twentsche Bank. Under the watchful eye of the elder Kalff, on 4 June 1964, Algemene Bank Nederland (ABN) was formed.

When they heard that they would both be working for ABN, Jan and Gerard Kalff phoned each other excitedly. With its 10,000 employees, it would be the country's leading bank, that was clear. They understood their father's concern and agreed immediately: we'll make our own way in ABN. They promised never to do each other favours and to avoid any hint of impropriety. Integrity: that was the key. Their father had rammed that in since infancy.

That ABN would be the country's dominant bank proved an illusion. Its creation brought the sluggish discussions between two other major commercial banks, Amsterdamsche Bank and Rotterdamsche Bank, to a head. Precisely one week after the launch of ABN, the formation of Amro was announced: even larger, in the Netherlands at least.

If he had followed his father's advice he would have been working at Amro, Jan Kalff realised. Then he would have joined his brother's bank 26 years later, when Amro merged with ABN. Would his career have been as illustrious? Would he have risen to the top in such a different bank? He'd never know. But he knew this would be his final year. Next year he would be retiring.

His successor would have to be announced before the end of the year. He wasn't overly worried. Naturally it had originally been arranged that Dick Meys would be appointed. After that tragic accident, it had been more or less clear that the charismatic Michael Drabbe would pick up the baton. Even if only for a couple of years. Now that Drabbe was ill, there was only one obvious candidate left in Kalff's view: his right-hand man, Jan Maarten de Jong. The calm, presentable De Jong was good with clients, he was good with credits and, crucial for Kalff, he could keep a team together.

If they went by seniority, the two Amro bankers would take precedence. Rijkman Groenink and Rijnhard Van Tets had joined the Amro board in the spring of 1988, a year before Jan Maarten de Jong had joined the ABN board. But De Jong had worked longest at the bank.

Everyone knew that Groenink wanted to be in charge. So did Jan Kalff. Kalff had never noticed any such ambition in Van Tets. Kalff didn't see Van Tets as a chairman. He was too reserved. For Kalff it was clear: it had to be De Jong.

The 53-year-old De Jong expected Kalff to choose him, but didn't know for certain. The chairman had given him several major assignments in recent years and introduced him on international forums, where Kalff enjoyed considerable respect. But Kalff never told him he was his candidate. De Jong understood that. Kalff was no Machiavelli; he preferred to handle these processes cautiously. The chairman didn't want to express his preference openly since this would raise expectations and possibly lead to disappointments.

Moreover, the situation would need careful preparation. Kalff knew that some members of his managing board and some on the supervisory board would raise questions regarding De Jong's candidature. Would he be tough enough to take major decisions, decisions that would be needed to take the bank into the new millennium? Did De Jong know in which direction the bank was heading, did he have strategic vision? Some would be shocked; Rijkman Groenink for one. Yet another ABN man at the top.

Kalff suspected that Tom de Swaan would also find it hard to accept. While he had not been at the bank more than a year, it was clear that the former supervisor at the Dutch Central Bank wouldn't have minded taking over the chairmanship from Kalff.

After eight months on probation, Tom de Swaan had formally been accepted as the bank's first chief financial officer on the managing board. He was enjoying his new job, but was surprised too. Where was the bank heading? The strategy seemed to be based on two vague premises: the enormous love of Rob Hazelhoff and Jan Kalff for the United States, and the opportunist desire to follow the wishes of the client and provide the best possible service. The bank that he thought he had understood as its supervisor, apparently had no clear strategy.

De Swaan had also been surprised by the inadequate management information system. The bank often had no idea where it was earning money and what things were costing. The lack of accountability was also disturbing. Few people were ever called to account for not meeting their budgets.

His assignment was clear: to ensure transparency and accountability. To make certain above all that costs were reduced. That was vital. Compared to similar institutions, the bank's efficiency ratio had deteriorated even further in recent years. While other banks scored an average 64 per cent; ABN Amro stood at over 69 per cent in 1998. That meant that the bank was spending almost 10 per cent more to make the same euro in earnings.

To *Bankwereld*, De Swaan commented that, "We have to bring an end to the situation of the last few years in which percentage costs rise faster than earnings. Shareholders and analysts are right to wonder about how it's possible for us to be apparently unable to control our costs. Especially if you look at the other banks in the so-called peer group, the category of banks we belong to." The new CFO announced that he would be holding people accountable for their actions. "Managers who are considered capable of running their section of the organisation should make cost control an integral part of their day's work. If they can't do that, they're sitting on the wrong chair."

De Swaan felt that the managing board should set the right example. It was irritating that members of the board had vague spheres of influence, rather than solid responsibilities. He wanted to jettison the notion of collective responsibility. De Swaan quickly aligned himself with the managing directors who had been criticising the twice-weekly discussions of stacks of credit dossiers. He realised that this gave a false impression of being in control. He explained to Kalff that the bank had been forced to write off hundreds of millions in bad loans in Indonesia, yet not one of these credits had been discussed by the board because they were all too small.

On the subject of Kalff's succession, De Swaan was cautious. He considered himself too new; he was not familiar enough with the organisation. Yet he wouldn't have refused if he had been asked, and he was not averse to anyone knowing it.

Kalff felt that the situation was too delicate to allow a plenary discussion; he decided to talk to each of his colleagues individually. He hoped to arrange a flexible, unanimously approved succession. As tradition dictated; as it should be. With meticulous precision, he compiled a list of when he would talk to each managing director, in what order and what about. He planned to speak to them at the beginning of the year and then after the summer, having taken the time to let it sink in and having spoken to the home front, he would discuss it again. He would ask the same questions each time: where do you stand, do you want the job yourself and who do you think would be a better successor? Who would be best at forming a team?

These were intense discussions. Rijkman Groenink was the most explicit regarding his own candidacy. Tom de Swaan didn't rule out the position of chairman either. He was not in favour of appointing Groenink either way.

Dolf van den Brink indicated that he had no ambition to be chairman. He had seen in his father what working a hundred hours a week could do to a person. Wilco Jiskoot had no ambition to take over either, he was clearly in favour of Rijkman Groenink. Jiskoot considered De Jong more of the same. It was time for change.

Rijnhard van Tets was absolutely against Groenink. He couldn't stand him, and he found the tension and conflict that his fellow managing director generated tiresome. Michael Drabbe and Dolf van den Brink hesitated. Jan Maarten de Jong was not against appointing Groenink. However, several managing directors wondered whether Groenink had sufficient empathy and ability to unite. They pointed to the endless squabbling between Ten Cate, Rutgers and Collee.

Kalff drew a preliminary conclusion: based on who would be able to lead a team better than anyone, De Jong should have implicit preference. The chairman took his results to the head of the supervisory board.

Aarnout Loudon and Frits Fentener van Vlissingen saw that Kalff clearly preferred De Jong. They decided to make up their own lists and agreed not to tell each other in advance who their favourites were. Like Kalff, Loudon believed at that time that Jan Maarten de Jong was the logical choice. He noted that the bank in general saw De Jong as the logical successor.

The two governors took different approaches for their discussions. What does the bank need in the coming years? What should be done and who is the best person to do it? And there were four candidates after all. De Swaan cautiously intimated that he was interested.

Rijnhard van Tets, a cousin of Aarnout Loudon, also said that he was available. But he refused to push for the job. Van Tets wanted to be asked. And he made no bones about it; under his leadership the main priority would be to expand the investment bank, perhaps even to take over a major American institution. He told the governors they would have to make a choice.

De Jong stated in clear terms that under his leadership, the bank would continue in the current line. De Swaan and Van Tets again stated that they were vehemently against appointing Groenink. Twelve years earlier, De Swaan and his wife had spent a week with Groenink and his first wife Lucia in the United States. It had not been particularly pleasant. His wife had concluded that Groenink didn't like people, which made him unable to communicate normally. Having worked with Groenink for a while, he had to admit that his wife had been right. He respected Groenink's intelligence, but didn't believe he would make a suitable chairman. He was too pugnacious.

More opposed to Groenink than any was Rijnhard van Tets. He realised that Groenink had the intellectual capacity, but also that he suffered from a major character flaw: for Van Tets, Groenink was too much of a prize fighter. Van Tets went even further, he told them he would resign if they chose Groenink.

The two governors were not pleased to hear that. Because in the same round of interviews, Fentener van Vlissingen and Loudon realised that Rijkman Groenink had prepared best of all for their discussion. Groenink told them exactly what should be done and how he would kick-start the bank's strategy. His core message was: it was time to take the interests of the shareholders seriously. Groenink emphasised his irritation at the lethargic pace of Jan Kalff's decision-making.

Aarnout Loudon then began an initial round of talks with the various governors. A couple, including Antony Burgmans, favoured Rijkman Groenink. Like former DSM chief Hans van Liemt. They wanted to see more movement, and at least Groenink was not afraid. Furthermore he was the smartest of all the managing directors. Yet the majority, including Maarten van Veen and Rob Hazelhoff, were for De Jong. They felt reassured by his typical ABN approach. Furthermore, De Jong was good with people.

Wim Dik was not in favour of Groenink, nor for De Jong. The former was too unpleasant to be a chairman, the latter too soft. He conceded that Groenink was hard enough to make good plans, but warned that he wouldn't be able to realise his plans if he kept making enemies. Dik tended towards Van Tets as he considered him decisive and able to create unity.

Hazelhoff was also against Groenink. He felt that a good board chairman needed sufficient insight and analytical ability to know that he couldn't do the job on his own. He wondered whether the macho Groenink had the required capacity.

Other doubts were expressed on the supervisory board. To what extent was Groenink driven by personal ambition? It was clear that his ego was unusually well developed. Was Groenink there for the bank, or was the bank there for Groenink?

Loudon noticed that while most of the governors preferred De Jong, they also felt that it was high time some key decisions were taken at the bank. The time for gentle adjustment had passed. That was Loudon's conclusion to Kalff. They decided to schedule another series of discussions later in the year.

Meanwhile, the bank's future in Europe was once again under discussion in the upper echelon. Following the blunders in Belgium and France, the horizon was extended further south. Italy had often been mentioned as an attractive possibility for a substantial presence. Italian banking was deeply fractured and offered all kinds of theoretical opportunities. ABN Amro was especially interested in the affluent north.

An added impetus came from a growing infatuation with Italy as a holiday location among various managing directors. Rijkman Groenink had bought a second home with his first wife near Bordeaux; since the divorce she now owned that house. He was looking for a new holiday home in Italy with Irene.

His parents loved Italy and he had enjoyed many holidays there as a child. Jan Maarten de Jong and his wife were helping them find a good house, as was the artist and Italy-lover Jan Dibbets, a friend of Groenink's.

Jan Maarten de Jong had already owned a renovated Tuscan ruin for ten years; his Italian was fluent. That was to prove useful. A month after De Jong had taken over the ailing Michael Drabbe's overseas portfolio, the head of ABN Amro's Italian operation, Francesco Spinelli, paid an extempore visit. He came with a complex but energising story about new opportunities in the Italian market.

Antonveneta, in which ABN Amro had held a small stake for some years, was apparently prepared to offer the Dutch a serious holding of 15 per cent. In return, the bank wanted ABN Amro's help in financing the takeover of Banca Nazionale dell' Agricoltura. Banca Nazionale was being put up for sale by Banca di Roma, which had been performing poorly. They didn't want to sell but were being pursued, apparently benignly, by Banca Commerciale Italiana. The head of Banca di Roma, Cesare Geronzi, had asked permission from the president of Italy's Central Bank, Antonio Fazio, to look for a way out: a party willing to invest in Banca di Roma. Geronzi had just become acquainted with ABN Amro. He made a proposal: if ABN Amro bought a stake in Banca di Roma, he would give up his interest in Banca Nazionale. There was a lot of money involved; the proffered stake in Banca di Roma of 9.65 per cent would cost around 1.4 billion guilders.

De Jong realised that this was the opportunity they had been waiting for. They could be joint owners of an Italian bank. Jiskoot and Groenink backed him. Kalff hesitated. He associated Italy with opaque structures and mafiosi. He feared for the bank's reputation. Through Rothschild's consultants in Italy, investigators went to work to screen the protagonists with which the bank would be dealing.

Kalff was reassured, trusting above all in Jan Maarten de Jong's expertise; he knew the country. Following the abortive attempts to take over banks in Belgium and France, the board now dreamt of a second domestic market in Italy.

De Jong was appointed vice-president of the board of Banca di Roma and was immediately made aware of what it meant to be a player in Italy. The ink on the contract had scarcely dried before he had was called by Geronzi to say that he was expected on 3 March in Turin to meet Giovanni Agnelli. The 78-year-old grandson of the founder of Fiat held shares through a construction in Banca di Roma and wanted to know if the Dutchman fitted in. De Jong spoke with 'l'Avvocato' for an hour and a half about this and that. The moment he drove out the gate, his telephone rang. It was Geronzi with an unambiguous message. "Welcome to Italy." For a while, the prim and proper Jan Maarten de Jong felt as if he were playing the lead in a thriller, with an uncertain finish.

All at once ABN Amro was involved in two major Italian banks, as part of the shareholder conglomerate that ran those banks. In the press conference, De Jong radiated pride. Yes, of course they had put the lessons they had learned in Belgium the previous year into effect. Since the failure to acquire Generale Bank, ABN Amro's top realised that participation as a shareholder was the way to gradually increase the bank's involvement in a potential acquisition. As De Jong remarked, "This time we took care to have the agreement of everyone who mattered in Italy. Including the Italian government."

He reserved judgment regarding a future combination with the Italian banks. "That is not the question now. But this does give us access to a second domestic market in Europe's fourth largest economy, the sixth in the world."

A few weeks later, on 27 March, Michael Drabbe died at the age of 57. 'The departure of Michael Drabbe is a great loss for the bank and for everyone who knew him. Not just for his expertise and his tremendous involvement; above all for the warm humanity that he radiated,' wrote Jan Kalff in a press statement.

Drabbe's death affected him profoundly. In recent months he had visited the ailing Drabbe often in his apartment in Amsterdam. They had many conversations there. Kalff enjoyed the stories of the *bon vivant* and had come to realise how strange it was to work with a person for ten years, and for something as horrible as this to be necessary to actually get to know them.

Kalff asked Joost Kuiper to make up the numbers on the board. To his surprise, Kuiper hesitated. He felt that this level might be too high. He told Kalff openly about his doubts. Kalff assured him that he fitted in. Kuiper felt flattered: the idea of power tempted him and a place on the board was the rehabilitation he sought after his dismissal at Fortis. It was an opportunity to show that he was up to it.

Late in April, the bank announced that Joost Kuiper would join Jan Maarten de Jong in leading the overseas division. The statement intensified speculation that De Jong was being groomed to succeed Jan Kalff. Kalff made no comment, suffice to say that he believed his successor would emerge from the ranks of the present board. Pundits noted that based on seniority and experience, Rijkman Groenink would be in the running as well as De Jong.

A suggestion was made in a strategy session at Duin & Kruidberg that this would be a good time to merge with ING. It was a particularly good moment because Godfried van der Lugt was then temporarily chairman. The consequent relative weakness of the ING board would give the managing directors of ABN Amro an advantage and allow them to dominate the bank. Those were the only terms on which ABN Amro would join forces with ING. All other Dutch rivals were treated with disdain. What they used to think of Amro at ABN, ABN Amro bankers now thought of their colleagues at ING; they laughed and called them the white-sock brigade.

Jan Kalff asked Gerhard Zeilmaker to do some research. The figures were persuasive, the combination would produce an instant global player. A powerful bank in Europe, a major asset management company and an insurance bank in the United States. With total assets of 830 billion dollars an ABN Amro ING combination would rank first, ahead of Deutsche Bank (732 billion dollars), UBS (685 billion dollars) and Citigroup (668 billion dollars). In May, Kalff paid a visit to Van der Lugt.

DNB welcomed the initiative and they were enthusiastic about a merger. Director of supervision Arnold Schilder, who succeeded Tom de Swaan, had said the previous year that the Central Bank would not throw any obstacles in the way of a possible large Dutch merger. To *Het Financieele Dagblad* he remarked that "If two of the three big Dutch banks were to merge it would be less important to view the global playing field in terms of local Dutch market shares." DNB considered the chance to be supervising one of the largest global players an interesting idea. The Central Bank would still be relevant as a supervisor. An international merger would hollow out DNB's authority.

Despite the enthusiasm among some associated with the two banks, the conversation between Kalff and Van der Lugt was cool. ING had little time for their ABN Amro colleagues, even though they would soon to be neighbours: ABN Amro's new head office on Amsterdam's Zuidas was almost ready. On the ING board, ABN Amro was the principal enemy, their great arrogant rival. It went deep. If an ING director were explaining to his son how bad Surinamese strongman Desi Bouterse was, the boy would assume that Bouterse probably worked for ABN Amro.

In part, their aversion was envy. Time and again ING's directors would wake up to find that their main rival had walked off with the prize. They knew ABN Amro to be technically proficient, with plenty of competent people. Lower down the hierarchy, ING staff exhibited a certain jealousy towards the all-round bankers and the tremendous history the institution embodied. ABN Amro's history as the supplier of the nation's bankers went back 150 years. More than any other institution, ABN, Amro or ABN Amro, they produced the country's top bankers.

And they paid their staff more too. Both members of the managing board and the lower ranks below board level: ABN Amro colleagues generally earned 60 to 80 per cent more. Headhunters noted that an ABN Amro regional manager in Groningen for example, would probably earn twice as much as his counterpart at ING.

ING's managing directors felt that ABN Amro simply paid too much. It irritated them to be told whenever they met that as the best bank, they were obliged to pay the best salaries. That they aimed to be among the top 25 wage payers in the salary league tables published by agencies such as Towers Perrin and Hay.

ING chairman Godfried van der Lugt had little love for his colleagues at ABN Amro. His career had been with Postbank, he had built up the bank and throughout his working life he had endured the jibes of ABN and Amro bankers who had refused to take him seriously. Van der Lugt didn't even deign to use his rival's full name; he called them AA.

While Kalff's visit sparked a discussion, at the next ING board meeting they concluded that ABN Amro was little more than a reasonably profitable bank in the United States, a poorly performing Dutch subsidiary and an adventure in Brazil. Presumably the poor performer in the Netherlands would merge with their successful Postbank ING subsidiary. Why should they want that? The combination would lead to thousands of redundancies in the Netherlands. And what would a merger mean for ING's insurance division?

They knew that the new combination would be a bank first and foremost. And that would have major consequences for their position in the organisation. Meanwhile, ING Bank, a young bank, was afraid that a combination would lead to many of the best jobs going to ABN Amro bankers, who were after all better. The takeover of Barings three years before had taught them a lesson. There too, many of the best jobs had gone to the arrogant Brits. Not that they had been such a success. In the end, the board concluded soberly that it wouldn't be a particularly good deal for ING.

Kalff's proposal to continue talks was considered in ING's supervisory board. The new president, former Shell president Cor Herkströter, was not enthusiastic. He feared a bloodbath; thousands would lose their jobs. Herkströter wondered whether the two banks were suitable. The governors proposed a follow-up study. At Van der Lugt's insistence, that too was dropped. Yet they did decide to continue talking, to keep the option open; one day it might prove unavoidable. They knew that DNB's president favoured a merger.

At DNB there was disappointment. Nout Wellink realised it would be difficult to bring the two banks together, their cultures were totally different. The supervisor knew how domineering ABN Amro could be, even arrogant. How little affinity there was for the bank at ING. Yet Wellink felt that arrogance was something felt by those who considered themselves less experienced. At DNB they concluded that ING suffered from an inferiority complex.

Kalff's fellow managing directors called on him to examine the major issues. Was the bank's universal bank strategy still feasible? Now that the principal exponent of the universal idea, Michael Drabbe, was no longer with them, that question kept resurfacing. Was the bank taking on too much? The two sworn enemies, Van Tets and Groenink, each appealed to Kalff individually to reexamine the bank's strategy more carefully.

Kalff was proud of the bank's growth under his direction. Net profits had increased from 1 billion euros to 2.5 billion. When he became chairman, the bank was worth 8.3 billion euros, now it was around 36.3 billion. He was particularly proud of the enormous assets ABN Amro had in the United States and Brazil. He was glad that the bank had not lost any of its reliability following the merger. They had made no major mistakes. Kalff realised that they would now have to devote effort to improving efficiency. Not least to pacify the shareholders. And perhaps it was time to make new choices. But Kalff didn't want to start down that road, that would be his successor's task.

So who would succeed? With a more or less absent, almost distant chairman, this was the time to start building a power base. Van Tets tried to steer the board in the direction of an investment bank. He was still focused on the United States. It might be far away, but it was the world's largest capital market, and that was where the bank should be, otherwise there would be no future for ABN Amro as an investment bank. Fortunately, unlike Europe, there was plenty to buy in the United States. It was only a question of money.

He pointed out that, apart from ABN Amro, three other European universal network banks were also trying to enter this American-dominated market: Swiss giants UBS and Credit Suisse First Boston, and Deutsche Bank. Their movements were being watched at the bank's head office. A year earlier, Deutsche Bank had paid almost 10 billion dollars for Bankers Trust. Rumour had it that UBS was acquiring PaineWebber for 11 billion dollars.

Rijkman Groenink was also forging his own path. He had set Europe as his priority. Based on his experiences in the domestic division, Groenink proposed to create a new European division. He had been thinking along these lines during the Generale Bank takeover attempt. The introduction of the euro as the new currency in eleven countries on 1 January 1999 reinforced his idea. Groenink wanted to organise the bank into three broad divisions: Europe, United States and Asia. He assumed that he would be heading the European division.

For Groenink it was clear that the activities of the apparently vague and intangible corporate business division should be placed at the service of the regional leadership. His lack of awe for investment banking led to a constant battle between Wilco Jiskoot and Rijnhard van Tets on one side, and Rijkman

Groenink on the other, supported by Jan Maarten de Jong and Dolf van den Brink. The latter three had little faith in the investment bank idea. The spiralling costs, the dearth of major transactions. Investment bankers had big mouths and small profits. In turn, the investment bankers were horrified at the idea that they might be tethered to geographical boundaries. To that old-fashioned ABN world.

At a managing board strategy session on 21 and 22 June, Rijkman Groenink's proposal to create a European division was adopted. The recent successes in Italy had created a sense of optimism that a truly European bank was possible. It was formulated differently in the official statement. 'The realisation of a European market and various technical developments have forced banks to reconsider their position. An increase in critical mass is needed to enable the enormous investments in IT, marketing, new distribution channels and product development.'

"We need to become Europe's most European bank," Groenink explained enthusiastically. He put Dolf Collee in charge of a workgroup to develop his plans. They realised that Groenink was out to prove that he had a vision for the bank's future, to show he could be a strategist. They spent a couple of months working hard on the project.

Almost sixty senior managers were invited to a meeting at head office. They were all country managers, or managers of regional offices. This was clearly a meeting to launch the new European division. The atmosphere was good. Especially among the former ABN bankers. They were glad to have a clearly defined geographical plan. They hoped this would finally do something about the alarming rise of the investment bankers.

The plan was laid out in the thirty-page 'Creation of the European Division', largely written by Jan Peter Schmittmann, responsible for the special credits department and a confidant of Rijkman Groenink. Groenink had told Schmittmann that if he wasn't appointed chairman, he'd take power through the European division.

The document opens solemnly. 'Viewing ABN Amro's position in Europe, it is clear that we must move forward. In the Netherlands our position is strong, but that position is coming under attack.' On the rest of Europe the authors wrote, 'Although we are one of the few banks in Europe with a presence in every EU country, we operate as a typical foreign bank, with limited scope, a limited client base and limited product range. The network's strategy lacks a forceful pan-European approach. There is clearly also room for improvement in relations between the corporate business division and the network. Moreover, earnings are disappointing and costs are high. Our means must be employed far more efficiently.'

Their ambitions were on a grand scale. In six months the new European division would be up and running. Groenink emphasised that the bank was a universal bank, offering commercial and retail products (especially loans) as well as investment bank products (mergers, share issues and commerce, etc) to the same clients. In addition he emphasised the need to increase the private customer base, especially through Internet banking. The basic idea in these plans was to make the matrix work. 'We have to ensure the best possible cooperation between the corporate business division and the new European division.'

Four different client groups were defined: global clients, financial institutions, regional European players and private banking clients. Country managers needed to start working. They would keep their central leadership role, but there would be 'a shift from general management tasks to a more client-directed focus. They have to present themselves as Mr ABN Amro in the local market. He implements the strategy worked out by the collective management of the European division and the corporate business division. He coordinates the cooperation this requires. He is responsible for the profit and loss account in his country and shares this responsibility in each client group with the relevant colleagues in the corporate business division.'

In chapter six, the authors discussed the most sensitive subject: collaboration between the European division and the investment banking division. 'There is a clear need for hard and fast agreements between the European division and the corporate business division to provide the best possible service to the selected clients. The corporate business division endorses that the regional client managers are the people that clients contact, that their products are offered exclusively through these client managers to the client. In short, that the client's principal connection is through the regional client manager. Together we will create a campaign strategy to attract clients. We will formulate our targets together. Service to clients must be a joint responsibility.'

Groenink stated categorically that 'the responsibility for all clients is geographically defined'. The country bosses, in effect. He also felt that the 'the corporate business division should reorganise, to clarify which part of the division will focus on European clients. The country managers will be the chairmen of the new local collaborative effort.'

In the workgroup everyone knew that the investment bankers in the managing board would refuse to accept the plan. Dolf Collee warned Groenink: this meant war, Jiskoot and Van Tets would never agree. It would mean the end of the corporate business division as a single unit. The bank would be ripped apart. Groenink responded in true power-play style, as one of the managing directors later recalled, "Then let them leave. That's their loss."

In an interview with *Het Financieele Dagblad* Groenink laid out his plans. "We were certainly serious at the time of the Generale Bank takeover about the European division. ABN Amro must expand in Europe and the best way to do that is through a European project."

Groenink said that the Generale Bank episode had left him sadder but wiser. "The staff and management of Generale Bank would have preferred to continue with us. But that wasn't sufficient. It is clear to us that the European idea hasn't really taken hold among bank governors and national governments. Solutions tend to focus on national interest."

He sensed that time was pressing. If the merger of three French banks announced in the press were to succeed, it would create a European bank with 15 million clients. This was the kind of rival ABN Amro feared. As Groenink remarked, "We can't predict when we'll be able to make an acquisition or possibly even merge. And even if I did know I would still have to assess whether I could do something else in the meantime." He explained that the new European division would create an organisation that would above all enable the bank to serve large companies. At the same time, the *pièce de résistance* of the European division would be "The capture of the European retail market." To attract new European retail clients without acquisitions or mergers, Groenink had turned his attention to the Internet.

Groenink explained enthusiastically that this would lessen the bank's reliance on the formation of a second European domestic market – which had failed so dramatically twice the year before. Indeed, the Internet would put the whole of Europe within reach. "We're not just talking about a second domestic market here. The entire European market will be the domestic market," continued Groenink. He was convinced that ABN Amro should put the Internet at the centre of its strategy. The domestic division was leading the European division at present. As the division chairman explained, "That's logical, since the domestic division has the expertise."

Until then investment in e-commerce had been sporadic. The bank decided to put a tighter Internet strategy in place, led from head office. Jean-Paul Votron was appointed general manager with orders to expand the bank's Internet activities. The 49-year-old Votron was not considered a real banker in the bank. He had worked for Unilever as a marketeer for sixteen years and for six at Citibank as head of marketing for Europe, before moving to ABN Amro in 1997. For this new job Votron reported directly to Groenink.

Other appointments followed. The men from het Gooi had decided long ago that it was time to bring some non-Dutch personalities into the managing board. The United States country manager, Harrison Tempest, was invited, but preferred not to come to Holland. So the bank looked to its own nest of foreigners. Besides the Belgian Votron, the Brit Hugh Scott Barrett and the Brazilian Sergio Lires Rial were appointed general manager (SEVP).

Meanwhile, speculation about Jan Kalff's succession was mounting. Rijkman Groenink's formal appointment as board chairman of the European division fed rumours that the chairmanship of the bank as a whole would go to Jan Maarten de Jong. Moreover, De Jong's room at the new head office was next to Jan Kalff's room, and he had been appointed chairman of a committee to examine the development of the ABN Amro brand. A typical role for a new bank figurehead.

At the press conference in early July, Groenink was unable to suppress a derisory chuckle at the speculation. "We do things here logically. My appointment to this position says nothing about who will succeed Kalff. No one can say anything at the moment."

He was right. Jan Kalff was doing his second round. These talks were different. Uncertainty had been increasing in the international financial markets. There was a sense that the bank would need a different sort of leadership in the coming century. He asked his colleagues: who is the most suitable candidate in that case?

Kalff noted that the opinions voiced six months earlier had become more entrenched. Van Tets's implied candidacy, a man considered by his fellow managing directors to be far too patrician, found little support. Doubts about De Jong and De Swaan had grown. Kalff moved De Swaan onto his reserve list. A large majority considered that De Swaan had not been with the bank long enough. Only two serious candidates remained: De Jong and Groenink. Support for Groenink had grown, but also opposition. Jiskoot was now adamantly for Groenink, and Joost Kuiper also indicated his support for Groenink.

Kuiper considered that it was time the bank abandoned its rather aristocratic manner of appointing a successor. He was a good friend of Van Tets, but felt the managing director was too close to Loudon. Something had to be done with the bank. He had left Amro in 1986 because the pace had been so lethargic. Thirteen years later he was shocked to find that almost nothing had changed at the bank, its introvert culture and its utter lack of energy and creativity.

Dolf van den Brink believed that Groenink would shake the bank out of its sleep, although he hoped that Groenink might not be quite as wild as in the past. Jiskoot, De Jong, Van Tets and Van den Brink all agreed that the whole question would have been a lot simpler if Dick Meys hadn't been killed.

Groenink was brimming with confidence. He told Kalff that he was ready: I think carefully, I'm well balanced and I sleep well. He told Kalff he was the only managing director with the courage to take the difficult decisions that lay ahead.

Once again Kalff reported to Loudon. Personally, the chairman was against appointing Groenink. It irritated him that Groenink rarely had any contact with clients. He was afraid Groenink would go too far, that he was all about showing muscle. He feared Groenink was edging towards the Anglo-Saxon CEO model of an omnipotent chairman. Kalff worried that the unity of the board, which had until then determined policy collectively, would be lost.

Jan Kalff made it clear to the supervisory board that he preferred Jan Maarten de Jong. Nevertheless he knew that the governors would follow their own course. It used to be simple. The next in line according to seniority would be the chairman of the board's right-hand man at ABN, and would be groomed as the next *primus inter pares*. They used to say that the board chairman was like an English lawn. Both were the product of years of care and attention. Which was why many assumed that Jan Maarten de Jong would follow. But Kalff sensed that his candidate was losing ground. He knew that Fentener van Vlissingen, a close friend of Groenink, was for the latter. And he noticed that Loudon was shifting in the same direction.

Seniority and bank traditions didn't mean much to Frits Fentener van Vlissingen. He preferred to analyse. It was clear to him that ABN Amro had some major decisions to take. He was a strategist, he understood power. He was like a spider in a web, forever looking out for the continuing interests of one of the wealthiest families in the Netherlands. For them, a close relationship with the chairman of the country's largest bank was important.

Fentener van Vlissingen was above all impressed by Groenink's courage, and he admired his energy. He also noticed that Groenink respected him, listened closely to him. In recent years, the family's connection with Groenink had grown closer. For four years he had been governor at Flint, the holding company through which the family engaged in various activities. Occasionally the family invited Groenink for dinner. Fentener van Vlissingen wanted Groenink to be the new chairman of ABN Amro. After eight years of ABN propriety it was time for some modern energy from a former Amro man.

The governors were increasingly critical of the bank's direction. Where was that promised second European domestic market? Had the bank wasted its advantage in Europe at the time of the merger? Could they win back their lost terrain? Reviewing the failed takeover plans of the previous year, it was clear that the bank needed a new type of manager.

And how successful was the broad universal bank anyway? In terms of cost efficiency it still had a long way to go. And what about the investment bank? The stagnant share price indicated that the shareholders were not enamoured either.

Kalff understood the criticism. He recognised that there was not enough accountability for results and he knew that thinking about strategy was not his strong point. He found it hard to be decisive. He preferred to make decisions together, as a team. If a decision wasn't taken, or too late, that was of course unfortunate. Perhaps he had remained chairman for too long. Although six years had been the agreement.

According to the statutes the decision regarding the succession was made by a joint meeting of the managing board and the supervisory board: twenty-three men together. Ideally, the managing board would submit a new chairman unanimously to the governors who would then give their assent. But there was no unanimity. No single logical candidate.

In the supervisory board one governor wondered whether it might not be possible to bring someone in from outside. The name Hans de Gier was mentioned, a Dutchman who was doing well at UBS. But the suggestion was immediately rejected. It would be a sign of weakness if an institution like ABN Amro was unable to recruit a leader from its own ranks.

Loudon and Fentener van Vlissingen also started on a second round of discussions. De Swaan seemed less assertive. But Van Tets's anger at a possible appointment of Groenink had only increased in the intervening months. He threatened once again to resign if Groenink were to become boss. Loudon thought it would be a bad signal if the appointment of a new chairman were accompanied by the departure of such a senior banker.

Kuiper was for Groenink, although he added that the appointment did carry a high risk factor. He warned Loudon: he'd have to remain in touch and be prepared to criticise.

In their second conversation with Jan Maarten de Jong, Loudon and Fentener van Vlissingen sensed his doubts. De Jong had been soul searching. He knew that he was no prize fighter, he was not looking forward to being in charge of his colleagues. Moreover, he was not particularly enthusiastic about the growing focus on the share price. His wife had noticed his hesitation and had not been encouraging him to aim for the top job. She was appalled that Jan and Lydia Kalff had divorced, and half joked that De Jong's appointment might also eventually lead to their divorce.

De Jong had been working for the bank seven days a week for twenty-five years. Seven days with an occasional Sunday morning for a game of golf. Once in a while. He had begun wondering if there wasn't more to life than this. He told Loudon and Fentener van Vlissingen that he was ready to accept the role of board chairman if he were asked.

De Jong's reluctance to push his candidacy helped Loudon. The president was increasingly inclined to accept Fentener van Vlissingen's argument. His deputy made it clear time and again that he considered Groenink the only managing director with the courage to act decisively. Governor Hans van Liemt's increasing intimations of support for Groenink also prompted Loudon to question the wisdom of appointing De Jong.

The governors confined their discussions to members of the managing board and fellow governors. They felt that time was too short to include people who had worked under Groenink in their deliberations. Among the lower ranks, below managing board level, it was assumed that De Jong would follow Kalff. Many secretly hoped it would be Groenink.

Among them were Rutgers, Ten Cate and Collee, the three men who reported directly to him. They hoped that checks and balances would be put in place to keep Groenink on course. De Jong and Groenink were two extremes. Rutgers felt that De Jong was not decisive enough, but on the other hand he feared Groenink's unlimited ambition. They had experienced it for themselves. The aims articulated in Visie 2000 had not been achieved, as they had predicted three years earlier. Perhaps the bank had increased its profits; its market share and customer satisfaction had not improved. And now would be a time for cutbacks.

If Groenink were chosen it would not be because he had led the domestic division so successfully, his subordinates concluded. Despite thousands of new jobs, doubts were growing at head office: would they ever manage to make the branches client-focused? Henk Rutgers had already been asked to revise Visie 2000 and in particular to look closely at the enormous costs.

The mood among the division leaders was not good. Ten Cate and Groenink were barely on speaking terms. Yet Ten Cate supported Groenink for the job of chairman; he considered De Jong vague. Groenink's appointment had another advantage: he would certainly be promoting one or two of his general managers to the managing board. Rutgers and Ten Cate stood ready.

Jan Kalff had another problem. Léon Melchior was back. He had ordered his lawyer to send a summons. ABN Amro and in particular the central player in the HCS debacle, Rijkman Groenink, were accused of not fulfilling their duty and acting illegally. Melchior demanded compensation. The bank had let the matter lie, but now that the succession seemed to point increasingly to Groenink, action had to be taken.

Other old pains needed dealing with too. On 11 August, a special dinner was given at Fortis head office in Utrecht. Kalff felt that it was time to mend the fences broken in the previous year's spat.

Europe was caught up in the excitement of a total solar eclipse that day. The moon would be blocking out the sun around midday. On the eighteenth floor Jan Kalff, Hans Bartelds, Maurice Lippens and Wilco Jiskoot were gathered in a friendly conclave at the window. The four bankers were each holding up a CD to watch the disappearing sun.

Kalff and Jiskoot hadn't come to offer an explicit apology. Yet their visit was seen by their counterparts as such and it was appreciated. Lippens was surprised that his third adversary, Rijkman Groenink, hadn't turned up. He assumed that it simply wasn't in his genes to say sorry.

As the summer drew to a close, Aarnout Loudon informed his supervisory board that Groenink was in his opinion the right man to lead the bank into the twenty-first century. The governors realised what they had to do. They saw that the share price was stagnating and costs had still not been brought under control. They voted unanimously for Rijkman Groenink as successor to Jan Kalff.

At the Dutch Central Bank, DNB, where they had been following the whole process, they were surprised. The supervisor felt it was positive that Loudon was prepared to go for a candidate other than Kalff's preference, De Jong, a man cast in the chairman's own mould. The supervisor concurred that this was a time for change. ABN Amro would need to make choices. President Nout Wellink supported Rijkman Groenink's appointment. He believed that Groenink would be able to turn ABN Amro around.

Jan Kalff warned the supervisory board one last time. But they replied that they had already heard all the arguments, and so he gave up resisting. Kalff knew: the game had been played out. Resigning now and leaving in a huff would only harm the bank. And Kalff recognised that the bank could use the good sense and diagnostic skills of a man like Groenink. Especially his irrepressible drive to win every fight. Perhaps he hadn't been incisive enough and maybe it was time for a new style, a different model.

Moreover, the chairman felt reassured that De Jong and De Swaan would be playing a key role in the central credit department. They would be a counterbalance in a managing board which would soon be paying much less attention to credits. Kalff promised the governors to support their choice.

Kalff told Loudon straight that he would be responsible as president to ensure that the managing board maintained a good team atmosphere, to guarantee unity in the bank. Loudon would also have to watch out that the bank didn't turn into an investment bank. He had to keep Groenink on a tight leash. Loudon promised Kalff to keep his eyes and ears open.

Knowing that he would soon be working closely with him, the president had a forthright conversation with Groenink. His message was unambiguous: you're not a particularly empathetic person, it's something you need to work on, it's important to keep the managing board together.

Loudon spoke to Van Tets to ask him to remain on the board; he asked his cousin to acquiesce to Groenink's appointment. He advised him to have a chat with Groenink.

Groenink met with Van Tets. It was a difficult conversation. Van Tets said nothing about having threatened to resign, instead he put a simple question to Groenink: which did he give preference to, retail banking or investment banking? Van Tets distrusted Groenink, was he really in favour of the investment bank? After all, he was head of the domestic retail division. Groenink replied that he would give the matter some thought.

Two days later, he met Van Tets again. Groenink promised to invest heavily in the investment bank, in combination with something that was then happening in another section of the bank: loans to companies. This would allow ABN Amro to develop as a wholesale bank, a bank focusing above all on large corporate clients. Groenink promised Van Tets that this would be a dominant part of the bank's new strategy and asked him to head this division. Van Tets was enthusiastic and informed Loudon that he would stay with the bank.

In late September, Kalff and Loudon visited Groenink in his brand new office to tell him that he would be designated as Jan Kalff's successor at the November meeting of the supervisory board. Until then he shouldn't mention it to anyone.

Groenink, who had just turned 50, felt a new sort of excitement. This was his moment. He had never hidden his ambition. He had worked hard for this; he had been on the managing board over eleven years. This was his reward. This was what he had dreamed of and counted on for all those years.

They knew that the appointment would be controversial and would meet resistance from various key figures. They proposed that he speak to various members of the managing board, to iron out as many of the difficulties as possible. Groenink promised to do his best.

There was a sense of excitement at the bank: 1999 would be a good year, a record year. That was true for most banks and companies. Optimism was high, the media was full of stories about a new economy. An economy with unlimited growth of productivity: the sky was the limit. At ABN Amro it was the corporate business division that profited more than any from this optimism. The bank was involved in 111 share issues, including several high profile launches of Internet companies.

Great things were expected from the investment bankers. This was reflected in the layout of the bank's new head office on Gustav Mahlerlaan on Amsterdam's Zuidas. The dealing room that had been set up there was the size of a large football field. It was the largest on the Continent. And thanks to a permanent digital connection with the bank's colleagues in London, it was one of the biggest in the world.

In the summer, the bank moved into the new building. It was ceremonially opened on 13 October by Prince Claus, who noted with a smile that cutting ribbons was his core business. A proud Kalff remarked that the bank's staff had doubled since the merger to over 100,000, total earnings had tripled (to 1,000 billion guilders), profits had multiplied by 2.5 and market capitalisation had quadrupled to 65 billion guilders (29.5 billion euros).

The first copy of *Worldwide Banking: ABN Amro Bank 1824-1999* was presented. In his foreword, Kalff had declared, 'We are proud of the leading position that ABN Amro Bank has built up over a period of 175 years and look with confidence to the future.' The former editor of *Het Financieele Dagblad*, Christiaan Berendsen, had been invited to write the final chapter and concluded coolly that the contours of the universal bank envisaged by ABN Amro Bank might be clear enough on paper, 'but putting these into practice in a turbulent world will only become visible well into the twenty-first century.'

Dutch Central Bank president Nout Wellink accepted the book and noted, "As you know, supervisors never say anything about the individual institutions that they supervise. But I see no reason not to divulge that DNB is proud to be a supervisor of ABN Amro. In our country this bank is still considered a Dutch bank. Let's hold on to that feeling, because we can all be proud of what the Dutch financial sector has managed to achieve. It has become a major source of prosperity for the country."

A few days later, it seemed that Jan Kalff would give this patriotic fervour an added fillip by completing a major takeover. To *The Wall Street Journal* he confirmed that ABN Amro had been talking to France's Société Générale about ways of working together. The French bank had tried to merge earlier that year with Banque Paribas, but had lost the race to Banque National de Paris. It had been a French bloodbath and Daniel Bouton, chairman of Société Générale since 1993, was now looking for rescue outside France.

They had been discussing the matter for some weeks. At first Jan Kalff and the 49-year-old Bouton got on well. The Frenchman was in trouble, the French banking sector had been consolidating at a growing pace and his bank had remained empty-handed. Though wary of reactions in France, Bouton wanted to know whether some form of combination with ABN Amro would be possible. "They are a universal bank, just as we are, and so it's sensible to look for ways in which to do something together," Kalff told *The Wall Street Journal*.

But Jan Kalff laid down rigorous conditions. Tom de Swaan travelled back and forth to Paris; president Aarnout Loudon also sat in on meetings. Both found Jan Kalff's demands frustrating. He wanted everything. ABN Amro would remain the bank's name, ABN Amro would supply the chairman and head of the supervisory board. Kalff was being arrogant. They wondered whether he understood what the French expected of him. Bouton had approached ABN Amro with a request; it required tact. Everything seemed to be going wrong between Bouton and Kalff. It was a sad waste.

Other members of the board were equally surprised by the demands laid before the French. Managing directors such as Van den Brink, Van Tets and De Jong wondered whether he wasn't being a little high-handed. In a conference call, Van den Brink commented that if ABN Amro really wanted to do business with Société Générale, nothing much would come of it if they made demands like these. But everyone was more concerned with their own business. This was the chairman's responsibility.

Slowly but surely it became clear that the discussions were going nowhere. The French had their pride too; they had no wish to be swept up by the Dutch, they wouldn't be able to sell that to anyone. In theory, Bouton was for joining forces, but he would never be able to explain to his people in Paris that even the dealing room would be in the Netherlands. It was humiliating. It would be a takeover.

And so the third serious attempt to become a truly European bank failed as well. In the supervisory board it was noted that the discussions had failed due to the exorbitant demands ABN Amro had attached to the merger. It was a missed opportunity.

On 12 November, early in the morning, a bunch of flowers was delivered to Jan Maarten de Jong's house. The American *Wall Street Journal* had heard from well informed sources that De Jong was to be appointed ABN Amro's new chairman that day. It was a painful mistake, one that Jan Kalff would dearly have wished to avoid. That afternoon, it was announced to the world that Rijkman Groenink would be taking over the chairmanship from Jan Kalff the following May. Kalff, like his predecessors, would be joining the supervisory board. Once again, following Nelissen and Kalff, ABN Amro would be led by a lawyer.

De Jong congratulated Groenink and warned him: You're a man of strong views, but you can't run the bank on your own, give other people a chance. And preserve the bank's unity. He also advised him to inject young blood into the managing board and informed Groenink therefore that he would certainly not mind stepping down earlier than his envisaged retirement date in

2006. Groenink sent De Jong a brief note. In large unwieldy letters (his left-hand penmanship never really improved) he thanked De Jong for his support.

Most ABN Amro personnel were surprised. Happily surprised. That the supervisory board had the nerve to choose a man like Groenink, few had expected. A sense of excitement was felt: would the new man lay out a definite course and make real choices?

Surprise was also evident in the media. It wasn't a natural choice for the bank. Groenink was portrayed as a tough negotiator, an astute banker and one of the bank's leading personalities. Ambitious and determined.

Léon Melchior was delighted at the news. Obviously now would be a good time to press ahead with his claim for compensation. A day before Groenink's appointment was announced, ABN Amro's lawyer had sent a letter to Léon Melchior's lawyer in which, in polite terms, the bank advised him to think again about the wisdom of pursuing his claim. The bank made it clear that it had no wish to go to court. Melchior was unimpressed by the bank's stance and responded that the compensation he was looking for was in the order of 150 million guilders. Kalff and Loudon were taken aback: Groenink had only just moved into the chairman's seat and already the first claim for damages had arrived. This would be bad for the bank's reputation. ABN Amro suggested an out-of-court settlement. Melchior agreed. It was understood, however, the result of the arbitration would not be binding.

The press release announcing Groenink's appointment also revealed that the domestic division would become part of a brand new European division in the following year. The new division would be led by Jan Maarten de Jong. But he already knew that this was window dressing. The new chairman had other plans, the *Creation of the European Division* report had already been consigned to the bin.

A few days after the announcement, Rijkman Groenink called a meeting with three men who had already begun cautiously to think about the bank's strategy: Jan Peter Schmittmann, Arnold van Os and Gerhard Zeilmaker. His question was clear: what should we change in our strategy? The workgroup listened carefully to the man who was now their *de facto* boss. He outlined the direction for them: Get rid of the expensive network and think how we're going to make money, more money than in the bank's current developed markets. They also listened to Groenink expand on his idea of a combination of corporate business and credits to major companies: the creation of a wholesale division.

And he had another assignment for them. Groenink knew that if the bank hoped to win in the inevitable consolidation battles that lay ahead, only one thing would count: market value on the stock exchange. The higher the share price, the better ABN Amro's chances of finishing on top in the coming round of mergers and takeovers. It was time to give priority to the creation of value for shareholders. Groenink hoped that focusing on shareholder value would engender a sense of discipline and accountability.

In December, Rijkman Groenink asked Hugh Scott Barrett, head of the merger and takeover department, to head the project group. The Brit was glad to get the job. Especially since the assignment included identifying where the bank's profits lay, and its costs.

At first the four called their project group Shield, after the yellow-green ABN Amro emblem. But that seemed a little too defensive. They took another look at the logo and decided to rename the group Arrow. Project Arrow would examine every aspect of strategy. The bank would be brought into shape for the twenty-first century.

6

Euphoria

January–April 2000

There was a mood of excitement at Duin & Kruidberg. The new century was a few days old. The top 200 managers of the bank were gathering at the bank's conference centre in the dunes close to Santpoort. Rijkman Groenink was looking forward to the meeting. This would be his first major appearance as head of the bank. He would formally take over the bank's leadership staff only in May, but in practice he was already the boss.

During the Universal Banking Conference he had tried to get people interested in the dramatic changes that he was planning. A sense of urgency would be needed. The consultants from McKinsey were helping. They had organised a role-playing exercise in which the ABN Amro bankers were asked to answer the question: what would they do if they were taken over by Citibank, or even more exciting, by the Internet company, AOL?

Anything was possible in these turbulent times. AOL had just announced a merger with TimeWarner, proof to many that the new economy, which was characterised by a seemingly endless growth in productivity, would overshadow the old. It was clear that the client, whether he was a consumer or a company, was becoming more powerful. That would certainly mean extra pressure on the margins. Even with a bank like ABN Amro.

Or maybe it would just be banks like ABN Amro that would feel the pinch. The bank's Internet strategy had not yet really got off the ground. What was the bank worth, what was its price, and how did these figures relate to those of new economy companies? Was the bank really so big, and powerful and successful?

The excitement during the previous quarters on bourses worldwide had been enormous. Internet companies were launching in great numbers on the stock exchanges. Investment banks were earning bucket loads of money. Nasdaq, the American electronic stock market, had broken record after record. ABN Amro's corporate business division had been earning well. There was more, even: in a few months, ABN Amro would work with Goldman Sachs to bring the Dutch Internet company, World Online, which had been set up by the high-profile entrepreneur, Nina Brink, to the market.

When Rijkman Groenink showed the first of his 24 slides, the hall went quiet. The title of his presentation was 'Back to the Future, revising our strategy in the context of a fast-changing world.' The presentation had been prepared by the Arrow team.

Groenink wanted to show that the bank would now have to focus on the future. During the half-hour of his scheduled speech he wanted to make it clear that he was ready for this, that he believed in the future of the bank. But he also wanted to show his colleagues how much work would have to be done.

His second slide summarised ABN Amro's weak points. "We do not have a second European domestic market. We lack a strong wholesale/investment bank in the United States, in Brazil and in other important economic areas. Our operations in Hungary and Thailand are too small. There are too few transactions to support the enormous network. Our asset management and private banking activities are too small."

A number of governors and managing directors shifted uncomfortably in their seats. This was not appropriate. An hour before, they had listened to Jan Kalff's last big speech, and given him a standing ovation. Kalff was still chairman of the managing board, and he was sitting in the front row. They could see from his face that he also didn't think it appropriate that Groenink should have distanced himself so publicly from his policies.

But the new head of the bank continued. "How do we become one of the top three banks in Europe? How can we become a leading global wholesale bank? How can we ensure a high share price?" He mentioned a number of changes in the bank's environment, which it would have to face. These included globalisation, the future of the Internet, deregulation, the rise of the Anglo-Saxon model in business and the privatisation of pension systems. Groenink observed that the United States had been dominant in bank mergers in 1998, but that European bank mergers had dominated in 1999. In 1995, ABN Amro had had a market value of 13 billion euros and it had been in the top ten of the biggest European banks; five years later, it was worth 34 billion euros, and yet it was now only in the top fifteen. Its big neighbour, ING, had grown from 17 to 58 billion euros and was now in third place. He warned that ABN Amro might become too small to play with the big global players.

The hall listened breathlessly. Groenink knew that he had found the right tone. He sketched rapid developments in IT. "Technology is a key strategic driver. The Internet will bring far-reaching changes to every market. Investments in IT will be greater, and the IT goods and services it provides will be state-of-the-art for shorter and shorter periods. We will have to build unique value in every line of business. Cross-selling will be essential to improve our financial achievements. It is vital that we find the right balance between being a client-driven and a product-driven organisation. If we really want to know what our clients want, we must learn to be open to their criticism."

He sketched the urgency under the heading 'The endgame, a us example'. "In the us, the top 25 banks generated a third of the profit made by all banks in 1980; now they generate half of that." The next sheet had an even more intriguing title, 'The global endgame'. Groenink sounded threatening. "In the long-term, the top ten banks in the world will have a market capitalisation of 200 billion dollars."

He said that shareholders were becoming much more demanding of banks. "That's why our actions will have to be guided by the need to create shareholder value. We must always be able to demonstrate the synergies between the various parts of our bank, and what contribution our products and services make to the profit. Analysts are increasingly demanding financial, strategic and organisational transparency. Only then will we be able to compare ourselves to other banks, to our peer group. And let's be honest: analysts appear to be asking for radical action from ABN Amro. I cite from a recent report by JP Morgan, 'More radical change is necessary.' The ultimate management motivator – to avoid a hostile takeover – hardly plays a role at ABN Amro. There is a lot of unused potential," Groenink laughed. "They're wondering if there is still fire in the management's belly."

He arrived at his concluding message. "As a universal bank we are being increasingly confronted by strong, focused and innovative competition in all our markets. Opportunities to strengthen our position in all these markets through acquisitions are limited both by the financial reserves and the available management. We will therefore have to ask ourselves a question: what are we good at, and what should we let go?"

He said that ABN Amro's shareholders, some 70 per cent of whom were foreign, expected a transparent mechanism for the distribution of the limited capital. The mechanism would help to achieve real internal accountability. "During the coming months, we must ask ourselves the following questions: What our real roots? Speaking realistically, where are the most promising opportunities for our business? Which areas must we invest in to be able to compete effectively in the long term? Which activities are really global and which are regional or local? Do all these activities create value for our shareholders?

"We will also have to consider the question whether we have the right organisation to achieve our strategic aims. How do we ensure maximum levels of transparency and accountability in our organisation? And do we have the right management style and corporate culture to be able to achieve rigorous control of our costs, as well as to continually adjust to changes in the ever-changing external environment?"

The temperature in the room had risen considerably. Here was a man with ambition and daring. At last, someone who dared to think about the future. "We have a mountain of work to do in the coming months," Groenink concluded. "The managing board would like your input. I want to have some interim conclusions ready in the autumn of 2000."

The applause was deafening. At the end of the gathering, everyone was asked to fill in a form in which they were asked to give their view of the meeting. One of the questions was, 'Must we really continue serving all our clients with as many products as possible? Do we want to be a universal bank?' The top 200 managers of the bank were clear: No, it's time to make choices.

Groenink had made a considerable about-turn: six months before he had been making plans for a European division, in which the matrix and the universal bank were central, but now he appeared to be going for a functional division of the bank. Confusion reigned on the managing board. When members of the managing board asked Groenink how things were going with the Europe division, which had been launched with such a song-and-dance, he said that he thought it necessary to take some distance from his own ideas. The Europe strategy came from the time when he had been head of the domestic division. Now he was looking at the whole bank, and from the perspective of his new responsibilities.

The discussion about the bank now had a completely different focus. Groenink, Van Tets and Jiskoot were constantly saying that the share price wasn't moving. And that a higher share price would be necessary if the bank were to undertake anything in the future. Now and then there were even suggestions that the bank could eventually be taken over if the share price stayed low. This was an intolerable thought to everyone involved. This bank would grow on its own steam, and become a leader. It was in the bank's genes.

The share price, something that had been a marginal issue under Hazelhoff and Kalff, now became the main issue. A higher share price would put the bank in a position to take over other banks, and remain independent in the long term. Groenink had talked about a market value of 200 billion. More and more frequently, the discussion on the managing board was about ways to ensure that the share price rose.

Against that background, another question was being asked more urgently now too: what kind of bank was ABN Amro, and what were its roots? Was it not mainly a bank that serviced the corporate world, a merchant bank? Jiskoot said that ABN Amro was in its nature much more a corporate bank than a retail bank.

There was a lot of discussion of the new concept of a wholesale bank. This was a mix of the commercial bank, which made loans to (big) business, and the investment bank, which serviced share issues, sold shares and advised clients on mergers and takeovers. That would be a good way to put things together. And surely, then ABN Amro would become the best wholesale bank in the world.

Classical investment bankers were rather sceptical about the concept. Investment bankers look down on ordinary bankers, thinking them too stupid to do the real work, which in their eyes was providing consultancy services. Activities such as selling simple loans were beneath them. They felt that this combination of activities would not simply work by itself. But on paper it looked attractive, because the combination was logical from the client's point of view.

The idea was that client-orientation would bridge the gaps. A client coverage manager would ensure that the different bankers would be encouraged to forget their petty jealousies and focus on the interests of the client. Hugh Scott Barrett believed in this approach. As he saw it, the bank didn't have the best reputation with corporate banking products, while it did have a good reputation with client-contact. They could build on that power.

Groenink formulated it differently: the commercial bank wasn't nearly profitable enough, and the investment bank is too small, but put them together and the result would be a successful wholesale bank.

Groenink told the Arrow team to investigate the integrity of the present ABN Amro strategy in more detail. Jan Peter Schmittmann, Arnold van Os and Gerhard Zeilmaker were already working on this, full-time. Some bankers wondered if it was logical to give the assignment to people who were analytically strong, but with a background mainly in investment banking. Others were concerned that there was no country manager in the team. There was also no one from the Dutch retail organisation on the team. Also, why was there no one from ABN? But euphoria was dominant. A serious strategy for the bank was being worked out at last.

Around 50 senior managers were interviewed. Consultants from McKinsey & Company provided strategic and organisational input. Consultants from Marakon Associates provided explanations of value-based management for use at a later stage and NautaDutilh provided advice on corporate governance questions. A range of big clients, among them DaimlerChrysler, La Poste, Reed Elsevier, Unilever and Zurich Financial Services, were asked what they thought of the bank.

The transparency and effectiveness of the business was evaluated. All of this set against trends in the financial world. The researchers also took a good look at what the analysts really thought. Things were happening fast; Groenink was in a hurry. But within the workgroup the feeling was that a responsible strategic choice should only be made on the basis of precise information about how much money the bank actually made. Which clients did the bank earn most from and which products did they need most?

Zeilmaker, who had become the bank's group controller, was concerned. More than any other, he knew that almost nothing had been invested in a good management information system over the previous years. There was a total lack of standardisation. The names of clients and products were abbreviated in different systems in different ways, for instance. It would be a huge job to come up with a well-founded overview of the bank.

It was agreed that the project team would present an interim inventory to the managing board in a couple of weeks. On that basis, further choices would be made. The first session was on 22 February. It was emphasised that there was a great need for transparency, efficiency and, above all, accountability. It was time people were held to their responsibilities. Kalff had put the shareholder in third place, after the client and the employee. Now the managing board decided, with virtually no discussion, that creating shareholder value would become the main driver behind the actions of the managing board for a period of three to five years. The discipline of the market must be felt, and the managing board would have to feel it too. They knew that if they were successful, their remuneration in options and shares would be far higher than their remuneration they had received in the previous years. They were seeing this happen in companies all around them.

Loud questions were asked about the performance of the international network. Tom de Swaan had already observed that there was a total lack of synergy in the network: if profits rose by 20 per cent, the costs rose with them. If the profits were disappointing, the costs still affected earnings. He found this frustrating. Jiskoot shared this irritation: the countries in the network were being managed like independent shops.

Zeilmaker and Joost Kuiper had already said in 1999 that the money overseas was being earned in the United States and Brazil, and that the network only cost money. Kuiper was for closing large sections of the network. It was agreed that a set of clear criteria would be outlined by which it could be shown exactly what the overseas offices brought in.

During that first discussion it was also enthusiastically observed that ABN Amro was in a position to build a top slot in global wholesale banking. As regards retail banking (small companies and consumers), it was decided that ABN Amro would focus only on markets where it could achieve a sustainable dominant position.

Members of the project group noticed that the managing board talked a lot about the enormous potential of the corporate business division. The mood on the board was one of euphoria at the opportunities available to ABN Amro. Van Os and Scott Barrett thought that the managing directors were mainly interested in themselves and how the outside world saw them.

Most members of the board appeared to think they were investment bankers. All of them had networks, and they had been talking for years with the leaders of large listed companies in the Netherlands. The issue of the share price had also become more important among them. Stories about integrating systems in an area dominated by increasingly restricted interest margins now looked much less attractive than organising and facilitating a big deal on the stock market. The general rise in share prices, the excitement about the new economy and a tendency to focus on the company's share price ensured that the other activities of the bank were hardly mentioned.

The board asked the project group to compare five alternatives for the new strategy: a global wholesale bank, a global retail bank, a European universal bank, a universal bank in certain regions (the present strategy), and a bank-insurer.

The corporate business division had been hard at work all these months, working on preparations for a spectacular share issue. Nina Brink had asked Goldman Sachs and ABN Amro to launch World Online. The Internet company had been much discussed. Not everyone was happy with this client.

Rijkman Groenink had bad memories of Nina Brink. He knew her from his time in the risk management department and he felt that the bank should not be doing this share issue. Governor Rob Hazelhoff told the managing board that he didn't feel that clients of this sort belonged with the bank. Hazelhoff felt that clients should not be evaluated only by the profit-and-loss account and balance, but also on grounds of morality. But he feared he was fighting a losing battle. His feeling was that the managing directors were getting too excited, and that they would soon find themselves standing beside the tombstone commemorating this launch: a glass column in the form of a gravestone with the names of the banks that had played a role.

Wilco Jiskoot was enthusiastic. This was a big, prominent job. The banks valued World Online at about 12 billion euros. Jan Kalff had wanted the company, which he saw as celebrated and promising, as a client. Kalff knew Dick Wessels, a major shareholder in World Online, well; since 1997 he had been a governor at Volker Wessels Stevin. The reputable firm of Goldman Sachs had been given the lead in the global share issue, which had reassured Kalff. Jiskoot and Kalff had seen to it that ABN Amro got a share of the leading role in the launch.

On 17 March, Nina Brink gave the thumbs up and World Online went to the market. The launch was celebrated at a gathering of hundreds of guests at Okura Hotel in Amsterdam. *Het Financieele Dagblad* commented, 'Joe Cocker was the guest of honour because the surviving Beatles weren't prepared to come'.

The share issue was a drama. The shares were brought to market at 43 euros, but the bank had to buy a swathe of them to prevent the price from falling below the starting level on the first day. Goldman Sachs and ABN Amro had both committed to buy 10.5 million shares if that threatened to happen, as a sort of quality guarantee. And the bank had to shell out more money on the days following. On 21 March, the share closed at 37.40 euros and a day later at 29.95 euros. The fall in the share price cost the bank tens of millions.

The big shock was the discovery that Nina Brink had sold a substantial part of her interest months before the issue. Later it emerged that it had been reported incorrectly in the share issue prospectus. Instead of the verb 'sell', the word 'transfer' had been used in a crucial sentence. The move was the better option for herself and her family, Brink explained to the outside world; she had wanted to ensure their financial future.

Investors who had lost around half of their inlay at that point were furious and blamed the banks, as well as Brink and World Online. A range of lawyers and the Dutch association of shareholders announced that they would be instituting legal proceedings; at that point the total damage was around four billion euros. Even politicians joined in. "Attention has focused on the conduct of Ms Brink," Ad Melkert, the parliamentary chairman of the Dutch labour party, told *Het Financieele Dagblad*. "I think the role of the parties that helped to bring World Online to the market has not received as much attention as it should."

Hardly four weeks after the launch, Brink left World Online. From that moment, many people directed their anger at the supervising banks. The damage to the bank's reputation was enormous. It was the blackest day, and the most shameful, in the careers of many of the ABN Amro bankers involved.

ABN Amro didn't flinch, fearing the damages that might be demanded if it did. During his last press conference as chairman of ABN Amro, Jan Kalff sat next to Wilco Jiskoot, who had been responsible for overseeing the launch. Kalff was visibly tense, and read out a message about the unhealthy atmosphere around World Online. "Those were days of almost unlimited euphoria about Internet stocks. The feeling was that a lot of money could be earned without risk, [that it was] a lottery without losers." Kalff wondered if all the excitement was really about investing. "Let's not forget: a shareholder is someone who owns a share." As he saw it, the bank "had never paid so much attention to a prospectus." Moreover, the bank's leadership had insisted that branch managers should refer all their excited clients to the prospectus. There, they would have found 15 pages summarising the risks involved. He read out a number of clauses, and shook his head. "A banker of my generation can only shake his head at the rush to invest." He said he was ready for to any legal proceedings that might arise. The bank had done its best.

A governor of the bank walked up to Kalff and asked him if he should not have shown more empathy. A lot of people had lost a lot of money. Kalff, who was being advised by lawyers, shrugged his shoulders. There had simply not been the space to do so. Kalff was tired. Very tired.

His successor was steaming ahead, meanwhile, with the process of breaking up the universal bank. Of the alternatives presented on 3 April by the Arrow project group – a global wholesale bank, a global retail bank, a European universal bank, a universal bank in certain regions (the present strategy), or a bank-insurer – the board decided that the last three, including the present strategy, would 'not lead to a sustainable market position in the long term', and would therefore not lead to generating 'superior returns to the shareholders of the bank'.

On the issue of combining banking and insurance, the managing board said ABN Amro was of course a wholesale bank, while a bank-insurer tended to focus on retail banking. Moreover, potential partners like ING and Aegon were worth much more than the bank on the market at the moment; ABN Amro would be subordinate in any merger. And an insurance culture would dominate.

The managing board had some serious criticisms of the present strategy. 'We have three strong regional companies, but they work entirely independently and until now have appeared incapable of carrying the enormous costs of the international network.' They were led regionally, while more and more big clients were demanding an approach based on the line of business. The bank had not succeeded in building up the investment bank, asset management and private banking activities in the United States or Brazil, although there had been some success in the Netherlands.

A definitive choice would be made at the next meeting. The work group went to work again. There was a lot to do. Gerhard Zeilmaker's room was a hive of activity. Once a week, Hugh Scott Barrett came over from England to go through the results with Arnold van Os. Fully briefed, he would then go into a discussion with Zeilmaker and Schmittmann. During one of the meetings, Van Os noted that it felt sometimes as if the bank was getting ready to be taken over.

The pace on the Melchior dossier picked up too. It had to. ABN Amro wanted the case solved before Groenink was formally handed the chairman's gavel. A judge had been found who was prepared to take on the arbitration: former president of the district court Wijnholt in The Hague.

The former president of the district court in Amsterdam, B.J. Asscher, had been asked first, according to Dutch weekly magazine *Elsevier*, but he had declined.

On 6 April, Léon Melchior and Rijkman Groenink appeared with their lawyers before Wijnholt. He thought that Melchior had a right to damages. The sum of 35 million guilders was discussed.

Groenink was furious. The judge had given Melchior a foothold. Of course he, Rijkman Groenink, had not given guarantees to the three investors for their investments in HCS. He had only said that the company would have a chance of survival if they put money into it, nothing more. He felt that Melchior's claim was nonsense. He didn't think that the bank should pay, and wanted to take the matter further.

For Jan Kalff it was clear that whatever rights there were in the situation lay more on Melchior's side. It was a fact that Groenink had acted clumsily. In the hot summer of 1991, he had given the three investors the impression that they would not suffer financially from the rescue operation.

Kalff thought that the bank should pay. The alternative would be a legal battle with Melchior, and it would undoubtedly get into the media. It would cause a great deal of damage to the bank's reputation if the appointment of the new chairman coincided with a court case in which he was accused of misconduct. That simply wouldn't do. Kalff knew that the bank had no choice.

But now it was Melchior who put a spanner in the works. He had an opportunity to do so; it had been agreed that the result of the arbitration would not be binding. So Melchior kept his options open to go to court and pushed the tension up higher.

Tom de Swaan thought it was a painful business. He had talked with Melchior a number of times, without being able to come to an agreement. Now this had become a game of cat-and-mouse, and Melchior was the cat. De Swaan noted that money didn't seem to be the main factor for Melchior. He wanted Rijkman Groenink to suffer for a little while longer.

Meanwhile, Groenink was preparing for his new role. He organised a series of round-table discussions at his office in the run-up to his chairmanship. The new chairman wanted to know what was going on in the organisation.

Around ten highly promising colleagues were asked to prepare the relevant documents. Most of them did so as thoroughly as they could. Everyone was nervous, assuming that Groenink wanted to test their knowledge. So they tried to formulate the question as well as possible and to prepare a good answer. Much of their work proved unnecessary. Groenink would hardly wait for the question to be asked before he started issuing instructions. The participants were astounded by the sharpness of his analysis. The man appeared to have a wide knowledge of the bank. The experience humbled them. But when the session was over, and they were out of his office, a feeling of distance remained. The new chairman had not really engaged in discussion, and had not made them feel that he was interested in what they had to say.

A few weeks before Groenink took over the chairmanship, he told the Arrow project group that it was time to round off their work. He wanted to communicate on the situation to the external world as soon as possible. The four men were surprised. The intention had been to present the whole story in the autumn. But Groenink said that there was a lot of pressure on him to come up with something good. He wanted quick progress.

Zeilmaker and Van Os especially were shocked. They had not been able to round off their analysis because they didn't have the figures they needed. The bank's management information system was simply not up-to-date enough. Figures for countries and regions were available, but not in consolidated form. They still didn't know where the bank earned most of its money. Now they would have to round off their analysis without the key figures, and therefore without any real foundation.

On 1 May, the managing board got together again to discuss Arrow. There were still three strategic options on the table: to aim to be a world-leader as a retail bank, or a world top five wholesale bank, or a worldwide top-five wholesale bank in defined client and product segments.

The most aggressive wholesale scenario was rejected after considerable discussion, with most of the criticism coming from Van Tets. "To aim at being in the global top five, we would have to take over a big investment bank. We're talking about an investment of 15 billion dollars, in the case of Lehman, and 30 billion in the case of JP Morgan. The execution and integration risks are too great. We could only fund such a takeover if we sell our retail bank in Brazil or the United States. That would probably mean the end of the remaining retail activities, which are relatively small."

There was another argument. "Any takeover of a large American investment bank would probably be a reverse takeover in a number of respects, given the limited size of our investment bank. The head office would have to be in New York, for instance. Let's not forget: we will not persuade our shareholders, and we would have to move to New York. And that's a long way from our present business and culture."

The ambition to become a global retail bank was also definitively rejected. "The model looks attractive, but let's not forget that our roots are mainly in wholesale and that the top management of the bank has a clear wholesale culture." The focus on retail would be an enormous destruction of value on the wholesale side of the bank. The model required a second domestic market in Europe. Until now, that had proved elusive. The bank only had a top-five position in the Netherlands and the American Mid-West. Moreover, the earnings of retail banks were under constant threat from the Internet, as well as the convergence of markets.

And so the decision was taken, without the complete figures and without knowing where the bank earned most of its money. "We will stop the universal bank and transform the bank into three dedicated customer businesses." The geographic division would be replaced by a global bundling of different client groups.

'The bank's network will lose its central role,' the board stated in the final presentation. 'We will become entirely client-driven. The need to feed the network is history. We have decided to create three separate divisions, or strategic business units (sbus). These will decide the extent to which they want to use, and pay for, the network. There will be a decentralised structure with lean and mean head office.

The wholesale sbu would lead, and serve all the large companies, both with loans and investment banking services. Small companies and consumers would be served by the consumer and commercial clients (c&cc) division. Investment and consultancy would come under the private clients and asset management (pcam) division. The latter two divisions will support the wholesale division.' Formerly, the universal bank had not made choices between the geographical (primarily former abn) and the corporate business (mainly Amro's area) activities. That time was now gone. The wholesale sbu would play the leading role in the bank.

The first difficult question came quickly: where would they draw the line? Which clients would go to the wholesale sbu and which would fall under c&cc? Scott Barrett felt that a mistake had been made. c&cc should simply have been called retail; then it would be clear what it did. But retail by itself was not profitable enough and so a compromise had to be found. The smaller companies would also fall under this division. Scott Barrett noted that there was already a lot of horse trading over clients. This frustrated him, as he felt that it was not right.

The agreement was that the leadership of wholesale, the corporate division, would set the boundaries, and determine which clients belonged to them. The American subsidiary, LaSalle, was mainly a retail company, and it was also agreed that all American clients would fall under c&cc, at first at least. The assumption was that a client of c&cc would want to list at some stage, or would want to make use of the bank's investment banking services, which could be carried out only by the wholesale division.

The underlying financial analysis looked promising. 'We can create 8.5 billion euros in value, and that will make the bank worth a quarter more than it is at present.' Half the value would come from the integration of the investment bank and the commercial bank as a single wholesale bank (1.9 billion euros), and this would have to deliver significant profits (2.4 billion euros). This would require a significant investment in new investment bankers. It was decided to budget 450 million to hire 500 new investment bankers over the following three years. The sums assumed that the new investment bankers would deliver twice a much as they cost within three years.

Jan Kalff missed the last session. A few days before he assumed his new position, Groenink went to visit him, to report the Arrow conclusions. The departing chairman was seriously shocked. He said that he thought the changes were too rigorous, too drastic. He didn't agree with them, and would have liked to discuss them in more detail.

He understood some things in the new plans well enough. There was a need for more accountability; that had been made abundantly clear during the previous years. But his main feeling was that the division into three independent sbus would not be advisable. The people who were presently leading their countries would lose their jobs. All countries would now fall under the division that they did most of their work for. In most cases, that would be the wholesale division. Someone in that division would then have to act as the country representative in each case. Kalff thought it highly inadvisable to remove the country managers. Aside from the effects this would have on the people concerned, he was worried that the clients would find it hard to understand the new structure. And what would the national authorities think of it? They often demanded a single contact point with the bank.

But Kalff didn't take up the fight. He was busy organising his departure. His diary was filled with lunches, drinks and receptions. When he thought of all those engagements, he missed his wife. She should have been there with him.

In April, Groenink left his job as head of the domestic division. He invited the top 20 managers to his home, with their partners. Groenink lived with his wife, who was pregnant, and their young son in a beautifully restored windmill on the river Vecht.

Halfway through dinner, Groenink gave a speech. He told his colleagues

that a new organisation was being built. It would have an entirely new structure, and it would also be very different to the European division they had
been used to. With a mischievous smile, he added that his colleagues didn't
need to worry ... with this sort of thing, it was not about the organisation itself,
it was the fact that they were moving ... that they were changing. It was not
about the content of the change, but the fact of change.

7

Mistake

May–December 2000

It was Tuesday evening, 9 May. The next morning, Rijkman Groenink would be formally appointed as chairman of the managing board. But he was not in a party mood. He was flying with Tom de Swaan to the town of Beek in the Dutch province of Limburg. From there they would travel by car to Lanaken in Belgium, to meet Léon Melchior.

The 74-year-old Melchior had still not agreed to the bank's proposal of a settlement of 35 million guilders. He had even approached the chairman of the bank's supervisory board about the issue. Aarnout Loudon had not liked that; Melchior had a certain reputation. Loudon's message to the managing board was clear: sort this out. The damage caused by a court case on the day Rijkman Groenink took up his appointment would be greater than the cash Melchior would get.

Groenink was angry. He didn't want to settle at all. He was convinced that he had done nothing wrong. But he also knew that Kalff and Loudon had sent Tom de Swaan along with him to prevent the meeting from getting out of hand, and especially to prevent Groenink from walking away. Loudon and Kalff wanted a last effort to prevent the former building contractor and project developer from spoiling the new chairman's first day by instituting legal proceedings. They were determined. Melchior was capable of anything.

Tom de Swaan was not much happier. If the predecessors of the man sitting next to him had dealt with this matter years before, the bank would probably only have had to pay out a couple of million. And then he would not have had to be here, to deal with this sordid case. But he realised that it would have to be dealt with. Groenink was vulnerable on this, and therefore so was ABN Amro.

It was a strange meeting. Melchior went for everything he thought he could get. Groenink and De Swaan offered 40 million guilders. But Melchior shook his head, again. The two men left Lanaken empty-handed. The threat of a court case on Groenink's first day as chairman was now real. They flew home, disillusioned.

The following morning, at fifteen minutes to nine, Melchior phoned his consultant, Harry Langman, to ask him what to do. The former ABN banker had been having fun with this little game from the sidelines for years, but now he thought that enough was enough. He advised Melchior to agree to the offer. Melchior said he would.

Langman had hardly hung up when Groenink and De Swaan called him in a panic. They were worried that it was all going wrong. Could he talk again with Melchior, perhaps? Maybe the man would listen to him. Langman reassured them that Melchior would call them within a few minutes to confirm that the deal would go through. And he did.

The bank duly paid up and also promised to sponsor an equestrian event with which Melchior was associated. The threat of a court case concerning Groenink's supposed failure nine years earlier in the HCS case was gone. The top managers of the bank heaved a collective sigh of relief. Rijkman Groenink took up his appointment without further trouble when the shareholders' meeting began a short while later. The new chairman lit up a large Havana, his favourite cigar.

On 12 May, Jan Kalff held a farewell party at Amsterdam's Concertgebouw. Of course it had to be there, like the farewell parties of his predecessors André Batenburg and Rob Hazelhoff. Only Roelof Nelissen thought that the party was too expensive.

There were 1,500 guests. It was a strange farewell. Many people were annoyed by Rijkman Groenink's rather loveless speech. He didn't manage to say anything nice about his predecessor. And there was surprise that Lydia Kalff was sitting on the stage next to her ex-husband. Everyone in the bank knew that they had been divorced for nearly two years by then. Apparently the departing chairman had done everything he could to ensure that he was not there alone.

"I am not a man for huge, visionary changes," Kalff said in an interview in *Bankwereld*, about his six years as chairman. "My feeling is that that approach is excessive. I see myself primarily as someone who built on what his predecessors started. First and foremost, I wanted to strengthen the bank's culture. Mainly through my style of leadership, by phoning people who I knew were having a difficult time in business, and by organising meetings to promote unity."

As an example, he mentioned his Christmas meetings, which brought the ABN Amro family together. "My wife always did a tremendous job of decorating the venue. Together we would think of a gift, which all the guests would receive. She always remembered to take things on our trips – whether it was a pot of liquorice or peanut butter – which would be nice presents for the people we would meet."

Meanwhile, Irene Groenink was putting her stamp on her husband's work-life balance as the bank's new chairman. They had decided that Groenink had not succeeded in his first attempt to combine work and family, and they had agreed that he would strive for a better balance. That year, their second son was born.

Groenink wanted to be involved in raising his children. To be able to spend time with his young family, the new chairman decided that he would travel as little as possible and cut back rigorously on his evening commitments. These were usually dinners and receptions with clients, which he hated anyway.

Arrow project was thundering along. The last knots were cut on 15 May. Summarised, the strategy was as follows, 'We will become a leading integrated commercial/investment bank, and we will strive for a sustainable position in the top five in the defined client and product segments. Wholesale will lead. Retail (consumer & commercial clients: c&cc) and private clients & asset management (pcam) will play a supporting role.'

The concerns of some members of the project group, that they didn't have figures to justify the choice of a leading role for the wholesale sbu, were not mentioned explicitly by Scott Barrett, the chairman of the work group. Tom de Swaan observed that this decision was being taken without the necessary foundation, but he didn't intervene.

It was felt that the approach would deliver considerable costs savings. The retail bank was expected to achieve a structural saving of around 260 million euros. The asset management division (pcam) would cut back by some 50 million euros in costs. The rationalisation of the network of overseas offices would deliver some 325 million euros in savings per year; dozens would be closed. The savings at head office, which was to become more efficient, would be 373 million euros. From 2004 the bank's cost levels would be consistently lower by some 600 million euros. The total reorganisation would cost 725 million euros, aside from the costs of consultants and the installation of a new management information system, which would cost 400 million over two years. The pace would be quick. The leadership of the bank wanted to see the new approach implemented by 31 December of that year. In total, a provision of some 900 million euros was made to cover the costs.

Scott Barrett, who had been concerned for years about the lack of accountability, saw his chance and observed that the strategy would have significant consequences for the structure and principles of the bank. "We must finally get away from the present culture of excuses, which are made possible by matrices that allow everyone to point their fingers at everyone else, and endless steering committees etc," his work group said. "We must move to a culture in which personal responsibility and accountability are central."

Tom de Swaan was happy to hear this. It was exactly what the bank needed. Even fans of the matrix structure could understand the criticism. The matrix only worked if people were prepared to work together. If that was absent, the matrix could be used to blame other people when the results were disappointing. It was time for clarity.

The board noted the conclusion of the work group that a 'top-down approach is necessary to change the culture of the bank from the present practice of consensus and compromise to an environment that focuses on the creation of value. To achieve that, the bank must set clear targets based on real value creation.' Under Kalff, a cautious start had been made toward value-based management. To prevent confusion now, a new term was introduced: managing for value.

Value creation would therefore now be central. The bank's activities would focus on economic profit over the long term, that is, the net profit minus costs. The reasoning behind this was that capital in a bank is expensive and scarce, and it is always a question where capital can best be used, that is, where it will yield the best returns. The managing board thought this was a logical criterion by which to steer the bank. It required a clear picture of the profits and losses delivered by each unit, including the cost of invested capital.

'Both inside and outside the bank, we will communicate clearly that there are specific consequences for bonuses, and even for the continuation of employment,' the work group warned. 'The investment community must feel convinced that the bank is pursuing this rigorously and consistently. Some of them have doubts, wondering if investors will understand the concept of economic profit. We cannot publish our results in this way, because our competitors will see what we are doing. It also makes it impossible to make comparisons [between banks] because the costs can be chosen arbitrarily.'

These concerns were waved away. An enthusiastic feeling that at last a way toward transparency and accountability had been found was dominant. From now on the bank's three divisions, and the units that made them up, would be expected to create economic value for the shareholders.

And so it was that the morning of 15 May was used to begin a total conversion of the inheritance left by Jan Kalff. That afternoon was devoted to Kalff's farewell reception. An emotional Kalff received the title of Commander of the Order of Orange-Nassau from Dutch finance minister Zalm.

On Friday afternoon 26 May, the Arrow project was presented to the supervisory board. As always, it was a formal meeting. The governors sat across the table from the managing board. The longer their term of service as a governor, the closer they sat to the president. Requests to speak were channelled through the chairman. When this was given, the governor would be allowed to switch on his microphone and ask his question in English. The chairman and the president sat at either end of the table, opposite each other. They were the axis of the meeting, and they conferred with each other and agreed on the items on the agenda beforehand.

Frits Fentener van Vlissingen would no longer be following the discussion; he had indicated that he didn't want to extend his term as a governor. Hans van Liemt, who had been a warm enthusiast of Groenink's appointment, would follow him as deputy president.

The supervisory board would be reinforced by Trude Maas-Brouwer, who worked at Hay Management Consultants. During their introductory talk, Maas-Brouwer was impressed by the view from Groenink's 21st story office in south Amsterdam. A large portrait of a woman by the South African artist Marlene Dumas hung on the wall behind his desk. Maas was curious, and wanted to sound Groenink out.

But she noticed that answering questions was not his strong point; Groenink preferred to say how things were. When he talked about the bank's employees, he seemed distant. He saw people mainly in terms of their function. At the end of the talk, she asked Groenink what drove him, where he got his energy. The chairman was silent for a moment, changed the subject and let the new governor out. Trude Maas didn't get an answer to her question.

The other new governor, Jan Kalff, didn't need an introductory talk with Groenink. At this first meeting, his fellow governors noticed that he sat in silence, apparently sulking. Kalff had intended not to say anything at all, but he could not restrain himself when the Arrow presentation made it clear that the country managers would lose out. He thought it incomprehensible that the American division was being cut up into three pieces.

Kalff also thought that his successor in the chairman's seat was making an error by closing down large sections of the overseas network. The bank was withdrawing from eleven countries and closing offices in more than forty. As he saw it, they shouldn't be focusing on specific offices. He had warned often enough about this in the past: if you break the bank open, you break it up. Kalff was concerned that cohesion within the bank would disappear. He warned Groenink of this, and asked if the organisation, and the people who would have to carry it out, could support that.

Groenink had no patience for this, and said that he was now the boss. The other governors didn't support Kalff. Instead, they made an urgent appeal to him to support Groenink's plans, both inside and outside the bank. He had been present when the plans had been formulated, after all. The bank's interests were paramount. Kalff resigned himself to the new direction.

Most of the 100-page Arrow document was presented at the meeting, page by page. Hardly any questions were asked. The governors told themselves that these highly skilled bankers had spent six months on the plan, and you couldn't shoot it down without some preparation. In general, they were enthusiastic. The feeling was 'we're doing it differently' and 'we're cleaning out the stickiness'.

The focus on building up the corporate division was supported. The division delivered 20 per cent of earnings; in the new plan, it would deliver nearly 40 per cent within four years. That's where growth would come from. More advisory services, less credit, that was the future.

Loudon had an uncanny feeling that Groenink himself had serious questions about allowing the corporate division to become dominant. He felt that Groenink's main idea was that wholesale should be given a chance. But the president of the supervisory board didn't express his doubts. It was obvious that the investment bankers were dominant in the top management of the bank; they made a lot of noise, and you shouldn't underestimate their influence. Moreover, the market was good. Loudon was worried about all the attention that would be going to C&CC, the retail division. He noticed that the corporate bankers were condescending about retail activities.

Rob Hazelhoff, who would be serving out his last months at the bank as a governor, thought that this was a dangerous development. The bank ran the risk that it would become too focused on getting big deals in, rather than on the long-term interests of the clients. He thought that was stupid, because banking is all about the client. He was afraid that the universal bank would disappear.

Unilever headman Burgmans expressed some cautious concerns: did ABN Amro have the talent it would need to go up against the competition offered by the big American investment banks? If that was not the case, did the bank have any reason to think that that talent would want to work for ABN Amro in the future? Loudon jumped in to protect his new chairman, and warned his fellow governors not to try to think for him. Arrow got the green light.

There was one subject on which the meeting didn't agree. The project group had consulted with McKinsey's advisors. They suggested that Rijkman Groenink be made chief executive officer along Anglo-American lines. The four men felt that any far-going reorganisation would have to be led by someone who was decisive. Groenink responded to the suggestion with reserve. The new chairman thought that discontinuing the managing board and leaving him to make all the decisions would be too radical a break with the past.

But he did think that it would be a good idea for him to have more elbow room as chairman. He also thought that the bank suffered from a lack of quick decision-making and wanted more powers as chairman to intervene directly as he felt necessary.

Some of the governors, Wim Dik among them, supported this approach. To introduce and see through significant changes, a chairman needed to be able to intervene. But Hazelhoff, Kalff and Loudon were against it. Loudon said that a chairman with a strong personality had the same room for manoeuvre as a CEO.

The supervisory board was divided. After some discussion, those against had to give way. Loudon told Groenink that they were behind him, that they wanted him to carry out the changes. They had chosen him as their chairman, and they must abide by that decision. A few changes were made, though; Groenink did get a few more stripes on his sleeve. One change was that a motion could only be adopted if the chairman voted for its adoption with the majority. In other words, he had a veto on any majority decision, although he would not be able to push through a motion if the majority was against it. Moreover, control over the achievement of targets would lie with the chairman and his CFO. It was also decided to pay the chairman substantially more than his predecessor: 40 per cent more than anyone else on the board.

Groenink received a letter from the supervisory board stating that he had been appointed for six years, after which period his chairmanship would be evaluated and a further decision would be taken whether he would get another term.

From Groenink's first day, a lot changed in the managing board's approach. The endless discussions about credit were history. Groenink didn't feel it necessary to meet them twice a week; twice a month would be sufficient. The new chairman also put an end to the executive aspect of the roles on the managing board. Responsibility for client contacts, even for the important ones, would be carried at a lower level in the SBUS. The task of the board would be to focus on strategy.

People at levels lower than the managing board were appalled by this; many felt that a lot of goodwill might be lost this way. They were worried that the distance between the bank and its clients would grow. Clients would not understand why board members no longer had any time for them, and why they were talking mostly to shareholders. Lower-level employees also disliked it. People working in the field need to be able to spend some time with their bosses, to get a sense of what is going on at the top level of the bank.

Groenink was clearly enjoying his new role, shaking things up and provoking his colleagues. He even suggested that the name of the bank be changed to

ABN. Like many of his colleagues, he had been irritated for years by the long acronym of the bank's present name. It was not easily understood or easy to say, especially for people overseas. Groenink felt that he was the ideal person to make this suggestion, as a former Amro man. But there was a lot of resistance to the idea. Someone did some figuring, and showed that a rebranding exercise would cost several hundred million. The name remained ABN Amro.

The biggest change was in the tone of the discussions on the managing board. Under Kalff, members had rarely exchanged an unseemly word. But Groenink, who behaved more emphatically as the chairman, ensured that a completely different atmosphere reigned from the first meeting. Discussion was faster and more aggressive. Swear words were used more regularly, as well as remarks like "Well, you should have read the documents."

The heads of the three strategic business units (SBUS) would be held responsible for the results of their own divisions from January 2001. As had been agreed, Van Tets would head up the wholesale activities: the corporate business division. Jan Maarten de Jong would be CEO of C&CC and Dolf van den Brink would be CEO of PCAM. Groenink thought that each of them was the obvious man for the job.

De Jong and Van den Brink, both of them ABN men, were clearly not at ease with the situation. Things had been rather too calm under Kalff, perhaps, but now they bordered on hectic. The former sense of collective responsibility had been replaced by an every-man-for-himself feeling. De Jong wondered if the bank had taken the wrong direction by giving the corporate business division a leading role. After all, big American investment banks led the way in that world. Would ABN Amro be able to take its place among them? He was also worried about the focus on the interests of shareholders in combination with a bank led by the corporate business division, which was dominated by investment bankers. Many interests within the bank were being driven back. De Jong, reserved as ever, hardly expressed his concern: Groenink was now the boss.

Van den Brink felt that the managing board was becoming a sort of arena in which people talked but didn't listen. He was concerned about a unit that he had been responsible for under the old structure, the resource management division. He wondered if this large-scale decentralisation of a range of staff services such as a human resources and IT was well considered. He felt that the bank had become a huge test case. Van den Brink quarrelled with Tom de Swaan about this. He thought it wrong in principle that the coordination of human resource activities in the SBUS should fall under the CFO. The financial director would have to be strict, paying close attention to costs and intervening quickly if necessary.

Amro chairman Roelof Nelissen (left) and ABN chairman Rob Hazelhoff at the press conference in Amstel Hotel on 26 March 1990, where the merger of ABN and Amro was announced. 'There are similarities, and there are differences. That's what makes life interesting. But in some areas both will have to make changes.'
Photo: ANP

May 1991, the 41 year old Rijkman Groenink, member of ABN Amro's fourteen-man board.
Photo: ABN Amro

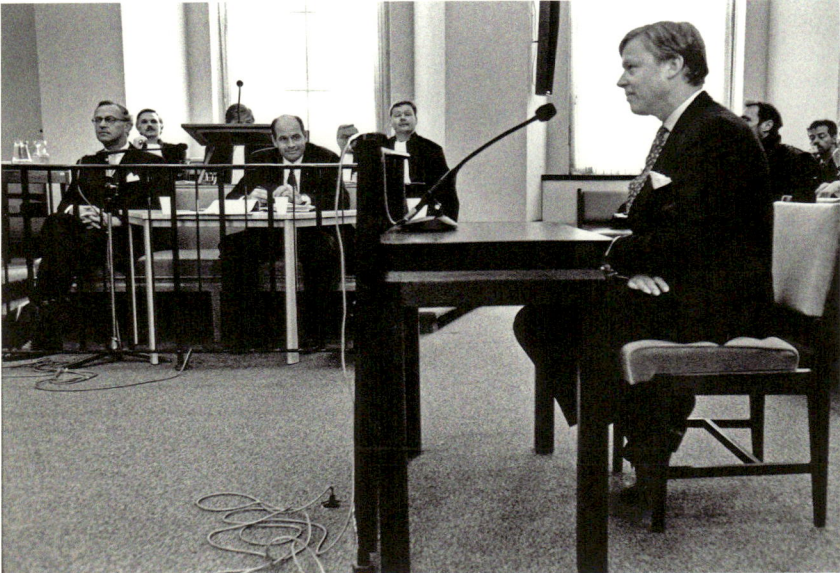

'So Joep, why don't you sell a couple of million shares?' On 3 October 1994, Rijkman Groenink explained to the president of the court, Huub Willems, that his remark had been meant as a joke. The judge was not amused and accidentally addressed Groenink as the defendant in the interminable HCS case. In the centre, laughing, is the defendant Joep van den Nieuwenhuyzen.

Photo: Willem Middelkoop /Hollandse Hoogte

Dick Meys, the flamboyant head of the bank's domestic division in early 1995. 'We've turned in on ourselves. More than anything, what we lack is quality.'
Photo: Ron Offermans

Chairman Jan Kalff flanked by the two senior Amro bankers, Dick Meys and Michael Drabbe. Others, from left to right: Rijnhard van Tets, Louis de Bièvre, Paul Ribourdouille, Ruud van Ommeren, Rijkman Groenink and Jan Maarten de Jong.
Photo: Picture Report

Under Jan Kalff, the board met twice a week, with the latest credit applications a fixture on the agenda. This meeting in late 1998 was Michael Drabbe's last. He was already extremely ill. Also present from left to right: Wilco Jiskoot, Rijnhard van Tets, Jan Kalff, Michael Drabbe, Tom de Swaan, Dolf van den Brink, Rijkman Groenink and Jan Maarten de Jong.
Photo: Bert Verhoeff

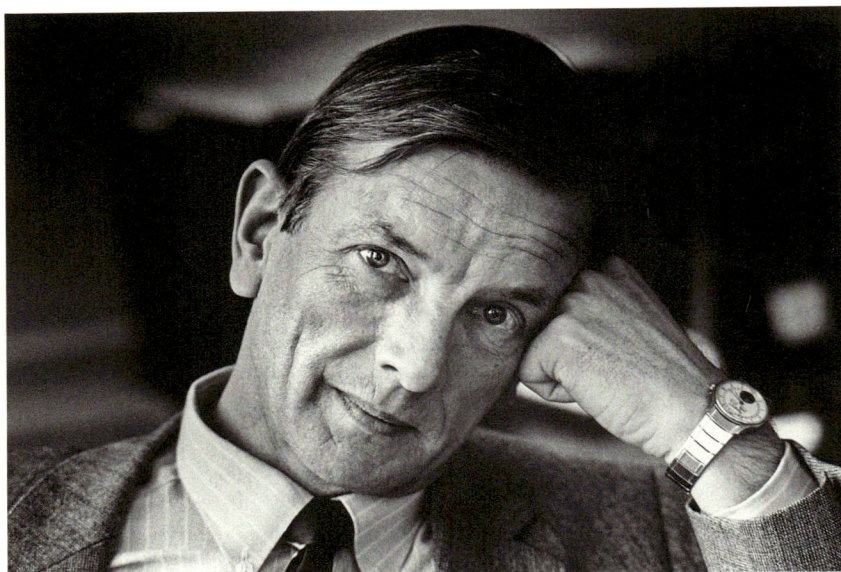

Frits Fentener van Vlissingen, vice-president of ABN Amro's supervisory board from 1973 (at Amro) to May 2000, felt that the bank needed someone with courage and decisiveness as chairman, someone like Rijkman Groenink.
Photo: Vincent Mentzel/Hollandse Hoogte

From left to right: Rijnhard van Tets, Jan Kalff and Jan Maarten de Jong at a press conference in late 1998. In 1999, Van Tets threatened to resign if Rijkman Groenink were appointed chairman. Kalff was also worried. He would have preferred De Jong to succeed him as chairman.
Photo: Bert Verhoeff

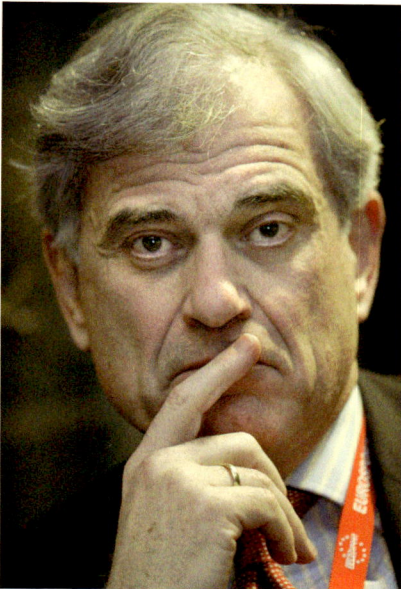

In 1999, Tom de Swaan also opposed Rijkman Groenink's appointment as chairman. For years, the chief financial officer felt like a nurse in charge of an endlessly bickering board.
Photo: Peter Boer

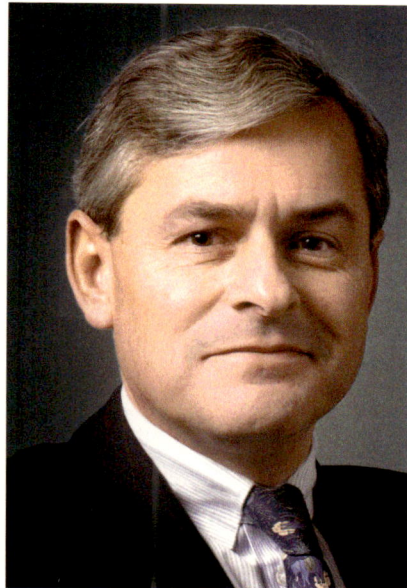

Jan Maarten de Jong was not sure he wanted to take over from Kalff; he wasn't convinced about the growing focus on the share price. He was more concerned with clients. When he left, in late 2001, he realised that the bank had failed to manage the increasing greed properly.
Photo: Picture Report

For years, Dolf Collee was one of Rijkman Groenink's loyalest subordinates. He was surprised to be appointed to the board in May 2000. In the summer of 2006, after two yellows, he was shown the red card.
Photo: Peter Hilz/Hollandse Hoogte

Henk Rutgers worked for Rijkman Groenink for fifteen years. In November 2000 he was replaced as head of the domestic division by Floris Deckers. Rutgers wasn't hard enough, his boss said. He had no stomach for bodies by the roadside.
Photo: Fotopersbureau Dijkstra

When Hans ten Cate heard that he hadn't been appointed to the bank's board he quickly moved to the Rabobank board, to the annoyance of Rijkman Groenink.
Photo: Peter Boer

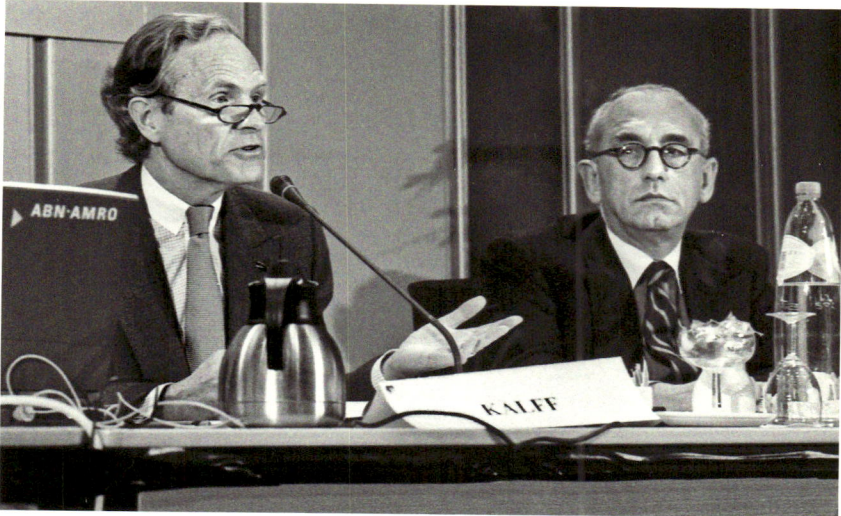

May 2000, at his final press conference as ABN Amro chairman, a tense Jan Kalff, flanked here by Wilco Jiskoot, read out a statement following the debacle surrounding the World Online share issue. 'Let's not forget: a shareholder is someone who owns a share.'
Photo: Peter Boer

In May 2000, Ewald Kist (left) had just succeeded Godfried van der Lugt as chairman of ING. The year before, Van der Lugt had clearly stated his opposition to a merger with ABN Amro. In early 2003, Kist was toying with the idea of combining forces.
Photo: Peter Hilz/Hollandse Hoogte

Floris Deckers took a hard line between 2001 and 2003. In the controversial No Detours operation the bank discarded almost half its workforce in the Netherlands. Deckers was amazed that action hadn't been taken earlier. When he heard that he wouldn't be appointed to the board, he accepted the post of chairman of Van Lanschot.
Photo: Peter Boer

Deckers's successor Jan Peter Schmittmann, one of Groenink's protégés, organised leadership training trips. He wanted to purge the bank of its often inward looking arrogance. When he found out that he wouldn't be appointed to the board in 2005, he turned against the chairman with a vengeance.
Photo: Peter Boer

On 6 May, Van den Brink expressed his concerns in a memorandum sent to the managing board. He wondered if the basic assumption of the reorganisation – more focus on the client – was also the correct assumption for the bank's IT function. With IT, it would be important to look for economies of scale. He was concerned that cutting the bank up into small pieces and bringing these under the various SBUS would 'bring large and expensive inefficiencies'.

The managing board discussed the document several weeks later. Van den Brink said that the split into SBUS should be continued on the client-side of the bank, but that the back office activities should remain bundled. One example would be to use a single, shared IT platform. In his memorandum he calculated that the bank would save around one billion euros. The wholesale SBUS expenditures on IT activities would be some 250 million lower. Wilco Jiskoot didn't agree. He was worried that a central organisation would not be able to deliver the computer-related supplies he needed, as quickly as he needed. In his market, it was all about speed.

After two hours of discussion, Van den Brink's proposal was shot down. The 53-year-old former ABN man was disappointed. He believed in the universal bank, and in teamwork, and worried that this approach would create little synergy. But he felt himself giving up, psychologically. Van den Brink indicated to Groenink that he would not be averse to an early retirement before the official date planned in 2008.

After discussing it with Groenink, Van den Brink went to see Van Tets, also 53, to discuss the issue. What did he think of the idea of all three SBU chairmen taking early retirement simultaneously? Van Tets told Van den Brink that he wasn't interested. The corporate banker believed that now, finally, he had the room to achieve what he had always dreamed of achieving. Van Tets wanted to turn ABN Amro into a successful international investment bank. That's what he had agreed with Groenink, and that was why he would be staying.

Groenink felt that the managing board needed new, younger blood. He also felt that it should not be too large. In the longer term, he wanted to get rid of some old hands. It wouldn't be complicated. Dolf van den Brink and Jan Maarten de Jong indicated that they might be prepared to step down in 2003 (De Jong) and 2004 (Van den Brink). 'Might' meant: if tactfully arranged.

Groenink already knew who he wanted to appoint to the board and reported this to his colleagues. The 47-year-old Dolf Collee, who had started at ABN, was appointed to the managing board, to his surprise. He would strengthen the leadership of the C&CC division. It was immediately clear to Aarnout Loudon that Groenink wanted his own men on the managing board. That was logical. After all the aggression of the corporate bankers, it was time there was a retail man on the board.

Hugh Scott Barrett, 41, was rewarded for his strategic contribution and given a job in the leadership of the corporate business division. Van Tets was happy with the appointment. He thought Scott Barrett a good, clear thinker, a real staffer. He was also pleased at the growing Anglo-American influence. Some general managers didn't understand the appointment. The Brit was smart, but hadn't made much of an impression yet. He had been working for four years for the bank, but still behaved like an outsider. They thought him unsure of his own achievements.

Scott Barrett himself was surprised. The ambitious leader of the Arrow team would have thought it more logical if the managing board had been reinforced by someone from the retail division. In addition to Van Tets, Jiskoot and Scott Barrett, the 39-year-old Brazilian, Sergio Lires Rial, had been appointed to the leadership of the corporate business division. In total, four managing board members would lead the wholesale SBU.

Proudly, the supervisory board observed that foreigners had finally made it to the bank's managing board. Moreover, 'the ages of the members are conducive to the continuity and quality of the management'. From now on, all meetings of the board would take place in English.

The supervisory board reported the appointment of Alexandra Cook-Schaapveld and Carole Anne Menzi Collier. Now women had also made it to the level of general manager. Both worked in the corporate business division.

The Saturday morning after the meeting with the supervisory board, former Amro man Hans ten Cate heard that he would remain as general manager. He was furious, though, when he heard that Dolf Collee was getting a place on the managing board. Ten Cate thought that he was better than Collee. When he ran into Groenink that afternoon at the Cor van Zadelhoff annual polo picnic, the chairman didn't ask if Ten Cate was happy with his new role. At that moment, something snapped inside him: Hans ten Cate, who had worked 26 years at the bank, decided to leave.

It was quickly arranged. In February, he had been approached by Rabobank, but hadn't been too receptive. This was the moment to reopen those talks, he felt. Within four days he had a deal: an appointment to the managing board of Rabobank. When he told Groenink about it a few days later, the chairman was surprised. He thought it was wrong, that it shouldn't be allowed, that Ten Cate belonged to the bank. The departure of one of his team would be interpreted as a loss of face within the bank.

When Ten Cate stood his ground, Groenink grew angry. He threatened to call the Dutch Central Bank to ask them to prevent the move to Rabo from going ahead. Rabo was, after all, a competitor. Ten Cate said coolly that his new employer had already arranged that side of things. Groenink grew angrier. He told Ten Cate that he wanted him out the following day, and that he would be allowed to hold a small leaving reception, but that the managing board would not be present. In the jargon of the bank, Ten Cate was a bad leaver.

Henk Rutgers was also disappointed not to be appointed to the managing board. Rutgers was upset to hear it from Jan Maarten de Jong, and not from Groenink himself. After all, he had worked for the man for fifteen years. That evening, an emotional Groenink called Rutgers; the chairman understood that he had made a major error in communication. He explained to Rutgers that he thought him a good general manager, but that he needed a product man on the managing board, someone like Dolf Collee. He said that Rutgers was too soft, that he had too much pity for victims along the way, and that he invested too much energy in the final sprint. Rutgers was asked to come up with suggestions for the follow-up to *Vision 2000* sooner than had been planned.

Other people, too, threw their towels in the ring. E-commerce general manager Jean-Paul Votron, felt that he and his expertise deserved a place on the board as well. But the managing board felt that Votron had not succeeded in shaping the bank's e-commerce activities, and that a place on the board was therefore out of the question. Votron refused to report to Dolf Collee and left. His fellow managing directors were not really surprised. A few remembered a flashy presentation by the Belgian – a long story with lots of concepts but far too few hard numbers. They felt that the marketeer Votron had talked more than he had delivered.

After the successful takeover of Banco Real, former ABN man Floris Deckers had also reckoned on a place on the board. He thought it incomprehensible that Collee was now sitting in that seat. Michael Drabbe had said that it might be possible for him to succeed Harry Tempest in America. But that didn't happen either. Deckers accepted the request of the new managing board to take over responsibility for all the activities in Asia.

Rob Kleyn (another former ABN man), the general manager who had been responsible for human resources for many years, also decided to leave. He was only 58, but he was tired. He would take a sabbatical and not return to the bank after that. "It's good for the bank and for me to leave," he told the Dutch trade magazine *Bank- and Effectenbedrijf.* "I want a better balance in my life. Every evening there's piles of paperwork to go through. You want to get rid of that pressure after a while."

The supervisory board wondered if there was someone in the bank who would be able to take his place quickly. But the board decided that the new head of human resources would come from outside the bank.

On Monday 29 May, the top 200 managers of the bank were invited to Gustav Mahlerlaan to attend an information session about the new strategy of the bank. Groenink emphasised the need to listen much more closely to the shareholders. Developments in the share price must push the bank to a new discipline and costs savings. The top managers agreed.

Groenink said that the geographic hierarchy would be scrapped. He said that the products and services of the bank would lead the functional division in SBUs and explained that the bank would emphasise on building its corporate business activities. He also announced the appointments to the managing board. The ten managing board members appeared on the stage. He indicated that De Jong and Van den Brink would retire early, in 2003 and 2004 respectively, after laying the foundations of their SBUs.

Many country managers were surprised. Their function would cease to exist. Most of them were from the old ABN stable. They saw this as the great Amro revenge; Amro people had been complaining for years about the costs of the network. They were angry with the investment bankers, who apparently exerted major influence at head office in Amsterdam. Was this still their bank? This plan had clearly been put in place by people who had never managed a country.

The two most main country managers (and big profit-makers) were also disappointed. Harry Tempest, CEO of the American activities, symbolised the fury of dozens of country managers. He stood up and left the hall. Fabio Barbosa, who had been nominated as the next boss of Brazil, also could not believe his ears. Banking was all about the power of the local market, knowledge of local clients. They were happy that head office was a ten-hour flight away.

There were immediate concerns in the Dutch organisation too. Would they still get access to the overseas offices under this structure? They would be led for the most part by people from the corporate business division – people who were mainly interested in making deals with big clients.

The media were enthusiastic. 'Groenink takes ABN onto the banking highway,' ran a headline in *Het Financieele Dagblad*. The sub-header was, 'After Kalff's tinkering, Groenink is the man to go in search of the big kill.' The newspaper observed that shareholder value was now central at the bank, and that Groenink would undoubtedly go for a big deal when the share price was right. The newspaper thought that something would happen. For the last three years, the share price had been about 20 per cent behind the rest of the sector.

The newspaper also considered the news that Groenink had given his management more responsibility. 'This means that disappointing results will have consequences, which wasn't always the case in the past. However, the glittering prize of the modern options package offers some compensation for the risk. This week, Groenink indicated that he was inspired by the options package recently introduced by Reed Elsevier. The publishing group rewards its management by giving them a share in the additional shareholder value created after a number of years. Under Rijkman Groenink, ABN Amro will become a quite different bank,' the newspaper concluded. 'The new managing board chairman is certainly not a man who will just sit and mind the shop. That means that the bank, which has always held caution high as a value, will become less cautious. It is indeed the case that higher yields mean higher risks.'

The top managers of the bank were aware that it would be a considerable effort to pervade the entire bank with the new thinking in terms of economic profit, that is, net profit minus the costs of capital invested. Every business unit would have to be informed, and the meaning of economic profit would have to be worked out again and again in context. And then the ambition and the capital provision for the coming years would have to be determined.

Since the board was only concerned with the strategic side of the business, the layer below it had to be significantly strengthened. In total, eleven new general managers were appointed, seven in the wholesale SBU. The total number of general managers was now 28.

Two consultants were named to the Arrow project to help with the introduction of the managing-for-value concept: McKinsey and Marakon. McKinsey, mainly through Buford Alexander, had been doing business for years with the bank. There were about 40 McKinsey consultants walking round the bank, mainly advising on strategy. The contact with Marakon, relatively unknown, and with its 250 staff a relatively small consultancy, came through a young colleague of Zeilmaker's, who had been at Insead with someone who had then gone to Marakon. It helped that the American consultancy was already carrying out similar work with two British banks: Barclays and Lloyds TSB.

Tom de Swaan was enthusiastic about Herman Spruit, who had been appointed as a partner at Marakon only a few weeks before. His Dutch was rusty, because he had left the Netherlands when he was young, but he always had a good story to tell. He explained that the way you organise a business is what drives the strategy. Spruit said that it was essential that everyone spoke the same language. If the boss decides that something is a good decision, everyone must know what he means by good.

Marakon could help ABN Amro to create that common language. The recipe sounded simple: first, you use the concept of economic profit to make it clear what everyone brings in and what everyone costs. In this way, you force all departments and people to take responsibility. That results in a lot of fighting, because everyone will try to charge costs on to everyone else. It was therefore important that people and departments communicate well with each other and find a way to start working on the basis of their new, clearer responsibilities.

Spruit wasn't coming cheap. Consultants were paid between 5,000 and 7,500 euros per day. The Marakon man said that the whole operation would cost the bank between 20 and 30 million euros per year. The Arrow team advised Groenink to talk to Marakon anyway. He was also impressed.

McKinsey man Buford Alexander wasn't amused when he heard that this relatively unknown American competitor was stealing the assignment from under his nose. He demanded some time with Groenink for a chance to bring in this highly attractive assignment for McKinsey. He said that McKinsey's great advantage was that they had been advising the bank for ten years already, and knew the bank through and through. Alexander suggested that McKinsey be remunerated in proportion to the degree to which the bank became more efficient.

This suggestion offended Tom de Swaan. He wanted a consultancy that had learned the concept of value-based management in the hard American school. He wanted to see some real clarity. He felt there was another advantage in Marakon: the office was so small that making a success of such an assignment would be of vital concern.

Spruit gave another presentation to the managing board. It was an eye-opener. Here, people left the boardroom in order of seniority. It was a sort of club, really. One press on the button and flunkeys appeared bringing coffee, fruit juice, fresh cigarettes. The bank directors lived in their own world.

Groenink told the consultants that the Arrow approach was a fact. The new organisation would have to be ready from 1 January 2001, and everyone would have to be convinced of the need for accountability. Spruit had done his own calculations and observed that the bank was not doing particularly well, if the cost of capital were included. Apparently people at ABN Amro still had no idea about the costs of using capital. It was time for clarity.

Groenink was enthusiastic about Spruit's sharp analysis. The Marakon consultants would be engaged to help the bank become more transparent and accountable during the coming two-and-a-half years. About 30 consultants would move around the bank full-time, advising and informing departments. Their job was to show people where the bank was destroying value and where it was creating value.

De Swaan and Spruit felt that the chairman should also start selling the value story throughout the organisation, just as his colleague at Barclays had done – he had spoken to 70,000 people. It was important that the chairman should stand on as many soap boxes as he could and show that he himself was taking responsibility.

Spruit explained to Groenink that his job as the boss of the bank was to go around repeating the same message every day; it was the only way to make sure he would be heard. But he quickly saw that this chairman had no interest in this. Groenink delegated this assignment to Tom de Swaan and the corporate development department.

People throughout the organisation were asked to help Marakon to communicate its message. Wietze Reehoorn, a member of the domestic managing board, and the manager responsible for credit risks, took up the invitation. He was assigned to persuade the leadership of the c&cc division of the usefulness of the managing-for-value concept. It wasn't an easy task. He gave a presentation on the subject at one of the first sessions of the leadership of the retail division, and found that they simply weren't interested. They felt that their focus should be on the big questions of strategy for the division. They were working these out in further detail with McKinsey consultants. Reehoorn felt that Groenink had not persuaded people like De Jong, Collee and Kuiper of the importance of managing for value. In the United States, Reehoorn was more or less stared out of the room by Harry Tempest.

Reehoorn detected an attitude among the leadership of the bank that managing for value was appropriate for lower ranks. He wondered if you could ask people in an organisation to do things that you didn't do yourself.

Many employees at lower levels were looking forward to the arrival of the Marakon consultants, not so much for themselves but because they felt that they would help to reveal parts of the organisation that didn't earn anything, after subtraction of costs. It was high time that this was made clear. A lot of ordinary retail bankers were looking forward to the figures with regard to the wholesale/investment bank. They were convinced that this capital-intensive division earned very little money.

Marakon consultants visited every unit of the bank within the next few months, and they went through the results in each case with a fine-tooth comb. They were after figures that would clearly show the economic profit of the business. But it turned out not to be easy. The main difficulty was the distribution of costs. This was especially difficult where one department charged costs to another; there were often quarrels about this. The receiving department naturally wanted to keep the costs as low as possible, while the department making the delivery wanted to increase its turnover.

In fact it proved impossible to define the costs: this was the element that was always lacking in analyses. The result was that managers might be told to double their economic profit by the end of 2004, for example, but that it was unclear what that was, since no one knew what the total costs would be.

The move to a functional approach, and the arrival of Marakon, were the subjects of a lot of discussion in the overseas network. It had been relatively easy to distribute costs when the business was divided into countries. The costs would simply be charged to the country organisation. But now everything went through the SBU of that country (or of a part of that country). In each country, the three activities (corporate business, retail and asset management) would be asked if they thought they could achieve a top five position in that country. The main activity (in most cases corporate business activities) would lead the country, and it would provide a manager to represent the company in contact with the authorities.

In cases where several of the bank's activities would remain active in a country, a decision would be made as to who would pay the costs. This had previously been organised by the central management of the country. How much would they pay for human resources, accounting, rent, and so on. The SBUS in a country would now have to agree about who to charge the costs to. The agreements would be recorded in service level agreements. It would all mean endless discussion. Everyone wanted to limit their costs.

The exercise was supposed to bring clarity, but instead it produced a situation in which no one had any idea what was profitable and what was not. The entire organisation was thrown into a big and complex discussion. Enthusiasm for Marakon ebbed. It was clear that it would take some time before the bank's 100,000 or more employees would work in a disciplined way under the new system. If they succeeded at all.

The central banks in the countries where ABN Amro did business were finding the reorganisation difficult. This was certainly the case with the American supervisory body that dealt with the banking world: the Federal Reserve Bank. The Fed body asked Joost Kuiper, who worked for C&CC and was responsible for the United States, who would be their contact with the bank in the United States.

Kuiper explained that the corporate business activities would be under the functional leadership of the corporate business division. LaSalle's retail activities would fall under him, and in the United States, under Tempest. The Fed said it would like to see a single contact point in the United States. Kuiper asked if the structure the bank had chosen was illegal. That didn't turn out to be the case.

In the summer Groenink gave an interview to *De Young Banker* in which he explained why the bank was now focusing on growing the corporate business division. "Germany and France are locked up. If there is to be consolidation, then our preference is for concentration at the national level and not for expansion across our borders. The conclusion must be that the merger process is making little progress in those countries and where it is that foreign banks are not really welcome. That's why we've stopped saying that we want to create a second domestic market or that we are going to do a takeover in another country, because those opportunities aren't there. We must direct all our energies at what is possible … the expansion will come from global wholesale banking."

When he was asked how it could be that the share price remained unaffected despite the fact that the bank was achieving all its financial targets, he answered, "Here we're talking about the mysticism of investment. The price of a share is of course driven by expectations regarding the future cash flow of an enterprise. And then you have to say that the market apparently does not believe in a high-grade achievement in the future, despite the fact that we have realised an average of 30 per cent growth in shareholder value over the last five years. The market apparently does not believe that we can sustain it. The only way to turn the share price around is to build that belief. To do that, you need a credible strategy, and a credible management model, and a team that the market thinks is capable of managing it. Also, the share price is relatively low at the moment because it does not include a takeover premium. No one believes that ABN Amro is a candidate for a takeover. One of the reasons for this is that we are a large conglomerate with a lot of different activities."

Groenink said that he planned to be the bank's chairman for at least ten years. "I hope that the bank is still an independent organisation when I do retire, and that it still has control over its own future. I hope that we will be proud of ourselves then, and also that we have an open, honest, unpretentious and transparent organisation. I would also like to be able to say that I really enjoyed doing my job and that the whole organisation now has an atmosphere that is fun to work in. And lastly, I hope that we can say, in retrospect, that together we achieved a balance between work and our private life."

Henk Rutgers thought differently. He had stayed on as head of the domestic division, and he was working on *Vision 2005*, the follow-up to *Vision 2000*. It called for 2,500 jobs to be scrapped and 150 branches to be closed. But the results were disappointing. The managing board, among them Dolf Collee, observed that more direct intervention was necessary. The domestic division would also have to double its economic profit during the coming years.

Groenink didn't believe that Rutgers was the right man for the job. He was too close to a lot of the people he was talking to, and he would never be able to carry out cuts. He offered Rutgers a job as head of the real estate company,

Bouwfonds, which the bank had taken over at the beginning of the year. Rutgers refused. He felt that he should lead the reorganisation of his division. He had been fiercely against that takeover, anyway.

In the summer of 2000, three young managing directors on the managing board, Arnoud Rikkers, Chris Vogelzang and Leo Peeters Weem thought up a plan to scrap 6,000 FTES. The 6,000 full-time positions were filled by around 8,000 employees. But Rutgers didn't succeed in compiling a workable budget for this to happen in 2001. His wife saw him wrestling with the assignment and warned her husband that he wouldn't be able to carry out the task. A lot of the people involved were friends, and he would find himself quarrelling with everyone. Rutgers followed her advice and went to Jan Maarten de Jong to ask if the job as head of Bouwfonds was still open. He was just in time, as they were on the point of naming someone. Groenink would have to find a new head for the domestic division, and fast.

The Arrow project had established that the bank's main priority would now be to maximise profit for shareholders. It had also been stated that the share price had to rise, fast. That would be necessary to give the bank a leading role in the consolidation of the banking sector. A high share price reflected confidence among investors, and that confidence would be necessary to be able to take over other banks. A high share price also meant that the bank would be worth a great deal, and would therefore not be easy to take over. A bank that is worth a lot is a predator. Some solid promises would have to be made to get the shareholders enthusiastic again about ABN Amro.

Under Jan Kalff, some cautious comparisons had been made with the achievements of a peer group, a group of similar banks. The euphoric managing board said that the bank should strive for a top five position in a new competitive peer group of 20 banks.

Scott Barrett was one of the proponents. In the Brit's view, such a comparison was necessary for clear agreements about management remuneration. If they succeeded in persuading shareholders to like the bank's shares again, the managers would also profit. The proposed peer group was just as diverse as the bank itself. It included investment banks (Morgan Stanley, Merrill Lynch), a bank-insurer (ING) and a pair of genuine retail banks. At the time this ambition was communicated, ABN Amro was tenth on this list.

Joost Kuiper had doubts. He didn't believe the bank could get into the top five. ABN Amro would always be somewhere between the sixth and sixteenth place, just because it had corporate business, asset management and retail activities under its control. Jiskoot had doubts. He was sceptical anyway about multi-year prognoses.

Groenink didn't like their views. They didn't fit with the atmosphere he wanted. He wanted to hear people saying: of course we can, we can do that. New lists were produced with other banks, and other calculations. In the end, the board agreed – mostly because they all wanted more accountability, and this comparison would ensure that.

Some members of the supervisory board also had their doubts. It was Burgmans again who asked if the ambition was not too much for the bank. The other banks would simply innovate and do even better. To climb such a list, ABN Amro would have to perform at a level that was higher than its average best. They thought it would be better to promise investors that the bank would always be in the top ten of its peer group. But the consensus on the supervisory board was that the move was, anyway, an attempt to improve the bank. Burgmans often sounded cynical, and his criticism was dismissed.

To achieve the ambition of reaching the top five of the peer group, Groenink enthusiastically increased the targets for the share price profit growth from the present 10 per cent to 17 per cent. The return on equity would now have to be at least 25 per cent, instead of the present 18 per cent.

Groenink received his formal letter of appointment on 17 July. He would be paid a basic salary of 1.5 million guilders, 20 per cent more than the rest of the board. There were a number of variable components as well. Groenink would need the supervisory board's permission to take up a position as governor on another board. Like the other members of his managing board, he would retire at 62, and the costs of security at his home would be paid by the bank for three years after he left. Like them he would also have a leased car (with chauffeur) to the value of 3,068 euros per month while he worked at the bank. The letter also stated that Groenink and his fellow managing directors would receive a new remuneration package as of 1 January 2001.

The supervisory board brought in consultants from Towers Perrin to set market-related levels of remuneration. From 2001, Groenink would be paid a basic salary of 1.96 million guilders. His annual bonus could be as much as 100 per cent of his salary if ABN Amro 'achieved substantially more than the targets set'. The bonuses of the other managing board members would be related to the performance of the division for which they were responsible. If the bank as a whole achieved its targets, they would in principle receive a bonus of between 60 and 75 per cent of their salary. But if their division performed 'substantially below the target set', they would have to give up 20 per cent of that. Groenink would decide the extent to which his colleagues had achieved their targets and discuss the extras with Loudon.

The managing board members also received substantial options packages. An ordinary member of the board received 80,000 options, and Groenink 112,000. At the end of 2003, the bank was expected to achieve a return on equity of 12.5 per cent. Under their management, the bank would also have to ensure that economic profit rose each year. If it didn't, they wouldn't be able to cash in their options. Their performance against the targets they had been set would be evaluated at the end of a period of three years. The options would be valid for ten years.

The supervisory board felt that the remuneration package was rather conventional. They therefore suggested an additional stimulus: the members of the managing board would receive shares that they could cash in if the bank achieved a position in the top ten of the peer group on the basis of the total return for shareholders. 'Given the highly demanding targets that the bank has set itself, we have decided to provide some additional incentives,' the supervisory board wrote in Groenink's contract. 'All members of the managing board will receive 70,000 shares over the next two years on a conditional basis. Groenink will receive 98,000 per year. If the bank has indeed achieved a position in the top ten at the end of 2004, the members of the managing board may cash in (part of) their share portion.'

A tenth place would mean that they could cash in 10 per cent of their shares, and a fifth place would mean they could cash in 100 per cent. If the bank achieved first place, they could cash in 150 per cent. In that case, if the share price stood in the region of 40 euros, Groenink would receive an extra reward of six million euros.

The various forms of remuneration added up to an impressive sum, certainly by Dutch standards. Dolf van den Brink figured out that each person on the managing board could earn at least 150 million euros if the bank achieved all its targets in the coming ten years. Tom de Swaan observed that they might all become rather wealthy.

That summer saw speculation that ABN Amro was working with Aegon on a takeover of bank-insurer Fortis. *Het Financieele Dagblad* got Maurice Lippens on the line, who laughed when he heard about this. He said that Groenink had called him to say, "I burned my fingers once, and I'm not going to do it again."

But the speculation wasn't all that strange. Lippens was worried about the future of Fortis. "If we don't want to be the victim of a hostile takeover, we have to focus on the areas where we're really good."

To facilitate this, Fortis took a number of drastic decisions. As co-chairmen, Lippens and Bartelds were shifted to the supervisory board, in Belgium an important position. There, the head of the supervisory board has far more power than his equivalent in the Netherlands.

Anton van Rossum, who had been a McKinsey consultant to the Belgian branch of Fortis for many years, was asked to become chairman. Van Rossum was Dutch by birth, but he lived in Belgium with his French wife. The consultant was given a one simple assignment: make a single company with one culture. One thing was certain: head office would be in Brussels. As predicted, Fortis had been a mainly Belgian company since the takeover of Generale Bank.

To the outside world, the new chairman communicated a different message to that of his Dutch colleague. "The challenge is to treat the client as we ourselves would like to be treated. If we do well with our clients, shareholder value will come of itself."

At the presentation of the half-yearly figures, Groenink responded cryptically to the speculation about ABN Amro, Aegon and Fortis. "Our most important emotional ambition is to stay in control of our own future. That means that if an opportunity for a merger presents itself which is in the interests of our shareholders, employees and clients, and if there is no alternative, we will be prepared to take it up."

Groenink also announced that the total return for shareholders (the rise in share price plus the dividend) would at least double over the next four years. "Maximising shareholder value is all-determining from now on." Marakon consultant Spruit had insisted that this ambition be communicated externally. "It's a target that you can check every day," said Groenink. "We have to get away from this mentality of clubbing together and not sticking our head out."

Reading the press, Spruit warned Groenink that he had communicated a rather too concrete ambition to the outside world. It would have been better to formulate it as a potential ambition. Groenink complained about the media; journalists understood nothing. He had an especially strong dislike of Dutch journalists. They enjoyed representing him as cocky and arrogant. They had been stereotyping him since the HCS affair. He had decided not to pay any attention to the Dutch media. It was a fight he couldn't win.

The shareholders gave Groenink the benefit of the doubt during the first months of his chairmanship. Between May and August the share price rose from 22 to 29 euros. But shareholders and analysts weren't impressed by his ambitions. They were shocked at the disappointing results, and observed that the bank's efficiency ratio had declined over the previous half year, and so the share price fell by 2.3 per cent.

They wondered what had happened to the Internet strategy of a year ago. Then, as head of the new Europe division, Groenink had promised that the bank wanted to have 10 million European Internet clients in 2004, some 6.5 million extra clients. What had happened to the European division? Groenink had been the initiator of the plan, hadn't he?

The commentary in *Het Financieele Dagblad* was direct. 'Kalff's departure didn't remove all the caution from the top level of the bank. On the contrary, it looks as if the bank is rather uncertain in seeking a way forward. Doesn't the bank know what to do about the lack of appreciation for its share on the markets? It can't be the results. Despite everything, the bank has achieved all its targets, and more, in recent years. What does seem to be the problem is the bank's ability to communicate its successes to investors. Clarity and consistency are advisable, especially for a new managing board chairman.'

On Share Day, Groenink tried to interest investors in the bank. "Our most important target is to achieve a position among the top five of a group of twenty banks that operate globally within four years, based on our returns. That means, roughly, that the share price and the dividend together will double over the coming four years. This doesn't look like a bad outlook for shareholders." With Marakon's assurance in the back of his mind, he promised investors that the bank would strive for a situation "in which we know exactly what is earned by every business unit, product, client, distribution channel and market segment. On the basis of that, we will be able to deploy our people, resources and capital as optimally as possible."

Within the bank, there was a lot of concern about this enormous ambition, which had now been made public. At the end of August, the corporate development department did its sums and came to the same conclusion that the Arrow project team had earlier wanted to come to. Finally, they had an answer to the question as to where the bank earned most of its money.

The analysis made it clear that ABN Amro earned most of its money from the retail bank, serving small and medium-sized companies and individuals. A lot of people had thought that anyway. Van Os and Zeilmaker realised that the strategic discussion might have gone in an entirely different direction if there had been less haste. With these numbers, the position of retail-oriented bankers like Joost Kuiper, Jan Maarten de Jong, Dolf van den Brink and Jan Kalff would have been much stronger during the Arrow discussions. But nothing was done with the figures that now came to light. That ship had already sailed.

In the autumn, Fox-Pitt Kelton presented a similar analysis. The American investment bank warned that ABN Amro's wholesale division was lending money mainly to large companies. A lot of capital was involved, and it was delivering small margins. The returns were around half of the margins that could be achieved by lending to medium-sized companies. The American bank advised ABN Amro to focus on the medium segment and not to bother with the large business segment. 'As far as that's concerned, you've already missed the boat.'

Fox-Pitt Kelton did see possibilities for the global transaction service (GTS), the worldwide cash control system, which had matured. This was the bank's ace card. If the bank intended the wholesale division to earn a lot of money from consultancy, where the bank's balance was less needed, then a considerable investment would be necessary. 'A real consolidation battle is taking place in this sector.'

The first takeovers in the Groenink era were not made by the wholesale bank. In the United States, the bank bought Alleghany Asset Management for 825 million dollars. The capital being managed by the bank rose from 105 to 150 billion dollars. Dolf van den Brink was happy. "It was above all important for us to access the institutional investors on the biggest market in the world."

A month later, Michigan National Corporation (3,600 employees and 184 branches) was bought for 2.75 billion dollars in cash, to strengthen the retail activities in the United States. Jan Maarten de Jong and Joost Kuiper were happy that the board had been convinced to undertake a takeover of this American retail bank. The bank now had the same number three position in the Chicago-Detroit belt as it had in the Netherlands. It fitted with the strategy of the c&cc division, which wanted to grow in the three domestic markets. Investors were frightened and the share price fell by 5.5 per cent. Only four months later, it became clear that the takeovers had largely been financed by the sale of the European American Bank in New York, for 1.6 billion dollars, to Citibank.

Meanwhile, the corporate business division was picking up tempo. It had decided to focus on service provision to the 4,000 biggest clients. That's where the money would be earned. The bank would maintain contact with another 6,000 clients, said Van Tets; they would be potential key clients. It cut contacts with some 30,000 clients, mostly smaller enterprises that had been getting credit and advice on share issues or takeovers – these clients put too little money in the till. In his view, the bank was in a position to do this without suffering too much damage because in many cases it had had a subordinate relationship with the client anyway.

A lot of good people would have to be brought onboard quickly, to achieve an optimal and profitable service provision within the corporate business division. The division was expected to double its profits from six to 12 billion euros within four years. The executive recruiters licked their lips at the thought of the ABN Amro assignment: find 500 quality investment bankers. A number of agencies were invited in to ABN Amro to pitch. In the letter, they were asked how much they would charge to locate 500 investment bankers.

Hugh Scott Barrett and Sergio Lires Rial made the selection. Russell Reynolds, where former ABN Amro banker René de Zwaan worked, got the lion's share of the dream assignment. A small part of it went to Sainty Hird &

Partners, a small player in London. They got the assignment because the company's founder, Julyan Sainty was a neighbour of Hugh Scott Barrett's outside London.

Investment bankers were being sought with urgency. The bank wanted rainmakers, originators who would enable the corporate business division to bring in large share issues, or supervise mergers and takeovers. The new people would be required to deliver twice as much as they had cost the bank within three years.

Groenink looked around the bank as well. In the staff magazine, *De Young Banker*, he explained that the bank wasn't looking for 500 classical investment bankers. "That's a misapprehension. Wholesale banking is a cooperative venture involving both the commercial banking business and the investment bank. That's why we need more originators, people who can generate business from client contacts. And they could come from either the commercial side or the investment bank."

De Zwaan thought it was a complicated job. Not everyone understood the combination of investment bank and corporate bank. Investment bankers were not interested in chasing loan deals. They couldn't understand how the cooperation – and therefore the distribution of bonuses – could be made to work. The headhunter concluded that it was investment bankers who would be needed, since the bank focused mainly on earning money from so-called share-of-mind business: services related to mergers and share issues. But they would have to be investment bankers who could also talk about loans. Within the bank, they were called client coverage managers.

Another problem was ABN Amro's image. In the banking world it was seen as second-tier, and therefore not the first bank that came to mind. It was a vicious circle. The bank was not in the top ten of many lists as regards delivery of services. If it was not on those lists, companies wouldn't consider hiring its services, assuming that it didn't have the best people. If no assignments came in, there would be no large bonus pool, and that meant that the bank couldn't attract good people. And so on.

Nevertheless, De Zwaan noted that many bankers were interested in talking. They thought that ABN Amro, like Deutsche Bank (the other European bank that was trying to buy its way into the top markets for investment banks) might well make a success of the move. They were both banks with deep pockets and staying power. From October, new rainmakers were being hunted so aggressively that general managers from different departments within the wholesale SBU found that they were sometimes tugging on the same candidate.

In an interview with Dutch weekly magazine *Elsevier*, Groenink said that the hunt for new people for the wholesale division was going well. "The remuneration that such people can command is staggering. London is now at New York levels. In Frankfurt, and even here in Amsterdam, things are going the same way. We can't ignore that totally, but at the same time we also can't simply go with the flow. So we're offering an attractive, cheaper alternative: the new people who come to us won't have to work eightyhour weeks. They won't have to work from seven in the morning until half past nine at night. If you do that, you don't have a life. No time for relaxing, family, friends, cultural activities. That's how we've been able to recruit around fifty people in London in the last few months. Without American salaries."

It was his first big interview as chairman. He had chosen *Elsevier*, and therefore Hans Crooijmans, the journalist who had revealed the claim filed by Léon Melchior. Groenink enjoyed confrontation. "It's unbelievable," he said, greeting the journalist. "You've been trying to bring me down for eight years, and now you're the first to get an interview ..."

He explained where his thirst for action came from. "Looking back, I think that we have made things too easy for ourselves. Let's be honest, we had the wind in our sails. Strong economic growth, greater prosperity, advantageous interest rates, a great climate for the markets. Our financial targets were raised twice, and yet we achieved them with ease. But those targets were simply too low. I was partly responsible for that.

"Things were going too well. Our people were never driven to do everything they could to find revenue, open up new markets, bring new clients in. We were also never successful in carrying out strict budget discipline. People felt safe when they exceeded cost limits, because things were going so well that they felt the bottom line would compensate and the targets would be reached anyway. That culture must disappear. A shock can be a good thing sometimes. From now on, we will have ambitious, hard targets internally that everyone will be required to achieve, at every level."

About his own strong points he said, "I feel that I am good at analysis and the strategic long view. I can also keep a balance between the demands of entrepreneurial banking and dealing with risk. I am not simply a manager. And I don't put the whole enterprise at risk." On his weak points, "I sometimes don't give people the opportunity to come into their own. I'm too quick. I will already have drawn my conclusion and made my decision. I do sometimes cut short discussion on the managing board that I consider unnecessary. It does annoy people, yes."

He told the journalist that he was working on the weaker points in his performance. "It's an important part of managing a managing board to give people room to move. I am trying to pay attention to that aspect and I also try to be open to criticism. Colleagues sometimes come to my office after a meeting to say, 'Rijkman, you shouldn't have done that.' I really value that." Laughing, he added, "And I won't be going to see a shrink about it either."

He admitted that his second marriage and being the father of two young children were leaving their mark on his life. "My wife and I have passionate discussions about this, and we have come to the conclusion that the present work-life balance isn't entirely bad. But far from ideal either."

Encouraged by his wife, Groenink tried to bring more women into top positions in the bank. At the annual get-together of the management development department, Groenink told interviewer Jeroen Pauw that the bank was doing everything it could to ensure that women got the same opportunities as men. "Moreover, we also need to offer women the opportunity to stop work temporarily, or to work shorter hours if they want to spend more time with their families. We must also offer men the same opportunities to spend more time with their families, without letting that have an effect on their careers."

Within the bank, Groenink's colleagues understood what he meant. He was seldom at work before half past nine in the morning and he usually left at around six. On the one hand, they had respect for a boss who gave a good example, and showed that being a father was important to him. Some of his colleagues were annoyed. They felt that his job required a commitment of 24 hours per day, seven days a week. You couldn't do the job otherwise.

They complained that the boss's wife wore the pants at home. Groenink idolised her. He practised his speeches in front of her and discussed everything with her. She knew the bank well, of course. A lot of jokes were made within the bank about Irene Groenink-Verboon. One of them was that she wanted to be to Groenink what Hillary was to Bill Clinton.

In the autumn, Groenink found a successor to Henk Rutgers: Floris Deckers. Deckers had only been working for two months as head of the Asia region when the bank suddenly no longer needed country managers and his job ceased to exist. The 50-year-old Deckers was appointed on 15 November. On the same day it was announced that Fabio Barbosa would be the new head of ABN Amro in Brazil.

Deckers was not happy with his new assignment. Half his working life in the bank had been spent working overseas and he had always disliked returning to the Netherlands. He thought there were a lot of bad bankers in the Dutch company. But the bank had treated him well over the years and he was not yet in a position to leave and live off his savings, so as far as the bank was concerned it was payback time.

Deckers and Groenink had had a tense relationship for years. Deckers admired the chairman's analytical skills, and he was also impressed by his energy. Deckers thought that Kalff had brought the bank's development to a standstill over the last few years. Kalff had been afraid to test the success of the merger, and a lot of questions had remained unanswered about its capabilities. But you would walk through fire for a man like Kalff, while you wouldn't risk a finger for a man like Groenink. Groenink had no personal magnetism.

Deckers thought that Groenink was a typical staffer, a head office man who had never lived or worked overseas; he had never got his hands dirty. But he agreed that greater transparency was sorely needed. He was enthusiastic about managing for value and Marakon.

So he was shocked by what he encountered in the domestic division. And he saw that Henk Rutgers was astonished when he asked him for the profit-and-loss accounts, as well as the balance and internal accountants' report for the domestic division. There was no such thing. Rutgers explained that the Netherlands was primarily a sales organisation, and it didn't have its own costs centre. His people in the Netherlands spread money around, but they didn't know how much it was costing; that was a secret kept by the bank's treasury, the dealing room. That side of the bank wasn't keen on anyone finding out what it cost to attract money, since they were afraid they would lose their margin.

Deckers realised that the domestic division was an organisational mess. He also thought that the division into three SBUs had in effect split up the domestic division. In the end, the domestic division would lose around 6,000 clients. 1,000 big companies would go to the corporate business division, and 5,000 wealthy clients would go to the asset management division (PCAM).

At Groenink's request, Deckers had a talk with Martin Simon, the man behind *Vision 2000*. They didn't click. Simon thought that Marakon and Deckers' way of thinking totally contradicted his own, while Deckers thought that Simon didn't understand what he was saying. In his view, bankers were not entrepreneurs. It was a brief conversation.

Deckers' task was clear. The domestic division, which fell under his responsibility, was now realising an economic profit of around 200 million, and that would have to be one billion in four years. The Netherlands would be a showcase. Operating in a small, saturated market with narrow margins, Deckers understood immediately that he would have to cut costs significantly. And because nearly 70 per cent of the costs of a bank go on the personnel, this was where most of his savings would have to be made.

Deckers suggested that 13,000 (nearly 10,000 FTEs) of the 35,000 (26,000 FTEs) people could go. The managing board was worried and thought this too rigorous. Dolf van den Brink phoned Deckers to warn him: be careful, you're in the Netherlands. The new head lowered his sights and came up with a new suggestion: 8,500 jobs, or 6,250 FTEs, could go. In December, the plan was presented to the managing board, which agreed.

That December, the top 200 of the bank met to listen to the plans of the chairmen of the three SBUs. Rijnhard van Tets, Jan Maarten de Jong and Dolf van den Brink had been busily tinkering with the strategies of their divisions during the previous few months. Whatever else they achieved, these would have to result in a doubling of value by the end of 2004. They had wrestled with the information available, which was not high in quality.

It was clear that the three men would have to get used to their new assignment. In the presentations, the focus was on the new accountability. The time for mollycoddling was over.

A number of the managing directors present thought that the presentations lacked cohesion. They thought it suspicious that the three SBU chairmen all assumed they would double their earnings. That didn't appear credible.

Van Tets had warned Groenink: give me time, building a new division takes time. But Groenink had made it clear that Van Tets's earnings would have to double in four years. At the corporate business division, there had been weeks of feverish consultation with McKinsey on how to bring commercial bankers, who focused on loans, together with the corporate bankers, who focused on deals.

De Jong explained that growth of 15 per cent in the operational profit would be possible if profits increased by 10 per cent annually, and costs by 7.5 per cent. He reckoned on an improvement in the efficiency ratio from 66 to 59 per cent. But some parts of the new strategy had yet to take shape even by the time he got to version 7.0 of 'Consumer and Commercial Clients SBU Strategy'. Now and then someone would observe that it was important to establish which costs each department was responsible for, before definitive plans could be drawn up.

Stuart Graham, analyst at JP Morgan, didn't seem to be impressed. The authoritative Graham had been invited to give a speech. Few analysts had followed ABN Amro longer than him. Graham referred his audience to the growing scepticism amongst analysts. They were wondering where the bank was going, what the strategy was. They were worried about the continuing high costs; the bank just didn't seem to be able to get its cost efficiency in order. The analyst sounded threatening, even: he told them to make sure that the bank didn't end up in the sin bin. Once there, everything would always be interpreted the wrong way.

Groenink made up a balance at the end of the year. He wasn't happy. He was worried that the market would decline severely following the bursting of the Internet bubble. After reaching a high point of 29 euros in August, the share price had fallen again to 24 euros.

A bank is like an oil tanker; you can't turn it around in a hurry. This was another aspect of the situation that he didn't like. Groenink was in a hurry, but his room for manoeuvre was limited. The chairman was frustrated by the endless complaining about deficient figures. Many people in the bank simply didn't know where they stood. For years, they had focused on generating turnover. They had no idea, no concept at all, of costs. The bank was investing furiously in the corporate business division, but too late; it had become clear that there was no logical foundation for this.

The chairman was also angry at his predecessor, at the history of the bank. With Hugh Scott Barrett and Tom de Swaan, he had observed that ABN Amro had gone astray during the years under Kalff. There were a lot of loans to large companies that earned the bank hardly anything. The loans the bank had taken out to finance the takeovers of Standard Federal and Banco Real were also exerting pressure. Overall, there was little room for an entrepreneurial approach. Jiskoot also observed the lack of balance. He was angry at himself for not paying more attention to this in previous years.

Moreover, Tom de Swaan observed that the climate in the markets was declining so rapidly that there was little room to ask shareholders for new capital. De Swaan had been working at the bank for two years. Slowly but surely it was becoming clear to him that the merger between ABN and Amro ten years earlier had been based on major compromises. Not only had existing inefficiencies been tolerated, new ones had been created. Cost discipline had gone out of the window. It was a tall order to get the bank back in shape. He warned Groenink that there was no room for investment or expansion on the basis of the available capital.

Groenink didn't want to hear this. He didn't want to tell the outside world that the bank was actually in bad shape. It was dangerous for a bank to shout 'Fire!' The bank existed because of the trust of its clients, and to damage that was to invite disaster. He also realised that he had been on the board throughout the years this had been happening.

Groenink worked off some of his frustration on Aarnout Loudon. He went to see the head of the supervisory board in Arnhem, where he lived, and told him that he had no idea of the real rundown state of the bank. When Loudon reminded Groenink that he was just as responsible for this state of affairs, given that he had been on the managing board during those years, Groenink said that he had never found the bank's accounts to be transparent. He called the finances of the bank a black box. He warned Loudon that there was no more growth to be found. The bank would have to work hard on its balance to create more room for investment. Groenink made it clear that they would have to do their best during the coming years to save the merger between ABN and Amro.

Loudon was shocked. This was the first time he had heard any of this. If what Groenink was saying was true, then it was his responsibility too, since he had led the supervisory board for five years. The two made an agreement: costs had to be reduced, and clear choices would have to be made.

At his first Christmas dinner, Groenink's message sounded severe. Anyone who thought they had been working hard had been mistaken. Next year, everyone would have to go the extra mile. The partners of all those hard-working people (mostly men) were irritated. What did he mean by saying his managers weren't working hard? Was this an appropriate Christmas message? You certainly didn't motivate people this way.

The general managers were told to downgrade their evaluations of their subordinates on a structural basis. Everyone would have to take a step back. They should aim at stimulating 30 per cent of their employees by giving them unsatisfactory scores in their evaluations. At the top levels of the bank, the friendly tone that had been customary in performance evaluations disappeared. Only three of the top 200 bankers were described as very good after their evaluation.

8

Settlement

January–August 2001

Rijnhard van Tets never really got used to Rijkman Groenink being chairman. There were times when he felt he should have left the bank. The head of the corporate business division had warned his friend Jan Kalff and his cousin Aarnout Loudon about Groenink's confrontational manner. After a year under his leadership, Van Tets was sure that Groenink would never bring unity to the board. It was simply not in his nature to work cooperatively with other people.

Van Tets was known throughout the bank for his detailed knowledge of clients' dossiers. He was convinced that ABN Amro would have to combine forces with another bank. Now more than ever the bank needed a chairman who could make friends. From his network he was hearing that few of the leaders of other European banks were prepared to do business with Groenink. He was afraid to think what this might mean for the bank's future.

He understood their aversion. It was Groenink's way of speaking, his arrogant tone. His baby face didn't help either; it made him look young for his age. Together, these qualities could make the ABN Amro chairman seem callow. And this didn't fit well in the banking world, which was dominated by solidly respectable managers. Van Tets knew that world well. He had always seen Groenink as a junior. A junior who might be of use to Van Tets on his way to the top.

Van Tets had fallen in love with investment banking a long time before. Halfway through the 1970s, the 28-year-old Van Tets had worked for a small investment bank in New York that was allied to Amro. When he was required to return to the Netherlands after two years, he resigned, because he wanted to stay in New York, the Mecca of investment banking. The discipline was just beginning to mature in New York in those days. He had worked at First Boston for five years, and then Fop Hoogendijk had brought him back to Amro. After the merger with ABN, Van Tets, with Jan Kalff, was given responsibility for the overseas business, and then from 1993, with Louis de Bièvre, for building the investment bank.

His fellow managers knew that Van Tets wanted ABN Amro to buy a large American investment bank. PaineWebber, Donaldson, Lufkin & Jenrette – he suggested these and more. A couple of years ago, Van Tets told *De Young Banker* that ABN Amro wanted to be one of the top three investment banks in Europe. He added that this was no idle ambition and that "the real challenge is in directly competing with the bulge bracket banks." These were the world's top banks, and the list was dominated by American institutions. It was clear to him that ABN Amro would not achieve this goal without taking over a large American investment bank.

More and more, though, he was wondering if that takeover would ever happen. It seemed to him that a precondition was the appointment of an investment banker as board chairman. Deutsche Bank was his model. In 1998, the bank had appointed corporate banker Rolf Breuer specifically for this reason. Because Breuer was made chairman, the Germans had dared to buy American Bankers Trust for nearly 10 billion dollars.

The decision a year earlier to make the corporate business division the leading division within ABN Amro was an important victory for Van Tets; it might open new worlds for the bank. But while the bank was keen to supply its clients with investment banking activities, he still felt that it would not go further than that.

ABN Amro was the only Dutch bank that was still active in that area. Rabobank had sold its loss-making activities in London; after the Barings fiasco, ING had decided to rein in the corporate business division's ambitions. ING's managing board said that the corporate business division had not become successful enough quickly enough, and had got caught in a downward spiral of hiring ever-worse bankers at ever-higher salaries.

The American part of ING Barings, called Furman Selz, which was good for 20 per cent of the corporate business division, was about to be sold. Goldman Sachs had been commissioned to find a buyer but soon reported that no one was interested. ING's board was surprised when ABN Amro said it was interested at the end of January. They wondered if their neighbour had gone crazy. But mainly, they were relieved to let these loss-making activities go. ABN Amro paid 275 million dollars.

Van Tets thought that the bank would have to invest quickly in people who were capable of bringing large assignments to the bank in the United States. His feeling was, "Well, let's do it." Tom de Swaan had doubts. The signs were not good, and the markets were declining fast. But he understood the hunger. Late the previous year, the asset management division had bought Alleghany in the United States, and after that the retail division had bought Michigan National. So of course the wholesale division also wanted to purchase something in the United States. That's how it went.

Jiskoot was enthusiastic about one part of Furman Selz, the so-called prime brokerage platform, a service to professional investors, which looked as if it would fit in well. A question that arose immediately was the quality of the merger and takeover consultants. But the desire to play a meaningful role in this area, in the financial centre of the world, was so great that an attempt was made to hold onto a few dozen rainmakers, according to Jiskoot. One hundred million dollars was budgeted for this. "If this is successful, we will be able to strengthen our position on Wall Street," Jiskoot told *Het Financieele Dagblad*. "Because we're gaining critical mass, we are able to attract better people. That's the flywheel effect."

The outside world was surprised. Even the newspapers voiced misgivings. 'Things have not been good at ING Barings in New York for five years. Because of the trouble in the bank, and the boom in investment banking over the last few years, all the real talent there has left. ING Barings and ABN Amro are ranked between ten and twenty in the key American bank league tables. Even together, they wouldn't make the top ten.'

In February, *The Guardian* reported that British bank Barclays was to merge with ABN Amro. Barclays was wrestling with problems in its investment banking department, and the combination would build a strong corporate business division. Analysts didn't believe this, and were almost unanimous in saying that ABN Amro would gain little from such a merger with Barclays, which was bigger but also largely local. However, many thought that the banks would be a good fit culturally. With Bank Brussels Lambert and Dresdner Bank, Barclays and ABN had been part of the Abecor Group during the 1970s and 1980s; this meant that their staff had followed the same training programmes. Moreover, Barclays had engaged Marakon, the same consultancy as ABN Amro.

Barclays was considerably larger than ABN Amro in terms of market value. Groenink denied that they were talking and insisted that if there were a merger, the smaller party would disappear. "And that's not our ambition. We want to be the leading party in any merger of equals."

In mid-February, Floris Deckers and his boss Dolf Collee presented plans for the domestic division at Amsterdam's RAI conference centre. Neither of them was looking forward to it. There were thousands of people present, and they were told that many of them might soon lose their jobs. To their surprise, though, the mood remained positive and their colleagues were happy to go for a beer together after the meeting. Had they understood the message? During the coming months, the managing board would be touring the country to explain what was going to happen. They would be talking to the unions about the shape of the company after it had been reorganised. The problem was that a new social agreement had been signed recently, and it ruled out involuntary redundancies.

Deckers found the upbeat message from head office about the bank's earnings annoying. It hardly encouraged a sense of urgency. Groenink announced that net profit for 2000 of 2.45 billion euros "was satisfactory for a transitional year". Excluding the provisions made for the reorganisation, profits had risen by some 20 per cent.

Analysts saw through that quickly enough. There had been a fall in profit over the previous six months of nine per cent. Investors were concerned that costs were rising faster than profits and the efficiency ratio had risen from 68.3 to 71.5 per cent.

Costs were rising fastest in the corporate business division. There they noted that the efficiency ratio was 86 per cent. "We have deliberately allowed costs to rise to strengthen our personnel potential," Groenink explained, reluctantly. Internally, he was hard on the four managers responsible for the corporate business division; he told them to see to it that costs were brought under control. Analysts laughed and said that at any rate the bank now had the costs structure of a first-class investment bank. All they needed was the big assignments that would justify the expenditure.

The managing board was riddled with doubt. Hugh Scott Barrett wondered if the bank would ever be prepared to pay the real price for talent. What they were getting at the moment was still second-rate. He knew the market in London. The Brit noticed that Groenink continued to resist paying the necessary bonuses. Jiskoot jumped as if stung by a wasp when De Jong wondered aloud if ABN Amro would ever be able to attract real rainmakers and reach beyond the Dutch border. He hastened to outline the many successful deals that his division had already done and added that there were more in the pipeline.

The top managers of the corporate business division were under constant attack. The internal numbers were even more dramatic. Marakon man Herman Spruit had made an inventory of the division's services: in 2000, it had booked an economic profit of minus 600 million euros. There was immediate discussion of the cause. Van Tets and Jiskoot explained that the results were not really so bad, if you considered only the pure corporate banking activities. In fact, the bank had been reasonably profitable, according to Jiskoot. The men referred to their mega-expensive global transaction services (GTS) department, which still had too few clients, despite huge investments, mainly in IT. Van Tets complained that the setbacks were mainly due to the expensive network which fell mostly under the corporate business division, and it had not yet been cleaned up. Scott Barrett was annoyed by the endless discussion about whether to close countries or not. Only around ten countries had actually been shut down; by now it was supposed to have been thirty.

The New York branch was part of that network. Kuiper had been quarrelling with Jiskoot about who held responsibility for New York since the start of the three strategic business units (SBUS). The people in New York were managed according to function by colleagues in the corporate business division in Amsterdam or London. The Brazilian Sergio Lires Rial was responsible for corporate business activities in the United States. Lires Rial wanted to move things along. As Jiskoot said: the flywheel has to start turning. In the United States, they set about strengthening the corporate business service. Tempest was angry when he heard that the people in New York, who identified more with their colleagues in Europe than with the Chicago retail people, were setting up their own human resources department.

Tempest refused to accept his new role as a sort of upgraded sales representative. He didn't understand it. Tempest was CEO of North America and that included New York, period. Joost Kuiper agreed. Groenink was irritated by the American tendency to think in black-and-white terms. But he left his colleagues to resolve the matter.

Since the audit and control of the New York operation were still Tempest's responsibility, the Fed was sending its inquiries to employees in Chicago. The Fed was concerned that client information was being withheld by employees in New York.

The Fed wanted to know about a growing number of overseas accounts of Russian and Cypriot banks. Thirty accounts that had been taken over from Bank of New York in 1999, under the auspices of Tempest and approved by Jan Kalff. These accounts were mainly owned by Russian financial institutions which had been used to transfer money belonging to Russian clients into the United States. Servicing other banks and financial institutions was a typical corporate business activity. Bank of New York wanted to close these, because the Fed was asking whether the accounts were being used to channel criminal money from Russia into the United States.

The Fed assessed that the number of Eastern European clients managed by ABN Amro in New York had tripled by 2000. There were about 30,000 accounts. The Fed claimed that the bank was unable to provide adequate information about these clients. This indicated a substantial danger that an attempt was being made to launder money.

The Fed wanted to know if ABN Amro could prove that this was not the case. It also wanted to know if the people who supervised these activities had been adequately trained. But many of these questions were never even communicated to Amsterdam. On the one occasion on which Groenink heard of the Fed's inquiry, he told the people involved that it was unacceptable and that the problem must be solved immediately.

Joost Kuiper and Wilco Jiskoot ran up against each other time and again at meetings of the managing board. They had completely contrasting personalities. A good example is the way they presented themselves at role-playing sessions at a gathering of the bank's top 200 managers. Kuiper stepped forward with a rose in his hand and said that he was a child of the 1960s: peace, love and happiness. Jiskoot commented that he was also a child of the 1960s: sex, drugs and rock 'n' roll.

Jiskoot and Kuiper had entirely different views on the bank's strategy. Kuiper believed in the power of the local franchise, that the wishes and needs of the local medium-sized clients should form the basis of the bank's strategy. He thought that corporate bankers should understand that their interests were subordinate.

Jiskoot believed that there was only one way to realise synergy between the three retail companies (the Netherlands, United States and Brazil): with the products of the corporate business division. The development of state-of-the-art products and services in the corporate business division would have to lead the business, or the bank would never be a global player. If they had to choose, he said that it would be better for the bank to sell the retail activities in Brazil and the United States.

Kuiper thought that didn't make sense. The bank had been benefitting for years from the profitability of the United States. Both foreign subsidiaries were worth many billions more than their book value. For Kuiper, these were the geese that laid the golden eggs, and the bank shouldn't sell them.

The conflict between the men also concerned the bank's affairs in New York. Jiskoot thought Arrow had established that the corporate business division would lead the business, and that retail people like Tempest would play a supporting role. But Kuiper thought that Jiskoot should have more respect for the successful American subsidiary.

Rumours soon abounded that Jiskoot and Kuiper didn't see eye to eye.

This didn't help solve the many conflicts in the field. Retail was supposed to support wholesale and it often happened that corporate bankers asked for the lists of (medium-sized) clients of retail managers in, for example, the Netherlands. Often Brits or Americans, the bankers would then fail to report that they didn't see any profit in a particular client, and no one would follow up. The retail staff would then feel that they had been left to clean up the mess.

The rest of the bank thought that the leaders of the corporate business division, and especially Hugh Scott Barrett and Sergio Lires Rial, behaved like boors. They would toss clients who they thought uninteresting, or who they didn't like for some reason, to the retail division. Their arrogance was a cause of much bad blood in the bank.

For example, Jan Maarten de Jong heard that a colleague was dealing with a company named Geveke. The company worked with Caterpillar and was thinking of making an acquisition in Scandinavia. De Jong asked Jiskoot to close the deal with Geveke. After a while Jiskoot returned with the message that his people at Alfred Berg weren't interested in Geveke because they thought they could earn more money elsewhere. To a client-oriented man like De Jong, leaving a customer in the cold like that was the worst thing they could have done.

There were constant fights about who should be allowed to charge costs and why. The corporate business division needed the domestic network to be able to sell their products. The domestic division was therefore allowed to charge costs to the corporate business division. The compilation of service-level agreements was another source of conflict between the two divisions. To many the conflict was only too real, since bonuses were largely determined by the results of their own division. This resulted in vehement confrontations between Hugh Scott Barrett and Dolf Collee (responsible for the domestic division) on the managing board. The two men were not friends. At one time some people in the corporate business division were threatening to go to another Dutch bank, because they would be charged less there.

Floris Deckers thought that the corporate business division had been focusing on Dutch clients too much. He believed that there were between thirty and forty companies in the Netherlands who needed the services of specialised corporate bankers – companies that would not be intimidated by an aggressive investment banker. However, there were certainly not 1,000 companies looking for such services. Most Dutch companies would not need super-specialised product knowledge. And they would not understand the bonus-driven bankers, who were interested in the client only as long as there was a lucrative bonus in it for them.

There was an attempt by some general managers, former ABN people, among them Lex Kloosterman, Jan Willem Meeuwis and Floris Deckers, to form an old-fashioned workgroup to stop SBUs viewing clients as possessions. The idea was shot down by the managing board. Such universal thinking didn't suit a strategy based on each SBU holding its own.

As Marakon consultant Herman Spruit saw it, each member of the managing board was only capable of seeing things from his own perspective. The other members of the board would listen, and after four hours of talking, agree – without knowing exactly what they were agreeing to. Then a few days later, they would suddenly realise what they had agreed to, and scramble to undo it. That meant that decisions were always being revisited. The consultant suggested that the managers should stop preaching to the converted. They should try to present more alternatives, which would help to keep their audience interested and make it possible to make real choices.

Spruit noticed that the discussions were often long and that Groenink seldom intervened. Did he think he was forging a stronger team by letting everyone talk as much as they liked? He often asked Groenink if he followed up on instructions that he had given to subordinates. The chairman always said that he had told the person concerned what was expected of him.

At that time the supervisory board had no idea that there was so much bad blood on the managing board. One governor wondered if Tom de Swaan was capable of being firm enough with a man like Groenink. At any rate, De Swaan was usually busy keeping his beige book, a ring binder containing the quarterly figures, in order. It was quite a job in itself, of course. The governors were careful not to be too harsh on De Swaan; his wife had been ill for some years.

The supervisory board met around eight times a year, and the meetings were always much the same. They started at one with a simple sandwich, with perhaps a croquette, and continued at two with the meeting itself, which usually went on until six.

The managing board's plenary sessions with the supervisory board seldom yielded any concrete results. The members of the managing board thought them a waste of time. Why should they meet seven or eight times a year with people who didn't understand banking? Of course the managing directors were arrogant; they were a breed apart because they practised a difficult profession. But that didn't take away from the fact that the governors didn't offer any added value. They laughed about Louise Groenman, who had been a government-appointed member of the social economic council. Whenever she asked a question, she began, "I don't understand any of this, but ..."

Hugh Scott Barrett was frustrated that the meetings of the supervisory board were carefully scripted. Groenink and Loudon would discuss the agenda in detail, and list the results they desired from any discussion that might arise. A number of the governors noticed that Loudon grew irritated if questions were asked on topics that had been suggested by Groenink, and about which it had been agreed that there should be a positive result.

Scott Barrett thought it was not satisfactory that governors seldom asked questions about the operational management of the bank and seemed to be interested only in discussing strategy. The Brit thought that the governors should ascertain if the bank was being managed well. There should be more interest, he felt, in helping to achieve operational excellence.

The managing directors saw the supervisory board mainly as a part of the network. A few years before, most of them had been important clients of the bank, although there were fewer of those now. Still, the main function of the supervisory board as they saw it was to provide people who could help the bank through their contacts at home and abroad. As regards content, the managers didn't take the governors seriously. Except for Jan Kalff, but he had marked himself from the start by criticising the choice of Groenink as chairman and the bank's new strategy. No one listened to Nelissen and Hazelhoff, they were from a bygone age.

The composition of the supervisory board was decided by Groenink and Loudon. For instance, they decided to ask Cor Boonstra to join the board after he retired from his position as president of Philips. In the annual report, Loudon said that the bank expected that Boonstra's expertise in successful complex reorganisations would of great value to the bank. But this turned out to be a disappointment.

In April, Boonstra was accused of insider trading in Endemol shares, and he became the subject of a criminal investigation. The appointment was postponed and eventually rescinded. In May the managing board announced that future appointments to the supervisory board would be made only via an independent asset management corporation or investment funds. The bank insisted that this limitation was not connected to the Boonstra case, whose appointment was suspended for the duration of the investigation.

Van Tets was another hunter. He hadn't given up his plans. Of course, the economic climate could not have been worse. Rijkman Groenink was making it increasingly clear that he didn't want to extend the bank's traditional investment banking activities. But he still made one last attempt to realise his dream. He thought that the bank should buy that quintessential American investment bank, Bear Stearns. They wanted 80 dollars a share, while the share price on the markets was 55 dollars. All in all, the takeover would cost over 10 billion dollars. Van Tets and Lires Rial did an audit and were pleasantly surprised. They thought that it would be a cowboy operation, but that turned out not to be the case.

Van Tets had dinner with Jimmy Cayne, the CEO of Bear Stearns, in New York and invited him to come to the Netherlands to meet the bank's top management. He was hoping to counter the scepticism that he noticed when he talked with certain colleagues about the opportunity. It was seriously discussed by the managing board. Cayne was keen, Van Tets and Jiskoot were also for it, although the latter had reservations about the differences in culture between the two organisations.

But Rijkman Groenink hit the brake hard. The chairman was beginning to realise that there were still some people who thought that ABN Amro should become a classical investment bank. Wherever he went he had to explain that the corporate business division was also about lending loans, and that ABN Amro was still, after all, a wholesale bank.

Groenink was playing with two ideas about the future of the corporate business division. On the one hand, he was irritated that Van Tets, Jiskoot, Scott Barrett and Lires Rial continued to talk about the importance of the league tables – the lists of big deals that you had to be on as an investment bank. On the other hand, he could use a couple of big successes in the corporate business area. In any big share issue or merger, the supervising bank puts a couple of per cent of the deal in its pocket. Fees earned in this way can involve tens of millions of dollars.

Groenink often talked with Herman Spruit about the problem. He pointed out that the corporate business division still didn't have a clear strategy. He asked Van Tets about it, but he only said that Bear Stearns was a once in a lifetime opportunity. They agreed that Marakon would try to make clear agreements with the corporate business division about its performance.

But Groenink didn't want to run the risk of a takeover of a bank like Bear Stearns. He was even concerned that the deal might end up bankrupting the bank. De Swaan was also vehemently opposed; he was convinced that the two cultures wouldn't match. With the Americans it was always every man for himself. Groenink consulted Loudon and told him that the corporate business division, and especially Van Tets, wouldn't be pleased if he let Bear Stearns go. Loudon said he would support him.

Groenink told Van Tets that he couldn't see it working. He indicated that the market wasn't right. When the Internet bubble had burst, it had left little work for investment bankers. That year, the volume of share issues, mergers and takeovers had been 65 per cent lower than the previous year. In the first six months of that year, the corporate business division had booked 53 per cent less profit than for the same period the previous year. They were often sidelined. ABN Amro had stopped hiring new bankers, and only 180 new people had been taken on, compared to the targeted 500. Even so, the market assumed that the headhunter, Russell Reynolds, had earned some 20 million euros from the assignment.

The new people were often expensive, too. Some of them would only join the bank with a contract that guaranteed bonuses of between two and three million dollars a year. Sometimes for two years. A lot of people in the bank were uncomfortable with this. The new recruits often appeared to be living off past successes, because the big deals didn't come in. The investment bank was surviving largely on Wilco Jiskoot's contacts. The majority of the activities were also still in the Netherlands. It was decided to intervene, as the competition were doing, and scrap at least 600 of the 12,000 jobs. That wasn't difficult in itself, although it would cost a lot of money.

Van Tets saw that he wouldn't get what he wanted and that his position had become difficult. The takeover of Bear Stearns was supposed to have been the great victory that would give the bank access to the all-important American market. It would have put the investment bank on the map.

Groenink realised that he had moved too fast. He regretted putting the corporate business division at the centre of the bank's strategy, he regretted communicating the peer group ambition too enthusiastically. He had been working with the wrong information; he had been too euphoric. If he had waited half year before formulating the targets, the goal would have been considerably less ambitious. And he would not have communicated the less ambitious goal externally. It was time to put some things right.

He felt responsible for what had happened and decided to steer things more actively, and in the desired direction. Under Jan Kalff, the annual reports had been signed by the entire managing board; now they would be signed by the chairman.

Groenink didn't like the fact that there were so many people on the managing board, and he was especially irritated by the wholesale sbu, which had four representatives on the board and tended to dominate.

The chairman worked his frustration off on some of his colleagues. He wasn't pleased that Van Tets, De Jong and Van den Brink had come forward with some attractive prognoses for the coming four years, although they had done so at his request. The prognoses were clearly unrealistic, given the worsening economic climate. As had been agreed, the three acted as heads of their own sbus. They weren't much concerned with the rest of the bank. And therefore also not with the chairman of the board, who was responsible for the whole show.

Groenink had no grip on the board and this frustrated him. He wrote a memo in which he observed that the board was too large, it had become unmanageable. The memo was widely discussed by the board, and supported. The chairman told the board that he would work with the president of the bank to decide who would have to leave the board.

Herman Spruit supported Groenink in this. He noted that Groenink was dealing carefully with the three board members who would have to leave. On his own initiative, Spruit wrote a letter to Aarnout Loudon in which he explained that the bank was being led by four chairmen at the moment, and that was three too many. Loudon agreed. Groenink suggested to the president that the three longest-serving members of the board should leave. Groenink and Loudon decided to ask Jan Maarten de Jong, Dolf van den Brink and Rijnhard van Tets to give up their seats on the managing board. The three would not be fired. Instead, they would continue at the bank as consultants until their retirement.

Loudon thought it a pity that De Jong was leaving, but understood that it was important for clarity in the bank. He thought that Van den Brink was troublesome and as far as he was concerned there was no longer a place for Van Tets because the takeover of Bear Stearns was not going ahead. This was a turning point for Loudon. Now, he felt, the retail activities would receive more active attention.

Van den Brink was angry. He no longer felt at home at the bank. He believed passionately in the sort of cooperation that had been achieved in the old universal bank. What was happening to the bank now was awful. A culture of every man for himself was being created, and he worried about the future of the bank. He was disappointed with Tom de Swaan, who identified with the new policy and never offered any opposition to Groenink.

Things were not going so well for his division, PCAM. The markets were bad, the bar had been set too high. The managing board often found itself stumbling over Van den Brink. Some of the other managing board members were annoyed by his professorial tone. But psychologically, Van den Brink had already left, and he agreed with Groenink and Loudon's proposal that he retire early.

De Jong was at his holiday home in Italy when Groenink phoned him and asked him to take early retirement, one-and-a-half years earlier than in May 2003, as had originally been agreed. De Jong was shocked, although he himself had noted a few months before that his retail division could do well under the leadership of two men, and that he was now a supervisor of Collee and Kuiper more than anything else. But he was being asked to leave the bank where he had worked for 32 years, and suddenly, within a few months. He phoned Aarnout Loudon to tell him what had happened. Loudon responded curtly. The president told De Jong that these things happen. It was a short conversation.

The conversation with Van Tets was more forceful. As he saw it, Groenink had not delivered what he had said he would two years before, in exchange for Van Tets's support for his candidacy as chairman. But Van Tets also knew that his time had come.

The three men then agreed to what one of them would later describe as the best retirement package ever negotiated in the Netherlands. The exact amount was not made public, but a calculation did the rounds within the bank that came to a total of some 60 million guilders. They got an office with secretary, a car with chauffeur, and were on full salaries until their official retirement. In return, they would do a little work now and then as consultants. The negotiations for the separation went relatively smoothly. In December there were more departures. De Swaan made a sour joke about the departure of the three managing directors to other members of the managing board: no, they hadn't been fired, they had just ceased to exist.

The central role of the corporate business division had also ceased to exist. The worsening market, combined with a critical report by Marakon, saw to that. Marakon thought that the level of service within the corporate business division was low. Spruit told Groenink that they might feel like investment bankers, but they were really just ordinary corporate bankers. The bank would have to change its strategy, and this only a little more than a year after they had announced that the corporate business division would play a leading role.

Some on the board were cheerful enough about the situation. Joost Kuiper observed that they had all failed to see the worsening conditions in the markets. He was happy with this result. As he saw it, the reality check had been badly needed. Now the bank would get back to business.

The die was cast. The figures delivered by the corporate development department in August the previous year showed that the corporate business division was too weak to be the basis of the entire bank's strategy; PCAM was simply too small. From now on, it would not be the wholesale division but the retail division that would play the leading role within the bank.

The mood of the managing board was that it was better late than never.

Jiskoot and Scott Barrett were disappointed. They said that it would take time for the investments in the corporate business division's network to become profitable. They were only getting started. They thought that ABN Amro should push on, and invest more. Their protests made no impact. Scott Barrett indicated that there were still problems with discipline and transparency; when that was in order, the investment bank would show that it could do quite well. But Tom de Swaan agreed with Groenink. He also thought that they had been caught up in the euphoria of 2000. To him, a retreat now would be a sign of power.

Jiskoot changed his tack and said that Marakon had indeed been critical of his division, but he added that ABN Amro would never make it to the top five in its peer group by focusing on the retail division. He had figured out that the profit of the corporate business division was made in nine countries, and suggested that the other 41 countries be quickly closed. Groenink was against this and underlined the importance of the bank's unique network. There were only a few banks with a comparable network, and during takeover or merger negotiations that network would be an asset.

There was a lot of anger in the corporate business division about Spruit's performance – especially when it became known that Spruit had advised that Hugh Scott Barrett should head up the corporate business division. The consultant thought Scott Barrett a better manager than Jiskoot. He had a lot of respect for Jiskoot; he was the only world-class banker on the board, aside from Groenink, in his view. But he didn't have a high regard for Jiskoot as a manager. Like every deal maker, Jiskoot liked to keep his options open and he found it difficult to make choices.

General manager Alexandra Cook, who was close to Wilco Jiskoot, thought that Groenink had sold his soul to Marakon. Spruit was a sort of Rasputin who talked only with Groenink, and was therefore out of the loop as regards what was really happening in the corporate business division. But she had no need to worry. Groenink didn't dare to take on Jiskoot.

On 15 August 2001, the supervisory board was surprised to receive a document called 'European Asset Gathering Model'. The piece, written by Arnold van Os of the corporate development department, began with a cheerful remark: that the decision to focus on wholesale for the strategic endgame taken the previous year had 'not actually been made, that a real strategic choice between wholesale, retail and asset management could not be avoided. And that it is high time that that choice was made. Not least because it is clear that shareholders and analysts still do not know enough about the direction the bank is taking. It is also important to make it clear what direction the banking is taking to management and employees.'

During three sessions of discussion, the managing board had decided on the European Asset Gathering model as the bank's strategic endgame. The governors were surprised: until recently, everyone had been talking about the corporate business division. So much so that the division had had four members on the managing board. And they wanted to know what asset gathering actually was.

Even Jan Kalff didn't know what it was. Did it have anything to do with savings accounts? The board couldn't say exactly what it was either. Jan Kalff persisted with his questions. Eventually, it was explained that in Europe banks would strive for as many clients as possible, and for as great a share as possible in their savings accounts and investment needs.

Arnold van Os understood why there was so much confusion. He believed that it would have been far better simply to say that from now on the retail division (C&CC) would play the leading role within the bank. But Groenink said that the name of the division was too sensitive psychologically to be used.

After some further questioning, another description was found: what it meant was the consumer & corporate clients division would lead in combination with asset management. The managing board had decided that 'the primary focus on the corporate business division is no longer a credible option for the endgame'.

From now on there would be much more focus on Europe at any rate. 'The shortage of capital limits our options outside Europe,' the document read. It was even suggested that a European merger was unavoidable. The role of the domestic division would be crucial, 'the Netherlands must be a showcase.'

The managing board observed that the 'the attitude of the bank with regard to a merger has changed. It has proved difficult to create a second domestic market in Europe through a takeover. Acceptance of a merger as an alternative means that this is again a realistic scenario.' The bank remarked that it would have to consider the sale of activities outside of Europe in order to realise the European ambition. The non-European activities will be regarded as 'the exchangeable chips that will make a European strategy possible'.

Van Os and Groenink followed their presentation with a plan to focus the bank's activities on opportunities to play a leading role in France, Germany or Italy in the retail and asset management markets. In addition, an attempt would be made to build a stable relationship with an insurer. A 'successful cross-border IT platform' would be built.

As regards the desired merger, the managing board said that a large merger would take place between 2002 and 2003 that would ensure that the bank would have a market share of at least 20 per cent in that second domestic market. ABN Amro would have a market value of between 80 and 100 billion at the end of 2003.

Between 2004 and 2006 another large takeover would be carried out, to create a third European domestic market. Toward the end of 2006 the market share of the bank would be between 160 and 200 billion euros. During the last and final phase the bank would build an integrated multi-country platform that would mean that it was servicing at least 20 million clients in Europe by the end of 2006. The bank would then be 'a leading European asset-gathering platform with a clear brand and an open IT platform'.

In closing, the supervisory board was told that the managing board would strive for an equal merger. A list of sixteen European banks was brought forward. Seven of them, among them Barclays and Fortis, were worth more than ABN Amro. Seven others, among them SocGen, HypoVereinsbank, Unicredito and Nordea, were worth less.

Groenink was clear that he would look around Europe in search of a merger partner. In the first instance he would look for banks whose size would mean that ABN Amro was the dominant party. He would also see to it that contact was maintained with banks that were much larger than ABN Amro, among them RBS and Santander. Here his mission would be to talk with them, learn more about what was on their minds, and prevent them from becoming hostile.

The governors nodded in agreement. As usual, almost no questions were asked. Apparently a majority of the managing board thought that this change of direction was necessary, and there was nothing else to do.

9

Gulf

September 2001–April 2002

"Smart thinking and accurate formulation," Floris Deckers said with a grin, in answer to questions from the bank's internal magazine, *De Young Banker*, about his great passion. Deckers went on, "You have to think smart about what you do and what your capabilities are. As managers, a lot of us are seriously short of people skills in relation to the way we deal with our colleagues individually, but it is important that we get this right more generally, and that we are better than the rest."

Deckers had been the boss of the domestic division for ten months. He hadn't worked in the Netherlands for a long time. The fact that he was Dutch was not important to him. Indeed, he had unlearned his Dutch ways of thinking, because they were no use in the many countries where he had worked.

This made the challenge that he was now faced with all the larger. On the desk in front of him lay two letters. One of the letters would go to 25,500 employees, the other to the remaining 8,500. The first group would read that they would be allowed to leave the bank with a severance package, while the second group would not be allowed to make use of the severance stimulation package. The intention was to get rid of 6,250 full-time jobs out of 26,000; this worked out to about 8,500 people. Now he would have to sign the letters.

The plan to scrap 25 per cent of the jobs was the result of a calculation. Thanks to Marakon, it was clear that the domestic division earned only around 200 million euros. But the economic profit of the domestic division would have to become five times higher within four years. And that could only be achieved by cutting down on jobs – jobs that were between 15 and 20 per cent better paid than at competitors. They'd called the operation No Detours.

So the Netherlands was getting some attention again. Deckers felt that some major maintenance work was seriously overdue. No Detours would ensure that ABN Amro would be running at the front again. Some 570 of the 863 traditional bank branches would be transformed into bank shops offering elementary services. Another 80 advice offices would be opened to offer more complicated services. The old-fashioned counter clerks would be better educated and made into client consultants.

Deckers' mood darkened as he thought of the numbers involved in the huge reorganisation. They should have done this eleven years ago, when ABN and Amro merged. He wondered why Rijkman Groenink had not intervened more actively, as head of the domestic division in the late 1990s. But the more contact he had with his boss, the more he understood why. Groenink reacted to incidents and to advice. He didn't initiate. Deckers didn't think his boss was a strategist.

The two letters had been carefully compiled in cooperation with the unions. There had been a number of sessions at the head office of the domestic division in south-east Amsterdam. Four men from ABN Amro, among them Floris Deckers and Rob Mommers, and four representatives of the four unions concerned, among them Huug Gorter of the FNV, had attended the meetings. The unions had referred to the new social agreement, which had just been renewed, and which established that no forced resignations could occur in future reorganisations. Their view was that everyone should be offered the same severance package. But the bankers thought that would be dangerous. People with talent or an exceptional ability would simply cash in the package and then get taken on again. The bank said that people who were indispensable would not be allowed to leave.

The discussion turned into an endless totting up of plusses and minuses. The unions wanted to ensure that as many people as possible would be eligible for the severance package, while the bank had a long list of people they didn't want to offer it to. Finally, an agreement was reached in the middle of the night: 25 per cent would not be offered the package, 75 per cent would. The unions said it was a good result.

The bankers had suggested that a general announcement be made, and that the execution would be carried out at a lower level of the bank. But the unions didn't agree. They were worried that local managers would seize the opportunity, and make their own choices as to who would or would not receive the package. And they didn't think that would be fair, because it might allow favouritism. They thought it better that each person should receive a letter from Floris Deckers addressed to each of them personally, stating which category they were in.

There had been some haggling about the exact formulation. The people who would not be allowed to leave would receive a letter stating, 'You belong to the group of employees to whom we can offer an appropriate function at your present level of seniority or higher. The specific function for which you are eligible will be made clear at a later stage, from 15 January 2002, as well as its location. This means that the severance stimulation package does not apply to you ... I count on your commitment, support and flexibility during the coming period. I request you to show some tact to those of your colleagues who have a less certain future ahead of them, and thereby to give expression to two core values of the bank: teamwork and respect.'

The people who were being let go received another letter. 'The bank cannot offer the certainty that there is an appropriate function for you in the new organisation. This means that you can indicate whether you wish to make use of the severance stimulation package. You are requested to do so between 15 September and 15 January 2002. If you do not wish to make use of this, selection for a matching place will take place from 15 January 2002. It will then be clear whether you can offer the competencies that will be required in the new bank and if there is an appropriate function for you. If the answer is No in either case, you will become part of the mobility organisation in due course. I am painfully aware that the contents of this letter, and the question whether to make use of the severance package, will be of concern to you over the next few months. That is very understandable. In the end, it is a choice that you must make for yourself, and your personal circumstances will play a large part in your choice. Nevertheless, I hope that you will continue to give of your best, both with respect to clients and colleagues. I wish you success in determining your choice. Yours sincerely, Floris Deckers, CEO Netherlands Business Unit.'

A number of psychologists and other experts have since looked at those texts, and they agree that it was a smart approach. And the package was good: one monthly salary (gross) for every year worked; employees over forty got one-and-a-half months' salary per year worked, and those over fifty got two months' salary per year worked.

Deckers was concerned that the announcement might cause agitation in the bank. The organisation had known since the RAI meeting the previous February that this was possible. During the previous few months they had been doing road trips throughout the country to prepare the way for the announcement, telling people about the No Detours plan. Representatives of the staff council were present at all meetings. The somewhat distant tone adopted by Deckers and the younger managing directors, among them Chris Vogelzang, who had come from Shell and was reckoned to be smart, was not appreciated by everyone. People missed the fatherly tone of former managers, such as Gerard Kalff and Henk Rutgers. But on the whole they were not unhappy with the reactions that they got. The percentages had already appeared in a newspaper in July. The decision whether or not to take the severance package had been the talk of the day at the bank for some time. No, this letter would not be a surprise.

Before he signed, Deckers checked again to see that the introduction and the date were correct. The letters were dated 11 September 2001. Later that day there was a sudden disturbance at the head office of ABN Amro in the Netherlands. Everywhere, TV's were turned on and work put aside. Two aeroplanes had flown into the World Trade Center in New York.

The next day there was a lot of confusion. The world was suddenly in flames and the employees were wondering whether they would have a job in a few months. The people who knew they would not be staying were ashamed, both of themselves and of the bank. How could you work for a company for so long and then suddenly hear that they didn't want you? When even the secretaries of the managing directors started complaining, they began to have their doubts. These women had followed the whole process from close by, and it was worrying that they were worrying.

Rumours immediately started going round that some people had received the wrong letter. An example was what happened to Theo Kraan, one of the bank's most popular analysts. Kraan, who had represented the bank in the media for years, was told that he wasn't needed, and it made him furious. He phoned Dolf Collee, Deckers' boss, to tell him so. But the letter proved to have been a mistake. Theo Kraan had been given a job in private banking, which was part of the PCAM SBU (asset management). Salary administration was running two months behind the reorganisation, and his new appointment had not been recorded, because he was still registered as part of the domestic division. But that explanation didn't help; the damage was done. After 38 years at the bank, Kraan decided to take his severance package.

Deckers got piles of angry letters and emails. Someone even threw a stone through the window of his house. The banker wasn't too concerned; he hadn't lived all those years in Brazil for nothing.

Action had been taken at the domestic division, then, but the analysts remained sceptical. Groenink had been chairman for nearly one and a half years. The reorganisation of the whole bank, though, was taking too long, costing too much and it was not going ahead forcefully enough, they chorused. Some thought that Groenink was flogging a dead horse: ABN Amro didn't have the scale to be a winner on the global banking stage. The share price declined further; it had fallen 20 per cent in eight months.

There was some grumbling at the message that the bank would be giving priority to its retail activities from now on. Why had it taken the managing board so long to come to such an obvious conclusion? The message was being interpreted in such black-and-white terms that Groenink hastened to say that the corporate business division would remain a fully fledged and integral part of the bank.

There were more interventions. The corporate business division was given 20 per cent less capital to work with and was now supposed to concentrate on the 2,000 most lucrative clients. The corporate bankers would have less room for discretion in extending loans that the bank would earn little from anyway. They would have to sell new services, and they would have to earn money. Groenink asked Jiskoot, Van Tets's successor, to make some smart decisions. At present the corporate business division was selling too many products to too many clients, and that was causing costs to rise.

The top of the bank was worried about the activities they had bought in New York six months before. On the recommendation of Herman Spruit of Marakon, strict targets were set that Furman Selz would have to hit by April the following year. If the targets were not achieved by then, they would have to intervene, and hard.

In the rest of the organisation, many people were angry about the whole-sale adventure, which they felt had never fitted with the bank. Stories buzzed around of people who earned a lot but didn't perform. One name was a symbol for many others: Jim Carrabino. Carrabino had come from Merrill Lynch, and was being paid a guaranteed five million dollars for two years, but he was said to have earned little for the bank. Carrabino was taking home substantially more than the members of the managing board. However, at the presentation of the annual report, it emerged that Carrabino and others had received increases to their basic salaries of 12 per cent the previous year. That was also painful to many.

"It's easier to set a lower bar for your ambitions," Rijkman Groenink told *Management Scope* in an interview about the ambitions of the bank. "Then you go home every evening feeling calm about things, and weekends are also more restful. You're not lying in bed worrying."

Around 25,000 of his Dutch colleagues were certainly lying in their beds worrying. By the first week of December, only 1,650 employees had registered for the severance package. Another 23,000 people still had to make a decision during the coming four weeks, before 15 January. After all the turmoil over the letter, it was time for the reorganisation to begin.

Wednesday 12 December was the fourth wedding anniversary of Rijkman Groenink and Irene Groenink-Verboon. He had not had much time for the marriage since then though. The domestic division had asked him to play a role in the biggest multimedia show that the bank had ever organised.

Some 10 million euros were budgeted for the communication of the bank's plans and ambitions to the employees. The managers were ready; they had been working on this reorganisation for two years. They thought they were through the first phase. The letters had been sent. Everything had been communicated, and now they felt ready for the next phase. They wanted to explain in more detail why the reorganisation was necessary, where it would lead, and what the future would look like.

It was a crucial error. The top management were ready, but the rest of the people in the bank weren't. Various managing directors, visible on huge, linked screens, found themselves facing angry audiences in Utrecht, Amsterdam, Eindhoven and Rotterdam. Most of the employees felt that the bank had let them down.

Dutch television presenter Paul Witteman was asked to interview employees from a studio in Hilversum. He was happy to do so, on one condition: he wanted to be free to ask critical questions. The journalist received the assurance that this was exactly what was intended. The management of the bank was ready. For hours, Witteman listened to the anger and frustrations of the employees of the bank. One frequent comment was that the merger in 1990 had been carried out carefully, and virtually no one had been fired then.

At the end of the event, Rijkman Groenink walked onto the stage at Utrecht's Jaarbeurs. Witteman saw Groenink, but Groenink didn't see Witteman. The journalist confronted him with all the worries he had been hearing. Things weren't so good for all those people, were they? Groenink responded immediately in an authoritarian tone, taking on both Witteman and the audience. The chairman explained that from now on the bank would be focusing on creating value for its shareholders. This was the last message that the people in the hall wanted to hear.

Paul Witteman saw that he had hooked a big fish. He reflected that Groenink was not very authoritative, for if he had been, he would have kept the meeting under control. The questions became more and more confrontational. Why was he taking the shareholders' side? They were talking about the future of people who had lost their jobs, after all. Groenink, who appeared not to be able to hear Witteman well, was apparently totally unprepared for a confrontational question-and-answer session. He was furious at Witteman, at the people who had organised the event, at the people in the hall. He had to win this fight. But he couldn't win it.

Boos began to echo in the hall. Some of the employees turned ostentatiously away from their chairman. Some people even threw beer. The example was followed in other places in the country. "You men in your shining suits," people yelled. "What do you know about banking? You don't visit the clients, you don't visit the branches in the country ..."

The anger grew. The employees felt that they were the heart of the bank, but now they were making sacrifices and economising while the bank was hiring hundreds of young, expensive, English-speaking investment bankers, who talked a lot about big deals involving millions but never seemed to bring any business in. The employees commented on the "stupid arrogance" of the top management. The atmosphere got worse. Bank directors on a number of different stages felt that anger, physically. They were not being taken seriously, and could not speak above the shouting. The managers found themselves stepping down from the stage fearful and disillusioned.

For the first time, many bankers were wondering if ABN Amro, *the* Dutch bank, would see its 200th anniversary as an independent organisation. Things were not going well.

The management of the domestic division is distraught. This was a catastrophe. They had been caught up by their tunnel vision. They had wanted to start looking to the future. Meanwhile, though, the employees who had lost their jobs were still in mourning, and still wanted recognition of their sorrow. We forgot that we are dealing with people, a department manager sighed afterwards; they simply weren't ready for this.

There was great consternation among the top managers of the division. They could feel the anger of the people who worked for them, but they also felt that of the managing board. Groenink was furious and blamed them. The managers were receiving hundreds of angry emails, and it seemed as if the whole bank was angry with them. Almost all of them were considering tendering their resignation.

Afterwards, Floris Deckers reflected that the Dutch were even more emotional than the Brazilians. He understood where the emotion was coming from; 70 to 80 per cent of his colleagues worked in the back office. They were people who had chosen a career with a bank because they wanted security in their lives. Many of them might even have preferred to be civil servants. These were risk-averse people. Moreover, many of them felt that ABN Amro was their bank, the country's bank. They had never heard that things were not going well. And now they were paying the price for having been kept in ignorance.

There was an advantage in all the drama. The number of people who were registering for the severance package was increasing by the day. It looked as if they would achieve the target of 8,500.

There was anger on the supervisory board too about No Detours. What were the managing board doing? Was this the way to go about things? They warned that it would not be good for the bank's reputation. Groenink was advised to stay out of the press for a while. Things seemed to go wrong whenever he went outside.

The supervisory board attempted to present a united face to the world. But a crack appeared when Trude Maas said in an interview that No Detours had been an enormous mistake. Aarnout Loudon called her immediately. She was right, of course, he said, but she should not have said so. It should have stayed in the bank.

In December, Rijkman Groenink gave an interview to Dutch weekly magazine, *Vrij Nederland*, in which he said that he regretted the letters that had been sent. The letters had been seen by Jan Maarten de Jong, who was leaving, but not by the chairman. "That letter did a huge amount of harm, and I regret that a lot. We simply underestimated the harshness of the message. People felt that they had been dumped. Everyone involved in the negotiations, including the unions, had simply missed that aspect. We should not have made a distinction between people. We might have lost some people who we needed, but we would not have had to deal with [thousands of] grieving, demotivated employees."

In December, Rijnhard van Tets, Jan Maarten de Jong and Dolf van den Brink left the bank. There was a big dinner at Duin & Kruidberg. The guests noted that the three men had not entirely accepted their departure.

During the final meeting with the supervisory board chairman, Dolf van den Brink made some critical remarks about Groenink. He told Loudon that the chairman continued to bully his colleagues, that Groenink was always fighting fires, that he was no strategist. He had found, and left, the domestic division in chaos. Loudon simply listened.

De Jong now expressed himself openly too. More and more, he wondered if it had been a good idea to open the bank to investment bankers. It had broken up a lot of traditions, and the bank was full of tradition. In his generation, it had always been about the bank, the relationship with the client. There was value in that. They had been proud to work for the bank. But he didn't see much of the same spirit today, looking at all the new faces around.

De Jong didn't trust the investment bankers. As he saw it, they were people who were only interested in themselves – their network, their opportunities to make deals and their need for an infrastructure that supported them and also paid them well. They changed banks as easily as other people changed cars. It was impossible to get them to work in a team. And all of this so that they could invest in things that might yield a profit in a couple of years. The investment bankers had no sense of a shared horizon. They were interested in only one thing, and that was their own wallet.

De Jong had learned something in all these years, and that was that money had an even stronger influence on people than sex. Money was at the basis of everything. In a bank, it was therefore essential that remuneration and bonuses were well managed. He was depressed by all the fighting on the board during the previous two years. Smart colleagues had fought tooth and nail over costs that they were always trying to transfer to each other, and simply because they wanted to improve their own result, and thereby their bonus. De Jong was concerned that the bank had not managed the growing greed well.

That evening, De Jong gave Groenink an antique edition of *Il Principe* by Niccolò Machiavelli. He referred him to an important point in the book: the new leader must get rid of all the supporters of his predecessor. There was a huge laugh at that. Some guests thought there was another relevant lesson in the book: divide and rule. To Machiavelli, a sixteenth-century thinker, it was all about position. His basic assumption was that people tend to the bad. One of those present knew the work well and remarked that there was another point that did apply to Groenink. Machiavelli's view of things was in a sense amoral; he saw people primarily as functional creatures.

At the dinner, some former managers realised that it was really the end of an era for the bank. They were worried. Would Groenink succeed in bringing the growing tension and disunity under control? Jan Kalff was not pleased at all about the way things had gone. Men like Van Tets, De Jong and Van den Brink could have provided the counterweight that would be necessary as long as Groenink was chairman. They would have been in a position to ensure that the values that they had so carefully formulated four years before would remain central in the bank's behaviour.

Knowing that men like them were surrounding Groenink had given Kalff some reassurance. That was now gone. Kalff had been totally surprised when he heard that these three men would be fired. It had simply been reported to the supervisory board. He realised that this had been cooked up by Loudon and Groenink. The former chairman had registered his protest and warned about this, but no one had listened.

One of the governors shared Kalff's concern about Groenink's power. He was too dominant. Groenink had been on the managing board for twelve years, and the most senior board member after him was Wilco Jiskoot, who had been on the board for five years. The rest were fairly new arrivals. The governors had not yet got round to looking for a successor to Groenink. It also didn't help that Rob Kleyn's successor in human resources, Garmt Louw, who was coming from Shell, would join the managing board only in March 2002.

They had at least come up with a plan if something should happen to Groenink. This was something that couldn't be excluded, and certainly not with a man like Groenink. Good friends said only half-jokingly that a man who liked taking risks as much as he did would probably not die peacefully in old age. If Groenink got hit by a bus, Joost Kuiper would be his temporary replacement. The governors called Kuiper their bus candidate.

The markets were bad, the Internet bubble had burst. A lot of banks were having trouble, among them ABN Amro. The profit for the first half of 2001 had been dramatically lower. And what was worse, the bank was in last place in its peer group. This fact was explored in detail in the media. Commentators said scornfully that Groenink was a windbag. What do a turkey and Rijkman Groenink have in common? stock exchange traders joked. Answer: neither is going to see Christmas!

For the first time, many of the ordinary department managers had not been invited to the annual Christmas dinner. There were now so many managing directors that not everyone of the same rank could be invited. This applied especially to regional managers, old hands who had made decades-long careers in the domestic organisation. The reasoning at head office was simple: they didn't invite regional managers from other places in the world either. A shock went through the dometic organisation. They were no longer part of the family.

Rijkman Groenink thought that the managing board should focus on strategy. The responsibility for better efficiency and operational excellence would lie primarily with the general managers. Of his own role, he thought it logical that he should focus on finding suitable candidates for mergers or takeovers. Members of the managing board noticed that Groenink spoke more often with staffers like Arnold van Os than he did with them. The staffers seemed to know more about what Groenink was doing than they did.

Van Os presented his last document in April. As the manager responsible for the corporate development department, he would be succeeded by Wietze Reehoorn. Because there were still many questions about the new strategy of the bank, Van Os had set out a number of points for the managing board's consideration under the title 'European asset gathering, our strategic endgame updated through ten questions'. In it he observed that communication on the strategy of the bank had been 'much too aggressive and far from clear'. Instead of taking a step-by-step approach, the concept of asset gathering had been thrown into the organisation, and it had not helped to create any clarity. We have to communicate much more carefully, the document stated. To do so, a work group should be set up, called Restoring Faith, which would restore trust in the leadership as regards strategy.

'As a group, we can no longer pretend to global aspirations. We are too small. We should focus on Europe. The consolidation of the European banking sector is unavoidable,' Van Os wrote, with Groenink's approval. 'The coming three to five years will result in a top league of players with market shares of 100 billion and an average of about 20 million retail clients.'

The document went further. 'If we want to be in the top five in Europe, we will have to find a merger. And because we are a second-tier bank with a market share of less than 30 billion, we will have to watch out. We fall into an intermediate category where it is not clear whether we are predator or prey. Are we going to eat, or will we be eaten? We must be careful to ensure that we don't miss the boat.'

It would be the British banks in particular, which were consolidating fast, that would bring the pressure to bear. For ABN Amro this would mean increased focus on Benelux, France, Italy, Spain and the Scandinavian countries. 'Our goal in the long term is to achieve a top position in personal financial services in one or more large European economies.'

It was cautiously hinted that the subsidiaries in the United States and Brazil would no longer be part of the core company. They would be sold when capital was needed for survival in the process of European consolidation. At any rate, 'requests for investments from these regions will not be given priority. The managements there know that we have placed the accent on Europe and therefore have doubts about ABN Amro's strategic commitment as a group. Head office must make it clear that the goal of the businesses in the United States and Brazil is now to maximise their value on a stand-alone basis.'

Or, in other words, as Van Os continued, 'We must ensure that these subsidiaries can be sold for the best possible price.' He added a warning, 'But we must be careful with our communications, because the new focus on Europe could have a demotivating effect on the people in the United States and Brazil.'

The same was true of the people in the wholesale division, which was no longer leading. 'The asset management and corporate business divisions must be prepared for the focus on Europe. The domestic division remains the real core of the bank. No Detours will ensure that the Dutch business unit becomes a showcase.'

In the short term, according to this analysis, non-core activities would be shed, such as the interests in Bouwfonds, Banca di Roma, Bank of Asia, the Hungarian bank and banks in Taiwan and Greece. 'These disinvestments are consistent with the results of the managing-for-value process.'

The document emphasised again that 'a rigorous implementation of managing for value in all our day-to-day activities is essential to success in achieving our ambitions. In the short term, we must show results to our shareholders, the share price must rise. The investment community has a short horizon. A strategic vision will only be appreciated if results are delivered in the short term.' There was another warning, 'Our independence from mergers or takeovers in playing out our strategic endgame makes us vulnerable. Our credibility will be at issue if we do not find and carry out a big merger.'

Groenink realised that this was his assignment. ABN Amro was a leading bank because it had resulted from the largest merger in the country. He must now ensure that the bank would lead the consolidation process on the European continent. He was talking to a number of different parties. The starting point was that list of fifteen banks, neatly ranked in order of market value. Groenink aimed at HypoVereinsbank, SocGen, Unicredito, Intesa BCI, Abbey National, San Paolo IMI and Nordea. These were banks whose size would mean that ABN Amro remained the dominant party in any merger of equals.

The chairman began at the bottom of the list. The Swedish-Finnish-Danish bank Nordea had a market value of 20 billion euros, and was therefore a third smaller than ABN Amro. His first appointment with the Danish CEO, Thorleif Krarup, was promising. The business case looked good. The Finns also believed in a combination. But the Swedish government said it didn't see anything in it, mainly because the unions were afraid that it would be followed by high job losses. The deal didn't happen.

Groenink's road trip through Europe brought him for the second time in a few years to Société Générale in Paris. In this case too, the new organisation that would result from a combination was worked out, and the business plan looked good. But the French decided not to go ahead. They were worried that their arch-enemy, BNP, would make a knock-out offer as soon as the deal with ABN Amro was announced.

Nothing stays secret for long in the banking world. In London, investment bankers were making jokes about ABN Amro. Why was Groenink searching so desperately for a bank to take over? Jiskoot was annoyed. He thought that Groenink had not handled things well. The chairman always went to the crucial first meeting alone. Jiskoot didn't understand this. Lesson one in the world of mergers and takeovers was: principals never talk to each other alone. If things don't click, it means that nothing moves any further. It was much better to allow two subordinates to do the negotiating, because they could say that they were in agreement, but that they still needed to get their boss's okay. That allowed some room for discussion.

Jiskoot also didn't understand why Groenink didn't ask him to attend the meetings. He was, after all, the bank's expert. But when he asked the chairman about this, Groenink answered: I'm the boss, this is my responsibility, I'll do it.

But the head of the corporate business division didn't have much time to talk to Groenink anyway. One year after they had bought Furman Selz in New York, its results were so bad that they would have to close the equity section. The targets that had been formulated in October had not been achieved, not by a long shot: in fact, the business had made a loss of nearly 100 million dollars. The bank was simply not up to the aggression of its American competitors. Jiskoot's flywheel in New York had not started turning. The manager responsible, Nick Bannister, was fired. To be able to fire a total of 550 people, the bank made a provision of 205 million euros. All told, the New York adventure cost more than half a billion dollars.

Jiskoot put things in perspective and tried to explain that there was still enough value in New York. He didn't agree with the decision and thought that ABN Amro should simply soldier. But in the banking world, the Furman Selz fiasco was often cited as yet further evidence that the corporate business division was only good at wasting money.

Marakon consultant Spruit was happy. This was the first clear decision he had seen Rijkman Groenink make. He had regularly complained that it wasn't easy to get Jiskoot to agree to targets for his performance. Jiskoot tended to play his cards close to his chest.

But the results of the corporate business division were disappointing again that year, and it became clear that there were problems with the division. Joost Kuiper repeatedly expressed his concern. Kuiper's criticisms, as well as those of Collee and De Swaan, began to gain ground on the managing board. It was inevitable: the representation of the corporate business division on the managing board had been halved.

After the departure of Van Tets, Sergio Lires Rial had also decided to tender his resignation. It was the Bear Stearns courtship that led to his departure. The Brazilian was beginning to believe that the Dutch bank would never realise its ambition to be a global player in the corporate sector. It was reported that Lires Rial was rewarded with a package of 25 million dollars by Bear Stearns. Groenink thought it a pity that a foreigner was leaving, and regarded it as a sort of treason. He had brought Lires Rial onto the board only two years before, and he had not finished the task he had been given.

Most of the rest of the board were relieved. They thought that the 41-year-old Lires Rial was a hard, arrogant man who sometimes gave others the impression that he felt that he was the only one among them who could take the bank to a higher level. He was brilliant, but troublesome, able to focus on details and occasionally capable of being extremely direct.

The two remaining managing directors from the corporate business division, Hugh Scott Barrett and Wilco Jiskoot, fought like lions for their division. Again and again, they responded to the growing criticism by saying that the pure investment bank was doing well, but its results were being contaminated by other activities.

That explanations were necessary was clear from the dramatic quarterly figures. The corporate business division had had a difficult time. They were earning hardly any money (11 million euros), and the efficiency ratio had risen from 86 to more than 91 per cent. The profits had fallen fast, while the costs had risen further, partly as a result of the multi-year guaranteed bonuses that still had to be paid.

The rest of the bank had also had a difficult time. The economic climate remained problematic. The quarterly profit had fallen by 47 per cent. The decision to make C&CC the leading division was supported by the numbers, because retail was good for 72 per cent of the company result.

Within the SBU, Floris Deckers was reasonably content with the first result after the introduction of No Detours. In total, 6,673 people had registered to leave. That was immediately visible in the figures. The costs of the office network decreased by 7.5 per cent over the first three months of 2002. The efficiency ratio started falling at last, by a couple of per cent, to 81.5 per cent, but that was still high in comparison to the competitors.

For Rijkman Groenink there was a sting in the tail. In an interview with journalists from *Het Financieele Dagblad*, he said, "Now it's clear who's leaving and who's staying, we're seeing an atmosphere emerging in the spirit of We, the stayers, are loyal and They, the leavers, are profiteers." According to Groenink, the employees who had stayed at the bank were more motivated to make the bank a success. And that was nice to see.

There were shocked reactions from within the bank. The chairman was saying that people whom the bank had asked to leave were profiteers. The supervisory board was also angry. Why was the chairman so clumsy, and so often, in his communications? They invited Groenink in for a disciplinary meeting. Aarnout Loudon, Antony Burgmans and Trude Maas (all three of them members of the selection and remuneration committee of the supervisory board) explained to Groenink that this sort of thing was not acceptable and warned him not to allow it to happen again. The warning was confirmed in a letter. Groenink offered his apologies. He hadn't meant it that way.

10

Weakness

May 2002–May 2003

The ABN Amro top brass flew to southern Morocco in two Falcon jets. They were to spend the next four days travelling together. The programme was secret. All the almost thirty men and one woman knew was that they were being sent into the desert to learn how to find each other.

Building bridges, that was the theme. The bank's leadership was to become a close-knit team. After two years of managing for value and peer group thinking, the bank's managing directors were primarily involved with themselves and their own results. The three strategic business units had turned into little empires, as a result of which a great deal of money and energy had been lost. The bank's leadership realised that Marakon's story was primarily analytical and harsh. A listening leadership now had to make the message softer, more human and more empathetic.

Empathy was thin on the ground at the bank. Over the last few months, its top two hundred had looked into the mirror and been told what their personal leadership profile looked like. For this 360 degree analysis – which was carried out by the Hay Group's consultants – the colleagues above, alongside and below the banker in question filled in questionnaires and attended interviews. Each top manager was then evaluated on the basis of five or six of these assessments.

The vast majority were labelled with the same profile. They were pace-setting: leaders who tell their subordinates how they should do things and then begin to march. Assuming that the troops will follow, they never look back. Pace-setting leaders explain but rarely communicate. They are often described by the outside world as being arrogant, and their actions are based on the assumption that they are always right. They have relatively little respect for other people's opinions. This raised a laugh, even among the bankers themselves. They were well aware that lacking empathy was now no longer acceptable, and certainly not at a service provider with so many highly educated people. So this was something that they really had to work on.

Rijkman Groenink was also given feedback. However, in his case, it hadn't been the full 360 degrees because Loudon had not been interviewed. Groenink felt that this was logical: Loudon was not his boss. He didn't have a boss. But the remaining 270 degrees had been sufficient to establish that Rijkman Groenink was also extremely low on empathy, a fact that the board chairman already knew. Groenink also believed that a different tone at the top was needed. Only when a team had been established there, would the cooperation among the lower levels improve. He hoped that this trip would help.

The bank's leaders had been inspired to make this journey by one of their governors: Unilever chairman Antony Burgmans, who had taken his company's top one hundred into the jungles of Costa Rica. Burgmans had explained the benefits of top managers, who lived in five-star hotels and chauffeur-driven cars, spending some time together in an awkward situation. He described how they became people again, once they had sat together around a campfire in a strange environment and told each other personal stories. Although he didn't find it easy, Burgmans had discovered that professional detachment and internal competition soon made way for real human contact. The resulting trust was a condition for effective cooperation.

The supervisory board, with the recent addition of the American Arthur Martinez, was delighted with this initiative. The body language of the managing board had been more than obvious of late: this all-male club was plagued by conflict. Although the departure of Dolf van den Brink, Jan Maarten de Jong and Rijnhard van Tets may have made the meetings more orderly, it was as if the conflicts had become more deeply entrenched. Dolf Collee and Hugh Scott Barrett were almost constantly fighting about where which expenses should be defrayed. In addition, there was the continuing battle between Jiskoot and Kuiper about the position of the corporate division in the United States.

Shots were frequently fired at the chairman for not solving these conflicts. When Groenink was tackled about this, he would simply repeat his belief that quarrels were healthy, that they brought out the best in people. In short: may the best man win. Colleagues in the managing board and at the level below felt that Groenink was mainly concerned with his own position. His refusal to opt decisively for one side or the other and his strategy of divide and rule meant that he encountered relatively little opposition and that plenty of energy was being squandered in personal discussions and feuds.

Several managing directors were also critical of their board chairman. Where was he? He seemed isolated. Groenink had always been extremely detached but, with his appointment as chairman, he operated increasingly as an elusive lone wolf, as a loner. Clearly he had wanted to be the boss. However, once he became boss, Groenink sometimes didn't seem to feel like being one at all. He hardly travelled and rarely visited the troops to spread his message. Nobody dared to say it, but they felt that their boss preferred staying at home. With his young family. With his wife and his two little sons aged four and two.

Yet what they found far more worrying was Groenink's unclear message. Did the board chairman have any idea of the direction the bank needed to take? The rapid zigzagging of the previous two years had damaged his authority. Was Groenink really the strategist he claimed to be? Apparently even he had his doubts. His attitude was becoming increasingly vague. They noticed this in meetings. Generally the chairman seemed to wait to see how the game developed. How the group reacted. Who assumed which position. But what was his own position? His colleagues were desperate for clarity. Sometimes they wanted to cry out "Take a stand! Tell us what you represent! You're the leader!" Groenink's standard reactions of "That's the way it is", "It'll be all right" and "Trust me" worked while his colleagues still felt safe with him. But this was no longer the case.

The two planes landed just before midday at Ouarzazate airport in southern Morocco. The bankers could stay in their comfort zone for a little longer at the five-star Le Berbere Palace. The afternoon was for relaxation.

The first evening would be devoted to a constructive discussion of the bank's strategy. Groenink had asked Jan Peter Schmittmann to talk about the impossibility of setting up a European investment bank. Three years previously, Schmittmann had been the main author of the bank's European strategy. The piece that had ended up in the rubbish bin at the end of 1999 when Groenink became chairman. And also the piece that explained that investment bankers mainly needed to provide support and to serve the country managers.

Schmittmann knew why Groenink had asked him for this lecture. A new dream was unfolding at the corporate division. Following the previous year's turn of events, the departure of Van Tets and the partial cessation of activities in New York, ABN Amro was to become a major European investment bank.

Schmittmann didn't believe in this. He explained to his audience that there was only one playing field in the world of investment banks and it was global. But ABN Amro was not a part of that game: if we had wanted that, we would have had to take over a major concern, like the Swiss or the Germans.

Groenink realised that he was back with his plans of three years ago. The difference was that they were no longer easy to implement. There was now a powerful wholesale division. This was what he would have to deal with first. The genie would have to go back into the bottle. He was cautious; the strategic choices were being discussed in a general sense. Groenink did most of the talking. But the atmosphere was good. The evening ended with no firm conclusions. A Bedouin leader presented Groenink with a leadership stick. He swore to Groenink that as long as he kept the stick with him, he would be the boss.

The next morning, eight jeeps were at the ready. The bankers were to set off for their camp and their campfire in the desert. Each jeep was assigned four people representing various parts of the bank. Everyone wanted to be behind the wheel. The members of the managing board took precedence. Apart from Joost Kuiper, who allowed the group's only woman, Alexandra Cook, to drive. Jokes were made about Groenink's sabbatical four years ago when he had had plenty of opportunity to practise.

The plan was that the jeeps would drive the distance to the desert in a neat line, one after another. In a convoy. This completely failed to materialise. There was much excitement. Pedal to the metal. It turned into a competition. The bankers raced along the road, overtaking each other and blocking each other's way. They were having a great time. The first dents were felt on all sides.

The final stop before the desert was at a hotel with a swimming pool. Someone threw a ball into the water and the men soon saw each other for the first time in swimming trunks. It was initially a little uncomfortable, but once there were points to be scored in a game of water polo, they were soon crowing with pleasure. Rijkman Groenink observed the proceedings from the terrace.

They were then to enter the desert for first time, in search of the camp where they would spend the night. It was a drive of some 200 kilometres; the instructions were precise and strict. A GPS receiver showed the points where they would meet. They would wait there for each other.

Groenink's jeep failed to turn up at the last but one meeting point. People were jokey at first, but after half an hour they began to get anxious. It was becoming cold and dark. Mobile phones didn't work here. The organisation was nervous: Groenink and his team hadn't got lost, had they? After an hour, they decided to continue driving carefully, in wide bends, in the hope of encountering a stray board chairman along the way.

Once the group arrived at the camp, it turned out that all their worries had been in vain. Groenink was sitting there having a beer, and laughed as he wondered what had kept them and why they had been so slow. His colleagues realised that for him, everything was a competition. A competition that he intended to win.

That evening around the campfire, Groenink held forth passionately about their bank. The main message was that it would not be easy, that we could only save it if we worked together. We had to work together. Groenink was never really personal but no one had expected him to be. He became slightly emotional and waved his wooden sword ... For a little while, those present were once again aware that this was their leader.

Becoming a person, appreciating each other as people and creating a bond: that was the plan. That was why they were sleeping four to a tent, why there was just one shower tent, and why defecation was to occur in a hole in the ground. For the rest everything was perfectly organised. There was enough drink to ensure that any embarrassment could be quickly swept aside. The rosé was particularly popular. So much was consumed that halfway through the stay in the desert, the organisers had to make a round trip to replenish the supply.

The next morning Fabio Barbosa, the boss of Brazil, stood on a dune and asked for permission to speak. Barbosa was popular in Amsterdam and had repeatedly declared his love for ABN Amro. He liked the fact that, despite the SBU structure, he had been given plenty of space to work more or less independently. Yet he still missed the contact with the rest of the bank, and he would have preferred a higher level of interaction with his colleagues.

The Brazilian's speech was inspiring. He talked about the importance of the human aspects along with all that calculating through managing for value. Barbosa wondered about the bank's position. Of course, no one's going to find inspiration under the shower along the lines of "and now I'm going to create some shareholder value ..." But what then should it be? Does the bank have a clear objective in mind? An objective that people care about. In a solemn tone, Barbosa concluded that it should be the interests of the client. Understanding them and serving them to their best advantage, that should be the common objective. If the client is satisfied, the shareholder value will follow of its own accord.

The rest of the day was devoted to games. A rally was held in the afternoon. Floris Deckers' jeep got stuck in the sand. Alexandra Cook, who was sitting next to him and had been given training the previous day by one of the guides, wanted to explain to him how to get free. She was shocked by his humorously-intended reaction, "I'm not going to have myself helped out by a woman, by someone who's ten years my junior, and certainly not by someone from wholesale." Cook was made well aware of the yawning gap between the SBUs.

Hugh Scott Barrett's jeep also got stuck. The British banker stood on the top of his car in order to attract attention. The Deckers and Cook crew decided to help him out. Scott Barrett matter-of-factly described how Rijkman Groenink had driven past at high speed when he saw him standing there. Wilco Jiskoot's team experienced the same thing. Jiskoot was having problems with his GPS receiver and had asked for help. Rijkman Groenink had sped past without stopping. However, fifty metres short of the camp, the chairman had also ended up stuck in the loose desert sand.

Joost Kuiper was furious when he heard that, on two occasions, Groenink had refused to stop to help his colleagues. Kuiper was a yachtsman, and you never abandon anyone in an emergency, no matter how much you want to win. You just don't do that; you don't leave someone behind. His colleagues realised that the loyal Kuiper effectively represented the chairman's conscience. Groenink giggled and reacted awkwardly to Kuiper's fury: it's just a game. But Kuiper refused to back down: the desert can be even more treacherous than the sea.

The final evening was a colourful circus. The group was divided into three; they had to prepare short plays. There was a dressing-up box, a lot of laughter and plenty of drink. Rijkman Groenink played the ring girl. Dolled up in a dress and a wig, the chairman announced the various performances. The atmosphere was good.

The next morning, two helicopters were waiting to fly the ABN Amro leaders back home. Apart from Hugh Scott Barrett, the entire managing board was sitting in one of them. A passenger made a joke: if we crash and the bank ends up being led by Scott Barrett, will the share price go up or down? This was greeted with much merriment and the remark that the prices could in fact go up.

At the Dutch customs it transpired that Rijkman Groenink had forgotten his passport. After he had somewhat impatiently made it clear that he was the boss of *the* bank, ABN Amro, he spent the next hour or so stuck at the airport.

Following their four-day caper, the participants felt relieved. They had played and talked with each other, and they had once again discovered where they stood. A great deal still needed to be clarified in terms of strategy. But Rijkman Groenink had turned out to be remarkably receptive to criticism. The earth had been ploughed. Now was the time to sow the seeds.

Jiskoot and Kuiper spent the next year quarrelling about who was to be responsible for what. While Groenink failed to come to a clear decision, these two tough guys were given plenty of scope for their personal interpretations. Whereas Jiskoot tried to gain greater authority, Kuiper defended the interests of Harry Tempest, the United States boss. Following Sergio Lires Rial's departure, Hugh Scott Barrett was put in charge of the corporate activities in the United States.

Meanwhile, the Fed continued to ask questions about the Russian and Cypriot clients. The supervisor was still not convinced by the answers. As a result, these questions were becoming more incisive. Since the attacks in New York and the growing fear of terrorism, pressure was being exerted to keep a careful eye on whether money entering the United States was being used for illegal purposes. Indeed, those behind the Al-Qaeda attacks had had enough funding in the United States to be able to pay for expensive flying courses. Along with the offices of several other foreign banks, in New York ABN Amro found itself increasingly in the American supervisors' firing line.

Most of the Fed's angry letters were still being addressed to Harry Tempest. But he had virtually turned his back on the activities in New York. These letters either stated that 'this can be solved in the course of ordinary business', or that 'this cannot be solved in the course of ordinary business'. In the latter case, the Fed wanted the bank to undertake the large-scale sealing of loopholes. ABN Amro received a letter from this category, but those in Amsterdam had failed to recognise the far-reaching implications of the little word 'not'.

Moreover, it now seemed that a report by the internal auditing service had been circulating for some time; it expressed the usual doubts about the extent to which the people in New York were familiar with their clients. For obscure reasons, this report was not sent on time to Amsterdam.

The Fed's assessments established that the bank had still not proved that it had fulfilled the regulations of the Bank Secrecy Act, which describes in detail the measures banks must take to counter the laundering of illegal funds. The American supervisor concluded that ABN Amro didn't have sufficient documentation concerning the clients for whom money was being channelled into the country.

According to the supervisor, ABN Amro had no documentation whatsoever for 50 per cent of the corresponding accounts. Up till February 2002, the bank's sole action involved a single employee, who occasionally went through the transactions by hand. This was despite the fact that this task actually required a computerised system.

Although the Americans were making increasing demands that the banks improve their compliance, at ABN Amro's Dutch head office this was generally interpreted as meaning the auditing of share transactions as implemented by colleagues. Here, lawyers checked whether staff members had acted properly and had filled in all the forms.

Moreover, along with many other central sections, this department – which was led by general manager Jaap Kamp – had been drastically reduced as a result of Arrow. Every strategic business unit had been assigned its own staff. The head office's compliance department still had three staff members and a secretary. Kamp reported to De Swaan but he was not even aware that there were Russian accounts in New York. Furthermore, there was a rule that if something happened in New York, the colleagues from the corporate division would be the ones to deal with it.

Those at head office had finally realised that something had to be done. In August, the entire activity in New York, including audit and control, was transferred to the corporate division. Tempest was not amused. This was re-ferred to internally as the divorce.

Hugh Scott Barrett was given the task of mopping things up. The British banker was shocked by the harsh tone of the Fed's letters. He also realised that the problems were deeply rooted, that they could be traced back to the 1990s and the way in which the organisation had been mismanaged for all those years. Scott Barrett set up a large team: there was a great deal of work to be done.

In the United States, the bankruptcies of such major companies as Enron in the summer of 2002 resulted in strict, new regulations. The Sarbanes-Oxley Act was rushed through Congress. To restore investor confidence, the Bush administration demanded that published figures now had to be signed by the top management of not only American companies but also all foreign compa-nies listed on United States stock markets. If anything were wrong, the com-pany would be made personally liable. Fraud could lead to a twenty-five-year prison sentence.

At the presentation of the half-year figures, Rijkman Groenink announced that he and Tom de Swaan would be signing the third quarter figures. This meant that ABN Amro would be the first Dutch company to be listed in the United States. Peter Diekman, head of the bank's internal auditing service, was shocked when he heard this. In his diary column for *Het Financieele Dag-blad*, the accountant wrote that this was more than simply a signature, that it could even lead to criminal prosecution. He wondered whether his chairman actually realised that.

For some time, Diekman had been a member of a working group that was to ensure that the bank dealt adequately with this new American request. He discussed the situation with Gerhard Zeilmaker, who was responsible for the consolidation of the group figures. They discussed how they could give Groenink and De Swaan the confidence to add their signatures without qualms. Zeilmaker came up with the solution: all 350 managers of the busi-ness units would be sent a questionnaire concerning the reliability of their fig-ures. They would have to fill this in, sign it and send it to Amsterdam. The members of the managing board would then endorse this sum. Finally, Groenink and De Swaan would sign the whole thing.

That autumn, to understand how Sarbanes-Oxley would affect the bank, Jaap Kamp invited the new governor Arthur Martinez to a dinner with the general managers. At that meeting, Martinez mainly emphasised the importance of a strong supervisory board. He described how a third of non-executives at American companies simply made themselves useful and regarded their position as an honorary job. In his view, another third were far too busy working as CEOS and managing directors at other companies. Only the remaining third had the time, the desire and the qualifications to make the necessary effort. Martinez considered this to be far too low.

As he explained to his audience: we have now learned that things must change, that the quality of supervision is not up to the mark. Martinez was astonishingly honest about the calibre of the supervisory board to which he had just been appointed: It's not good enough. He felt that the governors were far too passive. In his view, the task of a supervisory board was to support and challenge. He had seen far too little of the latter. Nonetheless, the new governor was confident of the bank's direction. Martinez was also enthusiastic about its most important consultant: Marakon. In November 2002, he was to become a member of Marakon's advisory council.

Martinez was enjoying this mainly European adventure. To his absolute amazement, he was phoned at the end of 2001 by the headhunter Heidrick & Struggles and asked whether he would like to be a governor at ABN Amro. The American governor Silas Keehn had just turned seventy and was due to step down. Martinez wanted to broaden his horizons and felt that there was plenty to be learned in Europe. He had already been the Fed's chairman in Chicago.

Following a friendly meeting with Groenink in New York, Martinez phoned Silas Keehn and asked him about the functioning of a two-tier board. Keehn explained that, as a governor in this system, you keep your distance and you won't make that many decisions. Martinez wondered whether there was anything he had to watch out for at ABN Amro. Keehn felt that there was nothing he needed to be warned about. Martinez hoped that the Dutch were not under the illusion that he was a banker: the Fed chairmanship in Chicago could have caused confusion. In fact, he was first and foremost a businessman and a former top manager at Sears, Roebuck & Co.

Loudon was also enthusiastic, and Martinez took office in May. He was astonished and intrigued by what he encountered. As the youngest governor, he was given a place at the end of the table. It was much more formal than he had expected. Hardly any questions were asked. He immediately noticed that Van der Hoeven, Burgmans and De Rothschild were top-quality people. In addition, he soon realised that the governors didn't participate in the bank's decision-making process. He also discovered that Aarnout Loudon (the chairman of both the supervisory board and, for many years, the audit committee) actually agreed with everything in advance. All the other governors needed to do was to concur. The supervisory board acted as a giant rubber stamp that in principle approved everything.

The markets were bad; all the banks experienced difficulties in 2002. Over the first six months, ABN Amro's returns fell by more than 16 per cent. Fiduciary loans to companies that had gone bankrupt through mismanagement and fraud (such as Enron and Worldcom) cost the bank at least one hundred million dollars. Hence, it was going to have to set aside approximately 1.6 billion euros for serious financial setbacks.

In the media, Groenink expressed his annoyance at the way in which these companies had been led. Yet he also predicted that this malaise had reached a watershed. Because he didn't announce the expected profit warning, analysts were moderately optimistic for the first time in ages. They finally expected to see the results of the expenditure savings. During 2001, the efficiency ratio had again risen to a record high of 73 per cent. This would have to come down. In any case, the savings in the domestic division would exceed the reorganisation costs. The closure of offices in eleven countries had also saved money. At last, ABN Amro was once again the pacesetter on the stock market: its share price rose by 11.5 per cent to 16 euros.

Groenink announced that the bank intended to continue building in Italy. There could well be potential in the bank's interests in Antonveneta and Capitalia, previously known as Banca di Roma. ABN Amro's share in Antonveneta had increased from 7.6 to 10 per cent. Groenink was optimistic, "The Italian Central Bank will probably allow us to acquire a larger share."

The corporate division had been through several major setbacks but seemed resigned to its new role as second fiddle. The closure of Furman Selz in New York, which had been purchased just a year before, was particularly painful. In the previous quarter alone, 1,237 expensive employees had been fired. Of the 850 merger and takeover specialists, almost three hundred were back on the streets. 1,350 of the 2,700 equity market and investment research jobs had been scrapped.

The corporate division had made a loss of 108 million euros against a profit of 182 million euros the previous year. Groenink complained, "We don't earn much from the really big multinationals." The low revenues on credit loans were not counterbalanced by the high fees requested during mergers and takeovers. This was because the major transactions, the elephant deals, simply didn't materialise. Jiskoot and Scott Barrett admitted responsibility in an interview with *Het Financieele Dagblad*. "Two things are important if you provide credit: you must make the right demands so that you get your money back, and you must insist on a good interest rate. We're generally extremely good at the first, but then we give the money away for practically nothing. That has to change."

All this sounded extremely promising. Although the bank wouldn't reach the peer group's exulted top five, there was a growing belief that it might make it to the tenth, ninth or eighth place. In that case, the bonus scheme meant that the managing directors could receive 10, 20 or 40 per cent of the conditionally allocated shares.

They felt that this was not enough. On behalf of the managing board, Groenink expressed his displeasure to Aarnout Loudon. It was the only occasion on which the other members of the supervisory board's rewards committee had seen Loudon angry. He was horrified to hear Groenink complain about his reward and what he would not be able to do with it. Yet the board chairman won the day. The percentages were adjusted on 16 August 2002. If the bank were to reach the tenth place, 25 per cent of the shares could be cashed, the ninth place would produce 40 per cent and the eighth 55 per cent.

In a letter to Groenink, the governors wrote, 'The performance share plan aims at providing a superior reward as befits a superior achievement.' Because the managing board was still facing the task of steering the bank's radical transformation in the right direction, this year they once again received 70,000 shares. Groenink was given an additional 98,000. 'We trust that we have satisfied your expectations in respect to the making of these adjustments. Yours sincerely, A.A. Loudon.'

At the end of 2002, a long-awaited meeting was finally to be held at the bank's head office. Here, managing for value was to be linked to the reinterpretation of human resources. General manager Garmt Louw had been working on this for six months, and would present his findings.

His fellow managing directors were shocked at the insubstantial story that this former Shell man served up on old-fashioned plastic sheets. Was this what they had been waiting eighteen months for? It was a technical story that frequently stated the obvious. But above all, this presentation revealed Louw's profound lack of affinity with ABN Amro. They wondered how long he would last.

In November, Groenink was proved right. The summer of 2002 was indeed a watershed and there were no new scandals. Because expenditure savings could be deposited and the rainy day fund no longer needed to be so full, the bank's profits rose over the third quarter by 25 per cent. It also did relatively well over the next few months. Even the investors seemed to appreciate this. On the stock market, the bank proved more successful than the banking sector as a whole. In the course of 2002, European banks lost on average 30 per cent of their quoted value while ABN Amro lost only 14 per cent. The bank rose to the twelfth place in the peer group.

This new confidence encouraged Groenink to contact ING. Could this possibly be the moment to merge? The ING board chairman, Ewald Kist, rather liked the idea. Groenink then approached Wietze Reehoorn who, two years previously, had been one of the most important messengers of the Marakon story, and was now head of the corporate development department. He was asked to prepare the merger, which he did in cooperation with his counterpart at ING, Hans van der Noordaa. The two bankers had to disappoint their families: Christmas would be a washout.

In January six men met at Rijkman Groenink's home. Ewald Kist and his right-hand man Michel Tilmant discussed the possibilities with Rijkman Groenink and Joost Kuiper. Reehoorn and Van der Noordaa also explained their ideas. Kist and Groenink had already made agreements about their division of roles. The 58-year-old Kist was to be the first CEO of the new combination; Groenink would succeed him two or three years later. In addition, the Dutch Central Bank clearly liked this merger.

There were all kinds of questions. The most difficult point concerned the extent to which the new combination should take on the insurance market. It was also apparent that the merger would lead to many thousands of redundancies, particularly in the Netherlands. Van der Noordaa and Reehoorn believed that the way to convince any political opponents of the merger was to explain it in a European perspective. In other words: this was not a Dutch bank, it was truly European. The discussions went well. It was obvious that both Kist and Groenink were enthusiastic.

But the ING managing board still had its doubts. Tilmant, who was hoping to succeed Kist as chairman in the not too distant future, was worried. He discussed the current proposal with the bank's experienced CFO, Cees Maas. They were afraid that ABN Amro would be overly dominant. In addition, the bankers questioned the deal's structure. They feared that ING would be taken to the cleaners. Maas and Tilmant argued that ING should be playing the leading role and didn't believe that Kist was strong enough to safeguard its interests. They also thought that ING was doing better than ABN Amro at that point in time. ING director Alexander Rinnooy Kan agreed with them. Ewald Kist was eventually summoned by his board. The merger had been called off. For the time being, the involvement of this comprehensive financial service provider was to be limited to an interest of 15 per cent of the shares.

During his New Year's speech of 2003, Groenink couldn't resist returning to his joke of several years previously. "It's been written that I won't survive until Christmas 2001. Well, I'm still here, and next year I will also be here." He was clearly enjoying himself now that the bank's criticism had abated and the share price was going up. He challenged the press and asked them to answer four questions in their analyses, "Will ABN Amro still be independent in a year's time? Will Groenink still be sitting in his chair? Will the 2003 results be an improvement on 2002? And will the bank reach the seventh or an even higher position in the peer group?"

A month later, the bank announced that strong cost containment and the good results of the United States mortgage companies had resulted in profits rising by 2.1 per cent to 2.4 billion euros in 2002. The bank's efficiency ratio had improved by three per cent to 70.1 per cent. This result was entirely due to the retail bank. The corporate division saw the 200 million euro profits of 2001 become a loss of three million euros. Groenink let it be known that he was proud of this result. "The fact that the net profit has risen, is more than most other banks can claim under such difficult circumstances. The bank has been transformed. We now have a customer-oriented, transparent organisation with – at least at the present rates – an attractive dividend."

Groenink fantasised with analysts about mergers and takeovers in Europe. Takeovers were extremely expensive. He argued that the alternative was to merge with an equal party so as to increase their size. But how would the interests be divided? Where would the head office be? And who would be chairman?

Clearly Groenink had no worries about being taken over. He announced that next year the bank would be looking into ways of abolishing protection structures. Groenink also proposed opting for organic growth with new offices in the United States and Brazil, where various brands were to be supported by the green-and-yellow ABN Amro shield.

At the end of February 2003, the bank played a leading role in salvaging Ahold. The supermarket concern was in extreme difficulties. This was because US Foodservice, its American subsidiary, had exaggerated its profits by many hundreds of millions of dollars through supplier credit that had never been received. And could never be received. ABN Amro, Goldman Sachs and JP Morgan tried to agree on extended credit, but the Americans had no desire to burden their balance sheets with credit running into billions. Their proposal was to let Ahold go bankrupt and to sell it off in parts.

The Dutch bankers blamed their colleagues for having no sense of history, that Ahold was an item of cultural heritage. They pointed out that for years the banks had earned plenty of money from this client who, in less than ten years, had conducted takeovers amounting to 19 billion euros. Together with his boss Wilco Jiskoot, the bank's team leader Rob Meuter had developed a back-up scenario: a Dutch solution. In the greatest secrecy, they phoned Hans ten Cate of Rabobank and Jan Zegering Hadders, a board member of ING Nederland. Both of them were former Amro bankers, and they were prepared to be involved. Groenink spent some time alone with Jiskoot during the ABN Amro tennis tournament. They discussed the figures, and briefly spoke with Tom de Swaan. "Do what you like," was the message. By mobilising their network, the ABN Amro bankers prevented the collapse of Ahold. Once it was obvious that extended credit could be found without their involvement, the Americans made the best of a bad job and came on board.

The Cor Boonstra debacle meant that the bank had lost another governor. Cees van der Hoeven also announced his resignation when his company's problems got out of hand in December 2002. Groenink made it known that ABN Amro was looking for bankers who would emphasise its international character.

The bank heaved a sigh of relief. The first three years under Groenink had not been easy. The strategy alterations, the focus on creating shareholder value in combination with the doubling of economic profits for internal achievements: all this required a fundamental change in the ABN Amro culture.

The bank was still extremely hierarchical. Whenever an ABN Amro banker was asked what they did, the answer consisted of the name of the job in question. This was quickly followed by how important the work was, and that naturally the employee was listed for promotion so they could become even more important. An individual's success was determined by their relative position vis-à-vis other colleagues at the bank. A general manager was better than a department manager. So every department manager wanted just one thing: to become a general manager.

Not much had changed regarding the bank's introspective attitude since Dick Meys' departure seven years ago. There was still a strong tendency towards self-absorption and little by way of transparency and accountability.

Some of the bank's consultants had noticed a void in the leadership. Those who made it to the top two hundred seemed to be overcome by a certain lethargy. At that level, and often with the help of countless consultants, all kinds of measures were being devised for the rest of the bank. But, as a leader, you needed to provide a good example if you expected other people to be cost conscious.

British consultant Tom Cummings had been working at ABN Amro since 1996. In 2000, he was asked by Groenink to become managing director of the leadership programme. Cummings was to ensure that that the bank had future leaders in its ranks; now was the time to cut across the twin groups of ABN and Amro, and construct a real ABN Amro leadership culture. An eye was still being kept on each important appointment to see whether the two groups remained in balance.

226

Tom Cummings was one of Groenink's confidants. He regularly attended the managing board's offsite meetings, where he was free to share his opinions. Cummings developed the programme for the leadership trip to Morocco. As a foreigner, he observed ABN Amro's headstrong and extremely Dutch top brass with astonishment. He expressed his concerns to a number of colleagues. Was the leadership of this bank prepared to face the brutal facts?

Cummings was worried. He observed the board's growing hostility and resulting paralysis. So he asked Erik van de Loo to try to do something about this. Van de Loo was not only an adjunct-professor at Insead, he was also the joint founder of Phyleon in The Hague. 'Our inner motivation is the source of confidence in the world around us' was the motto of this consultancy that specialised in 'the development of leadership, the individual and organisations'. Phyleon coaches had been involved with ABN Amro since 1999. They charged 500 euros an hour and were – at least in terms of price – at the top end of the market.

Groenink asked Van de Loo to supervise the board's meetings so as to link the bank's strategic agenda with the behaviour agenda of the individual managing directors. In this way, he hoped to alleviate the tensions at the board and to increase effectiveness. Van de Loo was to make sure that members could be critical of each other without putting personal relations at risk.

There were major differences between the men that Van de Loo tried to work with. It was usually Collee and Kuiper who took part in his careful attempts to dig deep in search of the reasons why processes had become locked. The other members found it difficult; for them it was a load of softie hogwash.

But Groenink was impressed with the psychologist and also hired him as his personal coach. He liked the fact that Van de Loo had clinical experience, and real knowledge and expertise concerning the workings of the human psyche. Groenink believed that Van de Loo could help him to become more empathetic.

But that wasn't easy. To be able work effectively, Van de Loo believed that a good coach occasionally had to delve into the depths to get at the roots. Groenink rarely felt like doing this and was seldom open to real coaching. The chairman also had trouble with Van de Loo's message that a great leader dares to steer from his inner compass because you cannot use your intellect for everything. Groenink found this complicated. He was a man of rational action: his natural inclination was either to fight for something or to flee from something. In his experience there was nothing in between.

Van de Loo explained to Groenink that he needed much more space for buy-ins: moments when subordinates could enter his story. A leader creates buy-ins by showing his followers that he really listens to their side of the story. They will then know whether they are being taken seriously. The only problem here was that a large number of the people surrounding Groenink simply didn't dare to challenge his leadership.

In many of his coaching sessions, Van de Loo did little more than provide an example of a good listener. This was because good listening was precisely what pressurised bankers and managers rarely did. And that's what he explained to them. Van de Loo told them how to achieve fair process in their leadership role: First tell your staff what the problem is, then ask them how they feel about it and then make a clear decision. It sounds logical but many managers forget to listen.

Van de Loo believed that leaders who impose solutions on organisations on the basis of their own right, and are unable to listen to alternatives, are perceived by the other side as being insecure. A strong leader is well able to listen to alternatives and even adopt them. The coach described the path from authoritarianism to authority. He tried to make it clear to the bank's top managers that their personal insecurity meant that they were stuck in that pace-setting leadership style, that this insecurity meant that they didn't really dare to enter into discussion with colleagues reporting to them. The consequence of this was that they would not be taken seriously as leaders. If they wanted people to listen to them more attentively, they had to make themselves more vulnerable. And that began with actively seeking the opinions of others and adopting them.

The bank's top two hundred were invited to select a personal coach. Speed dates were organised where ABN Amro managing directors could meet various bank-approved coaches. The overwhelming majority of bankers participated, and a small army of approximately thirty coaches was soon on hand to teach the bank's leaders how to listen better. Armed with the notes of the Hay consultants' leadership profiles, they now knew which qualities they needed to develop. The same applied to most of them as to Groenink: the need to listen properly.

The coaches' job was to hold up a mirror. This revealed what the bankers' pace-setting leadership did to their subordinates. Under the motto of 'Only if you can lead yourself, can you lead others', they were to acquire a more complete image of themselves. Together with the coaches, they had to discover what the alternatives were for their actions.

Bankers with serious career ambitions were expected to master at least three of the five leadership styles that the bank deemed important: pace-setting (dominant, guiding), democratic (listening), authoritative (commanding), coaching (supporting) and affirmative (validating). They had to be able to switch between them with ease. The degree to which they succeeded in this, was central to the performance interviews. Each year, direct reports measured whether managers felt that their bosses put a number of these styles into practice.

Generally the coaches were wrestling with the same dilemma: how do you counsel arrogant, essentially insecure people? Bankers wanting to show that they know it all. The only point of having a coach is if the person involved is aware that things have got stuck. Then it's a matter of reducing the boundary between reason and the subconscious so that, step by step, they will increasingly dare to play it by ear.

To reinforce cooperation and team spirit, the more than 130 management teams reporting to the bank's top two hundred were invited to attend the velocity programme. Each workshop was led by the department manager in charge. The participants received a two-day training. Here, the objective was to accomplish something practical together. The training's central message was: you can't manage it all on your own. Listening to each other carefully and mutual respect were essential here.

For instance, each team was given materials to build a little windmill. But in order to do this well and within a certain timeframe, they first had to create an optimal division of tasks. To find out what this would be, they needed to listen to each other. Who is good at analysing? Who is good with their hands? Afterwards, the trainer came round with an electric fan so as to test whether the windmill rotated properly. That was the proof that a successful team had been built. The velocity programme swept through the entire bank and cost tens of millions.

While the lower echelons were breezing around with their windmills, the bank's higher levels were once again stricken by doubt. After Morocco they had felt like a team for a while. But little had come out of that sense of hope. The bickering continued between the investment bankers and the others. The market malaise, the relatively low share price and the lack of success abroad had resulted in the analysts becoming increasingly acerbic in their criticism. Where was this bank heading? ABN Amro was still hopping between two thoughts. And the chairman had not yet succeeded in uniting them.

Groenink hoped that he would be able to announce a good merger of equals within the foreseeable future. This would automatically impose discipline on the bank's persistent strategic and organisational issues. He was gambling on Fortis, and had already spoken several times with Maurice Lippens. The bank was now number four in the Dutch league table, a position that Lippens considered too weak. For him it was clear: something had to happen in the Netherlands.

But Lippens was also sceptical. He had heard plenty of stories about Rijkman Groenink, who had been knocking on various doors in Europe: in Scandinavia, in France, in Germany and in Italy. All these stories were the same.
The Dutchman was charming at first, but soon became rude and demanding.
With the Generale Bank affair at the back of his mind, Lippens was on his
guard. Together with his CEO, Anton van Rossum, he travelled to Amsterdam
for open disscussions with Groenink.

The atmosphere of these discussions was good. Lippens's criticism of what
he viewed as the stupid and costly corporate adventure was received with an
assenting nod. It was agreed that the ABN Amro board chairman would draw
up a written summary of these discussions.

However, there was much disappointment when the summary arrived in
Brussels. Van Rossum and Lippens didn't recognise what they were reading.
Groenink was suddenly making all sorts of demands for any possible merger.
He informed them that ABN Amro was a major concern whereas Fortis was an
amalgam of little banks. For that reason, the head office should be in Amsterdam. Moreover, Groenink felt that the merged bank should largely divest itself of insurance activities. He also made it clear that he was to be the CEO of
the new combination.

Lippens broke off the negotiations. He wondered whether Rijkman
Groenink really didn't realise that all those European players had walked out
on him. Didn't he understand that these processes were not about individuals? Lippens felt that Groenink was narcissistic and arrogant. That was a
shame, because ABN Amro was a fine bank with good people.

Groenink regularly went through the 2001 list of banks at the supervisory
board's meetings. New banks were added and others were dropped. The order
changed. Sometimes he alluded to the talks he was having.

Reading these short reports, governor Wim Dik increasingly felt that
Groenink only spoke with those candidates who presented him with the
prospect of an impressive position. He wondered out loud whether there were
other banks that were better suited to ABN Amro. This irritated Loudon, who
found this suspicion improper.

Antony Burgmans approached Dik after the meeting. He felt that Dik was
right and wondered whether, as governors, they should remain answerable
for this vague and drifting policy. Or whether it was time to resign? Dik had
never considered it like this but realised that he felt the same way. However,
this discontent had evaporated when the two men met at the next supervisory
board meeting some eight weeks later. Not a word was said on the subject.

The supervisory board was critical of an interview that Groenink had given
to NRC Handelsblad. In it, he called on Europe to provide more active opposi-

tion to the threatening American domination of the global economy. He feared that the United States, stricken by terrorist attacks, would endanger globalisation by aggressively imposing its legislation on the business world beyond its borders.

Groenink was critical of the Sarbanes-Oxley Act, and warned, "These measures were announced and implemented in a completely unilateral way. That bothers me. It may mean that we will have less control over investments in other countries. If the board of our companies in America is to be structured according to American standards for corporate governance and have American supervisors, this could result in us having no influence whatsoever, even though we own every single share." Groenink continued, "The Americans are now threatening to dominate the harmonising of American and European accounting regulations. We must ensure greater unity in Europe, and we must try to win over the Americans with different ideas."

Martinez was already aware that the chairman didn't like Americans, and perhaps he was right in his criticism of the Bush administration. But the governor warned Groenink: why did he always get caught up in discussions? Why did he always let himself be seduced into making outspoken remarks? He found it extremely stupid that Groenink had got carried away like this. And particularly when the bank was in the midst of complicated discussions with an increasingly critical American Fed.

The Fed upped the pressure that spring and informed ABN Amro that all transactions involving Eastern European parties would now be regarded as suspect.

Meanwhile Arthur Martinez had become one of the bank's most important governors. Loudon had asked him to head the supervisory board's audit committee, which monitored the bank's figures. Martinez, who was already a member of three other audit committees, was once again amazed at the extreme formality of these meetings. Peter Diekman didn't attend the first meeting. Martinez asked in astonishment why Diekman, the head of the internal accountancy department, was absent from discussions where he was so clearly needed. Tom de Swaan explained that he was on holiday. Martinez found this incredible: the meeting had been planned a year ago.

Martinez mentioned that he would like to discuss the bank's results with the external accountants Ernst & Young, but without the presence of the managing board. Financial director De Swaan told him that he found this strange: did Martinez think that he wasn't telling him everything?

Martinez was familiar with the bank's issues. He was convinced that the corporate division was the major problem. The American felt that this needed to be solved quickly or that the bank should find a way to get rid of it. Yet the governors and the managing board rarely discussed these kinds of issues. It didn't help that Groenink kept his fellow governors on a tight rein during the meetings with the supervisory board. As chairman, in principle he was the one who gave all the answers. Sometimes Groenink indicated in advance that a member of the managing board could expect to be questioned by him. He also asked him to avoid getting bogged down in detail. Groenink's colleagues were constantly aware that he maintained an exclusive dialogue with the supervisory board. If anyone commented on this, Groenink argued that his answers were at a level that the governors would find easy to digest.

Wilco Jiskoot found it extremely annoying that Groenink prevented him from having contact with the supervisory board. But he also blamed the governors themselves for rarely communicating individually with members of the managing board. This meant that they had no idea of what was going on there.

Another banker vital to ABN Amro's image was also disappointed. Floris Deckers had been told that there would be no place for him on the bank's managing board. For that reason, Deckers had accepted the invitation of the former ABN managing director Harry Langman. Langman was president of Van Lanschot, and was looking for a new board chairman.

Groenink was unhappy that yet another important banker had defected to a rival, a fact that he also made known to Deckers and Langman. He then asked Jan Peter Schmittmann to be the new head of the domestic division.

There was growing tension at the bank between the investment bankers and the rest. Their verbal domination was considerable at the meetings of the top two hundred, where English was the language of communication. Many of the Dutch felt that they were no match for the eloquent English of their mainly British colleagues.

On 21 May, former board member Dolf van den Brink described his perspective on the lack of understanding and growing chasm at the bank. He was being installed as a professor at the University of Amsterdam, and was presenting a speech on Bank Strategy and Bank Culture. The crowded auditorium included a number of former colleagues such as Rob Hazelhoff, Roelof Nelissen and Jan Kalff. Of the current board only Hugh Scott Barrett was present.

Van den Brink passionately described the details of the major cultural differences between traditional bankers and investment bankers. He was convinced that large universal banks, such as ABN Amro, had to ensure that these two subcultures remained subservient to the organisation as a whole. He explained to his audience that traditional bankers focus on a long-term relationship with the client; they're conservative and avoid risks; they're loyal to their employer and involved with the interests of the entire bank. By contrast, investment bankers actively seek risks; they consider the relationship with the client to be secondary to the deal, have limited loyalty to their employer and are less involved with the interests of the bank.

"This means that the character structure and personality of investment bank officials are entirely different to those in traditional banking." He warned of the opportunism of investment bankers, who regard cooperation with other bank departments as unproductive and a waste of time. He also pointed out "that, just as in top sport, investment bankers have become increasingly aware of their market value. This results in an almost obsessive awareness of remuneration."

Van den Brink observed that enormous bonuses cause great tension at universal banks because regular commercial bankers often "earn just a fraction of that". These tensions can only be solved if "convergence occurs in some way". The professor continued in a serious tone, "I'm quite positive that solving this issue is essential to the future of banking. Particularly in Europe the implications will be far-reaching. The failure of the universal bank concept will inevitably lead to a hegemony of American investment banks." He also acknowledged that unfortunately no universal bank had succeeded in uniting these two diverse activities in a positive way.

In the appendix to his published address he explored the case of ABN Amro, 'which is extremely familiar to me'. He carefully highlighted the risks affecting the bank: the initial separation of the three strategic divisions and the desire to achieve synergy between the three strategic business units through asset gathering. Van den Brink observed that the cultural problem described in his speech had become more evident because 'the necessary focus, which was chosen in 2000, has further reinforced the subcultures'.

Van den Brink felt that the solution was to devote more attention to the relatively soft subject of culture, with its lack of emphasis on numbers. 'Banks keep their options open and assume, for the sake of convenience, that the parts strengthen each other or at least don't hamper each other. One of the causes of this is the fact that, starting with the CEO, not enough time is invested in this issue. Culture is far more elusive than numbers. It requires a certain spirituality to be able to examine and comprehend particular elements. Spirituality is a quality that does not score highly in banking careers.'

Finally, Van den Brink called on the bank's leaders not only to recognise this problem but also to want to do something about it. 'And that means far more than simply organising a few workshops.' It was essential that the leaders served as an example for others. They really had to believe in synergy and to project it. This was because the necessary cooperation would encounter much resistance from the many people who would initially regard it as being relatively unproductive and a pointless distraction. The professor banker appealed to the members of the supervisory board to assume their responsibility. He bemoaned their focus on numerical supervision and felt that they should be given a People and Culture committee to tackle this issue.

Jan Kalff was the only ABN Amro governor to attend this event. Speaking to a journalist from *Het Financieele Dagblad*, he argued that the cultural differences at ABN Amro had been dealt with reasonably well. He felt that bidding a radical farewell to one part of the company was undesirable. Kalff insisted that the supervisory board was far more involved with so-called soft subjects than it used to be. "And naturally Van den Brink is not aware of everything we discuss there."

II

Paralysis

June 2003–September 2004

Together they formed the undisputed leadership of the bank: the one because he was board chairman, the other because he was the face of the bank, both in the business world and particularly in the Netherlands. Although they should have been developing ABN Amro together, over the past few years Wilco Jiskoot and Rijkman Groenink had become increasingly alienated. The two men no longer understood each other. They avoided each other and annoyed each other. There was little by way of dialogue and that meant that the board had become deadlocked.

Groenink was deeply disappointed in Jiskoot. In the 1980s he had briefly mentored him. Things had gone well; at least Jiskoot delivered. But that was long ago. Over the past few years, the corporate banker had repeatedly claimed to have a firm position and had made firm promises. But those promises were never kept.

Nonetheless, there were countless statements and calculations that apparently showed that the corporate division's central operation was scoring some serious successes. Groenink was sick of Jiskoot's opportunism: if things went well, it was all down to the corporate division; if they went badly, he refused to accept the blame.

Groenink was also irritated by what he viewed as Jiskoot's constant nagging about selling their American activities. At least money was being made in the United States. Moreover, Groenink felt that thinking smaller simply wasn't in the bank's DNA. This bank had to be big and to become even bigger. He also believed that it was unwise to make yourself unattractive as a bank by rejecting opportunities. In his discussions with potential merger partners, it turned out that they were clearly interested in the American subsidiary.

However, if you don't want to backtrack, you must make choices. He also understood that. But it's only possible to make the right choices if you have a superior performance. Then your share price will rise and you can at least make the choice yourself. Otherwise other people will do that for you. He also demanded this of Jiskoot: Make sure that you deliver a superior performance. But the corporate banker had still not succeeded in this. Groenink was particularly disappointed in Jiskoot's refusal to make more incisive choices. Jiskoot still wanted to be a state-of-the-art investment banker, who did everything for everyone. And that was something that ABN Amro could not permit.

Privately Groenink had told Jiskoot on a number of occasions that, in his opinion, he was not a good manager, that he was incapable of making choices. This also meant that the corporate division's costs were far too high. Apart from new promises, these discussions produced absolutely nothing. Groenink found it hard to believe that Jiskoot truly thought that he was a good manager.

For him, it was not an option to involve Jiskoot at an early stage of the merger and takeover talks. The bank's strategy was part of the chairman's portfolio. Jiskoot would first have to lead his own division effectively and produce some good results.

It was now more than two years ago that they had decided that the corporate activities should be supporting the retail division. Little had come of this. Jiskoot was still sticking to his own plans, appointing his own people and doling out the bonuses. The man was fighting like a lion for his division, and still claiming to be convinced that the major successes were just around the corner. The chairman could well understand why Jiskoot was called the best deal maker in the Netherlands: the man always got his way. It was impossible to reach agreements with him.

On several occasions, Marakon had calculated how much money was being lost. It came to hundreds of millions a year. Since he could not keep the corporate division in line, the chairman was increasingly playing with the idea of sacking Jiskoot.

However, the question was whether he really could sack Jiskoot, who had a great deal of informal power both at the bank and elsewhere. Jiskoot was also popular with the supervisory board. The members were enthusiastic about the man who advised some of them directly. In addition, the people in his division supported him, and they were not without influence. They loved Jiskoot. Many ABN Amro bankers considered him to be their friend and their coach. His people were extremely loyal. Groenink suspected that naturally this was partly because Jiskoot always paid the promised bonuses on time.

Groenink had no desire for endless arguments with Jiskoot; he preferred to invest his time in considering the bank's strategy or conducting discussions with other banks. For years, he had allowed Joost Kuiper, the boss of the retail division, to handle the fights with Jiskoot. Groenink was pleased with the support of what he considered to be an extraordinarily loyal and honest managing director. Just like the chairman, Kuiper felt that the corporate division was failing to deliver what it had promised, and that the corporate bankers could therefore do with being a little less arrogant.

Kuiper's position was strong. If there was one part of the bank that had earned money over the past few years, it was the retail operations in the United States and Brazil. Jiskoot's criticism that the bank had not succeeded in linking the three domestic markets clearly had a point. On the other hand, these two foreign subsidiaries were by now worth many times more than their purchase price.

At the bank, the counterproductive collisions between Wilco Jiskoot and Joost Kuiper were viewed with disgust. They were two managing directors with completely different ideas about the bank's development. What many people didn't realise was that the two men did respect each other as people.

The major confrontation between Groenink and Jiskoot would be postponed for as long as Kuiper and Jiskoot continued to fight. The other members of the managing board were well aware of the tensions between these three former Amro bankers. Erik van de Loo, the managing board's coach, was regarded as being too soft to solve this growing hostility. In a sense, Jiskoot and Groenink were a real match for each other. The members of the managing board were virtually unanimous in their judgment: in terms of analytical ability and staying power, Jiskoot was the only one to hold his own against the board chairman. The two bankers seemed to balance each other out.

Wilco Jiskoot had known his boss for almost thirty years: for all the time that they had worked together and made careers together. Yet he never felt that he knew Groenink, who he regarded as distant and cold. Jiskoot often wondered why Groenink hadn't taken the initiative to work with him, to involve him in his camp. Why did the board chairman never phone him before an important meeting so that they could choose their position? This would have created a basis of trust that would have also benefited the bank.

When Jiskoot spoke about this with his colleagues, they explained that Groenink was primarily afraid of him. That Groenink couldn't pin him down because he would keep on discussing endlessly until he got his way. But the chairman seemed to feel particularly threatened by the fact that Jiskoot had plenty of support at the bank. In this respect, they were opposites: whereas Groenink had little personal contact with his colleagues, Jiskoot was intensely involved.

Naturally Jiskoot respected Groenink's analytical ability, but he also felt that he had become lazy and was too frequently absent. Recently, he'd noticed that Groenink was too quick to shoot from the hip, and that his latest opinions were overly based on people at the bank who were no longer relevant. Jiskoot didn't understand this at all: he had built his position on maintaining the right relations in the best possible way; he looked after those contacts, whether they were clients or colleagues.

Groenink had no reason to fear that Jiskoot would seize power. Jiskoot had no real ambitions to lead ABN Amro. He wanted to create a robust and successful bank and to implement agreements as drawn up in Arrow. If it had been up to him, they would have continued with that idea of 2000: to turn ABN Amro into a bank that focused on serving major clients throughout the world.

Jiskoot blamed Groenink for abandoning that strategy a year later and for not daring to make the necessary investments. He openly admitted that the corporate division's results were still disappointing. But it took time to construct a network of good people and clients, so you shouldn't overturn everything just a year after the division had been set up.

The mere suggestion of shutting down the bank's corporate section – which was sometimes made in the heat of the battle – made Jiskoot livid. There was no way you could do that. This was a leading Dutch bank. The logical consequence was that the bank could just as well reject the whole of the Netherlands because, as a retail bank, ABN Amro was clearly no leader.

Jiskoot certainly believed in all manner of combinations of corporate and retail, and also wanted to discuss this with his colleagues. But it never happened. This was partly because it irritated him immensely that Groenink and Kuiper, under the influence of outsiders such as Herman Spruit, constantly suggested that the corporate division was the cause of all the bank's problems. That was simply not true, and also impossible when you constituted a mere 20 per cent of the bank.

As he became more alienated from the chairman, Jiskoot increasingly focused on the interests of his corporate division. But he rejected as absurd the reproach that he preached only to the converted and was uninvolved with the bank's other interests. He still believed that there was only one way to achieve synergy between the three sections in the Netherlands, the United States and Brazil, and that was by selling the products of the corporate division.

Here, Jiskoot frequently suggested that the bank could easily lose LaSalle. The corporate division in the United States had not really taken off. He often proposed selling off 'the land of the downward dollar' and, if necessary, giving the money back to the shareholders. And so they kept on running around in circles. In fact, the discussion between Kuiper and Jiskoot had been going on for years without anything ever happening.

Jiskoot, in turn, felt that there was too much talking in the managing board and that nothing was ever completed. First it was half-heartedly decided to opt for the ambitions of the corporate division and then this was reversed. Jiskoot felt that all the decisions taken over the previous years under Groenink had been half hearted. There were gaps everywhere: gaps for fights and for discussion. And Groenink refused to solve those tensions in informal one-on-one sessions.

The managing board and the level below still had no idea of the chairman's plans for the bank. That lack of safety ensured that few people at ABN Amro were still prepared to say what they really thought. Jiskoot had stopped doing that a long time ago; he kept his cards close to his chest.

Just like his predecessor Rijnhard van Tets, Jiskoot was also convinced that Groenink lacked the ability to create trust among his staff. He believed that the chairman had no real human insight, or whatever he may have had was used far too rarely. Van Tets had been well aware of this five years ago. If only they'd listened to him. Groenink was incapable of creating a team, and he would never solve the tensions in the managing board.

In this respect, Jiskoot was also deeply disappointed in the supervisory board. Why didn't they investigate this malfunctioning managing board? Why didn't they intervene? Why didn't they question the other members? If they had, they would have found out for themselves what was going wrong. Wasn't that their responsibility? He suspected that the board chairman had been telling the governors that the other members of the managing board were not up to the work they were doing, that he was the only one who knew and understood everything that was going on. Jiskoot believed that Groenink had the governors by the tail.

The corporate banker found it bizarre that, both in the supervisory board and in the media, Groenink was constantly depicted as a powerful managing director who took decisions. In Jiskoot's experience, Groenink was a weak leader, who availed himself of divide and rule tactics so as to remain in power without intervening.

The two leaders had completely different views about the role of the managing board's members. Groenink thought that they should be mainly involved with their divisions' results and strategy. Jiskoot felt that this was nonsense. The members needed a predominantly hands-on approach, certainly in view of the board's considerable size.

In the autumn of 2003, this subject was on the agenda at the managing board's offsite meeting in the Spanish city of Seville. This was because the general managers had noticed that the managing board had become paralysed by all the conflicts. They demanded that the activities should be coordinated more effectively, and they also wanted to be involved more closely in the leadership's decision-making process. Moreover, it had been agreed to invest plenty of hard work in the synergy between the three SBUS.

At this meeting, Joost Kuiper and Dolf Collee, the two keen yachtsmen in their midst, surprised their colleagues with the idea of becoming the owners of a boat or two and promoting the bank's unity by participating in the Volvo Ocean Race. They were jointly responsible for the c&cc, the bank's leading retail division where Joost Kuiper concentrated on the Netherlands and the United States, and Dolf Collee was responsible for Brazil and new markets. Time and again, they'd noticed that colleagues outside of the Netherlands didn't really feel involved with the organisation as a whole, that they experienced no sense of unity. Without making any radical investments, they wanted to strengthen the bank's unity. Sailing around the world in the race, and involving all the subsidiaries, would propagate the one-bank idea. Their colleagues were reticent. Groenink had little interest in sailing. He remarked drily that you should only take part if you were certain that you would win.

During the offsite meeting in Spain it was decided that, under the managing board, eight general managers would be made responsible for implementing policy. Together with the board, these eight super GMs would comprise the business team group (GBT). This GBT would be chaired by Rijkman Groenink and, apart from the entire managing board, would also include the bosses of the United States, Brazil and the Netherlands: Bobins, Barbosa and Schmittmann. Also involved were Lex Kloosterman, the man responsible for private clients, along with Alexandra Cook (global clients) and Piero Overmars (global markets), who were Jiskoot's closest associates at the corporate division. The remaining GBT members consisted of Huibert Boumeester, who was in charge of asset management, and Ron Teerlink, who was to launch the new shared services group for Scott Barrett.

Lex Kloosterman, the former general manager of the corporate division, expressed his concerns in this new body. He wanted to discover where the bank was losing control over the operation. Kloosterman had realised that too many major loans were going to important clients, money that provided the bank with little return. He felt that ABN Amro should focus on medium-sized companies: clients who the bank had alienated over the past few years through its emphasis on major clients, who were relevant to the major investment banks.

Kloosterman argued that ABN Amro would never win over the major clients. He was tired of comparisons with the success of Deutsche Bank. It had a domestic market with many significant players and could therefore afford to invest in the knowledge needed for serving multinationals. ABN Amro didn't have that kind of foundation. He pointed to the advantages of focusing corporate services on smaller clients: ABN Amro's knowledge was sufficient here, and was also something that clients were willing to pay for.

The ensuing discussion included nothing about opting for either large or small companies. Instead emphasis was placed on the need to create a more effective exchange of knowledge between the corporate and retail divisions. 45-year-old Hugh Scott Barrett was given the task of forcefully implementing the desired synergy. All the SBU auxiliary departments were to be transferred to his Group Shared Services department, which Scott Barrett would direct in his new capacity as chief operating officer (COO).

With this new structure, the bank was hoping to counter the fragmentation of auxiliary areas such as IT, concern purchasing and staff administration. By combining them, it would gain the benefits of scale. In fact, Dolf van den Brink had already passionately argued for this back in the spring of 2000.

Groenink hoped that this would provide the managing board's members with more time to concentrate on the bank's strategy. But for him there was another advantage: Scott Barrett would be relieved of his duties as leader of the corporate division. Jiskoot would now have to run the division on his own. Groenink was therefore hoping to weaken his resistance considerably.

Jan Peter Schmittmann, who had been responsible for the domestic division since October, was working hard for greater unity. Over the coming years, he wanted to invite all the management teams for at least one leadership trip. He had embarked on this during his previous post as the general manager of the private clients department.

Schmittmann felt that he could only get the best out of his colleagues if they treated each other like good friends. Good friends who keep each other on the ball and are honest with each other. That bond was created by travelling together and, more importantly, by listening to personal stories. In fact, this plan closely resembled the bank leadership's trip to Morocco.

At first some of the bankers found it extremely difficult to acclimatise to the informal setting. Reinout van Lennep was the department manager of international private banking and an upright, client-focused veteran of the international network. His colleagues teased him when he turned up smartly dressed for a trip to a mud hut village in the desert. Van Lennep laughed. "You never know, maybe I'll bump into one of my clients or prospects here." This was greeted with much laughter. Van Lennep had ensured his place on the team.

The destinations of these leadership trips were also a surprise for the managers of the domestic division. Everyone had to leave their comfort zone so they were always sent to extreme locations. Everything revolved around an informal atmosphere where the boss of the team in question would be the first to describe what their life really involved. Experience had shown that if a boss revealed they were first and foremost a human being, the rest would follow. Everyone was allowed to react to each other without judging. The bankers had to keep a diary about themselves and to talk about this in the group.

These outings were dominated by emotion; they had to guarantee that, from then on, managers would dare to lead in an authentic fashion. Schmittmann believed that there was too much management and too little leadership. It was time to have done with that stupid and frequently introverted arrogance of so many executives at ABN Amro. Here, the idea was that you could only lead others if you could lead yourself.

Many people came back full of enthusiasm. Various old hands in the bank's upper echelons felt that these journeys were like a warm bath. They talked about having their old bank back: the bank that focused on the individual.

Management teams were renamed leadership teams. However, some people found it difficult to get used to emails from head office that began with the words Dear Leaders. When they received these emails, bankers such as Van Lennep felt uncomfortable: it smacked of North Korea.

Moreover, many bankers also noticed that it was extremely difficult to create enough space for all these new leaders. So they would tell their subordinates, "Fine, go ahead and assume leadership over yourself, but keep within my guidelines."

Hugh Scott Barrett was also a man of guidelines and of ensuring that everyone stuck to them. Groenink asked the somewhat unempathetic chief operating officer to become the chairman of the Marakon-proposed Resource Allocation and Performance Management Committee (RAPMC), which Groenink promised to attend occasionally. Some of the managing directors wondered why he was delegating such an important task.

In this role, Scott Barrett was to check whether the various business units delivered their promised results. This meant that, as the architect of his brainchild Arrow, he would also have to keep a strict eye on the corporate division. Scott Barrett was dreading this. He knew that it would put pressure on his relationship with Jiskoot, who would feel abandoned. Fortunately, the markets improved considerably that year; it even seemed that, after the previous year's loss, the corporate division would once again make a profit.

In addition, the ambitious British banker believed that he was on his way to the bank's top job. In an interview, Groenink had let slip that, in ten years time, Scott Barrett would be well suited to lead ABN Amro. He later confirmed this in a conversation with Scott Barrett. However, Groenink also pointed out that his colleague still had things to learn. He particularly felt that Scott Barrett needed to be more engaging and empathetic. They agreed that his coaching would focus on this. Scott Barrett was amused. He saw Groenink's own difficulties in this area. Scott Barrett recognised that resistance because he also tended towards the analytical. Team building was clearly not one of the chairman's talents.

When, in that same interview, Groenink was asked about the qualities needed for reaching the top of a company, he replied, "You have to be prepared to put up with a lot and to shrug off a lot. Emotional stability is a prerequisite, particularly at this point when the public keeps a close eye on Dutch business leaders."

In that respect, Groenink was to have no more problems with governor Jan Kalff. In the autumn of 2003, Kalff was preoccupied with his role as president of the Hagemeyer group. Through a combination of poor results and an exorbitantly expensive IT project, Hagemeyer was in deep trouble. Over 2003 a loss was expected of some 200 million euros. This meant that the company no longer fulfilled its credit conditions and had to return to the bank for a new loan. ABN Amro had already received the request.

At the same time, an aggressive private equity investment firm, the American Clayton, Dubilier & Rice, got wind of the problems. It announced that it was preparing a bid. A bid that the Hagemeyer leadership was unenthusiastic about. But before Kalff dared to convey this message, he phoned ABN Amro to ask how things stood. Kalff wanted to know whether or not they would secure the credit. Wilco Jiskoot had already told him that, in his view, a combination of a loan and issuing new shares would be feasible.

Tjalling Tiemstra, Hagemeyer's financial director, conducted the credit negotiations. Kalff felt that it was logical that a governor with a financial background should be involved in considering the financing of the company he supervised.

Groenink exploded when he heard about his predecessor's phone call. In comparison to Mr Integrity, Kalff, he was regularly depicted in the media as being something of a scoundrel. For him, this was proof that Kalff was not so perfect himself. Groenink felt that Kalff had traded on his background. In his opinion, Kalff should not have played any active role at the bank in the mediation of credit for a client in serious difficulties. It was not inconceivable that people at the special credit department would be in some way impressed by the involvement of their former boss. Would credit be extended on the right grounds? Groenink considered that Kalff could no longer remain a governor of ABN Amro. He raised the matter with Aarnout Loudon, who agreed with him.

In October, the members of both the managing board and the supervisory board set off on their annual excursion with their partners. This year it was London. And that's where the bombshell was dropped. During the day, Aarnout Loudon took Jan Kalff to one side and told him of the growing doubts about the way in which he, as Hagemeyer's president, had been involved in actively helping to acquire funding for that company.

It was a painful conversation. Loudon explained the situation carefully. Kalff defended himself: his involvement had never gone beyond that of a consultant. In his discussions with people from Hagemeyer, he may have occasionally suggested what ABN Amro would or what not support. But it was nothing more than that. He didn't understand the problem. After all, he was honest, wasn't he? How could they doubt that?

Loudon knew that the phone call had been made with no dubious intentions, and he never questioned Jan Kalff's integrity. But the bank's president stuck to his guns: you can't wear two hats at the same time, you really can't. Kalff realised that he had no choice: that this looked like a conflict of interests. Although Kalff could understand this intellectually, he found it difficult emotionally. He would have to choose for Hagemeyer, a company in trouble that needed his help. So he would take the honourable way out. That afternoon at the ABN Amro supervisory board, Kalff announced that he would retire as a bank governor. This was greeted by a deathly silence. Everyone saw the pain and the grief.

It all went wrong that evening. People gave speeches and the hours went by. Loudon, Groenink ... But nobody said a word about Jan Kalff's departure. Trude Maas asked Groenink whether something would be said. Hopefully someone had something nice to say about the man who had worked for the bank for more than forty years! But Groenink shook his head: no, nothing had been agreed. She approached Loudon. He had already spoken and suggested that a retirement party would be held ... But Trude Maas insisted. She pointed out to Loudon that everybody in the hall knew that this was Jan Kalff's final meeting. It would be excruciating if this weren't marked in some way. Loudon got the message. At the end of the dinner, he stood up and remarked humorously: We haven't forgotten you, Jan. Jan Kalff was given an elegant and eloquent send-off.

All this didn't really matter to Kalff. For him, it wasn't really a farewell, which was something he simply couldn't envisage. He was assuming that the supervisory board would ask him back once the Hagemeyer affair had died down. The bank needed him, and especially in a board with just one banker: Baron David de Rothschild. Kalff believed that Loudon and Groenink had promised in principle that he could return after the Hagemeyer issue was resolved. They had agreed that they would talk about this together at that point in time.

Loudon discussed Kalff's successor with Groenink. He always conferred with Groenink about the supervisory board's membership. The chairman regularly came up with suggestions for new governors. Loudon's point of departure was simple: the supervisory board needed people who could get on well with the people on the managing board. They agreed that the supervisory board would eventually need a new member with a banking background. Someone who really understood the workings of a bank. That was what they would be looking for.

In the New Year, the board would at least be reinforced with the presence of André Olijslager, who was retiring as the chairman of Friesland Coberco Dairy Foods. When Groenink asked him to join, Olijslager joked: Are you sure? I'm a difficult person. The 60-year-old Olijslager had been a member of the bank's advisory board for some time. He regarded his promotion to the supervisory board as a great honour.

At the end of 2003, Groenink was interviewed by the Dutch magazine *Intermediair*. When asked whether, after three-and-a-half years, he had to some extent built the bank that he had in mind, he said, "I think that halfway through next year I will be able to say, yes, it exists." Groenink was angered when the journalist observed that the bank was now probably stuck with its arrogant image. "But why? I don't understand that. We're no longer arrogant." Then he remarked, "Okay, no matter how much we believe that this is not the case, if people perceive us as being arrogant then we must do something about it. Nowadays there's enough humility concerning individual strengths and failures in this company. Of course, we've been rapped across the knuckles a few times, which we have taken extremely seriously. This has greatly increased our capacity for self-criticism. And that capacity also forms the basis of our attitude towards the outside world, for the way in which we approach our clients and deal with public opinion. And so on and so forth. But this is essentially different than a few years ago."

In this interview, Groenink described how proud he was of the balance he'd achieved between his work and his private life. "I've come to the conclusion that I used to give too little to the world around me. Moreover, I now think that well-balanced people make better employees. I'm consciously involved with this." He explained how this was managed. "It's a matter of planning your agenda, of considering the issues very carefully. For instance, how important is it for the bank that I do this? Or could I just as easily leave it out? And would I then be able to reserve that time for my family, friends or cultural things?"

When the journalist asked whether it had been a politically correct gimmick to appear at a press conference with his youngest child in a backpack, the ABN Amro board chairman reacted indignantly. "No it wasn't. I couldn't find a babysitter."

His fellow managing directors, themselves considerable workaholics, read this interview with mixed feelings. Almost all of them felt that Groenink was too frequently absent, that he had become lazy. Sometimes he seemed to be more involved with the architecture of his new house on the river Vecht than with the bank's prosperity.

Hugh Scott Barrett and Wilco Jiskoot regularly noticed that Groenink didn't read his documents. De Swaan also felt that he was definitely not a hard worker. Groenink's colleagues soon realised that the meetings took longer when he hadn't read his documents. The chairman appeared to listen to other people for as long as it took to understand what was going on. Here, he trusted in his immense experience and lightning analytical skills. But his immediate colleagues knew what was happening and it irritated them. If Groenink had read those documents in advance, he would have been far better equipped to direct the discussions.

In 2004, Gerrit Zalm, the Dutch finance minister, presented Groenink with a royal honour. He was made an officer in the Order of Orange-Nassau. The ceremony was followed by a dinner where Jiskoot gave a speech. With a broad grin, Jiskoot observed that Groenink had been praised to the skies, so now it was time to tell the truth. Jiskoot jokingly described Groenink's laziness, that he didn't read his documents and that he was the best at seeming to know it all. This meant that you didn't really get anywhere. Some of the governors were laughing so hard that they had tears rolling down their cheeks. The joke's serious undertone evaded them.

Groenink felt that it was unjust to reproach him for being lazy. He was not lazy: he worked at home almost every single evening and estimated that he still invested an average of eighty hours a week in the bank. However, he did accept the criticism that he had become less visible at the organisation. This was something that he was constantly being told, just as he was also hearing that he was not good enough at selling the bank to shareholders, clients and potential merger partners. Could they appreciate that, following the communication dramas of the past few years, he now knew that communication wasn't one of his strengths? And that he had come to realise that his clumsy humour was not always productive?

In his free time, Groenink liked to work on the land, not only in the Netherlands but also in Italy. Speaking to the Dutch magazine *HP/De Tijd*, a friend, the artist Jan Dibbets, remarked "Rijkman loves working in the outdoors. He really should have been a farmer. Ploughing, sawing and gathering wood are his real passions."

And that showed. The chairman was on crutches at the presentation of the 2003 annual figures. He apologised and limited himself to admitting that he had had a domestic accident.

Even in farming, Groenink liked taking risks. He had managed to overturn his tractor. Because one of his little sons was sitting on his lap at the time, he was forced to make a dangerous manoeuvre. Although he saved his son, the tractor landed on his leg.

Fellow board members shook their heads in sympathy when they heard this story. For them, this was the umpteenth piece of evidence that their chairman was a walking disaster. Whatever he did, the man took far too many risks. However, they did respect Groenink for returning to the bank without complaint just one day after the accident.

At the press conference Groenink was proud of the results. "The best trading results in the bank's history." Profits came to 3.16 billion euros. The corporate division was still not contributing in terms of economic profit, but it had turned negative trading figures of almost 300 million euros in 2002 into a positive input of nearly 400 million in 2003. Here, Groenink cited Ahold as an important profit source. According to some of the corporate bankers involved, the bank had earned between 80 and 100 million euros from Ahold's rescue.

During this meeting, Groenink predicted that major American retail banks would soon launch an offensive on the European banking sector. When asked whether he thought that ABN Amro could remain independent, he shook his head. "Now that the protection structures are gone, it's up to the shareholders to decide. They will determine the bank's future."

Groenink had been campaigning to have the protection structures removed that had been drawn up in 1990. This was prompted by an appeal in the Tabaksblat Code, a Dutch corporate governance document that mainly emphasised a more effective safeguarding of shareholders' interests. Groenink felt that the bank should lead the way. In his 'Back to the Future' speech of four years previously, he had quoted from a report by the commercial bank JP Morgan, "More radical change is needed. The management's ultimate motivator – the fear of a hostile takeover – plays virtually no role at ABN Amro. There is a great deal of unused potential."

De Swaan knew that there was only one real reason why the protection structures had to go. The bank's leaders hoped that it would silence the foreign shareholders' complaints about what they described as the Dutch discount, and that this would persuade them to become interested in the bank. They would keep their distance for as long as the bank was protected and shareholders had relatively little influence on its future. The main objective of removing the protection structures was to ensure a higher share price.

Aarnout Loudon, the bank's president, agreed with this plan. He felt that trust constructions were absurd. But the supervisory board was apprehensive.

Antony Burgmans warned that although he supported the abolition of protection structures, he still believed that the bank should first wait for a considerable rise in its share price. A high rate was the best protection against a hostile takeover.

The members of the managing board laughed when they heard this. Tom de Swaan declared that a hostile takeover would be inconceivable, and wondered out loud who would be able to cough up some 40 billion euros for ABN Amro. Groenink applauded De Swaan. He pointed out that protection structures would ultimately be forbidden by law, and added that hostile takeovers in banking were fairly improbable, given the sector's nature and the major involvement of both governments and supervisors.

The board then discussed at length the number of shares a shareholder would need to be able to add to the agenda of the shareholders' meeting. In anticipation of the legislative amendment, it was agreed that a shareholder with one per cent of the votes, an investment of 350 million euros, would be allowed to add items.

ABN Amro had asked the Dutch Central Bank for permission to abolish the protection structures. Its president, Nout Wellink, felt strongly that banks should not opt for optimising shareholder value. He consistently pointed out that deposit account holders had far more money in banks than shareholders, and that banks therefore had to focus on the interests of their clients. But ABN Amro's request never reached Wellink's office. One of his colleagues had already confirmed that it fulfilled the Tabaksblat Code requirements. The supervisor agreed.

Meanwhile it had become known that American supervisors had taken a close and critical look at ABN Amro. Apparently, an investigation had been conducted by the supervisor of companies (SEC) listed on stock markets. Groenink was noncommittal when questioned by the media. He told a journalist from *Het Financieele Dagblad* that there had been an inspection the year before. De Swaan then explained that SEC had requested all the documents that the bank had deposited at the Fed. He emphasised that it had been a routine investigation. SEC had sent a list of 75 questions and, once these had been answered, there had been a number of further questions. "Apparently it was our turn, but we passed with flying colours."

However, the Fed was not finished by a long shot. After it had announced in July 2003 that all transactions involving Eastern European parties would be regarded as suspect, Scott Barrett had been busy gathering information about any possible fraudulent funds that had passed through the New York office. The supervisor estimated that the New York subsidiary had made approximately 20,000 transfers between August 2002 and September 2003, transactions amounting to a total of 3.2 billion dollars. He noted that this frequently involved so-called shell companies: businesses where it was unclear where the money came from and what its use would be. The Fed was angry that ABN Amro had failed to check this out, that a year after the transactions had occurred – and only 'after much urging on the supervisors' part' – an analysis of these clients was finally undertaken to discover whether illegal funds were involved.

But the Fed was still not satisfied some eight months later. According to *The Wall Street Journal*, ABN Amro was now accused of 'drawing lines'. The bank was shocked and dug a little deeper. Its research revealed that fraudulent PO Box businesses in the United States, which were often linked with Eastern Europe, were using these accounts at ABN Amro. The bank decided to pull the plug on more than a hundred suspicious clients.

Because ABN Amro had discovered and reported both of these cases itself, the Fed allowed the bank to continue setting its own house in order. ABN Amro signed a contract with the supervisor on 23 July 2004. Herbert Biern, the Fed's director, was responsible for this agreement. The bank once again promised to invest more time and money in the monitoring of clients whose funds passed through its New York office. The bank's managing directors believed that the supervisor was finally satisfied.

Rijkman Groenink was still tirelessly searching for a merger candidate. He was checking the list of smaller European banks, which had been drawn up at the end of 2001. Groenink knew that the German HypoVereinsbank was in difficulties. For years, this Bavarian bank had struggled with bad credit on its balance sheets, and was regarded on the market as being ripe for a takeover. The bank's share price had been under considerable pressure for quite some time. It was now valued at a mere 7.6 billion euros. ABN Amro was five times as big.

Groenink knocked on the door of Dieter Rampl, the HypoVereinsbank's chairman. Rampl had tried to strengthen the balance sheet of Germany's second bank by selling off a 20 per cent interest in the Austria Creditanstalt bank, in which it had a 78 per cent interest. Groenink offered to help. ABN Amro wanted to acquire five per cent.

Rampl initially refused to discuss a merger with ABN Amro. But the Germans were under increasing pressure to join forces. The newspapers had announced that various banks were interested, such as KBC, SocGen, BNP Paribas, Credit Suisse and Santander. Groenink told the German *Handelsblatt* that ABN Amro was also interested. Rampl responded by informing Groenink that ABN Amro had been added to the shortlist of parties for further discussions. Also included was the Italian bank Unicredito. Groenink asked

Alexander Pietruska to help with these negotiations. He had been working at ABN Amro since 2000.

Pietruska, who began his career at McKinsey, had been amazed by his employer's behaviour for many years: why did the bank never make any clear choices? He was annoyed by what he regarded as the frequent stupidity of Dutch arrogance. The bank was big in the Netherlands but thought that it was also unassailable in the rest of the world. The way in which Rijkman Groenink treated Dieter Rampl was a prime example. None of the Dutch negotiation partners seemed to have any idea how this would benefit Rampl.

Groenink explained the current state of the world to Rampl along with the role that ABN Amro played in it. He described the retail division and informed the German that he could be the boss of the combined bank's German retail activities. Pietruska registered Rampl's shock at this meagre offer. HypoVereinsbank's board chairman was clearly unhappy. The Italian Unicredito eventually made off with HypoVereinsbank.

Groenink was extremely disappointed: he had invested a great deal of time. The bank's leaders also felt let down: this really should have worked out. By way of an explanation, Groenink told the board that these two banks would have a strong position in Eastern European, which they could now jointly develop. He knew what Unicredito had paid and could have offered more. However, he felt that this would have been unwise because ABN Amro could never achieve the same synergy advantages. A telling fact was that the Italians had invited Rampl to become the chairman of the joint supervisory board.

There was more criticism of Groenink's timing. In the spring of 2004, he decided that Bank of Asia should be sold, an idea that had been under discussion for several years. Making a success of the bank had clearly failed. Various bankers puckered their brows: was this really such a good idea? The Thai bank had been bought for a lot of money just before the Asian crisis, and was now to be sold off cheaply. The managers involved estimated that the total damage for ABN Amro amounted to at least 500 million euros.

The neighbours were carefully following the news about ABN Amro. ING's managing board was astounded by all its shifts in strategy. They noticed that Rijkman Groenink seemed to be given far too much room by his governors. Their own experience was that action was taken when things didn't work out. That spring Ewald Kist had been prematurely replaced by the Belgian Michel Tilmant.

This was the first time that ING had had a foreign chairman. Tilmant immediately made it clear that he sought a fundamental shift in culture. He wanted to get rid of that Dutch habit of endlessly discussing problems without ever coming to a decision. More attention had to be paid to clients, and

Tilmant also put the emphasis on share price into perspective. He announced that he wanted to run a bank and not shares, and decided that there would be no more profit predictions.

Groenink felt concerned after the disappointment of the failed takeover of the HypoVereinsbank. It had been agreed three years previously that the bank was to work as quickly as possible towards a merger of equals. "Because, with a market value of less than 30 billion euros, we're a second-tier bank and we have to watch out. We're a part of that in-between category where it's not yet clear whether we're the predator or the prey. We must therefore make sure that we do not miss the boat."

To his intense frustration, the market value had hardly improved, and investors still refused to believe the bank's story. This meant that he was increasingly being forced to talk with banks that were bigger than ABN Amro. Groenink observed that there was little opportunity to speak with banks elsewhere in Europe, that governments (such as in Scandinavia, Germany, Italy, France and Belgium) tended to protect the sector against foreign players.

And what should be done with the bank's interests in Italy? Since 1999 ABN Amro had owned interests in Capitalia and Antonveneta and the Italians had been uncooperative about any further extension of Dutch influence. But even two years previously, Groenink had still believed that Antonio Fazio, the Central Bank president, would allow ABN Amro to acquire a larger interest. However, that optimism had since faded. ABN Amro had an interest of 10 per cent in Antonveneta, and the bank played a dominant role in the shareholder pact that had been drawn up with other shareholders. This pact would expire next April when the bank would have to decide whether there was any point in going on. After all those years, the prospect of Italy becoming a second domestic market had scarcely improved.

Finance minister Gerrit Zalm and Nout Wellink, the president of the Dutch Central Bank, agreed with Groenink. It was time the Italians took the lock from the door. The chairman was invited to vent his concerns at the informal economic summit of the European Union's member states. This was held in Scheveningen and was attended by all the ministers of finance and the central banks presidents.

The board was pleased with this invitation. Some of the managing directors, such as Tom de Swaan, were worried about the bank's neglect of its political relations. Joost Kuiper agreed with this view when it was expressed at a meeting of the board. Kuiper knew that he was also guilty of this: for years he had resisted the urgent requests of the Dutch employers' organisation that he should join their trade missions.

Jaap Rost Onnes, a department manager who had retired in 1998, was the only person to promote the bank's relations with the political world and other social institutions. In that sense, Rost Onnes, who liked to describe himself as the man behind the throne, was the conscience of Hazelhoff and Kalff. In addition, he made suggestions to Rijkman Groenink about where ABN Amro should invest its energy.

The bank regularly asked Rost Onnes to accept invitations on its behalf from ambassadors and politicians. He also advised Groenink to accept, at least occasionally, invitations that were important for the bank's network. For instance, he ensured that Groenink attended a dinner with Princess Máxima to talk about microcredit, an area that had become suddenly popular through her efforts.

In Scheveningen, Groenink confronted his audience and told them that they constituted the most important obstacle to international mergers and takeovers. He denounced the general political obstinacy. He didn't mention his own experiences in any tangible way, but everybody knew that he was mainly alluding to the bank's problems in Italy. Antonio Fazio, president of the Italian Central Bank, was also present and knew that this referred to him.

The bank's chairman, who had recently scoured Europe for a partner, told the press, "That obstinacy means that banks have become extremely wary. Banks operate in a highly regulated sector and therefore attach great importance to a good working relationship with the supervisors."

Finance minister Zalm then announced that his colleagues had agreed that "nobody in the future may use purely national arguments against foreign bidders in the banking section, such as the desire to create national champions". The ministers even decided that an enquiry was needed here. In a slightly sceptical tone, Zalm added that "words and deeds are not always in line with each other".

Jan Kalff also discovered this when he had lunch with Groenink and Loudon, an appointment that had been promised in October the previous year. The plan was that they would discuss his return to the supervisory board of ABN Amro. With a certain wistfulness, Kalff took the lift at the bank's head office on the Gustav Mahlerlaan. The memories flooded back when he got out at the directors' floor. He had missed ABN Amro. Kalff was really looking forward to rejoining the supervisory board as had been agreed.

With gracious smiles, the gentlemen sat down at the table in the bank's restaurant. Aarnout Loudon, the president, began hesitantly and told Kalff that he had changed his mind. That he found it too complicated to explain to the outside world why somebody had first gone away and then come back again. He was dreading it. Kalff didn't understand this. After all, that was what they'd agreed: they had decided a year ago that the supervisory board needed to have someone with knowledge of the bank! Moreover, no new governor with this knowledge had yet been appointed.

While Loudon was talking, Kalff noticed that Rijkman Groenink was nodding his head vigorously. He realised that it was all over. In his view, Groenink had cut him out; he simply didn't feel like having him around. He didn't fancy the involvement of a man who knew the bank like the back of his hand. Kalff felt wounded by this postponed but final farewell to the bank. But he didn't discuss it further. Kalff didn't wish to create the impression that he desperately wanted to return. He had his pride.

Aarnout Loudon had his own problems. The bank's president wanted to stay on but he would turn 70 in 2006, and that meant that he was entering his final eighteen months. In fact, the bank should have already announced who would succeed his 10-year reign in May 2006. But that hadn't happened.

Maarten van Veen, the supervisory board's vice-chairman, was to resign the following spring. That would give the new vice-chairman a year to limber up before succeeding Loudon as chairman. In terms of seniority Antony Burgmans would be the natural choice. The Unilever board chairman had already indicated that he was prepared to take this on. However, on a personal level Burgmans provoked resistance in some quarters. Not all the supervisory board's members liked him. They found him rude.

But the greatest opposition came from ABN Amro's board chairman. Groenink knew that Loudon had told Burgmans that he was his intended successor. Groenink disagreed strongly with this choice: he felt that Burgmans was good and incisive in terms of content, but that he expressed himself in a way that was coarse and arrogant. In his opinion, that aggressiveness was unconstructive. Groenink didn't want Burgmans to be chosen, and sounded out a number of fellow managing directors.

Groenink told Loudon that the bank's managing board would not be happy with Burgmans' appointment. However, several of the managing board's members were unaware of this and had never expressed any opposition to Burgmans. The rest of the supervisory board also knew nothing of this.

Sitting at the corner of the table, governor André Olijslager had by now attended several meetings. He felt that the members were distinguished, old fashioned and formal, and considered the supervisory board to be essentially a ratifying board: it approved what it was presented with. He didn't say much. Olijslager felt that he first had to learn what a bank was. However, it struck him that, among the managing board's members, Rijkman Groenink was the only one to open his mouth. Occasionally Tom de Swaan would also say something. The twelve governors, with an average age of 63, were extremely reserved. The Brazilian Pratini de Moraes and the Italian Paolo Scaroni were distanced, both in terms of content and actual presence. They often participated in these meetings by phone.

Wim Dik and Maarten van Veen were in their final months at the bank. They had become governors at a time when ABN Amro was focusing on attracting major clients to its supervisory board. This was also in an era when governors were chiefly expected to keep their distance from the banking profession.

Of the two women Trude Maas was clearly the most involved, particularly as a member of the nomination committee. Louise Groenman didn't seem to play any significant role. The only governor to contribute in terms of banking was David de Rothschild, who was a banker, still a senior partner at Rothschild & Cie Banque and chairman of the Rothschild Group. Lord Colin Sharman of Redlynch, the British former chairman of KPMG, and Arthur Martinez knew enough about figures to be able to raise their hands occasionally. On balance Olijslager was not particularly impressed. Why on earth were these people members of the board?

Privately, a number of governors admitted that the real reasons for being an ABN Amro governor were prestige and the platform that the position provided. An ABN Amro governor was someone important, a fact that generated invitations. Although the bank's managing board never actually listened to you, the rest of the world did.

For Aarnout Loudon, his role as the bank's president was his most important position and certainly cost him a day a week. It wasn't easy to chair those meetings. He found that bankers were often arrogant, overconfident about their own knowledge and obstinate in terms of considering other arguments.

Everything was agreed with Groenink in advance. Loudon was still convinced that he had made the right choice by opting for Groenink in 1999. It hadn't been straightforward, given Kalff's strong opposition, but it was absolutely clear that something had to be done at the bank.

He dismissed the governors' concern that this supposedly uncomfortable appointment had resulted in Groenink becoming Loudon's man. Loudon also failed to understand why the governors not only felt that he was too protective towards Groenink but also described their association as a father-son relationship. He simply got on with Groenink.

The two Utrecht lawyers were rather similar. Loudon also loved nature. He was happiest when sitting on his horse. Loudon recognised Groenink's student humour and realised that the chairman was mainly looking for recognition and respect. The extremely tall Loudon wondered whether Groenink found it difficult that, on average, he was somewhat smaller than the people around him.

Aarnout Loudon trusted Groenink, and believed that there was nothing that the board chairman would avoid discussing with him. He never felt ill-informed. Their good relationship meant that they were able to go through things properly.

Naturally, the bank's president knew that the chairman had no real involvement with team building, and that many people didn't really like him. Creating personal connections was something that clearly didn't interest him. Moreover, Groenink was more concerned with being right, rather than getting things right. But, in the discussions he had had with Groenink, he found it significant and pleasant to discover that Groenink was not ruthless and that he checked out people's backgrounds. Groenink could describe with great concern the general managers and managing board members who failed to deliver. And how he would have to have a difficult conversation with them. When Loudon talked with the people who worked with Rijkman Groenink, he found that they had few complaints.

The exception was the corporate division. Loudon knew that they were furious with Groenink. Right from the start, the bank's president had felt uncomfortable with the corporate division's ambitions. He had always wondered about Groenink's commitment, and he understood his doubts and worries concerning the spiralling expenses and sluggish profits. But he was also shocked by Jiskoot's argument that closing parts of the corporate division would entail enormous reorganisation costs. Moreover, Loudon was impressed by the attractive prospects that Jiskoot presented. If the corporate banker turned out to be right, ABN Amro would become extremely successful.

Loudon also noticed that Groenink had no hold over Jiskoot, a man who presented himself fantastically well and defended his terrain tooth and nail. He questioned whether Groenink would ever bring Jiskoot to heel.

On balance Loudon thought that Groenink was doing well. It didn't worry him that the bank wouldn't succeed in coming anywhere near the 2001 objective of reaching the top five. Everyone already knew this when the objective was communicated in such an appallingly clumsy way. The outside world simply didn't understand that the top five was something that you strove towards as a bank, as a place where you would like to end up. This had been a major communication error.

In contrast to Loudon, Antony Burgmans felt that it was time to discuss Groenink's performance in depth. Following the appeal in the Tabaksblat Code, the supervisory board had agreed to evaluate all the members of the managing board including its chairman. Until now, Groenink had informed the supervisory board each year about how the other managing board members were performing. Now they would be doing this themselves.

At the first meeting of the supervisory board, there was a heated discussion about the absent chairman's performance. Some governors, and especially Burgmans, expressed concern about how he was functioning. Loudon failed to keep control and was ordered by his fellow governors to convey these concerns to the chairman.

It was decided that Loudon and Burgmans would talk to Groenink. They explained to him that he was too much of a prize fighter where he should have been more of a team player. Whatever had become of the agreements that had been made with him in 1999? Burgmans was particularly fierce. Groenink defended himself and promised improvements. After this discussion, several governors noticed during the plenary sessions that relations between Burgmans and Groenink had deteriorated further.

From various sides, Groenink was encountering increasing pressure to deal more harshly with the corporate division and Wilco Jiskoot. Although on paper some profit appeared to have been made, on a structural level the results continued to be disappointing. The corporate bankers created vast expenses for the little they managed to earn for the bank. This meant that the bank's efficiency ratio remained poor. Seven years previously, whereas the peer group scored an average efficiency ratio of 66 per cent, ABN Amro had achieved 68 per cent. The peer group now notched up an efficiency ratio of 61 per cent while ABN Amro had to make do with a lousy 69.2 per cent. For investors and analysts, this was the proof that, despite profits in the billions, the bank was essentially failing. Within the bank, an increasing number of accusing fingers were being pointed at the corporate division.

Jeroen Drost used the summer of 2004 to write a document that would serve as a preparation for the board's autumn offsite meeting on the Bosporus. Drost was the new head of the corporate development department and Wietze Reehoorn's successor. Each week, he spent many hours talking about the bank's strategy with Groenink and Dolf Collee, who was responsible for Europe.

The three men agreed that choices had to be made. Here, they were supported by Herman Spruit, Groenink's key external consultant, who emphasised that the bank couldn't lose any more time. Spruit calculated that the corporate division's economic profit had remained emphatically negative. During talks, Groenink and Spruit decided that it was time to eradicate most of the corporate division.

Drost drew up two models for the fundamental choices facing the bank. In Model A, the bank continued to operate at a global level while the basis for all its activities remained the development of good products and good skills. In Model B, the bank would opt to concentrate on medium-sized clients at a regional level. The second model effectively meant the end of the corporate division in its present form.

Wilco Jiskoot had indicated that he would not be able to attend this meeting. He had promised a nephew to watch him play for the Dutch hockey team at the Olympic Games. Jiskoot was a sporting fanatic and for many years had also played hockey at a high level.

Drost and Collee told Groenink that he could not allow this meeting to go ahead in Jiskoot's absence. All the leading players had to participate in such a fundamental discussion. Hence, Jiskoot was offered the opportunity of a round trip from Athens in a private plane. But Jiskoot asked Groenink for the documents and told him that he would fly back and forth if he felt that this was necessary. He first wanted to read the documents.

At the meeting Jiskoot's chair was empty. Irritated, De Swaan asked Groenink where Jiskoot was. Groenink explained that he had already gone through the plans with his fellow managing director, and that he would convey Jiskoot's opinions. Jiskoot had made it clear to Groenink that eradicating the corporate division at this point was not a good idea. He warned the chairman: This means everyone will down pens and we will not achieve the promised results for 2004. If you leave us alone, we will deliver what we've promised.

However, the meeting's managing directors had received no reports of the conversation that Groenink had previously had with Loudon. He had told him that he felt that radical intervention was needed in the wholesale division. The chairman had explained to his president that he could not exclude the possibility that Jiskoot might in this case quit. Or have to be forced to quit. Because, if Jiskoot obstructed the reorganisation, Groenink would be obliged to fire him.

Loudon had made it clear to Groenink that, as far as he was concerned, Jiskoot's departure or dismissal was out of the question. The president argued that the corporate banker made far too much money for the bank. In his opinion, Groenink could not sack a man like Wilco Jiskoot.

During the meeting, Joost Kuiper again emphasised the corporate division's dramatic exploits, but it didn't help. They didn't take the plunge. Jeroen Drost was deeply disappointed. Never had he seen an empty chair with so much power.

II

PREY

12

Blunder

October 2004–December 2005

Arthur Martinez, Maarten van Veen and Wim Dik had a problem. With Colin Sharman of Redlynch, the three governors made up the bank's audit committee. They had just been informed by Sullivan & Cromwell, the bank's lawyers in the United States, that Rijkman Groenink had suggested a few weeks before that a key document be destroyed. And now they didn't know what to do.

The two Dutchmen thought the incident might be a little worrying. But Arthur Martinez had been a member of the board at the American central bank in Chicago, and he gave them a rude awakening. The incident wasn't merely a little worrying. If things went wrong, it could mean the end of the bank. The American supervisory authority would have a serious problem with any manager who gave orders for an important document to be destroyed. And not only the manager.

Martinez knew the bank had problems with the Fed in New York. The supervisory board had been informed of the Fed's critical attitude soon after he had succeeded Loudon as chairman of the audit committee, halfway through 2003. It had also been established then that ABN Amro's office in New York was isolated from the various divisions and that good supervision of management was lacking there.

Martinez immediately expressed his surprise. ABN Amro's shares had been listed on the New York stock exchange since 1997. How could they have thought that they could get away with providing insufficient information to the Fed? But the bank had signed an agreement with the Fed in the summer of 2004, and perhaps it seemed that the air had been cleared.

Rijkman Groenink and Tom de Swaan had thought so, only a few weeks earlier. On 1 October they met with John Feigelson and John Nelson, two American lawyers who worked for the bank, at the Ritz Carlton in New York. The hotel is located on the southern-most point of Manhattan, and they could see the Statue of Liberty through the window.

The four men were preparing for a meeting with Fed officials. The head office of the Federal Reserve was close to Wall Street, and a few hundred metres from the hotel. They hoped that the bank's problems with the Russian-Cypriot bank accounts would be solved at the meeting. When Tom de Swaan had visited the Fed in August, he had been led to understand that the problems weren't insurmountable, and were, in fact, manageable.

But the bank had discovered a range of new problems since those agreements had been made. It appeared, for example, that employees of the bank in Dubai had made more than a hundred payments to the United States and that in this way several billion dollars had entered America. Some of the payments had originated from Melli, the Iranian bank, others from Libya's Arbift bank; in either case the transfers should have been reported. Money transfers from these countries had to satisfy strict rules in the United States since the attacks on the WTC. It had not shown that the money involved was dangerous or risky in any way, but the simple fact that the transfers had not satisfied American requirements was a problem.

Tom de Swaan had the Dubai report in his briefcase. Groenink was shocked when he saw it: this wasn't the moment to come up with a report like this, just when they would be meeting with the Fed. De Swaan swore that it was only a draft version, although nothing on the cover said so, and said he had some fundamental criticisms of the document. They had probably made a mistake in Amsterdam, and thought that it was a final version. But Feigelson had received the report to hand it to the Fed that Friday evening, and he was planning to deliver it as agreed.

Groenink said angrily that he didn't want draft reports like this to be available in the United States. To him it was unthinkable that the Fed should receive a copy. He ordered that the report had to be undone immediately, using the word destroy. Feigelson made it clear that he was obliged to deliver the document to the Fed as agreed, because it had been sent as final. And that is what happened.

As a lawyer, Feigelson was troubled by the incident and went to see De Swaan a couple of days later. The Sarbanes-Oxley Act states that a lawyer must immediately report any incident where a client orders a document to be destroyed in what appears to be an attempt to get rid of potentially damaging evidence. The American lawyer believed that he had to report the incident, or run the risk of losing his license to practise in the United States.

De Swaan didn't agree and tried to prevent Feigelson taking the report out of the bank. He didn't threaten to fire him, but asked him sharply why he wanted to report the matter. After all, nothing had gone wrong, had it? The Dubai report had gone straight to the Fed. But Feigelson wasn't impressed and reported the incident to the lawyers at Sullivan & Cromwell.

Groenink had no idea what possessed Feigelson. Was the man pulling his leg? Why hadn't Feigelson warned him not to use the word destroy? He should have been aware that he, Groenink, wasn't trying to hide documents in any way. In his view, this was a typical example of stupid American black-and-white thinking, which left no room for nuance.

Martinez didn't believe that anyone had intended to destroy evidence. But he was angry at Groenink's clumsiness, and with De Swaan. In his opinion the CFO should have intervened immediately. He should have said: Rijkman, you don't mean that, do you? And he should have said something to Feigelson, something like: it would be better if you didn't report this. Martinez thought that De Swaan hadn't grasped the seriousness of the situation. ABN Amro's president agreed with Martinez. Loudon thought that De Swaan had over-played his hand. The CFO could have provided some balance, but had not done so.

They discussed the situation in more detail and it became clear that members of the audit committee had been irritated by Groenink's laconic attitude. He apologised for using the word destroy, but said that he thought that the Americans were a bunch of bellyachers. But the members of the committee were seriously disturbed that they had not been informed about the rising tensions with the Fed. For it now appeared that Tom de Swaan had been receiving all sorts of worrying signals since the summer of 2003.

De Swaan confirmed that he had not got involved during those fourteen months. He explained that documents coming from the Fed had always suggested that the local organisation would have to solve the problem, and he had been reassured by this. From the CFO's point of view it was clear: until the Iran-Libya problems had arisen the whole matter could have been solved at local level.

De Swaan thought that the bank had solved the problem quite adequately. Groenink had made some clumsy remarks, maybe, and the Americans hadn't liked it. The CFO had noticed that Groenink had limited respect for supervisory bodies, and particularly for the Fed. But he didn't think that anyone had done anything wrong. He and Groenink then suggested an independent legal investigation.

Groenink told his colleagues that no laws had been broken, and he gave every appearance of believing this. However, a number of colleagues were disturbed to hear about the incident. After all, the bank's management had been drumming it in for some time that employees were required to adhere both to the spirit and the letter of the law.

In December the legal firm of Pillsbury Winthrop Shaw Pittmann delivered a report stating unambiguously that the bank's management had not broken any laws and that there had not been any intention to withhold information.

All the same, the Fed moved quickly. It was concerned about the content of the Dubai report. Moreover, it had been concerned for years about ABN Amro. Now, they felt, an example would have to be made. There were a number of foreign banks around that didn't always keep to the straight and narrow.

Martinez indicated to his fellow board members that politicians in Washington had got wind of the Fed's activities. Questions were being asked. Why was it taking so long, why was the Fed not acting faster and harder? Let's tackle these foreigners! The United States is threatened by terrorism, after all!

ABN Amro then received a cease and desist order. This meant that the bank had no more room to move in the United States, because it was not allowed to buy or sell banks. ABN Amro had been sent to the sin bin, and the bank would stay there until it could show that its house was in order. This gave the bank a mountain of homework to do. It would have to satisfy the Fed that it had introduced improvements on more than 200 points with regard to its internal supervision on compliance.

Martinez said that the measure was unavoidable. The agreement that had been made in the summer of 2004 would end on 19 December 2005. The bank would then hear what penalties the Fed would impose.

The head of the supervisory board was mainly worried about the American public prosecutors. The department of justice had already announced that it would look into the possibility that ABN Amro managers might be liable for criminal prosecution. ABN Amro's problems would be all the greater if the department of justice decided to move to criminal prosecution of the bank and its managers. Martinez decided that if it happened, Rijkman Groenink would have to be dropped immediately as chairman of ABN Amro.

The bank's top 150 managers got together at Duin & Kruidberg in November 2004. Working in teams, they developed a number of scenarios for the bank's future. What would they have to do to develop Italy as a second domestic market, for example? And what would they do if they were taken over by HSBC?

Now Groenink suggested for the first time that there was a possibility that the bank might have to consider becoming part of a larger organisation. General manager Rob Meuter could not believe his ears. Later he said that Groenink could hardly be serious. The chairman was apparently disappointed in the lukewarm reaction to the idea that he got from the bank's top management. Gesturing with his arm, Groenink said: you can't win a war with people like that!

A summary of the decisions taken by the board a few months before at the Bosporus offsite meeting was issued at the meeting. The big decision, to split up the corporate banking division, had not been taken there, but it had been decided that ABN Amro would focus on medium-sized businesses: the sweet spot. Jiskoot had angrily resisted this at the meeting, but had come off worst.

The announcement raised a number of questions. Colleagues in the corporate banking division asked themselves what implications this would have for their clients. The people in retail asked if there would be room for their small clients. For a while it looked as if no one was pleased.

The general managers involved felt that the managing board had not explained the strategy to the business team group (GBT), which had been set up one-and-a-half years before to ensure that the general managers who would have to execute the strategy were involved in its development. They insisted that GBT, which many saw as a talking shop, had failed. Things would have to change.

At the meeting, Eltjo Kok, who had taken over human resources from Garmt Louw two years before, presented an employee engagement survey. The picture it presented was worrying: employee trust in the company's management was dwindling. Questions and doubts concerning the direction of the bank remained. The human resources department had advised Groenink to be more visible within the organisation, to make it clear that he was there and what he stood for. Groenink had told them that he would think about it.

At the end of 2004 it suddenly occurred to Rijkman Groenink that he might have to resign. The targets set in 2001 had clearly not been reached. Moreover, the problems in the United States had not yet been resolved. But he reflected that he had at least presented a record profit for 2004 of nearly 3.9 billion euros. He consoled himself that things weren't looking too bad for the bank, after a difficult start.

At the beginning of 2005, the members of the audit committee noted that the Fed affair and the performance of senior managers had damaged the bank significantly. Martinez suggested that the men be tackled hard. Hard enough to demonstrate to the United States that the bank would not tolerate such behaviour.

Wim Dik didn't agree. He suggested that Groenink and De Swaan be fired. Maarten van Veen thought this was going too far. Martinez hesitated. He let it be known that he agreed in principle with Dik, but that he also felt that the bank would suffer a lot of damage if the two men were fired. He thought it better to await the decision of the American prosecutor.

The members of the board decided that the senior managers would have to feel the effects of all this in their pockets. They were forced to return part of the bonuses they had received in January for 2004. Groenink returned 40 per cent of his bonus, De Swaan 30 per cent and the other four managing directors 20 per cent. In the view of the committee they had all played a role and they were all therefore to some extent responsible.

Groenink was stoical. He thought it was irritating, and simply wanted to get back to business as soon as possible. When Tom de Swaan heard that he would have to return part of his bonus, his world collapsed. A few months earlier he had even been voted CFO of the year by fellow members of his profession, and praised for his strategic vision and integrity. 'Above all, the jury values the skill with which he led the enterprise through turbulent times,' they stated. De Swaan felt that the board's imputations were completely unfair. All his life he had focused on behaving with integrity. He had started as a supervisor at the Dutch Central Bank and had been at ABN Amro for six years. The implication that he had not behaved with due care was unbearable: he wept.

Tom de Swaan and Rijkman Groenink had not become friends in the seven years they had sat together on the managing board. They never learned to understand each other. De Swaan felt that Groenink didn't think about what he did. Groenink never seemed to doubt himself, and that couldn't be right. The CFO also thought that Groenink had no character judgment. He probably often thought of the warnings of his wife, years before.

The financial director thought that Groenink didn't manage the bank well, and focused too much on individual battles. The CFO felt that he spent the previous years shuttling between the board members, who were always quarrelling. As he saw it, he was the team's nurse.

De Swaan understood that it would be difficult to tackle a man like Jiskoot. The corporate banker had enormous status; everyone in Dutch big business wanted him. De Swaan also thought that it would be difficult to convince Jiskoot that any views other than his own were valid. He was an excellent debater, for one thing. A fight like that could go on for years.

De Swaan would be turning 60 the following year. It had been agreed that he would stay on until then. But Martinez pressed Groenink to let the CFO go. Groenink agreed; he thought that De Swaan should have protected him better in New York. The men had also understood from the Fed that they would not be averse to seeing a new CFO at the bank.

Groenink thought that De Swaan had not been forceful enough as CFO, especially with regard to enforcing accountability. De Swaan was first and foremost an intellectual, a professor who enjoyed talking, and receiving recognition of his knowledge and skill. His close advisor, Herman Spruit, who had been a consultant at Marakon before being brought into the bank – mainly under the influence of De Swaan – thought that the CFO had not ensured that people accepted accountability. The head of the supervisory board also thought that De Swaan had not challenged Groenink enough. From the records of the meetings of the supervisory board it is clear that the board chairman was not especially impressed by his CFO.

In his turn, De Swaan thought that the ABN Amro supervisory board was a pretty loose outfit at best, and that it was not up to delivering much. Why had the bank's governors not been more critical? The CFO was disturbed that Groenink and Loudon worked behind the scenes so much and that Loudon seldom spoke to the other managing directors. De Swaan had hardly spoken alone with Loudon in years. But he felt that it would not be acceptable to meet with him behind Groenink's back. A CFO only did that when he wanted to broach the possibility of his boss's resignation, and De Swaan didn't want to do that.

Tom de Swaan experienced his early retirement with mixed feelings; his last years at the bank had not been his best. It was perhaps better to see the positive side. His wife was pleased.

Investors reacted coolly, again, to the record profit that ABN Amro had achieved for 2004: the share price had fallen by 0.7 per cent. Many questions remained. At the presentation Groenink had to explain the bank's strategy again. Groenink emphasised ABN Amro's new focus on the middle sector of the market. "It will yield 200 per cent of economic profit."

Groenink repeated that the bank was thoroughly aware of the need to take a close look at the costs of capital invested. The threshold for the required yield had been set at 10.5 per cent, and everything above that would be economic profit. He said that the corporate banking division had been instructed to jettison all its less profitable clients. Groenink also announced that the bank intended to grow in Italy and was planning to go ahead with its role in shareholder pact connected with Antonveneta.

Marakon had already made it clear that ABN Amro had only three possibilities for growth: the United States, India and cost savings. Time and again, Herman Spruit had hammered away at the bad results achieved by the corporate banking division. The division had achieved a profit of 754 million euros over 2004, 18 per cent of the group result. The corporate banking side of the business had employed nearly a third of the bank's capital, and produced a return of 6 per cent. Spruit estimated that Jiskoot's division had already cost more than 3 billion euros and had therefore lost some 10 per cent of the bank's total value.

The top managers of the corporate banking division were furious. Jiskoot indicated to his colleagues that an important part of the rising costs had been incurred by the ever-growing head office. Five years before some 2,000 people had worked there, but now there were nearly twice as many as that. All those costs were charged on.

But after the stalemate around the Bosporus offsite meeting, Groenink, encouraged mainly by Spruit and Jeroen Drost, had set out some tough demands for the corporate banking division. One of these was that the division's costs would have to show demonstrable reductions by March. Jiskoot had rung the alarm with his people in October the previous year: it was imperative they reduce costs. The corporate banking division's structure was simplified. Alexandra Cook was given responsibility for client contacts (global clients) and Piero Overmars responsibility for all products (global markets). To reduce costs still further, clients whose business yielded too little would be let go.

It was too little, too late. Three months into the first year, it was already clear that the corporate banking division would again fail to deliver, that its costs were still not sufficiently under control. Accountant Zeilmaker calculated that about one billion euros had been paid in bonuses for 2004, almost all of it to colleagues in the corporate banking division. As he saw it, the profit side was not strong enough to carry this. More and more people at head office were coming to the same conclusion; the elephant deals were just not coming in. These deals would have to come from overseas, because the Dutch market was simply too small.

Groenink now intervened. In March, it was announced that Wilco Jiskoot would be his advisor on mergers and takeovers. Jiskoot remained responsible for the big division, but not for its day-to-day management, which was put in the hands of Piero Overmars, general manager of financial markets. Jiskoot didn't think that Groenink would take up even a second of his time.

Piero Overmars was different to Jiskoot. He was a deal maker who focused on service and clients. Jiskoot found it difficult to cut through knots, make choices, or scrap certain products and services. Jiskoot liked to keep his options open. You never knew what you might get out of it.

Overmars was better at taking decisions. He had started at the corporate business division, and dealers make decisions all day. He intervened quickly and hard. As he saw it, all the qualities of the corporate banking division should be offered to all the bank's clients. Only then would all that capacity be utilised, and the expected profitability delivered. Overmars felt that the platform built by the corporate banking division was too big for the present portfolio of clients. He understood that the walls around the division would have to be broken down. This was the moment to shut down the corporate banking division, five years after it had been set up.

Overmars would have to fire a number of heavyweight and expensive investment bankers. He wasn't looking forward to it, but he had Jiskoot's support. Jiskoot wasn't happy about it either, but he had decided to coach the younger Overmars through the process as well as possible.

Meanwhile, ABN Amro was doing all it could to satisfy the Fed's demands. Dozens of people in Dubai, New York and Amsterdam, mostly at lower levels, were fired. Although checks showed that not one transaction had a criminal or even a terrorist background, nearly everyone who had had any connection with the transactions was dismissed. At head office the word was that this was necessary mainly to get in the Fed's good books.

The people who dealt with compliance at head office were becoming concerned. They had been overwhelmed. A lot should have happened already and they had got almost nowhere. The bank was now way behind, and until now it had only been reacting to the Fed's anger. How much longer would the bank be the Fed's punch bag?

In early May, Herbert Biern was brought on board. During the summer of the previous year, he had negotiated a deal on behalf of the Fed with ABN Amro, and now he would be working for the bank, with responsibility for seeing that the bank's attempts to meet the Fed's requirements went smoothly. Groenink was proud of the appointment. "Biern is one of the best-informed and most experienced experts in the world on the area of compliance," he said. "With him on board, we will be adding further impetus to a series of initiatives that will strengthen compliance within the entire organisation. ABN Amro is hereby taking an important step in the direction of a compliance programme that that will establish us as setting standards for the financial industry worldwide."

Biern would report to Carin Gorter. She had been appointed general manager with special responsibility for insuring compliance at the bank. Gorter was head of auditing at the corporate banking division and she was not an expert on compliance. People at the bank asked why they hadn't appointed someone who knew enough about the subject to make the board listen.

The Fed had demanded that the subject receive attention at the highest level at the bank. Carin Gorter would report directly to Rijkman Groenink and to Arthur Martinez. Groenink wasn't pleased by that, but Martinez explained that it was necessary. The bank had made too many promises without delivering.

Some of Gorter's colleagues were irritated that she soon started talking in line with Groenink about the bank's ambition to set standards in compliance for the entire sector. Wasn't that somewhat overconfident? The bank had a lot of mileage to make up and it would entail a huge effort to achieve even to a modicum of professionalism.

A compliance oversight board was installed in the supervisory board, with Arthur Martinez as its chairman. The members of the board would keep a close eye on the progress being made by the compliance policy committee, which had been installed at the end of the previous year. Under Groenink's chairmanship, it was supposed to oversee the introduction of new integrity rules throughout the bank, and also ensure that they were observed. These rules covered client information, integrity-sensitive positions and the reporting of integrity-threatening incidents.

The chairman told the committee that he always felt that things were going on that he could not get close to. He was convinced that he had not done anything wrong, and that this had been confirmed. But Groenink realised that he would lose his job if the United States moved toward criminal prosecution.

He discussed with his colleagues and Martinez the risk that the bank might be prosecuted. They didn't think that there would be a prosecution. Both DNB and the Fed had made it clear that if this happened, the bank's credibility would be brought into question. DNB had been solidly behind ABN Amro in the matter, and had probably done everything it could to prevent any danger to the continuity of the bank. The condition for this was of course that the bank did all its homework for the Fed, and well.

Around 300 people were taken on to make this happen quickly. Huge investments of about 200 million were involved, not only in people but also in IT. The whole organisation would be examined. It all involved a lot of money and time.

Hugh Scott Barrett was concerned about the enormous costs, and especially the huge amount of time the matter was taking up. The bank's employees would have to answer countless questions about their clients, but they would hardly have time to visit them, let alone bring in new clients. They thought that the whole operation was taking the bank's eye off the ball. Moreover, all the clients would also have to be reviewed within a year, and many of them were not pleased at all about this.

It was evident that the investment would place considerable pressure on the bank's profit-and-loss account. The bank's board was frustrated that the Fed had said that they were not to communicate about this.

Many bankers were irritated too; all senior bankers would have to do an integrity test. The tests, often involving an interview with a critical interviewer, were considered humiliating. What it came down to was that they were being asked if they were honest. Many managers thought this was strange. The top managers of the company didn't appear to have their house in order, and now the people who worked for them were being tested for their integrity. They felt that Rijkman Groenink had spun the mirror: people say I have a problem, he had said, but it's you who have the problem.

All over the world, ABN Amro employees were wondering how long the bank would be held hostage by the Fed. As long as that was the case, the bank had no real grip on its own future.

Meanwhile Groenink was getting into discussions with a whole different calibre of bank, and without using his new advisor, Jiskoot. In February 2005 he met Fred Goodwin, the CEO of Royal Bank of Scotland (RBS). They discussed the general situation in the world of big banking. They also discussed the sense and nonsense involved in a possible combination of the two banks.

Groenink didn't know how to handle Goodwin. Analysts had been speculating since 2003 that RBS and Santander might be interested in a takeover of ABN Amro. These two banks were not in ABN Amro's peer group, unlike ING and Barclays. But whenever he asked Goodwin about it, he denied it.

Groenink didn't find Goodwin particularly sympathetic; he was clearly used to working to his own agenda. Goodwin was not someone who would take much account of the thoughts of the man sitting on the other side of the table.

Goodwin was 46 and he was a phenomenon in the banking world. In the City of London, analysts had nicknamed him Fred the Shred, because he had repeatedly demonstrated his ability to integrate banks and save costs rigorously.

In a certain sense Goodwin was much like Groenink. Goodwin was strong analytically and the people around him described him as fairly emotionless. He was also a man who expected a lot of himself. Many of his colleagues were afraid of him. RBS wasn't known for its friendly atmosphere. There, it was all about results.

Goodwin's biggest coup had been the hostile takeover of NatWest, a bank that was twice the size of RBS, in 2000. It made a big impression. When he was appointed CEO in 2001, he scrapped 18,000 jobs and saved 1.5 billion pounds in costs in a relatively short time. While the rest of the market was going downhill, the British bank, which was not known for its efficiency, was being smoothly integrated. This seamless takeover brought Goodwin the *Forbes* magazine title of global businessman of the year in 2002. In an interview, Goodwin said that he did things by his "five second rule": the first thought or impression is the most important.

Goodwin also believed in the consolidation of the banking sector. He was a deal maker and wanted to turn RBS into one of the biggest players in its sector. His aim was a broad-based bank that was present in so many markets, both as regards products and regions, that its results would be relatively invulnerable. Goodwin was well on the way to achieving that too. RBS was valued at more than 50 billion pounds on the stock exchange, considerably larger than ABN Amro. It was also larger than Barclays, JPMorgan Chase, UBS and Deutsche Bank.

There was another similarity: for years, Goodwin had spent part of his career focusing on cleaning up badly managed companies. That was while he was an accountant at Touche Ross. In 1990 he had been the central figure in winding up Bank of Credit and Commerce International (BCCI), which had been brought down by fraud.

Goodwin, who liked to tinker with classic cars in his free time, had little time for journalists. He did, however, have time for analysts and investors, who were enthusiastic about the Scot. Goodwin had a clear growth strategy, and as a former accountant he could explain RBS's figures in detail.

He differed from Groenink in another respect too. The son of an electrician, Goodwin was clear about what he expected from people, and held them to it. He was focused on the operational excellence of the bank. Every day was another opportunity for further improvements in efficiency. The Scot began work each morning with a 45-minute conference call with the top twenty managers of the bank in Europe and Asia. Known as the touchdown session, each manager had two minutes to outline the most important issues in his area, and they had to be more recent than twenty-four hours. A similar touchdown was held several times a week with RBS's managers in America.

ABN Amro's chairman started crossing the Channel more frequently in early 2005. On 18 March, Rijkman Groenink met with John Varley, CEO of Barclays, to discuss the results of a variety of investigations they had commissioned to look into a possible combination of the two banks.

They were looking for answers to questions with regard to the strategic and financial logic of a combination, the impact it would have on the market, the effects it would have on employment and the synergies that would be possible. It certainly helped that they both used calculating methods provided by the same consultant, Marakon. Groenink and Varley decided to talk again at the end of the year. As with RBS, Barclays was also considerably larger than ABN Amro.

Meanwhile there were rumblings on the supervisory board. The 2004 annual report, which appeared in March 2005, reported that Wim Dik and Maarten van Veen would step down as governors. The former would be turning 70, while the latter had completed his twelve years. It was also announced that the two positions would be filled by Anthony Ruys, former chairman of Heineken, and Rob van den Bergh, former board chairman of VNU publishers. Remarkably, no new vice-chairman and successor to Aarnout Loudon was announced. Groenink had already let it be known that he was opposed to Burgmans being appointed, and this had not helped to improve the atmosphere. It was also not helpful that Loudon and Van Veen had been irritated by Burgmans' lack of diplomacy for some time.

Burgmans wasn't pleased; he really had wanted to succeed Loudon. The Unilever top man was convinced that the bank didn't want him because he had said that he would call people to account as head of the supervisory board. Burgmans realised that the race was over. He told his astounded colleagues that he wasn't interested any longer anyway, because the ups and downs at Unilever were taking up a lot of his time. He said that he would resign at the same time as Loudon.

Burgmans took this message to Jan Kalff, the man who had brought him into the bank in the first place. Burgmans was sorry, but he wasn't interested anymore. Kalff was disappointed that Burgmans was dropping out now.

Groenink and Loudon decided to ask Martinez to become vice-chairman. This meant that he would soon succeed Loudon, and occupy the role for four years. After that, the intention was to appoint a Dutchman to the position. Discussions had already been held with Shell's chairman, Jeroen van der Veer, to sound him out.

Loudon and Groenink thought that Martinez had led the audit committee well, and that he had made an important contribution to the discussions with the Fed. The American had kept the peace and ensured that Groenink wasn't fired, as Wim Dik had suggested. Loudon and Van Veen thought that an American president would help the bank in these difficult circumstances. The move also fitted well with the bank's international ambitions. Martinez's to-the-point approach at meetings appealed to them too. His meetings were never long.

Groenink told various colleagues that he wouldn't mind if the new head of the supervisory board operated from a distance and only visited the Netherlands around ten times a year. Some of his colleagues suspected that Groenink would also not be averse to the size of the bonuses seen through American eyes.

Martinez was honoured and surprised when he was asked. A taboo was being broken, and he understood why. Martinez considered Burgmans arrogant; he talked mostly in negative terms. Martinez felt that it was yet to be seen whether ABN Amro would be able to resolve its problems independently. He knew that one of his major tasks in the coming years would be to find a successor to Groenink.

The appointment was simply reported to the managing board, and it was not discussed. Martinez's appointment as ABN Amro's new president would be announced at the shareholder meeting at the end of April. Martinez would take up the post in May 2006.

While Groenink was playing with the idea that the bank might be satisfied with a role as the smaller party in a merger, in Italy ABN Amro went on the attack.

The bank had been involved in Antonveneta, the eighth-largest bank in Italy, for nine years, with a 12.7 per cent stake. The bank also owned nine per cent of Capitalia. In March, ABN Amro announced that it intended to acquire Antonveneta, which was worth around 5.5 billion euros. Not everyone was enthusiastic. Zeilmaker warned that the bank was not significant, and that reminded everyone that they had agreed that any bank considered for acquisition would have to be in the top three in its market. With its market share of little more than three per cent, Antonveneta was not in the top ten. ABN Amro had always said that strategy would not be an argument for an acquisition, Zeilmaker said; any acquisition would always have to yield good returns, and make a positive contribution to the result immediately.

From the beginning it was clear that it would be a difficult fight. Antonio Fazio, president of the Italian Central Bank, wasn't keen on foreign intervention. It might result in a more efficient Italian market, and it would make bankers work harder for their money. Italian banks charged clients an average of 550 euros per year for their services. ABN Amro couldn't charge more than 36 euros a year in the much more competitive Dutch market.

Fazio therefore decided in favour of the Italian Banca Populare di Lodi, led by Gianpiero Fiorani, who was also interested in acquiring of Antonveneta. Antonio Fazio suggested during a first exploratory talk that Groenink should simply talk to Gianpiero Fiorani. When he did so, Fiorani enthusiastically offered ABN Amro an interest of 15 per cent in a combination that he, Fiorani, would run. Groenink rejected the offer straight away. Meanwhile, Fiorani doubled his stake to five per cent. Moreover, he and Fazio were sowing discord among the other shareholders who were part of a monitoring shareholder pact with ABN Amro. The pact ended in April.

Jeroen Drost warned the chairman that if they got into a fight, it would be dirty. But Groenink sensed an opportunity to show that ABN Amro was in a position to create a second domestic market in Europe. After so many years, this might well be the last chance to do so. At head office it was suggested that the chairman was motivated by the American debacle. The bank was unable to operate in the United States, and there were a number of possible mergers and takeovers in the pipeline. The Italian adventure was looking increasingly like an attempt to take the fight to the enemy.

On 30 March, ABN Amro went on the attack. Without discussing it with

Fazio, the bank made an offer of 7.3 billion euros, more than 25 times the bank's profit. If the takeover was successful, it would be the biggest in the bank's history.

The ABN Amro shareholders were asked to participate in a share issue of 2.7 billion euros. Bankers at the corporate banking division warned Groenink that it would be an insanely expensive purchase. Jan de Ruiter, who headed up equity capital markets, was in charge of the share issue. He let Groenink know that the shareholders were not interested. They didn't understand why ABN Amro should invest in a country where it was so obviously unwelcome. On the day the bank announced that it wanted to issue new shares, the share price fell by 1.4 per cent.

Others, Piero Overmars among them, complained that the takeover might look good if you calculated the economic profit that the combination would yield over a period of ten years, but in the short term the takeover meant a decline in the profit per share, because it was financed partly though a rights issue.

Groenink, who had few friends left in the corporate banking division, irritated his colleagues with his laconic attitude to preparations for the issue. It didn't appear to interest him whether the shares sold for 18 or 19 euros, a difference of some 150 million euros. He refused to rehearse the presentation, which was intended to convince analysts and shareholders of the move. His audience would be his colleagues who would be selling the shares. They got the impression that he was looking at the figures for the first time, and they found it demotivating.

In the weeks following, the two rivals built up further interests in Antonveneta. ABN Amro was fighting with one arm tied behind its back. Fazio quickly gave the Italians permission to extend their holding above 20 per cent. ABN Amro received permission only after it had submitted a complaint to the European Commission. Banca Populare di Lodi was able to increase its holding considerably to 30 per cent. Fiorani let it be known that he would send Antonveneta's incumbent board away at the shareholder meeting on 30 April. Fiorani then made an offer, a package of shares and bonds, which he said was several hundred million euros higher than ABN Amro's offer.

Fiorani knew that one of his colleagues had been persuaded to take potentially damaging material to ABN Amro's lawyers. A detailed reconstruction in *Het Financieele Dagblad* called the man Mr X and described him as a man who lived in the same village as a consultant at Rothschild, who were advising ABN Amro. They talked with him with for a while and got him to explain to ABN Amro's lawyers that 18 accounts had been opened at Lodi for business friends of Fiorani, and that some 545 million euros had been transferred to them. The interest was low and Fiorani's friends spent the money on Antonveneta shares. 'This is an important indication that the bank was indeed buying shares in Antonveneta through frontmen,' *Het Financieele Dagblad* reported. The bank took the evidence to the Italian department of justice.

At the end of April, only a handful of shareholders voted for a takeover by ABN Amro. Drost and Groenink played with the thought of offering ABN Amro's interest in Antonveneta to Fiorani. This would yield the bank a book profit of 600 million euros. But on the morning after the humiliation, the Italian department of justice raided the head office of Banca Populare di Lodi. An investigation was launched into manipulation of Antonveneta's share price. It seemed the tide was turning.

ABN Amro was supported in this fight by the Dutch minister of finance, Gerrit Zalm, and DNB president, Nout Wellink. The minister voiced his criticisms to his fellow cabinet ministers and let it be known that he thought it incomprehensible that one European bank was being prevented from acquiring another in today's Europe. Wellink put Fazio's questionable conduct twice on the agenda at the biweekly meeting with the European Central Bank.

Their efforts were not without effect. In the end, ABN Amro won official permission from the Italians to proceed with its offer. Fiorani was also forced to make a cash offer. Despite the setbacks he had faced, he let it be known that he would continue as he had been doing. In search of money he needed, Fiorani arranged bridging finance with Royal Bank of Scotland, Deutsche Bank and BNP Paribas. Groenink wasn't pleased by their support of his Italian opponent. He had reckoned on a more European solidarity from his peers.

Even the Italian press appeared to be sympathetic to ABN Amro's offer. At the end of June, *Il Giornale* published a telephone conversation between Fazio and Fiorani that had taken place a few months earlier. Fiorani was tense and wanted to know if he would get Fazio's permission to make an offer for Antonveneta. Some of Fazio's close colleagues had advised against this because the Banca Populare di Lodi's financial position looked too weak. But Fazio pushed his plan through and phoned Fiorani in the middle of the night with the good news. "Tonino, I am moved, thank you ... thank you ... I'm getting goose bumps," he replied. "Tonino, I'd like to give you a kiss on your forehead, but I can't do that ... I know how much you have suffered, I've also had to deal with the structure, with my lawyers, and if I could I'd catch a plane and come to see you." That wasn't possible, but it emerged later that Fiorani treated Fazio to a Cartier watch, a Prada bag and a number of rare religious documents. Many Italians realised that their financial sector was dominated by an old-boy network.

Still, it looked like ABN Amro would lose the fight. The offer would lapse on 22 July, and fewer than three per cent of the new shares had been sold.

Rijkman Groenink could console himself that he had been chosen European banker of the year that summer by Group 20+1, a group of financial journalists. 'Groenink has led ABN Amro since May 2000,' the jury reported. 'During the last few years he has succeeded in transforming a highly decentralised bank into a tightly led organisation that is among the top ten of the leading European banks.' Two Dutchmen received the prize before Groenink: former DNB president Willem Duisenberg and former ING chairman Godfried van der Lugt. Fred Goodwin, chairman of Royal Bank of Scotland, was also honoured.

The takeover fight for Antonveneta was on the agenda of the strategy session of the managing board and supervisory board in July. A number of governors were astonished when the managing directors suddenly started talking about a possible takeover of the Turkish bank, Garantibank. A lot of momentum had been created in a short space of time in favour of the Turkish adventure, while the takeover of Antonveneta had been put on the back burner. Dolf Collee said that he no longer believed in Italy. Jiskoot let it be known that he knew the Turkish owner of the bank well and that he was interested.

Jeroen Drost, in charge of corporate development, had been working day and night for some months on the takeover of Antonveneta, and he was disappointed when he heard this.

At this point one of the governors, De Rothschild, raised his hand. He wondered what ABN Amro's managing board thought they were doing. There had been a strategy, and Italy had been central to it as the bank's future second domestic market in Europe ... This proposed acquisition couldn't be right. It was decided to make one last effort to buy Antonveneta. Groenink told Drost later that he had gone through the entire scenario with De Rothschild before the meeting. They had brought forward the plan to take over Garantibank to be shot down.

A few days later the Italian stock exchange supervisory body, Consob, intervened. It decided to freeze the voting rights on shares owned by Fiorani and some of his friends. The men were frightened and started calling each other to make new plans. The public prosecutor had the calls tapped and the information, combined with what they had heard from Mr X, was enough to suggest that it was time for action.

It was not until 26 September that the last details of the Antonveneta acquisition were rounded off, and ABN Amro became owner of the bank. Britain's *Financial Times* complimented the bank, although it had always been critical of Groenink. On the evening of that day, a visibly happy Rijkman Groenink was interviewed on the Dutch current affairs programme NOVA by Paul Witteman. He said he was tremendously enthusiastic about the bank's victory. When Witteman asked him if ABN Amro had now made itself attractive for a possible takeover in its turn, the chairman's face sank. "If someone offers us a good deal that I can't turn away, I would have to advise the shareholders to accept it," he said. "But I don't expect this to happen while I'm at the bank. There aren't many banks that can put up 50 billion."

The investor relations department, meanwhile, thought that Groenink should not be advising the shareholders to do anything. Time and again they tried to make it clear to him that what the shareholders wanted above all was consistency, and that he should always tell the same story. Groenink wasn't interested. To him, telling the same story was simply boring.

To the despair of his colleagues, the board chairman allowed himself to be led into speculation during meetings with shareholders. He always liked to challenge his audience. Groenink told Richard Bruens, investor relations manager, that it's always good to attack your counterpart at a meeting, to scare him a little. In his view, you could learn a lot about a person from their reaction. But the approach didn't always have the desired effect.

In the summer of 2005, Bruens and Groenink went to visit an American shareholder of the bank. Federated was good for 300 million dollars in assets and it was considering extending its holding in ABN Amro. After a talk with the fund manager, a woman with an Asian background, they were walking out of the building at the end of the afternoon when Groenink indicated a large professional vacuum cleaner that was standing there. In an attempt at a joke, he remarked that their hostess could start cleaning the room. The fund manager was furious, and said that she would sell all the company's shares in ABN Amro and take Groenink to court. The ABN Amro chairman didn't understand her response; he thought he had simply made a joke. He asked Bruens to write a letter of apology. There was no court case, but Federated sold all its ABN Amro shares.

During the July meeting of the supervisory board there was urgent discussion of proposed changes to the bank's strategy and structure. Jeroen Drost and Dolf Collee presented their Petra story. Named after the supervisory board's offsite meeting in Jordan, the presentation followed Seville and Bosporus, and its core message was that the bank now needed to show that it was a real bank.

The presentation was shot through with urgency. 'We must create much more value if we want to be among the top five European banks,' they stated. 'Only a few of the bank's departments have achieved their ambitious targets. During the coming four years we really have to do better. We must focus on the so-called midmarket, that is, medium-sized companies and individuals.'

To do so, the bank would be divided into ten business units. Five were organised regionally (the Netherlands, Europe, North America, South America and Asia). The idea was that the bank should bring its global excellence to local markets. 'We must create value as an integrated bank. We are still not seen as one bank and that means that we have to absorb the discount through our portfolio.'

Only 550 big companies, world players, would be admitted as clients to a separate global clients business unit. The same would be true for a separate global business unit for wealthy private clients. Another three worldwide business units would be for specific products: global markets for the development of services during big share issues and acquisition programmes, transaction banking and asset management. To ensure that all business units worked optimally with each other, another two responsibilities would be created: one to ensure that the same types of clients could benefit from the same information across the world, and another to ensure value creation through the network of activities.

To manage this new and complex matrix, the managing board suggested that GBT be given real teeth by its transformation into a business committee group (GBC). Moreover, it suggested that the board be expanded by adding three new positions. In the new set-up, five members of the managing board would have direct responsibility for different parts of the business. With the ten directors, they would form the new GBC executive. This was where the business would be led.

The roles of the chairman, CFO and COO were kept separate from GBC; they would control the results achieved and were also responsible for general bank strategy.

The supervisory board thought this was all too complex. They wondered if the set-up would be manageable. Not for the first time, some of the governors felt that they were only there to rubber stamp programmes that had already been decided.

Rob van den Bergh and Antony Burgmans thought that it was a ridiculous plan. Van den Bergh thought that either the chairman or COO should chair of GBC. The suggested candidate, Joost Kuiper, was a paper tiger. Van den Bergh knew that Kuiper couldn't take on Jiskoot. Burgmans walked out, saying that it was a spurious solution to put a man with no power in such a key position. Olijslager also thought that no good would come of it, but said nothing. The structure would be unmanageable; the matrix was too complex, warned Scaroni, an ex-McKinsey man.

There was also a great deal of resistance within the managing board. Kuiper, Jiskoot, Scott Barrett – in fact no one supported the plan. Scott Barrett would rather have seen a small executive board installed on the Anglo-Saxon model, with a big group of operational managers below it. It even looked as if a majority of the governors would sign up for this approach. Kuiper was happy enough; he was thinking of retiring anyway.

Groenink simply pushed the GBC set-up through. He didn't believe in a small, three-man managing board. The whole discussion irritated him. He thought that some members of the board supported the idea of a smaller board because it would mean that their remuneration would become invisible. The salaries and bonuses of managing board members were reported in the annual report.

Joost Kuiper thought that the plan would create a monster. But Rijkman Groenink wanted it that way, and he also wanted Kuiper to chair GBC. Kuiper, however, refused the job. He felt far more at home in a role as supervisor or coach. Groenink said that this was exactly why he wanted to see Kuiper as chairman: the group would need his diplomatic qualities. Kuiper said again that he wasn't interested. But Groenink put him under pressure and eventually Kuiper, ever-loyal, gave way. He understood why Groenink wanted him in the chair: he wouldn't seize power. Groenink felt safe with Kuiper. Under his chairmanship, nothing risky would be discussed behind his back by GBC. Coach Erik van de Loo would be brought in to ensure that Kuiper got the mandate he needed from his GBC colleagues.

So the managing board would be reinforced by three more members.

Eltjo Kok was assigned to look for three people with the potential to succeed Rijkman Groenink. The quest was based on two lists of names of between ten and twelve possible candidates. The names in the first list were also people who could in principle be appointed directly to the managing board.

There was unanimity on the proposal to bring Fabio Barbosa onto the managing board. Jeroen Drost insisted that Groenink should fly to Brazil to persuade Barbosa and his wife, but Groenink delegated the task to Dolf Collee, who was unsuccessful. Barbosa liked living in Brazil and despite his view that the bank needed more of its employees to move around, he didn't want to move to Europe.

Eltjo Kok did the rounds of the members of the managing board to draw up an inventory of their preferences. Hugh Scott Barrett wanted Ron Teerlink to join them. Groenink asked Scott Barrett to take up the position vacated by De Swaan on 1 January. Teerlink had done well under Scott Barrett, and it was felt that he would be a good replacement.

Scott Barrett was not happy with the way things had been going, however.

With three potential successors to Groenink on the managing board, it looked as if his chance at succeeding him had gone. Nor did Scott Barrett like the fact that he was no more than a stripped-down CFO, and that he was not involved in determining the bank's strategy.

Jiskoot fought for the interests of the corporate side and made it clear that he wanted Piero Overmars on the managing board. As Groenink saw it, Jiskoot thought that his prestige would be affected if his work was taken over by a general manager, and this was why he was backing Overmars. During the discussion that followed, everyone agreed about the two names. They all thought it regrettable that Fabio Barbosa didn't want to join the highest level of the bank. And there was also some discussion about Lex Kloosterman, who some thought the banker with the broadest range of skills, but he was not seen as a potential board chairman. The name of Ann Cairns, the general manager responsible for transaction banking, was also mentioned. If appointed, she would be the first woman at the highest level of the bank, but it was felt that she was not yet ready.

There was a long discussion about Jan Peter Schmittmann, the head of the domestic division. He had supported Groenink for years, and he had promised him a place on the managing board if he succeeded in getting the domestic division back on the rails. Everyone agreed that Schmittmann had succeeded in doing so.

Schmittmann had been counting on the appointment. Groenink had just asked him to organise a leadership trip for the top forty managers of the bank with Huibert Boumeester. An outfitter had already been in to take their measurements for yellow sailing suits. On the 12 November the managing board would be present at the start of the Volvo Ocean Race in Vigo, Spain.

But the governors vetoed Schmittmann. They thought him impudent and confrontational. It didn't help that he had a bad reputation with the supervisory board. They thought that he was too much like Groenink, who was also not good at listening. A year and a half before, André Olijslager had complained about his poor reception by Schmittmann, during his introductory round of visits. Schmittmann hadn't made any preparations. Huibert Boumeester was chosen to fill the third position, after intercession from Groenink.

Loudon was impressed by Overmars, and saw him as a possible successor to Groenink. And as he saw it, Teerlink was needed to get costs under control. Loudon thought that it would have been better to bring a retailer on to the managing board; this would have been logical. But in his view it was also clear that it was the chairman's prerogative to appoint his team.

Schmittmann was furious when he heard that he wouldn't be appointed to the managing board. He went straight to Groenink, who denied that he had promised him a place on the board, although he also said that he had wanted

Schmittmann but that the others had been against it. He said that the bank badly needed Schmittmann in the domestic division, and that there would be another opportunity in the future. But Schmittmann felt betrayed and turned against Groenink.

Kloosterman also thought that he had earned a place in the boardroom and decided to do some hard thinking about his career, and especially whether he wanted to continue at ABN Amro. He didn't like the way the bank was being led and told Groenink so. Kloosterman thought that too much of the bank's money was going into loans to big business. He felt that Groenink was not up to dealing with Jiskoot, that Jiskoot had too much power. He told Groenink that he wanted to work at a strategic level and that he would leave the bank.

The main difficulties were dealt with during a meeting of the supervisory board on 11 October. This time the numbers were taken into account. Petra had promised that the gap in the economic profit would finally be filled. "Our ambition is to be among the best 25 per cent of banks as regards delivering value to shareholders. That means that we must make some 7 billion euros in economic profit over the next four years. If we don't intervene, however, we will have a deficit of 2 billion euros. There are three ways to drive up the economic profit by 40 per cent: a takeover or merger (but that's unpredictable), work harder in the business units, or ensure that the business units work more effectively together."

The lessons learned from the Fed drama were evident in the document that was presented. 'We will be led by our clients, every relationship with a client will have an owner, and he must ensure that he knows his client well.' At the Petra meeting it had been agreed that from now on the supervisory body in each country would only have contact with the responsible ABN Amro managing director.

The new organisational structure, a document as thick as a fist, was eyed with horror at the bank. It was enormously complex, and looked like a matrix with triple reporting lines. It was simply not clear who would have final responsibility, or for what. Many asked themselves why either Rijkman Groenink or Wilco Jiskoot hadn't been appointed to chair GBC.

There was also some anger at the appointment of three Dutchmen to the managing board, which hardly made it look like the board of an international bank. Where was the diversity which the top had always said was necessary, and which they had talked so much about? Various managing directors observed acidly that Groenink and Jiskoot had seen to it that each of them had a henchman on the board: Boumeester and Overmars respectively.

Alexandra Cook was also disappointed. She had counted on the appointment of a woman to the supervisory board at last. She spoke to Groenink about it, and wanted to know if the women who had reached levels just below the top weren't good enough. The chairman made a joke: it was a pity that his wife, Irene, no longer worked at the bank, or she would certainly have been on the managing board by now.

At the meeting of the top 150 managers of the bank at the end of the year it emerged that levels of trust in the bank's management hadn't improved at all. Remarks were made, again, about Groenink. People in human resources suggested that he would have to do something if so many people were unhappy. Groenink was irritated, and growled that anyone who was unhappy could simply resign.

The media drew their conclusions when the Petra story became public. *Het Financieele Dagblad* reported that ABN Amro was returning to a regional approach and that the bank had now definitely put the organisational structure that had been launched with so much bravura in 2000 behind it. 'The corporate banking division will be integrated with the rest of the bank,' the paper stated. 'Some aspects of ABN Amro's new management structure looked much like the structure that had been in place before 2000. Under Groenink's predecessor, Jan Kalff, ABN Amro operated a structure based on countries.'

On 14 December, Duin & Kruidberg invited the key analysts to an Investor Day, to be presented with information about the bank's plans. Groenink and Scott Barrett gave enthusiastic presentations and promised that the first fruits of the new strategy would ripen in 2006.

Speaking under the heading 'Unleashing the intrinsic potential of the group', Groenink explained in nineteen sheets that the bank would now work systematically, using its own power, and focus completely on the middle segment. The chairman said explicitly that dismantling the corporate banking division would deliver a fundamental contribution to unleashing the bank's potential. Groenink said several times that the bank would now work as cost-efficiently as possible.

That last point was central in Hugh Scott Barrett's presentation, which followed Groenink's. The bank's efficiency ratio of 68.3 per cent was still one of the worst in the sector, and would be improved. The new CFO, who would take over officially from De Swaan on 1 January, promised that the bank would strive to be one of the top 25 banks as regards efficiency. Scott Barrett told his audience that the bank would work more efficiently in 2006.

Groenink was chosen as Man of the Year in the Christmas issue of Dutch weekly *Elsevier*. 'He has pluck, thinks fast and gives his enemies no quarter, friends and (former) colleagues say about the banker, who successfully took on the corrupt Italian establishment in 2005.' A page-long ode in praise of Groenink followed, ending, 'Rijkman Groenink is the undisputed leader of ABN Amro. The successful takeover of Antonveneta has strengthened his position. He is 56, and has another five years to go.' The magazine hit the stands on 11 December. The story was in all the newspapers.

A report that appeared seven days later attracted much less attention. On 18 December, the Fed, with DNB, announced the sanctions that they had agreed to mete out to ABN Amro for its continued non-compliance in the previous years.

It was now publicly known that the bank had no room for manoeuvre in the United States and that all the senior managers had had to return part of their bonuses. Moreover, the bank would be fined a total of 75 million dollars, one of the highest fines ever levied in the United States. In the accompanying press release, Groenink admitted that errors had been made. 'We must unfortunately acknowledge that our compliance programme in the past did not satisfy the required high standards in certain areas.'

The managing board over at the bank's neighbours, ING, remarked cynically that Rijkman Groenink had saved his own skin with the Antonveneta takeover. ABN Amro's competitors had assumed that Groenink would not survive the Fed affair, and that it would give the governors the stick they needed to beat the dog.

Under the header 'Blot on copybook of man of the year', de Volkskrant cited Marcel Pheijffer, professor of forensic accountancy at the University of Nyenrode. 'It is incomprehensible that the top man at a major company has done this ... And it is especially incomprehensible that it even occurred to him to give orders to destroy documents. We live in the post-Enron era, after that huge accounting scandal, and after the introduction of strict legislation. This disqualifies Groenink as the leader of a major institution.'

Meanwhile Arthur Martinez, the man who would take over from Aarnout Loudon in a few months, was doing his best to ensure that the American department of justice didn't move toward criminal prosecution. If that happened, the Man of the Year would lose his job immediately.

13

Shop Window

January–July 2006

His appointment to the managing board was a huge surprise to his col-leagues. But Huibert Boumeester wasn't taken aback when Rijkman Groenink invited him for a cup of coffee. He was even less surprised when the chairman shook his hand when he arrived and congratulated him on his ap-pointment to the board. Boumeester knew that he was on the list and also that Groenink had pushed the board to consider appointing him. He understood the situation, as he and Groenink were much alike. Both thought that the primary quality required of people who worked at the bank was intellectual ability. Boumeester was also an enthusiastic hunter, and occasionally went hunting with Groenink.

Then 45, Huibert Boumeester had worked at the bank for twenty years, and he had never made a secret of his aspiration to be appointed to the managing board. He had started in ABN's overseas class, and had worked for years out-side the Netherlands. From there, he had always viewed the bank's head office with a certain amount of astonishment. It always seemed a long way away, and appeared to have no contact with the activities of the bank in the field.

Dutch small-mindedness had often vexed Boumeester, and in his view many of his colleagues at head office were seriously infected with it. Did they have any idea what ABN Amro stood for overseas? He had been worried for years about the lack of discipline at the bank, and the absence of any willing-ness to make real choices. This appointment of three potential successors to Groenink was a good example of that as far as he was concerned. The bank seemed unable to commit itself to making a choice, and was now sowing a number of seeds with the intention of waiting to see what developed. Bou-meester thought that there was too much tolerance at ABN Amro for mediocre businesses.

He had known Rijkman Groenink for some time. His uncle, Frits Fenten-er van Vlissingen, had told him years before that he had been impressed by Groenink's performance as a governor at Flint, the holding company that managed the family's capital. He thought highly of his analytical abilities and especially of his nerve. Fentener van Vlissingen had proudly told him that he had ensured Rijkman Groenink's appointment in 2000 as chairman of the bank in his own capacity as deputy head of the supervisory board. Boumeester had agreed with his uncle that the bank needed a man like Rijkman Groenink. The bank was desperate for change.

In February 2000, Groenink called Boumeester. He was then ABN Amro's country manager in Malaysia. Groenink told him that he had been promoted to department manager, and that he would be the investment bank's head of global clients. Groenink had warned him that they were working on the Arrow project, and that the role would not exist for much longer, and told him to go to London straight away. Boumeester was then a member of the implementation team that had been working with consultants from McKinsey for months to set up the corporate banking division. He had expressed his concern to Groenink about Arrow. In his view, the project hadn't been thought through, and he had told Groenink then that it lacked a basis in fact. The chairman hadn't liked his criticism.

But Boumeester's career hadn't suffered. Two-and-a-half years later, he was appointed general manager of asset management. That appointment had also come as a surprise to his colleagues. Using the services of a headhunter, Dolf Collee had suggested five external candidates for the job to the supervisory board. It was Boumeester who got it. Now, two years later, he had made the big step to the supervisory board.

Some of his colleagues on the supervisory board thought that Boumeester had too little experience for the job. But friend and foe alike were agreed that he had led the asset management department well over the last two years.

As far as Boumeester was concerned, he was now in a position to make a difference. He was responsible for the bank's risk management and he was also head of the corporate development department, and therefore responsible for the development of the bank's strategy. He knew what direction he wanted to take. Even before the formal announcement of his appointment at the shareholders meeting in November the previous year, he had told Groenink that the bank was collecting too many options, and that it would have to choose or it would never achieve its aims. Boumeester believed that making a couple of good choices and dropping some of the bank's activities would shorten the path to achieving the operational excellence and cost efficiency that it so badly needed.

He took over this advisory role from Wilco Jiskoot, who wasn't shedding any tears about it. In the six months that he occupied the role, Groenink had hardly ever asked his advice on anything. To Jiskoot it was clear that Rijkman Groenink was still not listening to him after all these years.

Boumeester started immediately. Meanwhile, Groenink was playing multiple games of chess. At the start of 2006, the chairman's eye had fallen on Lloyds TSB, once Britain's largest bank, now number five, and a former client of Marakon. There was another advantage: Dutchman and Shell top manager Maarten van den Bergh was chairman of the board.

Groenink presented the idea enthusiastically to the supervisory board. But there he encountered only incomprehension. Arthur Martinez said that Lloyds was primarily a big retail bank, and that they wouldn't be able to sell the merger to the shareholders. What would be the profit? Martinez didn't believe that ABN Amro would be able to put together a story that would convince shareholders. He told Groenink that he shouldn't bother looking into it any further. Martinez was disappointed in Groenink. To him this was further proof that Rijkman Groenink lacked strategic insight. Their discussions weren't followed up seriously.

The chairman kept himself occupied with testing the waters with a number of other large banks. In February, he paid a visit to Michel Tilmant. The two men circled each other cautiously. Two months before, ING's chairman had invited Groenink to a Christmas drink at his house on Amsterdam's Herengracht. Now Groenink wanted to know if Tilmant was ready for a merger. The ING chairman didn't reject the idea, but made it clear to Groenink that he was himself in the middle of a strategic reorientation, and that it would take another six months to complete.

On 3 March, Groenink talked again with John Varley, chairman of Barclays. The two lawyers hit it off. Both spoke Marakon's economic value language. There was one major difference: Groenink was nearing the end of his role as chairman, while Varley was just starting.

John Silvester Varley was 50, and dressed in the classic city outfit of pinstrip suit and bright braces. He had been chairman for two-and-a-half years. Varley had also worked nearly all his life for his bank. He was married to Carolyn Thorn Pease, daughter of former Barclays director Richard Pease, whose family's bank had become part of Barclays in 1902. Varley would never free himself entirely of the suggestion that this was why he had been appointed head of Barclays.

Britain's second bank's value on the stock exchange was nearly 50 per cent higher than that of ABN Amro and striving to generate more than half of its profit outside Britain within the foreseeable future. Varley told Groenink that he had brought Frits Seegers to work with him on his managing board. The Dutchman had made a career at Citigroup. His presence could well help settle any fears of a British takeover. Varley was in a hurry: his two biggest rivals, RBS and HSBC, were already a few steps ahead of him. The two bankers agreed that they would exchange documents outlining their views on the potential merger.

These documents were exchanged at the end of March. Varley and Groenink agreed to see each other in early May, to discuss the outline of a collective strategy for the two banks.

On the markets, meanwhile, rumours about ABN Amro began to gather pace. At the end of March, ABN Amro's share suddenly jumped by nearly three per cent on the back of rumours that the bank was in discussions with a Spanish bank, BBVA. But this was categorically denied.

The bank's results for 2005 were 13.4 per cent higher than they had been the year before. ABN Amro had booked a net profit of 4.4 billion euros. As a result of the share issue that had been necessary to pay for the acquisition of Antonveneta, the profit per share rose by only 4.3 per cent. Groenink promised shareholders that the Italian subsidiary would start contributing to profits within twelve months. He tried to fob them off by promising to buy up shares, to support the share price. To find the money, he put an end to Drabbe's expensive Hungarian adventure, the former Magyar Hitel Bank, as well as Bouwfonds.

Groenink reported proudly that the improvement in the result was mainly a consequence of improved cost discipline. The efficiency ratio had improved by one per cent to 68.2. The chairman promised once again that 2006 would also be devoted to further improvements in cost discipline.

One analyst totted up the figures and established that the bank had neither grown nor become more efficient after five years under Groenink. During his first year, it had booked 18.5 billion in profits, but that figure was only 400 million higher now. Back then, the bank's costs had been 13.2 billion, while they were now 13 billion euros. The question remained whether the bank would be able to maintain its cost discipline. The bank's performance was already declining in the fourth quarter, mainly as a result of quickly rising costs associated with improving its compliance procedures in the United States. Carin Gorter's department had doubled in size during the previous months, to 800 employees.

A big article at the end of December in *The Wall Street Journal* under the header 'How Top DNB Plunged Into World of Shadowy Money', revealed that ABN Amro had been under investigation by the American justice department. Groenink told concerned journalists that there was no question of any criminal prosecution connected with the Iran-Libya affair. As he saw it, everything was fine. "It's standard procedure for supervisory bodies to send their dossiers on to the department of justice," he said. "They disappear somewhere in an enormous building in Washington. Nothing's happened so far anyway."

Former Unilever CEO Antony Burgmans felt certain he would succeed Aarnout Loudon as head of the supervisory board. He was determined to act decisively. But Rijkman Groenink informed Loudon that the management board would not appoint Burgmans.
Photo: Peter Boer

Supervisory board president Aarnout Loudon at the general meeting of shareholders in late April 2005. Loudon told Groenink that Wilco Jiskoot was too important for the bank and could not be fired. When he stepped down as president the following year, Loudon noted that Rijkman Groenink's flag was flying high.
Photo: Peter Hilz/Hollandse Hoogte

Much against his will, the loyal Joost Kuiper was promoted to chair the global business committee in late 2005. It led to a major loss of trust among the bank's directors.
Photo: ANP

August 2006: ING chairman Michel Tilmant (right) and his chief financial officer Cees Maas wanted a friendly acquisition of ABN Amro before the end of the year, thereby creating one of the world's largest banks.
Photo: Peter Boer

On Friday 28 July 2006, Huibert Boumeester, another of Groenink's protégés, presented the conclusions of the bank's board to the governors: it was logical and inevitable that ABN Amro should merge with a larger bank. The bank would have to give up its independence.
Photo: ANP

ABN Amro president Arthur Martinez felt that if Michel Tilmant would be the first chairman of ING-ABN Amro, he should be the first head of its supervisory board.
Photo: Goos van der Veen/Hollandse Hoogte

ING president Cor Herkströter disagreed with Martinez. When they met, on 9 March 2007, Herkströter brought a copy of the Dutch code of civil law, to show the American what it said about the duties of the head of a supervisory board.
Photo: Marco Hillen/Hollandse Hoogte

Wilco Jiskoot, for years Rijkman Groenink's principal foil. On Sunday 22 April 2007, Jiskoot voted against the merger with Barclays which Groenink had brokered. He was in favour of a takeover by the consortium; they were prepared to pay more.
Photo: Capital Photos

Director Piero Overmars also referred to the merger with Barclays as a takeover. Jiskoot's protégé felt that if the bank were to be taken over, they should go for the highest bidder.
Photo: ANP

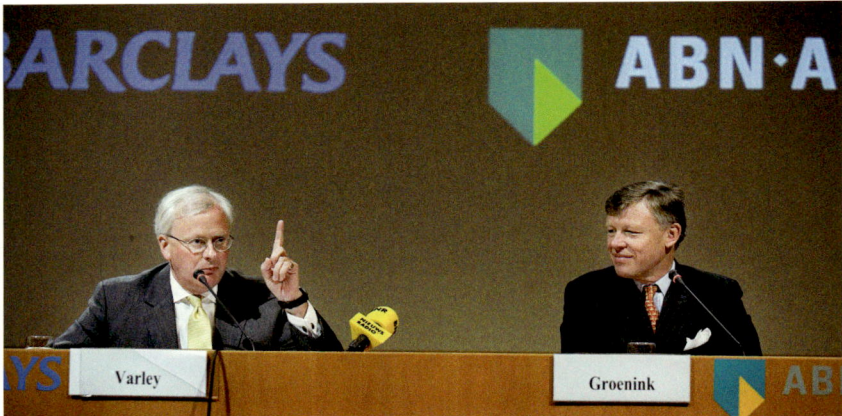

On 23 April, John Varley (chairman of Barclays) and Rijkman Groenink announced the 66 billion euro merger/takeover by the British bank Barclays 'the biggest international merger in the banking world, ever.'
Photo: Allard de Witte/Hollandse Hoogte

August 2007. 'One for all, all for one.' The leaders of the consortium were ready; there was no escape for ABN Amro. From left to right: Fortis CEO Jean Paul Votron, Fortis chairman Maurice Lippens, RBS CEO Fred Goodwin and Santander chairman Emilio Botin.
Photo: Murdo McLeod/Hollandse Hoogte

On 6 August, Fortis shareholders voted en masse in favour of the offer for ABN Amro. Here Maurice Lippens and Herman Verwilst arrive in Utrecht for the meeting with the Dutch shareholders. Lippens had spoken earnestly with Votron beforehand. 'Will we be steering the treasure ship into a storm?'
Photo: Maarten Hartman/Hollandse Hoogte

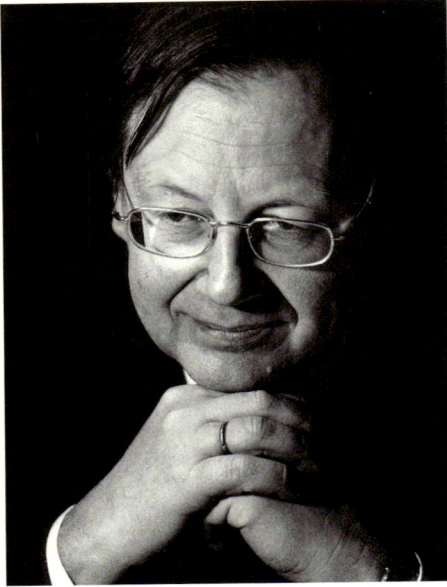

Nout Wellink, president of the Dutch central bank, feared that the solid Dutch banking system would fall prey to gold diggers and treasure hunters. For months he tried to convince the politicians in The Hague that a major bank like ABN Amro was more than just a company, and that it would be prudent to provide some form of protection. He was already worried in May 2007 that Fortis would be unable to support its acquisition of ABN Amro.
Photo: Peter Boer

Dutch finance minister Wouter Bos told Wellink that it was his responsibility as head of the Dutch central bank to decide whether to approve the consortium's offer or not. Bos reminded him that the consortium consisted of three licensed banks.
Photo: Peter Boer

1 November 2007. Here Rijkman Groenink is on his way to the last shareholders' meeting. In his wake are André Olijslager and Arthur Martinez, vice-president and president of the supervisory board. Within hours Rijkman Groenink would be out of office.
Photo: Peter Boer

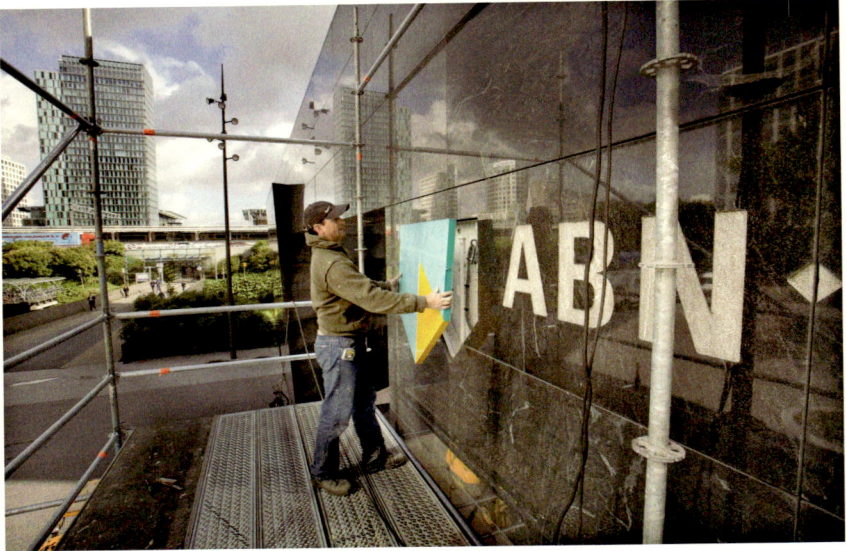

On 14 August 2008, ABN Amro's logo was taken down at its head office in Amsterdam. Less than two months later the green and yellow shield was back in place.
Photo: Peter Boer

Dutch central bank president Nout Wellink, prime minister Jan Peter Balkenende and finance minister Wouter Bos (left to right) on Friday 3 October shortly after the Dutch part of ABN Amro and Fortis were nationalised. Bos was satisfied. 'We have cordoned off the healthy parts of the Dutch bank from possible infection.'
Photo: ANP

An investigation commissioned by Aarnout Loudon into the effectiveness of the supervisory board did yield a result. The president had brought in a German consultant to hold a round of discussions with the governors and managers of the bank, intending the survey to be a sort of leaving present. He was keen to shake things up a bit.

The survey looked into both the personal effectiveness of each managing director and the effectiveness of the supervisory board as a whole. Each governor would be allowed to ring the consultant, to hear what the others thought of them. Not all of them did so. At any rate, the inventory led to the departure of Louise Groenman. Loudon advised Martinez not to extend her term, because her contribution had been insufficient.

The most important conclusion was that there was a need for more discussion. The consultant observed that more dialogue was needed between the governors and members of the managing board; at present this was minimal and the need for exchanges of views was felt on both sides of the table. In particular, the managing board would have to invest more in its relationship with the governors, and give them more opportunity to understand the business better. Groenink promised to make the necessary facilities available. He himself would lunch more often with the other governors.

As a first step, it was decided to get rid of the long board table, to allow the members of the boards to relate better with each other at meetings. The long table meant that meetings were mostly between the chairman and the president: they couldn't see if the other governors or managing directors at the table were asking for attention. To encourage discussions, a large round table was ordered, so that everyone present at the meetings could see each other.

Loudon thought that the supervisory board shouldn't consist of more than seven people. He also thought that the governors should be bankers – people who understood what was being discussed. Relevant knowledge was thin on the ground at present, and his successor would have to do more to correct this. He was pleased, at any rate, by Groenink's suggestion that Gerhard Randa be appointed. Until the previous year, Randa had been a manager at HypoVereinsbank. That unsuccessful attempt at a takeover had delivered a result, anyway. At last, there was a banker among the governors.

At his last shareholder meeting, Loudon was confronted by an uproar about a proposed increase to the bonuses paid to the supervisory board. They would receive 150 per cent, instead of 100 per cent, of their salary if they achieved their performance targets. Robeco, ABP, PGGM and the Dutch Railways Pension Fund voted against the increases. Representing the organisations that had voted against, spokesman René Maatman said that the proposed package was on the high side. The performance incentives placed too much emphasis on the short term. Loudon thought this was nonsense and referred to developments in the rest of the market. *Het Financieele Dag-blad* reported on the matter and noted that he had said, "We're far behind the other financial institutions on this. Mr Groenink gets a raw deal in comparison to the chairmen of Fortis and ING."

Loudon said that the increased bonuses were necessary because in some cases people who worked below the level of the supervisory board were earning more than them. "Of course, the basic salary of a general manager is lower than that of a member of the supervisory board. But I assure you that the bonuses paid to general managers are often higher." Loudon added that the bonus of 150 per cent would "not be earned automatically".

Aarnout Loudon knew about the meetings between Groenink and Tilmant. He also knew that these discussions might gain momentum in the coming year. When he left, he warned Rijkman Groenink that any merger with ING should not be allowed to fail on petty details. Although he himself didn't have a good relationship with Cor Herkströter, the chairman of ING's supervisory board, Loudon regretted that he was leaving the bank in the spring, as he would have liked to see the deal go through as smoothly as possible.

When he was handing over, Loudon referred Arthur Martinez to the letter that Groenink had received six years before from the suprvisory board. The letter had stated that Groenink would be appointed for a term of six years. Those six years had now passed.

Martinez had big plans. From now on, he wanted to the bank's managers to be evaluated each year by the supervisory board, and not merely on the basis of Groenink's opinion. He had mixed feelings about the chairman of ABN Amro. Groenink was quick at analysis and the new head of the supervisory board liked that. He also had some sympathy for Groenink the loner. He described him as an imperial CEO, a chairman who sought the endorsement of his governors, without actually earning it.

On the other hand, Martinez found it tiresome that Groenink always had his own agenda at every meeting, and that it was not always clear what he wanted to achieve. He was worried about his lack of openness and trust in others.

He was also concerned that Groenink paid too little attention to what was going on within the bank. As he saw it, Groenink was usually busy looking out for important people. He noticed that the chairman enjoyed talking about his meetings with them.

He had once told Groenink of his surprise that the chairman was only interested in the bank's future, and that he was hardly interested in the day-to-day organisation. Martinez suspected that Groenink wanted to lead the consolidation of the European banking sector, and that he wanted this to be his legacy. That was how he wanted to cement his reputation.

In fact, Martinez Rijkman thought that Groenink was deeply insecure. But he didn't tell him this. Not yet. He hoped that their relationship would develop to the point where he could tell him what he thought. One thing was clear: he was going to do this job differently from his predecessor.

Martinez realised that Aarnout Loudon had been too personally interested in Groenink's welfare. Groenink's appointment in 2000 had been down to him, mainly, due to the conflict with Kalff and certain other managing directors. That made it difficult for him to be critical; Groenink's failure would also be his. His predecessor hadn't thought it necessary to think about who would succeed Groenink.

The new head of the supervisory board assumed that he would be responsible for seeing to Rijkman Groenink's successor during his term. And even that Rijkman Groenink's position could become an acute problem in the short term. He knew that he would have to see Groenink off if the United States decided to move to criminal prosecution.

With Loudon's letter in his hand, Martinez decided after all to appoint the chairman for another period of six years. He didn't want to undermine confidence in the bank by messing around with the length of Groenink's next term.

Although he knew that the annual report would state that he would only become eligible for retirement in 2012, the 57-year-old Groenink also knew that his term as chairman of the managing board would not be endless. The American threat of prosecution hung like a black cloud over his head.

Halfway through April, Groenink agreed to join the supervisory board of SHV, at the request of Annemiek Fentener van Vlissingen. Frits Fentener van Vlissingen had died suddenly in March, and his daughter was looking for reinforcements to her supervisory board. She had been chairman of the supervisory board of the family company since the previous year.

Another attractive governorship soon presented itself. Aarnout Loudon would step down the following year as a member of the supervisory board of Royal Shell Group. Loudon, whose grandfather Hugo had been one of its founders and one of the first directors of the oil giant, had been urging Rijkman Groenink as his successor. It looked as if he would succeed in achieving this, too. Shell was looking for a governor with a banking background.

The supervisory board was busy again. Boumeester, Piero Overmars and Ron Teerlink had been attending meetings since October the previous year. And, because Tom de Swaan would retire only after he had turned sixty, in May, there were therefore nine people sitting at the board table.

The three new members were in a hurry. They knew that there was little time left. All three had a background in the corporate banking division and they all realised that the financial markets had less patience with funds that performed below expectations – however big they were. Moreover, they soon wondered what they had got themselves into. It looked as if Jiskoot, Kuiper, Groenink, De Swaan, Collee and Scott Barrett had settled into permanent conflict, and that the supervisory board was stuck fast. The entire Petra reorganisation had begun at least a year late, in their view.

The three potential crown princes ran into resistance from the 46-year-old Hugh Scott Barrett. Overmars and Boumeester were seen as Groenink's most likely successors. Scott Barrett didn't understand this. What, he asked himself, had the two of them really demonstrated they could do? The Brit realised that the arrival of these men, who were of his own generation, might mean the end of his dream of heading the bank. There were several signs that he was being sidelined. It might be true that Groenink had nominated him as CFO, but he was a CFO with fewer stripes on his arm than he would have liked. His predecessor, Tom de Swaan, had combined the function of CFO with that of risk manager. This had given De Swaan a strong power base. But the risk management part of the job had been hived off and handed to Boumeester.

The rest of the board thought it quite logical that the Brit was not involved in strategy. Scott Barrett was an Arrow man, after all. It had cost them years to correct that mistake. He noticed that there were seven Dutchmen at the table, who did their best not to speak Dutch, but all the same, he felt he was losing a sense of connection with them. He had done his best to learn the language as well as possible, but they still liked to crack jokes that he couldn't understand.

In addition to Huibert Boumeester, Rijkman Groenink had acquired a new conversation partner on the bank's strategy. In November the previous year he had asked Alexander Pietruska, the German who had advised him in his attempts to take over HypoVereinsbank, to follow Jeroen Drost as head of the corporate development department. Drost had been promoted as general manager responsible for the Asia business unit.

Pietruska quickly became a trusted confidant of Groenink's. The chairman liked people who didn't hide their opinions. Pietruska's first analysis was devastating. The Dutch, American and Brazilian activities were all performing worse than comparable rivals. He said that the bank was being undermanaged. During one of their first conversations, he pointed out the dangers of the Dutch consensus culture. He thought that Groenink should behave more like a CEO and offered the example of Josef Ackermann of Deutsche Bank. But Groenink said that there was no room for that approach at present.

Boumeester and Pietruska were Groenink's main conversation partners on the strategy of the bank. They were part of a select group of people who were privy to the talks the chairman was conducting with his fellow CEOs at Barclays and ING. Boumeester was somewhat disappointed. His discussions with Groenink and Pietruska about the future of the bank had convinced him that the bank was unlikely to survive, and that even rigorous choices might not ensure its future.

This was a subject that Groenink kept to a tight circle of people around him. Above all, he was determined that it shouldn't be discussed by the business committee group (GBC).

GBC met once a month, under the chairmanship of Joost Kuiper. They were following the two ABN Amro boats that were competing in the Volvo Ocean Race, and had already met in Rio de Janeiro and in New York. Now they were to meet in Portsmouth.

On 31 May, the British harbour was full of the boats taking part in the Volvo Ocean Race. In two days, they would be sailing the last stage of the race. It was already clear that ABN Amro One, captained by Mike Sanderson, had won the race. But it was not really a time to celebrate. Two weeks before, there had been a tragic accident on the second ABN Amro boat when sailor Hans Horrevoets had fallen overboard and drowned.

On the evening before their meeting, the entire GBC were sitting on a terrace. They would shortly be visiting the two boats, where the distressed crews were waiting for a visit from their bosses. The atmosphere wasn't great. The bank's results for the first four months of the year had been disappointing. They had again not lived up to their firm promises to investors that they would reduce costs.

Many of the unexpected costs that they were now facing had to do with the Petra reorganisation. The introduction of Petra had been received with a mixture of incomprehension and scepticism within the bank. Many colleagues didn't understand who they were supposed to report to. Outside of the bank, people were seriously confused. Analysts and investors complained that they couldn't work out how the figures were reported. They accused the bank of putting up a smoke screen to hide the continuing disappointing results.

Many of the costs were being generated at the centre, and they were being charged on to the various operational business units. This was driving the eight managers of those units crazy. They sat on GBC with five members from the supervisory board. General managers who had previously called the shots in the corporate banking division had a lot of difficulty with this. Alexandra Cook was furious when she heard from the various regions that she worked with that they had to pay these extra (central) costs. These were people who serviced the 550 biggest companies, after all.

Some on GBC were annoyed at the fact that Joost Kuiper was chairman of the body. As they saw it, Kuiper didn't know the business well enough. They thought that he was too focused on procedures and processes, and that he provided too little guidance and leadership. Either Groenink or Jiskoot ought to be in charge, they felt. Jiskoot, Teerlink and Overmars were particularly vocal on the issue.

Kuiper felt the resistance, and he was not enjoying himself. He thought it was unclear what GBC was in fact mandated to make decisions about. This was aggravating, not least because expectations were high. This was a group of people that was bursting with energy. Groenink had been angry that they had discussed the bank's strategy. But Kuiper had sworn that they hadn't taken any decisions. Groenink wanted GBC to focus entirely on business; it was their job to ensure that synergy developed between the bank's various activities. Groenink's mistrust of the situation was so great that he had asked to see the minutes of GBC meetings.

While they were enjoying their wine, they discussed the problems at the bank. A polemic arose about the sense of the bank's corporate activities. Joost Kuiper thought that it was wrong to talk about this at that time; he also felt that his colleagues were talking disrespectfully about Rijkman Groenink. He told them that he thought it better not to continue in this way. Ron Teerlink reacted as if stung by a wasp and told Kuiper he was out of line.

Kuiper exploded and stormed off, furious. He was frustrated, and had no idea how to turn the growing criticism of the effectiveness of GBC and its chairman around. More and more often now, signals were reaching him that the managers who had been brought together here felt that they were wasting their time. Everyone was worried by the way he had walked out on them. Dolf Collee went after Kuiper, and tried to persuade him to return. Kuiper refused. He phoned Rijkman Groenink, who tried to reassure him. The chairman would be arriving in Portsmouth the following day and asked Kuiper to leave the issue with him.

The next day it was Jiskoot who chaired the meeting. Groenink arrived at the end of the day. He and Jiskoot had a short meeting, during which Groenink promised that he would take speedy action. The following day the managers waved the boats out on the last stage of the race, without Joost Kuiper.

Groenink didn't do anything. After seven days, Jiskoot, Overmars, Teerlink and Collee were angry. A serious crisis had arisen in the GBC leadership, and in the presence of fourteen top managers. They didn't know what to do, or who to listen to. Groenink would have to show some leadership, and soon.

They felt that Joost Kuiper's role was played out, and that he was no longer credible as chairman of the bank's key management body.

The four board members decided to take action. Dolf Collee had been closest to Kuiper in the previous years, so they decided to send him to Kuiper telling him that they felt he no longer had a role to play in GBC. Kuiper was astounded: how could Collee dare tell him this? He told Collee that he had knocked on the wrong door and advised him to take his story to Rijkman Groenink.

The chairman reacted furiously to the four managers' suggestion. This was tantamount to mutiny. His subordinates couldn't decide whether Kuiper would continue to occupy his chair. He discussed it with Arthur Martinez. The American had only been head of the supervisory board for a few weeks and reflected, not for the first time, that he had got himself caught up in an unusual European adventure, to say the least. He had gained the nickname the Axe from Sax after his determined performance at the New York department store Saks Fifth Avenue in the 1990's, but he didn't know what to make of all this. If he agreed with the four managers, then he would have to fire Groenink. But to do so now would send out the wrong signals. No, Martinez agreed with Groenink, it shouldn't be tolerated. This was not good governance, and that would have to be made clear.

They decided to send a warning letter to the four, signed by both Groenink and Martinez. The letter contained a tough message: if you do this again, you will be fired. They were also asked to attend a disciplinary meeting. Martinez backed Groenink on this.

Groenink and Martinez told the managers, one by one, that they had behaved improperly. Teerlink understood the point straight away, and offered his apologies. Overmars also said he wouldn't do it again. These two managers were not held to be totally responsible for what had happened. They both had a lot to learn.

To Martinez, the fact that the four had sent Dolf Collee, Groenink's loyal vassal, to carry their message was proof that the top managers of ABN Amro sometimes behaved no better than kids on a school playground. Collee also offered his apologies.

Only Wilco Jiskoot was still angry. Now the other managing directors would never know what had happened. This would affect their credibility. But Jiskoot kept his mouth shut during the entire meeting. When Martinez asked him if he wanted to say something or ask a question in his turn, he shook his head.

After the meeting was over, Groenink suggested to Martinez that they should fire Jiskoot. But for Martinez that was going too far. He realised that at some deep level Groenink felt threatened by Jiskoot. The head of the supervisory board told Groenink instead that he should start managing Jiskoot better.

Dolf Collee was in a quandary. He was responsible for the bank's ailing European division and therefore for making the investment in Antonveneta profitable: and he would have to account to the managing board on these matters. But the first results from Italy were not great. He told the *Financial Times*, "Every day we get questions from clients about where all this is going to end." At the end of 2004, Antonveneta's market share was about 3.5 per cent. Now it was 3.2 per cent.

The Italians were amazed by their new owner. No one felt that they had been taken over. It looked like ABN Amro's approach would be to leave them in peace. They couldn't understand this. One Dutch manager even received a message to the effect that they should take the show over, fire the management, and put their stamp on things ... But Collee's attitude was that they had taken over a bank, to be sure, but banks are staffed by people and you don't fire people you've just taken over.

Collee trusted Piero Luigi Montani, who had been the boss of Antonveneta for three years. He believed that Montani would grow into the Italy's Fabio Barbosa. Because Montani stayed in place, the bulk of the Italian management did too. From the Netherlands they received the message that they were welcome to visit when they had time. When they did so, they would be free to tell the managers in the Netherlands what they could do for them

Only a handful of Dutchmen travelled to Italy to explain that some wonderful things were being developed in ABN Amro's Formula 1 factory in Amsterdam and London, and that ABN Amro was making it possible for the local banks to make use of their global platform.

Boumeester observed that the Italians were not merely expecting a takeover by ABN Amro, including the installation of a completely new management; they were hoping that it would happen. They wanted to see renewal under ABN Amro's leadership. So far as he was concerned, this was yet another example of Dutch clumsiness – the idea that the people at local level would surely know what they were doing. He thought it absurd that the people at head office seemed to have more faith in the people over there than in their own abilities.

Meanwhile, analysts were making it clear that they had little faith in the Italian adventure. They referred to the fact that ABN Amro had a bad track record with the integration of foreign subsidiaries. Hugh Scott Barrett, no friend of Collee, understood this well. He was annoyed by the bad management of the takeover. Why had the bank sent relatively inexperienced employees to Italy? It was the biggest acquisition in the bank's history, after all, and everything they did was highly visible.

Ron Teerlink observed that the whole approach was too friendly. All sorts of things were being offered to the Italians and a lot of synergy in products and in automation would be possible. But that kind of thing has to be enforced, imposed. As things were, it was not going at all well.

Slowly but surely it was becoming clear that Antonveneta would deliver half of the promised result of 500 million euros in its first year under ABN Amro. ABN Amro had therefore paid thirty times the profit for the takeover. Within a year most of the members of the supervisory board had come to the conclusion that they had paid far too much for the Italian bank.

Even Rijkman Groenink now regarded the takeover of Antonveneta as a tactical error. It would be years before the Italian bank would be profitable within the ABN Amro fold, and the shareholders had no patience for this. They were concerned above all by the decline in earnings per share which had resulted from the share issue that had financed the takeover. His colleagues in the corporate banking division had been proven right.

All this was becoming too much for Dolf Collee. His frustration erupted at the end of the Volvo Ocean Race on 17 June in Göteborg, Sweden, when he forgot to thank a fellow banker in a speech. The man's wife made a peevish remark about it. The remark went down badly with Collee, who fired the man on the spot. Joost Kuiper and Huibert Boumeester were there, and they could hardly believe their ears. They reported the incident to Rijkman Groenink, saying that this was just not done.

This was the third warning that Collee had received. A few years before he had received a warning after a strategy meeting at Duin & Kruidberg. Governor Antony Burgmans was furious with Collee when he remarked heatedly that the governors didn't understood strategy. The atmosphere became quarrelsome, and Burgmans had to tell Collee to moderate his tone. Burgmans had reported the incident.

As the governors saw it, Groenink had been patient with Collee for too long. Martinez thought that Collee had risen one rung too high in the bank. Now enough was enough. Groenink agreed. Collee was fired, but was allowed to leave quietly because the chairman had no wish to put him in the pillory; that had already occurred internally.

Collee said in a press release that he was leaving the bank with mixed feelings after working there for 26 years. Paolo Cuccia, ABN Amro's country manager in Italy, took over Dolf Collee's role as governor at Capitalia. There was now not a single ABN Amro manager on the supervisory body of the bank that ABN Amro had been so keen on absorbing.

Groenink was hoping that ABN Amro would be able to move quickly to take over Capitalia in Italy. The bank had owned a 7.8 per cent stake and was the largest party in the dominant shareholders pact at the Roman bank. Capitalia was twice the size of Antonveneta. The possibility of taking it over had been the subject of continuing investigation since the acquisition of Antonveneta.

Analysts fantasised about the combination. ABN Amro would then have a 10 per cent market share in Italy. That would make it possible to earn more money quickly in an unruly market. They observed that the takeover could be financed by selling ABN Amro's American activities. They were worth about the same amount as the cost of the remaining 92 per cent of the Capitalia shares, about 14 billion euros. They warned the top management of ABN Amro that a serious competitor was lurking in the shape of Unicredito.

The picture looked good to ABN Amro. But Groenink would have to convince two men in particular that the picture was also good for Capitalia. The board chairman, Matteo Arpe, who was still new in the position, had made it clear that it was 'highly unlikely that a foreign bank would take over Capitalia'. Arpe himself wanted to make his mark in Italy with a takeover.

Groenink had pinned his hopes on Cesare Geronzi, one of Italy's most controversial bankers, as he was always being accused of fraudulent practices and having to appear in court. Geronzi didn't make things easy for ABN Amro. *Het Financieele Dagblad* reported that the Italian had told a closed meeting of 2,000 managers that Rijkman Groenink had approached him arrogantly. According to Geronzi, Groenink came to Rome with a proposal to take over the bank and a demand for a quick response. Groenink had apparently said that ABN Amro was Capitalia's only option if it wanted to grow internationally. Geronzi concluded his speech, to thundering applause, with the conclusion that 'ABN Amro didn't know who they were messing with'.

But Groenink didn't have much time for Italy. He was shocked when he saw the first estimate of the figures for the second quarter halfway through June. A few months before he had promised that the bank would become more efficient, and that costs would be reduced. But the figures he was looking at were dramatic. Profits for the first half of the year had risen by eight per cent but costs had risen by 11 per cent. Cost rises in the second quarter in particular were causing the efficiency ratio to rise to the region of 70 per cent.

He went to see Scott Barrett immediately. What was the cause of all this and how would they convey the message? The CFO was also shocked. Costs had shot through the roof, especially during the last few months. Petra was supposed to deliver accountability, but it was doing the opposite. No one appeared to feel responsible for the costs, and it would take time to make this clear to people. Scott Barrett asked himself if the bank would get the time it needed. He blamed himself for not urging intervention more urgently two years before, at the Bosporus session, when there was still time.

Groenink had another explanation. He thought that the bank was now paying the bill for the costly sailing race around the world. During that time, it was as if his colleagues could only think about one thing – the race. Any meeting of any importance was planned at a harbour on the route of the race, when the boats would be there. The domestic business unit met in Cape Town, GBC in Rio de Janeiro and New York, the GTS conference was in Baltimore, the list went on. The sailing race had probably given many employees at the bank a sense of pride, and even the feeling that they were part of a real global bank. But it was an expensive feeling. The investors wouldn't like it.

In this sombre climate, Huibert Boumeester and Alexander Pietruska presented their most recent strategic reflections to the supervisory board. Their starting point was the bank's secret strategy to be one of the top five European banks in terms of shareholder value. They were talking about closing a huge gap. The top five were a long way off.

They concluded that the bank would have to achieve a market value of 100 billion euros in 2010 if it wanted to reach the top five. That would be necessary to achieve the strategic targets, and it would also be necessary to prevent becoming the target of a hostile takeover. They asked if the bank would be able to do this under its own steam.

There was some discussion of strengthening the bank's position in Brazil through a takeover of Unibanco. There was also some discussion of strengthening the bank's position in Italy through the takeover of Capitalia or of Monte dei Paschi di Siena Bank. And there was again some discussion of the necessity of more efficient management, and to improve the bank's operational excellence.

A new list of banks that ABN Amro might be able to combine forces with was also presented. Boumeester and Pietruska made it clear that the available alternatives were dwindling. The bank's financial elbow room had decreased considerably too. There was no money anywhere for anything after the Antonveneta takeover. The share price would stay low as long as investors didn't believe that ABN Amro was capable of improving efficiency.

A bank that is broke and troubled by a chronically low share price has little room for manoeuvre as regards mergers and takeovers. ABN Amro was worth around 40 billion. The target 100 billion could therefore only be realised by combining with a much larger party. On the list presented by Boumeester and Pietruska were seven names: ING, Barclays, Unicredito, BBVA, BNP, Lloyds TSB and Rabobank.

Pietruska and Boumeester thought that the last suggestion made no sense. Rabo was a cooperative bank; it would be impossible to merge with it, since permission would be needed from nearly 200 local managements. Groenink had talked with his former colleague, the chairman of Rabobank, Bert

Heemskerk, and made it clear that the option would have to be looked at seriously.

When the managing board considered the list in two meetings, they were aware that any merger with one of the larger banks would effectively be a takeover. It would mean that ABN Amro would cease to exist, and that it would have no control over its own future.

Wilco Jiskoot and Piero Overmars had more difficulty with this idea than Boumeester and Groenink. But in the discussion that followed, emotion made way for business logic. After some time Groenink noticed that there were no principled objections to the idea that the bank might no longer be the master of its own destiny. After two long meetings, Boumeester and Pietruska got the green light from the managing board to carry on and present these conclusions to the supervisory board.

On Thursday 27 July, the twelve governors and eight managing directors got together for their annual strategy session at Duin & Kruidberg. One of the governors had come with a firm resolve.

André Olijslager had been on the supervisory board for two years and, somewhat to his own surprise, he had become deputy president. He felt that he had not been much involved over the last two years, and now he wanted to get some things done at ABN Amro, an important Dutch bank. He had come to the conclusion that Groenink didn't have a realistic vision for the future of the bank. The man was no strategist, and he also paid far too little attention to operational matters, and this could not be right. Olijslager had decided to argue that a couple of big decisions should be made at that meeting at Duin & Kruidberg.

He had resolved to suggest that they sell their American operations, close operations in another thirty countries, and pay the shareholders an extra dividend. He thought that this would give the shareholders a year to work on a strategy. He also thought it should be communicated clearly that the bank would never be among the top five. Olijslager knew that it wouldn't be easy to get people to listen, because he was in effect asking whether Rijkman Groenink was the right man for the job.

The half-year figures were presented before Olijslager had an opportunity to speak. The faces in the room were sombre. It was bad news. Very bad news. The integration of Antonveneta was disappointing and costing more than predicted. The United States operations were considerably less productive. The costs of improving compliance were rising sharply. And the new matrix organisation that had been devised at Petra had also cost a great deal. The governors' earlier concerns that no one in the organisation seemed to feel any responsibility for costs were being borne out. There had also been the painful departure of Dolf Collee. And there was still no clarity on the possibility of a criminal prosecution in the United States.

On Friday 28 July, the second day of the conference, and surrounded by unhappy faces, Huibert Boumeester and Alexander Pietruska presented the conclusions that the managing board had come to the previous day. In their view it was both logical and unavoidable: they would have to sit down with some larger parties. ABN Amro would not be a leading player in the consolidation of the European banking sector.

After the presentation, Olijslager did what he had intended: he proposed the sale of LaSalle and closing thirty countries. The governor said that it was necessary to win time, and in this way the bank would remain independent for the meanwhile. There was some discussion about this, the other governors were not enthusiastic. After all the setbacks of the previous years, they no longer believed that the management of the bank was capable of much more. Yet they didn't feel that ABN Amro could ever cease to exist. Trude Maas thought that the suggestion of a junior role in any combination would be a respectful way to take an active part in the unavoidable round of consolidation without being the boss.

During the interval, some of the younger board members spoke to Olijslager, saying that they thought it a good idea not to wait any longer and instead take action, to show that the bank did have a vision for the future and that it wanted to achieve it. Piero Overmars in particular had difficulty with the general assumption that the banking world was consolidating and that you had to be big to survive in it, that ABN Amro would have to go with the trend. Why didn't the bank look instead at the relationship between size and profitability? Maybe the bank would even have to be smaller. And then it would certainly be possible to stay independent.

Olijslager tried to arrange a bilateral discussion with the head of the supervisory board to persuade him of his way of thinking. Martinez was reserved. He asked Olijslager what would happen if all his plans were realised. He thought that you should decide what you want, rather than what you don't want. He didn't feel that he would be able to explain the opposite approach to the shareholders as head of the supervisory board. And Martinez understood Groenink's position: it was the American subsidiary's network and assets that would be likely to be of interest to other banks. They were the assets that would allow the bank to sell at a higher price. Moreover, how long would ABN Amro be able to survive as a small bank? No, Martinez didn't see anything in Olijslager's plans. He thought it was more logical for the bank to talk to the large banks.

It was decided that the American subsidiary would be sold and that 30 countries would be closed unless an exceptionally interesting merger or takeover came around. For instance, if it should prove possible to take over Capitalia. But as long as that wasn't happening, Groenink would continue investigating a merger of equals with (one of) the top three on the list: ING, Barclays or Unicredito. Olijslager realised that the bank had decided to look for a larger organisation to hide behind. ABN Amro would give up its independence in exchange for the protection of a so-called white knight.

Wilco Jiskoot, who thought it strange that he had still not been able to arrange a bilateral meeting with the new head of the supervisory board, was worried. He warned two of the governors, one of them Martinez, not to allow Rijkman Groenink to conduct these talks on his own. Martinez nodded, he understood the message. He respected Jiskoot as a deal maker but as a manager he found him difficult to understand. He had often suspected that Jiskoot didn't always tell the whole truth, and that he played his cards close to his chest. Martinez was tired of Jiskoot. You had to ask incisive questions to get the whole truth out of him. He also thought Jiskoot was a bad manager who had cost the bank a lot of money over the years.

The head of the supervisory board knew that Groenink would not be open to suggestions from Jiskoot. He left things as they were for the meantime; he didn't see how he could force the issue. His predecessor had never done so. But he did tell Groenink to let him know if he had a discussion with another bank coming up.

To Martinez it was clear that Groenink wouldn't give him what he wanted. With Olijslager, he told a confidential meeting that they would have to start looking for a new chairman as soon as possible. The two governors realised that it wouldn't be easy. A panic would not be good for the bank.

On the Saturday after the session at Duin & Kruidberg, the chairman of ABN Amro gave an interview to financial press agency Bloomberg. "If someone came to us with a really good story and premium of 40 per cent more than our share price, then I don't think I could make a serious argument for saying no." The message went out to the world. Spokesmen of the bank worked themselves into a sweat and said that Groenink had not said anything new, only that offers for the bank would be seriously considered. And they were right, as every listed company is in a sense always for sale. But it was now evident that the managers wanted to sell the bank and that opened up perspectives for interested buyers. ABN Amro had put itself in the shop window.

Rijkman Groenink realised that his dream would never come true. He hadn't succeeded in turning ABN Amro into a leading European bank and that was painful. He reflected that until now he had always won. This was the first time in his career that he was not getting what he wanted. He resolved to sell the bank for as good a price as possible and ensure that ABN Amro's intellectual legacy was maintained in any new combination.

Meanwhile, another of his dreams had come true. Or nearly. He had moved his family at last to their new home on the river Vecht, on a picturesque stretch of some of the Netherlands' most desirable real estate. Because the windmill in Vreeland had already been sold, the family had to move, and they had to improvise and camp out until the new house was ready. The country estate had been enveloped in scaffolding for the last six months.

It had taken eight years in all. There were council commissions and licence procedures, and after that the architects and contractors. Called Vrederijk (Peaceful Realm), the estate included 16 hectares of woods and 17 of meadows, as well as a tennis court and a beautiful swimming pool. The modern house measured 16 metres by 16 metres and was four storeys high. It was equipped with every luxury. It was with this house, this impressive country estate that he had wanted to show the world that he, Rijkman Groenink, was successful.

14

Mutiny

August–November 2006

Arthur Martinez shook his head as he looked at the list of names. The head of the supervisory board had asked Spencer Stuart to undertake an executive search for a new chairman for ABN Amro. The list was the distressing result.

Martinez had been searching diligently for an alternative for Groenink. The American lawyers of the bank had told him that the department of justice would move to criminal prosecution of the top management of the bank. If this happened, he would have to dismiss Groenink immediately. It was out of the question that the bank should continue to be led by a man who ran the risk of being convicted in the United States.

Martinez thought that the bank should be led by a Dutchman. Because the head of the supervisory board was a foreigner, he thought that it would not be logical to appoint another foreigner to the position of CEO. But there was only one Dutchman on Spencer Stuart's list. That was Onno Ruding, and he had just turned 67.

Martinez decided not to invite anyone on the list in for a talk. He asked Joost Kuiper to take over Groenink's role as chairman until he had found a new chairman. Kuiper was not keen. He told Martinez that he had changed, that he no longer had any ambition to be the boss. Kuiper wanted to retire. Martinez promised Kuiper that he would only call on him for a short time. Kuiper felt a sense of responsibity for the bank and agreed.

To be ready to intervene as soon as the American prosecutor filed charges, Martinez asked the bank's new general manager of human resources, Pauline van der Meer Mohr, to compile papers in preparation for Rijkman Groenink's departure.

Van der Meer Mohr had been working in her new position for only two months. She had come from TNT and had had a number of gruelling discussions with Groenink about what would be expected of her in the job. She knew that she was facing a considerable challenge, as the role had been totally stripped down, and her predecessors had had little influence. She also knew that important appointments were regularly announced without human resources being consulted. The bank was shot through with backroom politics and the old-boy network. There was little accountability on this point; bankers looked after each other. There was a total lack of discipline, even with regard to remuneration and bonuses. Clearly a thorough professionalisation of the human resources function was necessary, and Van der Meer Mohr had demanded, and got, direct access to the supervisory board as a condition of taking the job.

She was impressed by her new boss. She understood criticism of Groenink, that he was not a binding force within the bank because he was always fighting with people around him. Van der Meer Mohr was also aware that he was worked incredibly well under pressure, and indeed that he flourished under such conditions. The respect was mutual. Groenink saw that Van der Meer Mohr was not afraid of saying what she thought. When he tested her during their meeting by taking a nasty tone, she hit back straight away. Van der Meer Mohr had demanded a veto on all appointments.

In return, Groenink also had a number of demands. Her group employed 1,850 people and had a budget of 450 million euros. Groenink wanted her to reduce costs by 80 million within two years. Van der Meer Mohr didn't think that would be a problem, as there was a lot of waste; she felt that she would be able to shed 600 people.

She noticed that many of the managers around her seemed to be oblivious of costs. Wilco Jiskoot looked like he would be most difficult to get into harness. The managing director liked to play with the bonus pot; he made it clear to Van der Meer Mohr that he would need elbow room if he was to make money for the bank. He explained, for example, that he sometimes needed to be able to pay a banker two million dollars to prevent that person from going to a rival.

Respect among investors for ABN Amro had by now totally vanished. The share price had hovered in the region of 24 to 25 euros in the first months of the year, but by the summer it was worth no more than 22 euros. The presentation of poor half-yearly figures at the end of July brought a further setback. On 11 August, the share price reached a new low of 20.64 euros.

Head of investor relations Richard Bruens and Hugh Scott Barrett found themselves defending both the awful figures and the complicated Petra strategy. They were massacred by analysts and investors. Time and again they were told that that Groenink and Scott Barrett had given emphatic promises in December the previous year that the new strategy would ensure that the bank's efficiency would improve significantly.

A deflated Bruens wrote up a report in a memo to the supervisory board.

The six-page document summarised the criticisms of the analysts. Six important analysts had changed their advice on ABN Amro shares from hold to sell. The number of analysts advising investors to sell had more than doubled, from three to seven. 'The overall sentiment around ABN Amro is negative,' Bruens wrote. 'Many investors have great difficulty in seeing anything positive in our story. They think that the results of the second quarter show that management is doing too little too late to deal with the problems. They regard the share as dead, and don't believe the promises of management regarding the promised efficiency improvements.'

Some analysts were irritated by Rijkman Groenink's and Hugh Scott Barrett's body language during their presentation of the figures. 'It's as if they were happy with these poor results and proved that there is no sense of urgency on the managing board.'

More and more often, and more and more emphatically, Anglo-Saxon analysts and competitors were saying that a deadly combination of ignorance and arrogance could bring ABN Amro down. Only one analyst was optimistic. 'ABN Amro was one of the worst-performing shares in the sector during the course of last year,' wrote Sigrid Baas of ING. 'It is now an average of 11 per cent lower than at the beginning of the year. Since 2000, ABN Amro has been among the top of worst-performing shares. The bank has now spent 1.3 billion euros on reorganising its corporate activities, without any improvement in profitability, because costs efficiency has only got worse.' Baas thought that all the trouble that the bank was going through would result in urgent action. She advised investors to buy ABN Amro shares.

What the ING analyst didn't know was that ING's chairman, Michel Tilmant, was thinking increasingly about a possible combination with ABN Amro. His right-hand man and CFO, Cees Maas, was also interested. In recent discussions with shareholders and analysts, Maas had heard how unhappy they were. The two ING directors thought it was time to do some investigating.

Your neighbour's house seldom comes up for sale, and when it does, you'd be advised to take a look at it. Tilmant decided to use the months of September, October and November to do the sums. He listed various categories on paper: the problems with corporate activities, with Italy, what to do about the United States. As a banker, Tilmant also realised that he would have to find an answer to what a combination with ABN Amro would mean for ING's insurance activities. Moreover, if it went ahead, competition law would require that a large slice of the Dutch retail business would have to be sold. The consequences would be enormous.

Michel Tilmant was cautious by nature. But ING's share price had risen sharply during the previous months. On the stock exchange, ING was worth nearly 50 per cent more than ABN Amro. ABN Amro's bad half-year figures had ensured even greater dominance for ING. That would be crucial for ING, Tilmant knew this. ING's people had been afraid of their haughty neighbours for years – afraid that they would be overshadowed in any merger. Tilmant had been worried, a few years before, when Kist had spoken with Groenink. But if ever there was a moment when there was no need to fear, it was now. If the two banks combined now, ING would play the leading role. That's what he told his fellow directors. The moment they had been waiting for had arrived.

Tilmant had three reasons for seeing possibilities in this merger. It would be good for the Netherlands, because it would result in a single strong world-class player that would benefit the country's open economy. The merger was also logical, in his view, when you looked at it from the perspective of banking history in the Netherlands. Not that he had suddenly become a patriotic Dutchman – he was Belgian, after all. The most important reason for the merger with ABN Amro would be that it was good for ING's shareholders. There was another reason, too: many of his colleagues were asking themselves if ING was big enough as a bank-insurer. Wasn't ING at risk of becoming the focus of a takeover bid in the longer term? Many investors had been critical for years of what they saw as the bank-insurer's incomprehensible strategy. In that sense, ING was in the same boat as ABN Amro. ING was also vulnerable.

Tilmant had not received formal permission from his supervisory board to start talking about a merger with ABN Amro. ING approval was not certain at this stage at all. It would not be easy to get everyone on the supervisory board to agree to the move, to win trust. Several governors thought that ABN Amro was a mess and they distrusted its management. They noted the fact that investors had long since ceased to believe their story. This was also true of ING, in fact; ING owned five per cent of ABN Amro's shares and was the largest (unhappy) shareholder. In the supervisory board it was mainly Godfried van der Lugt, a former ING chairman, who was adamantly against any combination with ABN Amro. He didn't trust Rijkman Groenink.

Moreover, chairman of the ING supervisory board, Cor Herkströter, was a cautious man who had some severe criticisms of ABN Amro. In the experience of this former accountant and Shell president, ABN Amro was suffering from serious levels of self-overestimation. The changes in strategy, the arrogant tone of its communications – these had not been good for the bank. It was now clear that ABN Amro didn't know what to do. Herkströter was proud of ING, which in his view always thought through its strategy carefully in a fast-changing world. And now he wanted to take his time too. He realised that Tilmant was primarily a banker, and that his main aim was to see the bank grow. The head of the supervisory board wondered what consequences this merger would have for the bank's culture, which was determined by the fact that it had both bankers and insurers on its staff.

Herkströter realised that this was probably the last time he would be able to put his stamp on things. He was supposed to retire as head of the supervisory board, after eight years. When Tilmant came to Herkströter to talk about a merger with ABN Amro, they both agreed that the strategy would be determined by ING. If that was clear, they would go ahead with talks about a merger.

ING was not the only party interested in ABN Amro. On 31 October, Groenink received a message from Fred Goodwin, CEO of RBS. Goodwin thought it would be a good idea if they met to talk. The two chairmen agreed to meet on 9 January.

Two days later, Groenink paid a visit to George Mathewson, chairman of Tosca Holdings, a hedge fund with a stake in ABN Amro. Mathewson suggested that ABN Amro investigate the possibility of a merger with RBS. This set Groenink thinking: Mathewson was a former chairman of Royal Bank of Scotland. Mathewson and Goodwin were good friends and they had initiated and carried out the hostile takeover of the British giant National Westminster (NatWest) in February 2000. To Groenink, this approach looked dangerously like an attempt by Goodwin to increase the pressure on ABN Amro in cooperation with aggressive hedge funds.

The talks with Barclays also gathered pace. Especially after the governors of the British bank had decided on 16 November that ABN Amro was an attractive strategic partner.

It was not only Rijkman Groenink who was actively looking for a new home for ABN Amro. ABN Amro was the biggest bank in the Netherlands, and its concerns were therefore also Nout Wellink's concerns. The DNB president did a regular round of the banks, and he knew the position ABN Amro was in. He felt that it was his duty to find out if other banks were looking at it. In September he went to Brussels.

Twice a year he met with Maurice Lippens, chairman of Fortis. In Brussels, they often met for lunch at the only restaurant in Brussels with three Michelin stars, Comme Chez Soi. That's where they met on this occasion.

The two men liked each other and they had their rituals. Lippens expected the DNB president to sound him out on whether Fortis was interested in ABN Amro around the time dessert was served. Lippens again made it clear that he was not interested. In a soothing tone, he let Wellink know that he thought that ABN Amro was too big, and Fortis didn't want to become part of ABN Amro. The Belgian said that Fortis would only proceed with a party that respected Fortis. He emphasised that in his view it wouldn't be possible to work with Rijkman Groenink.

When Groenink's name was mentioned, Lippens was reminded of the appointment of Jean-Paul Votron. Just as ABN Amro had two years before, he had needed a chairman with pluck. Fortis, which had become introverted, needed someone who could sell it better. Lippens had noted that Anton van Rossum preferred to remain a consultant, and worried too much about the bank's share price. In talks with the various members of the managing board, which he conducted personally every two months, it had emerged that Van Rossum lacked authority in his own board.

He expressed his concern to the Belgian paper *Le Soir*. "We are vulnerable to takeover. Everyone expects to see a cross-border merger, preferably on a friendly basis. But there's a big gap between intention and action. Enterprises of our size, with a capitalisation of between 15 and 25 billion euros, are vulnerable. We are relatively protected by our shareholder structure, but if a buyer turns up tomorrow who's prepared to pay a premium of 25 per cent for Fortis, no one will fight back."

A headhunter had told Lippens about the 52-year-old Jean-Paul Votron. After leaving ABN Amro he had returned to his former employer, the American giant Citigroup, and had been appointed to the board in 2002. But his wife wanted to return to Europe, and if possible to Belgium. For a while Lippens was worried that Votron would be too expensive, but he told him during their first talk that he didn't want to earn more than his predecessor. That was another worry removed. "In Votron we are choosing someone who demonstrates what Fortis will be within a few years," he told Belgian newspaper *De Tijd*. Lippens told Votron to guide Fortis's international growth.

Lippens was happy with Votron. Things had become rather American at the top of the bank, but at least it was clear what was going to happen. Votron took decisions and was clear about how he wanted them carried out. People who didn't like it were welcome to leave. There was unity again on the board. That unity derived from Votron's ability to get people to do things that they hadn't thought they could do, in Lippens' view. Lippens and Votron had agreed that the contribution to profits of countries outside Benelux would double to 30 per cent in 2009.

Lippens had only had to intervene once. Votron had wanted to move to a single Fortis brand as soon as possible. As a guest at a wedding of one of the Dutch royals, Lippens came to understand that people in those circles would appreciate it if the name MeesPierson was retained. He promised to see to it personally. And so the Fortis subsidiary, MeesPierson, remained MeesPierson.

At the time Lippens was meeting Wellink, he was working with Votron to see if Fortis could take over the activities of Votron's former employer, Citibank, in Europe. He decided to keep a close eye on ABN Amro. Lippens knew that the bank was in difficulties, that the people directly below the quarrelsome managing board had little faith left in the bank's share price. That kind of rumour goes around the financial world like wildfire. Especially when you've appointed a former general manager of ABN Amro to the managing board of Fortis.

Lex Kloosterman had talked to Rabobank about a job, but in January a headhunter approached him about a job at Fortis. An enthusiastic Votron asked his former ABN Amro colleague to be his director of strategy and a member of its executive committee. The two knew each other well, as they had both worked in the bank's overseas division in the 1990s. When he had taken up his appointment, Votron had felt that he himself should be responsible for the bank's strategy. That was why Joop Feilzer, Kloosterman's predecessor, had never been allowed to communicate that part of his job title externally. But Votron knew that Kloosterman would only be prepared to join the Fortis board if he had full responsibility for the bank-insurer's strategy.

Kloosterman took the bait, and resigned from ABN Amro after 23 years. He was moving to a competitor, and he was immediately branded a bad leaver. It cost him a lot of money, his options and other future bonus payments. Kloosterman sighed, but reflected that making one's own decisions can be a joy in itself.

Once installed in his new position, in October Kloosterman proudly showed a journalist from *Het Financieele Dagblad* around his new Fortis office, with a view of Utrecht's Dom church. 'It isn't odd that he gives the impression of being content,' the journalist wrote. 'After all, Kloosterman now enjoys one of the best views in the Netherlands.' The new Fortis director himself said, "Among other things, my role as a member of the executive committee will be to see to it that the image of the young Fortis brand, which is new in the Netherlands, is brought more into alignment with the important position that we have here."

Colleagues Kloosterman had left behind, who had not previously seen fit to express their criticism of the ABN Amro managing board now became more open. Rijkman Groenink was worried about the growing 'disconnect' between the two top layers of the bank. He had asked Pauline van der Meer Mohr and Alexandra Cook to prepare the meeting of the meeting of the top executive group (TEG) to be held before the end of October. The meeting, at which everyone who reported directly to a general manager or to a member of the supervisory board would be present – about 175 bankers – was to take place in

Venice. Groenink had asked the two managers to prepare a programme that would drive a single main message home with everyone in the top of the bank: One bank, no boundary.

Van der Meer Mohr and Cook decided that it was time for a serious wake up call. Everywhere around them they heard discontent. In preparation, they called about 120 of the participants during the weeks that followed. They were shocked at the response. Trust in the leadership of the bank had vanished.

They reported this to Rijkman Groenink and suggested that an attempt be made during the meeting of the top managers to improve the atmosphere. A commitment would have to be made to give the managing board another chance. It was agreed that all members of the managing board would explain why they deserved that chance from their colleagues.

Cook and Van der Meer Mohr decided to change the location of the meeting, although Venice had already been booked and paid for. They felt that it would be better to hold the meeting in a location with a more sober atmosphere, and decided on the Zuiderduin Hotel in Egmond aan Zee; which some of the bankers described as a sort of darts hotel with rooms at 75 euros a night. When the bank booked 180 rooms for three days, the director of the hotel asked Alexandra Cook if ABN Amro was okay.

Cook asked the members of the managing board to be at the hotel from Sunday evening, 23 October. This would give them all an opportunity to go through things together. For most of them this was not a problem, as the meeting of the business committee group would be held on the following Monday morning under the chairmanship of Joost Kuiper. Huibert Boumeester and Rijkman Groenink, who were not part of that meeting, indicated that they would rather turn up on the Monday evening. Cook convinced them that it was necessary to rehearse for the coming days.

The 175 bankers who arrived on Monday could hardly believe their eyes. They hadn't seen a hotel as cheap as this in many years. That evening, Rijkman Groenink kicked off. He told Alexandra Cook beforehand that he believed in his speech; that he had gone through it with his wife, Irene, and she had said that the story held together well.

Groenink spoke passionately about the 'One bank, no boundary' strategy and the various issues that the bank was facing. The board chairman admitted that the bank had a problem and said that the coming few days would be devoted to finding solutions.

The managing board had wanted Richard Bruens, head of investor relations, to speak after Groenink on analysts' and investors' views of the bank. But Cook and Van der Meer Mohr had insisted that this job should be given to the investment banker, Jan de Ruiter. De Ruiter was known to be critical and unafraid. He would be able to explain that the bank was not doing badly and indeed that on a number of points it had for some years been doing better than the much-praised RBS, under Fred Goodwin. In De Ruiter's view, the bank was fighting mainly against the perception that it was a loser. It was a perception, though, that threatened to become a reality if the bank wasn't careful.

Before De Ruiter began, the Beatles' song 'Help!' resounded through the Zuiderduinzaal (Southern Dune Hall) at the hotel in Egmond aan Zee. Speaking under the heading 'Investors' and analysts' perceptions of ABN Amro', De Ruiter launched into his talk. The third slide told the whole story, detailing the achievements of ABN Amro's peer group since January 1999. De Ruiter told his audience, "If you had invested 100 euros in the best performer, you would have made a return of 540 per cent after eight years. The same investment in ABN Amro would have yielded 190 per cent."

De Ruiter produced a similar slide of the picture since 1 January 2001, when the bank had told investors that it intended to become one of the top five. Now, six years later, ABN Amro was in eighth place. In that period Barclays had become one of the top five (after SocGen, BNP, UBS and Nordea). ING, Merrill Lynch, JP Morgan, Citibank and Morgan Stanley were in the fifteenth to twentieth places respectively. De Ruiter explained that ABN Amro had had the advantage of an early reorganisation in 2000, before the markets went under, but that it had quickly lost that advantage. Between 2003 and 2006 the bank was in sixteenth place. After 2003 things had gone seriously wrong. The top five had doubled their profit per share, while ABN Amro hadn't achieved more than a 19 per cent increase.

According to De Ruiter, the growing mistrust in the world outside ABN Amro could be simply summarised: there was no focus. The endless reorganisation of corporate activities and the bank's complex structure had also taken their toll. "I won't even mention the economic profit. No one talks about that any more. That's history," he joked.

The investment banker remarked that corporate activities represented only 20 per cent of the bank, but that it felt as if it had squandered 80 per cent of the bank's energy during the previous years. Talking about his own area, De Ruiter said that the bank still had a serious cost problem. The hall nodded in agreement.

He observed that since Petra, analysts had been complaining about the growing complexity and warned that it was becoming an increasing risk in the eyes of investors. Almost all analysts complained that it had become impossible to compare ABN Amro's figures over the years. "And let's be honest, I believe that many of us agree with these analysts: we have to run an extraordinarily complex report structure. When we're assigning costs or revenue, we think more in terms of every man for himself than in terms of one-bank behaviour."

De Ruiter closed with a message. "If analysts are expressing the views of investors, then their patience is nearly up. It is now time to deliver on what we promise, if we want to be bosses of our own future. I would like to be part of the solution, not the problem. I hope the same is true of all of you."

After Jan de Ruiter, the new head of human resources spoke on the latest results of the employment engagement survey. Again it appeared that the personnel had little trust in the managing board because it chopped and changed too much. With Groenink's permission, Van der Meer Mohr had included a subset of questions in her survey of the top 175 managers of the bank aimed at finding out what they thought of the bank's strategy and leadership.

The results of this part of the survey were even more negative. Groenink was facing a hall full of bankers who were on the point of giving up their trust in him and the managing board entirely.

To settle the atmosphere, Van der Meer Mohr said that it was good that the managing board had had the nerve to have a survey done, because it showed that they were open to criticism.

It was late, and everyone wanted a drink. In the morning they would start thinking about what the bank could do to address all the issues it was facing. Cook had asked the former coach of the New Zealand rugby team along to help raise spirits.

The following morning the senior managers of the bank were distributed around ten tables. Their assignment was to brainstorm on the question: What's going on? It was the first time the managers had had a say in the way the meeting was structured. Alexandra Cook had thought that it was time for them to go through the process without the assistance of McKinsey or Marakon. After all, there were 175 extremely smart people in the room.

After one-and-a-half hours, a general manager would join each table to spend fifteen minutes listening to their ideas and then produce a summary. The managing board, sitting on a stage, then listened to the resulting overview. It came down to a litany of complaints about the performance of the board. One table had a simple solution to all the bank's problems: Groenink should resign.

In the afternoon, the leaders of the thirteen business units worked on solutions. Each then got two minutes to present them. During the discussion at the end of the afternoon, Hugh Scott Barrett gave his personal commitment that he would resign if the finances weren't in order in a year's time.

On Wednesday morning, Fabio Barbosa led a discussion between Ron Teerlink and Piero Overmars. The two younger members of the board spoke from the heart: they wanted to get things moving. Cook realised then that

Boumeester, Jiskoot, Kuiper and Groenink hadn't yet given their commitment, that they hadn't persuaded senior management that they deserved their trust. She tried to get them to do so. Joost Kuiper promised that he would do everything he could to make his last year a success. Jiskoot indicated that he would do everything he could to make a success of the corporate activities, which were too diversified. Huibert Boumeester promised to contribute his ideas.

The hall was now waiting for Rijkman Groenink. Pauline van der Meer Mohr had warned him the previous evening that he would have to show that he had really listened. She advised him to stop being defensive, show his vulnerability, and demonstrate that he was really concerned. Make it clear to your colleagues that you are looking for solutions, she had told him. Let them feel that you need them.

With these words in the back of his mind, Groenink sent his chauffeur back to head office to fetch the bank's Moroccan leadership staff. Now, holding the stick in his hand, the board chairman of ABN Amro gave an inspired speech. Suddenly he was back. The pressure on him was enormous, and he understood what his colleagues wanted to hear. The hall felt that this man really loved ABN Amro. They saw that he really did want the best for the bank.

Rijkman Groenink promised to listen better to his colleagues. At the end of the short, fervent speech, Groenink held the leadership staff in the air and promised the hall that when he handed it over, he would also hand over a healthy bank. The people in the hall were relieved and felt a sense of unity again – for the moment.

That afternoon Groenink met with his advory board. This group of ten board chairmen, among them Jan Aalberts of Aalberts Industries, Henk Rottinghuis of Pon Holdings, Nancy McKinstry of Wolters Kluwer, Jan Bennink of Numico and Hans Struik of Struik Foods, were given an update on the bank at least once a year.

The picture Groenink gave them summarised the problems. "Our efficiency ratio has worsened again, despite our promise at the end of last year to improve it. The gap between us and our peer group is getting ever larger. The average of the top five is 55 per cent, and the average of the peer group as a whole is 62 per cent. ABN Amro's ratio is 70 per cent. We have to improve our productivity to provide a counterbalance to the forces that are squeezing our profit margins.'

Groenink reminded his audience that they had all been faced with real competition on price for some time. He named the best performers in a variety of industries: Walmart, Toyota, Philips and Southwest Airlines. The bank could learn from them. "We will have to deliver more value to our clients every year, while we will have fewer resources to do that," Groenink concluded. "Productivity must be drastically improved."

In the follow-up to the dramatic meeting at Egmond aan Zee, Cook suggested to Groenink that it would be good for him to start thinking about the steps that he would take to fulfil the promises that had been made. But Groenink told her that it was no longer her problem.

The managing board was not proud of Egmond aan Zee. The event had been a staged performance. They had been, and were still, in a scrape. The managing directors knew that there was a good chance that the bank would soon find itself caught up in a merger or takeover, and they also knew that they couldn't share this fact with their colleagues.

Cook, who had been a general manager since 2000 and was therefore the second-longest serving executive at this level, didn't know this. But now she felt that she had been dumped. She was furious and decided to meet with a number of other general managers, among them Jan Peter Schmittmann. Her plan was to go straight to the supervisory board after these meetings, accompanied by the most important general manager, to urge the chairman's resignation.

A number of talks and meetings were held. Most of the general managers understood her anger, and were extremely concerned. A number of scenarios were discussed, and estimates made of the degree of support they would receive from members of the managing board. In the end, a majority found that it would not be responsible to go around Rijkman Groenink. They didn't dare. The mutiny had failed.

The bank's management was creaking at the seams. In November, things went wrong again between Joost Kuiper and Wilco Jiskoot, when they quarrelled during a meeting of the managing board. Jiskoot thought that Kuiper was letting his people in the United States encroach on his investment bank territory. The deals were small, true – usually no more than ten million dollars. But the agreement was that Jiskoot and Overmars' people would see to the execution of such deals. Kuiper had given the boss of the United States operation, Norman Bobins, room to take on people to do that work. Jiskoot was furious. A fierce discussion ensued.

Kuiper said that he no longer believed that Jiskoot was capable of honouring the agreements that had been made about divisions of responsibility, and that he was approaching things in an ever more opportunistic way. Visibly affected, Kuiper said that he no longer trusted Jiskoot. Jiskoot wasn't going to take this. Kuiper had made a professional discussion personal. If you don't trust your colleagues, there's nothing more you can do.

The supervisory board was shocked at the breakdown in trust between Jiskoot and Kuiper. They asked Groenink to find a solution. They felt that he should manage the conflict. It was only a few months since Jiskoot had received his warning letter. Martinez hinted to Groenink that one possibility might be the resignation of both brawlers. It was time to intervene.

Groenink regarded the conflict as a consequence of the Portsmouth affair. Collee had just left, and it was unthinkable that they should lose another two managing directors. He would have liked to fire only Jiskoot. He discussed this with Pauline van der Meer Mohr. She looked at Jiskoot's dossier. They wouldn't get another opportunity to fire him soon.

Kuiper realised that his conflicts with Jiskoot had their origin in Groenink's indecision. If the chairman didn't make it clear what he wanted, and who he supported, Kuiper and Jiskoot would always have room for their own interpretations. But Kuiper also felt that he couldn't blame Groenink for his outburst. He was ashamed of himself. It wasn't acceptable to make the conflict personal. He offered his apologies to Jiskoot. Groenink told the supervisory board that Jiskoot and Kuiper were on speaking terms again.

ING's supervisory board met on Monday 27 November. During the strategy discussions the option of merging with ABN Amro became more central. A knot would have to be cut here, though: should ING approach ABN Amro formally? Tilmant referred to the fact that ING's share price had increased from 29 to 35 euros that summer. This was the moment. Tilmant was keen. He had been chairman of the ING managing board for two-and-a-half years, and this looked like a logical next step.

Tilmant had succeeded in bringing the head of the supervisory board, Cor Herkströter, around to his view of things. The main argument was that ING itself might become a takeover target if they didn't do the deal. Tilmant presented his plan. He would aim at getting a deal before the end of the year. Everyone realised that there was not much time.

The supervisory board had its doubts. There had already been a number of attempts to combine with ABN Amro, their haughty neighbour. They had now analysed the bank so often that there was a joke going round that they knew the bank better than their ABN Amro colleagues. Time and again, ING had decided not to go ahead with discussions. The bankers and insurers who worked at ING were uncertain of their own position and role after the merger.

Two of the bank's governors were totally opposed: Paul van der Heijden, who had been appointed in 1995 on the advice of the ING employees' council, and Godfried van der Lugt, the former chairman of the ING managing board. Van der Lugt thought that Groenink was a street fighter. He couldn't imagine Tilmant and Groenink getting on personally. The opponents were mainly afraid of a reverse takeover. ING was larger, but ABN Amro had positioned itself as the quintessentially Dutch bank and dominated in many ways. ABN Amro was also the Central Bank's darling.

The opponents also worried about the consequences of the move for its staff. According to Tilmant's sums, between 10,000 and 15,000 jobs would have to be scrapped. And it pained Van der Lugt that it was not clear if Postbank, his Postbank, would remain in the merged company. There was a chance that NMA, the Dutch competition authority or its equivalent in Brussels would demand that Postbank be sold.

It was a long discussion. This wasn't new to ING's supervisory board, where relationships weren't good. There was growing support for new blood in the supervisory board. The 69-year-old Herkströter came in for criticism. Some of the governors thought him too careful, too distant and not always easy to access. They insisted that Herkströter should retire at the end of his second term, the following spring. But the chairman thought the bank wouldn't be ready for this. He was concerned about the staffing of some of his committees.

The two governors refused to agree to the proposal to talk to ABN Amro. The head of the supervisory board asked them what they would do if it was indeed decided to go into talks. Van der Lugt and Van der Heijden made it clear that they were against it, but that they would remain loyal to the bank if the majority decision went that way.

It was decided that Michel Tilmant would speak formally with Rijkman Groenink at the earliest opportunity. The aim would be to sign a letter of confidentiality, expressing the view of both sides that the two banks would merge within the short term. The merger would have to be short and sweet.

A day after receiving the approval of his supervisory board, Tilmant went to the Dutch Central Bank. DNB president Nout Wellink reacted enthusiastically to the news. He had envisaged this combination of forces for some years, and now, finally, it was going to happen. Each time a move had been made, ING, afraid of being dominated, had slammed the door. Wellink was pleased that ING was now taking the initiative. Together, ABN Amro and ING would combine to form a bank that would be one of the two largest in Europe. The combination would give the Netherlands one of the five or six banks that would dominate the financial world in the future.

Tilmant told Wellink that he would go to see Rijkman Groenink the following day to begin negotiations. If it was up to him, the two banks would announce that they were in talks before the end of the year.

15

Gamble

30 November 2006–22 February 2007

Michel Tilmant knew that you had to act quickly when opportunities present themselves. This was even truer when listed companies were involved, because there would always be rivals around. So the ING chairman wanted to move fast. But at his first meeting with Rijkman Groenink at ABN Amro's head office he didn't get the feeling that his neighbour felt any sense of haste.

Although ING was much larger, Groenink immediately said that he wanted a merger of equals, that is, a merger without a premium. He was making it clear to his ABN Amro colleagues that they didn't have to feel inferior.

Groenink told Tilmant about the way Hazelhoff and Nelissen had created the ABN Amro merger sixteen years before. He explained how two extremely different bankers had been able to put aside their differences in character to speak in unison to their constituencies. If they had done it, anyone could. They had achieved a phenomenal feat and brought two former arch-rivals together. ABN Amro's chairman suggested to his ING colleague that they work things out together first. If we do well, then the rest will happen automatically, that's how it went with ABN Amro.

Groenink also made it clear to Tilmant that he thought it logical that he, as the older of the two, should become the first chairman of the new combination; Tilmant would then take over after him. But the chairman of ING indicated that his constituency would expect him to be the first chairman. They decided to put the issue aside for the moment and look into other areas where they would be able to reach agreement more quickly.

They met again on 8 December. They identified seven subjects on which they had to reach agreement: strategy, brand, location, supervisory body, share price, board chairman and who would head the supervisory board. There were several subjects that they would not have to spend much time on. The bank would be based in Amsterdam, DNB would be the supervisory body and the bank would certainly be listed on the Amsterdam stock exchange. Groenink agreed to call the new bank ING. He was keen to ditch the long abbreviation. He was annoyed though when Tilmant suggested that the orange lion should play the lead role in the new logo.

Their strategic problems were not insurmountable. Along with many of his colleagues, Groenink didn't believe in combining banking and insurance. He felt that ING should close its insurance activities. That was a considerable demand, but, ING had already been making moves in that direction. A little more than half of ING's profits came from the bank and Tilmant said that they had already agreed to shed the damage insurance activities. He told Groenink that he didn't have to worry on this point. The bank would be dominant. They agreed that ABN Amro's insurance activities would be taken over by ING and that ING's retail banking activities would be taken over by ABN Amro.

The enormous size and dominance of the combination on the Dutch market was one point of concern. They knew that the Dutch competition authority, NMA, would demand that the combination should leave four banks active in the Netherlands, in the interests of healthy competition on the Dutch market. Tilmant and Groenink thought that they would be able to combine about 300 branches or offices and sell them to a third party. This would mean that only around 2,000 jobs would be lost in the Netherlands.

Tilmant didn't really understand the serious concerns that some of his governors had about Rijkman Groenink. He enjoyed talking with him, because his analysis was sharp. He noticed that Groenink had a tendency to reason from his own perspective, his own position. Tilmant understood well enough that Groenink wanted to operate from a position of strength, and that he wanted to present the deal to his constituency as a merger. That would keep everyone motivated. But he would have to tone down his approach somewhat, given his bank's poor results. Tilmant felt that his attitude was wrong in principle. ING's chairman might be vain, but his main drive was his sense of responsibility for his bank's future.

There was a lot that Rijkman Groenink had to get used to. This was the first time he was talking to ING as the smaller, subordinate party. During its previous attempts to talk to ING, ABN Amro had always been the larger party, and in a position to make more demands.

During their second talk, Groenink repeated his view that it would be necessary to agree to merge as equals. To support that idea, Groenink didn't want ING to pay a premium. If ING paid ABN Amro's shareholders more than the share price, the merger would quickly be perceived as a takeover. The roles might have been reversed in terms of numbers, but this would not mean that ABN Amro people had gained more respect for ING. Many of his colleagues still told stories about the white-sock brigade. Groenink was convinced that he could only sell this merger to his constituency if it really was a merger of equals.

Tilmant understood the reasoning, but immediately warned that other bidders might try to seduce ABN Amro's shareholders by paying a premium. And those shareholders would be easy to seduce, because they had been complaining for years that they were earning hardly anything on their shares. The ING chairman emphasised that this was a window of opportunity, and they would have to hurry.

Tilmant was concerned about ING's share price. Until November it had been 35 euros on average, which was good. In November it fell to 34 euros, which was all right, but it was now 32 euros, and that was less good. Moreover, ABN Amro's share price, which had hovered fairly constantly between 21 and 22 euros, was now rising. This was why he wanted to announce to the world that ABN Amro and ING were talking. That would enable them to establish a time frame in which they would negotiate undisturbed and exclusively. He warned Groenink: they had to announce that they were talking.

Groenink said he couldn't do that. He told Tilmant that he wanted to keep his options open for the meantime. ABN Amro was exploring the possibility of taking over Unibanco, the third-largest bank in Brazil. He wanted to round off negotiations with the majority shareholder, the Moreira Salles family, and not complicate this. He told Tilmant that there was a good chance that the takeover would succeed and that ABN Amro would then be a much more attractive proposition for a merger.

Groenink had long been impressed by the growth of the bank's Brazilian activities; with this takeover ABN Amro would become the biggest bank in Brazil. He thought that he would be able to finance the takeover partly through the sale of LaSalle. This would turn ABN Amro from a bank that operated in mature markets into a specialist in developing markets. He told shareholders that he expected investors to show their approval with a hike in share price of five euros. However the race had not finished yet: the owners wanted a lot of money.

Tilmant, Herkströter and a number of hired investment bankers were meeting regularly to talk about the progress of the talks with ABN Amro. Under strict confidentiality, the situation would then be communicated to the supervisory board and the managing board.

Cor Herkströter was shocked when he heard that Groenink had been taking a high tone during the first talks. Of course ABN Amro would want to shed ING's insurance activities as soon as possible, because the ING bank that remained would be smaller than ABN Amro. The head of ING's supervisory board didn't think that Groenink was in a position to make demands. He asked Tilmant if it was clear what the other members of ING's managing board thought, as well as ABN Amro's supervisory board.

Tilmant explained that Groenink had told him he didn't think it necessary to involve his managing board at this stage; as he saw it, they wouldn't understand what was going on. So it was some time before the talks took on a formal character. A legal advisor suggested to Tilmant that a letter be sent to the head of the ABN Amro supervisory board, to explain what they talking about. This showed ING's senior executives the extent to which Groenink was dealing on his own. The letter wasn't sent. Herkströter and Tilmant weren't pleased.

Groenink thought it was way too soon to inform his colleagues of what was happening. He felt the governors had given him a mandate in July to talk to ING, Barclays and Italy's Unicredito. And he was concerned that his colleagues would be worried about their own positions if they heard about developments at this early stage. That would needlessly complicate the negotiations.

Groenink told Tilmant that he would deny it if he was asked if he was talking to ING. A number of ING governors warned Tilmant that Groenink might be playing on a number of other boards too.

On the financial markets, speculation about ABN Amro's future began to increase. One rumour followed another. A number of hedge funds bought swathes of ABN Amro shares. We can get something out of this, they told each other, working each other up even further. Lists of possible takeover candidates during 2007 appeared in the media, and ABN Amro was usually prominent in them. Many investors sold their shares in ING to buy shares in ABN Amro, because they didn't want to be committed to two Dutch banks.

Groenink saw this. The fact that the two banks were moving towards each other in market value was good. Firstly, it improved his negotiating position, and it would be easier to force the equality that he needed in this merger. It also helped to know that the bank's senior executives would earn more from the merger, because of the higher share price. The strike price of most of the options that had been handed out over the previous years was around 20 euros. ABN Amro bankers had been complaining for years about the low share price. Groenink's own package was also gaining in value. Groenink wanted to sell or merge ABN Amro at the highest share price possible.

Tilmant and Herkströter were concerned. They knew that every passing day made any merger with ABN Amro more expensive and harder to explain to the shareholders. Moreover the negotiations were not even official yet. Where was all this going? Now the markets were suggesting that both Royal Bank of Scotland and the Scandinavian bank Nordea might make a bid for ABN Amro.

The last rumour in particular led to a rise in the share price of three per cent, making ABN Amro more than a billion euros more expensive.

Tilmant went to see Nout Wellink. He told the DNB president that he was frustrated that it was already halfway through December and the merger, which he had sketched out with his governors and consultants weeks before, was still no closer to completion. As he talked, Tilmant noticed that Wellink still seemed to be more concerned about ABN Amro. He talked about ABN Amro in a different way than he did about ING. Wellink assured him that he would do his best to get the talks moving.

On 18 December, Michel Tilmant invited Groenink to his home. They shared a passion for vintage Bordeaux and Cuban cigars, and this helped considerably to smooth things along. Again Tilmant emphasised that they were losing valuable time. Again Groenink asked for more time. He talked again about Unibanco.

Groenink was angry when he heard that ING had already been to Brussels to find out if the combination would encounter resistance there. The demands they had heard there didn't seem insurmountable. But Groenink let it be known that he was not ready for the deal and said again that there was no agreement of any form with ING.

ING's chairman accepted Groenink's reasons for not moving on to a deal. Now that it appeared that ABN Amro thought the Brazilian adventure was more interesting, Tilmant decided to go on holiday for two weeks. He said he would return if necessary, though. When Groenink heard that Tilmant would be on holiday during the weeks around Christmas, he concluded that Tilmant wasn't in a hurry either. If it had been necessary, Groenink had been prepared to put off his holiday, but now he could spend two weeks with his family in South Africa.

Just before Christmas, Groenink told Arthur Martinez that he was in talks with ING. He explained to ABN Amro's president that he had been talking to Tilmant for some time, but that they had been exploratory talks, and not at a mature enough stage to discuss yet with Martinez.

Groenink's colleagues on the managing board now heard that he had been talking to ING for some time. Kuiper, Jiskoot and Scott Barrett were angry; why had they not been involved? Groenink explained to his managing directors that they had only been exploratory talks. They supported the strategic logic of a combination. But Jiskoot didn't believe at all in the possibility of a merger of equals. Mergers were never between equals: one of the parties was always leading; if not, no decisions would ever be made.

Knowing that Martinez was now in the loop, Cor Herkströter phoned the head of ABN Amro supervisory board. Herkströter soon noticed that Martinez knew little about what they were discussing. The men agreed to meet in January.

Tilmant and Herkströter were frustrated by the way things were going. When asked if he was talking to other parties, Groenink had said that he had good contact with Barclays. ING now knew that there was another player in the game. This gave the bank even more of a sense of urgency. But they didn't think it would be realistic to force the merger in a more or less hostile way. Neither bank believed that it could lead a hostile takeover and turn the result into a successful combination. It would succeed only if the bankers on both sides were interested in the combination.

When Michel Tilmant told his impatient supervisory board that there was still no confidentiality agreement, that there was not even a letter of intent in sight, Van der Lugt saw his chance. He said again that it would be difficult to trust a man like Rijkman Groenink. The short and sweet scenario faded away.

Just before Christmas, a number of bankers and consultants warned ABN Amro's senior management that the bank's share price was rising, although this was a time when trading was traditionally slack. They indicated that it was mainly aggressive hedge funds that were buying shares. Groenink knew this already. He had spoken with Tosca by then, and he had a meeting with TCI in his diary for the beginning of January.

It was clear that the financial markets were convinced that a huge, wounded elephant was stumbling through the jungle, and that it would not see morning. The only question that remained was who would catch the elephant. The ABN Amro share price had risen to 24.50 euros.

On Tuesday 9 January, Fred Goodwin visited Groenink. The 47-year-old CEO of RBS denied that he was working with Tosca Holdings, the hedge fund that had urged Groenink to merge with RBS a few months before. The men talked mainly about the possibility that RBS might buy ABN Amro's American activities. The bank was still unable to move in America because of the Fed's cease and desist order. Groenink promised Goodwin that he would contact him when plans for that sale had been made.

That evening, Groenink dined with Tilmant at his house on Amsterdam's Herengracht. The men hadn't spoken for three weeks. Groenink again asked for time. The ABN Amro chairman repeated that he wanted a merger of two equals, without a premium. Tilmant wondered whether Rijkman Groenink knew why the share price of his bank was rising. Tilmant was convinced that another party would soon make a concrete offer for ABN Amro. He warned Groenink again that they would have to pick up the pace – this was the eleventh hour.

There was a breakthrough of sorts. This time Tilmant agreed that Rijkman Groenink would be the first chairman of the combination. The ING chairman didn't want this to be a deal breaker. He wanted to ensure that the merger went through. Despite the warnings of his own governors, Tilmant was not at all afraid of Groenink, who was three years older than him. If it was clearly communicated from the start that he would take over from Groenink in two years, he would still be seen as an important driver of the process. He was still only 54, and he would be able to put his stamp on things for quite a few years after Groenink.

Tilmant and Herkströter decided to pay another visit to Nout Wellink, to ask him to move things along. Wellink observed that Groenink seemed to be delaying. He phoned the ABN Amro chairman and told him that it was taking too long to get the deal through, and that he should get a move on. But Wellink also understood that it was not easy for Groenink and ABN Amro to negotiate as the junior party with ING. The idea took time to get used to. He realised that the delay was contributing to the rise of ABN Amro's share price, and that this would give the bank much more to bring to the table. He had to concede that Groenink was right to recall that ING had closed the door on ABN Amro several times before.

Cor Herkströter didn't like Wellink's attitude. He understood his point of view that it was not up to the DNB president to be the deal maker. But ING people were constantly being reminded of ABN Amro's historical importance, as well as of the bank's size and international character. They felt that Wellink was more concerned about ABN Amro. This wasn't news, but it didn't make it any easier to accept.

On 10 January, Groenink received a visit from Davide Serra and Chris Hohn. Serra, a former banker with Morgan Stanley, had calculated in the summer of 2006 that splitting up ABN Amro would deliver a lot of money to the shareholders. The separate segments of the bank were worth more than the whole. Serra, owner of the small hedge fund Algebris, had told Chris Hohn, founder of the Children's Investment Fund (TCI) and persuaded him to join his scheme.

Hohn, 39, was the son of a Jamaican car mechanic; he had set up his hedge fund five years earlier. It had been a success. Over the previous three years, TCI had delivered an average annual return of nearly 50 per cent. It was one of the best-performing hedge funds in the world, and managed around 10 billion dollars.

Part of the money earned by the TCI went to the Children's Investment Fund Foundation. This foundation, managed by Hohn's wife Jamie, had around one billion euros in funds. Chris Hohn had transferred some 230 million pounds to the fund in 2006, making him the biggest philanthropist in England. People like Bill Clinton regularly asked him for money for their projects, which were mostly aimed at improving health care and providing better education for children in developing countries. "Chris really wants to do something for children in developing countries," Jamie Cooper-Hohn told the *Financial Times*. "In his first job, Chris worked in the Philippines. He saw children there who lived on garbage heaps. I think he was deeply affected by it."

Hohn, who lived as a recluse, was known mainly because he had ensured that the Deutsche Börse's bid for the London Stock Exchange failed. One of Germany's business tycoons, Werner Seifert, had been forced to resign. TCI and Chris Hohn were names that sent fear through many a managing boardroom.

Rijkman Groenink wasn't trembling though. They had a pleasant meeting on the 21st floor of the ABN Amro building. Groenink listened patiently to the expositions of the two hedge-fund managers. They were critical of the bank and warned that ABN Amro shouldn't go down the takeover route. It would first have to show that it could achieve cost efficiency.

Groenink nodded in agreement. He promised the two shareholders that the bank would show a clear improvement in its results in the next six months. The chairman felt that his guests had accepted his explanation and promise. And half a year would be more than enough time to merge ABN Amro with either ING or Barclays.

As they were leaving, Chris Hohn had one more thing to say. He told Groenink that he feared a merger between ING and ABN Amro. Even an aggressive hedge fund would find it difficult to go up against the love that was blooming between the two local giants.

The merger was still a long way away, however. ING's supervisory board had made it crystal clear to Michel Tilmant that they would not agree to Rijkman Groenink as first chairman. He would therefore have to withdraw that offer. Cor Herkströter was fervently opposed to it. The whole process was looking ridiculous. He thought it was absurd that he still didn't know what ABN Amro's governors thought of the potential deal. He also thought that such a merger would have to be worked out in detail before it went ahead.

Tilmant understood that his governors wanted him to be the first chairman and they were reaching agreement on the role of Rijkman Groenink. Herkströter let his governors know that he would attend future meetings along with Tilmant, and that he would insist to Groenink that Arthur Martinez also attend the meetings.

On 11 January, Tilmant informed Groenink of his supervisory board's displeasure and told him that he, Tilmant, would be the first chairman. Groenink immediately agreed and suggested that he follow Tilmant after two years. Groenink then said that Arthur Martinez should be the first head of the supervisory board of the new bank. Tilmant was happy with that.

The Belgian indicated that he now wanted to sign a confidentiality agreement, and that he wanted to announce that they were officially in talks. Groenink said that he also wanted that, but that he wanted to complete the Unibanco programme.

Tilmant was finding this increasingly incomprehensible. It was all taking too long. They agreed that they would have lunch with the heads of the supervisory boards in a week's time, on 16 January, at Tilmant's house in Amsterdam. ING's chairman had the idea that the deal would be formally struck then. Peter Jong, head of media relations, was told to prepare to announce the news. Tilmant told Cor Herkströter that he didn't have any problem at all with Arthur Martinez as head of the supervisory board.

On 11 January, shares analyst Stuart Graham presented his report on ABN Amro. More than six years before, at Rijkman Groenink's request, the bank specialist had warned the Dutch bankers that analysts had doubts because they didn't understand the bank's strategy. JP Morgan's analyst had frightened ABN Amro bankers by warning them to ensure that the share didn't end up in the sin bin. Once there, a share would always be analysed incorrectly.

And now it was time. Graham was still welcome at ABN Amro and he got a lot of information about the bank. There was one difference: Graham now worked for Merrill Lynch. In his report, 'Now or Never', he called on investors to buy shares in ABN Amro. 'If the bank doesn't deliver this time, there will be increasing pressure to find radical solutions. There can be no more excuses for cost excesses.'

During the previous year, ABN Amro's performance had been 8 per cent worse than the sector average, and since 2004 it had been 21 per cent worse. Graham calculated that ABN Amro's profit could be 37 per cent (2.1 billion euros) higher if the bank's various divisions were as cost effective as those of comparable banks. Graham was convinced that the share would soon rise above 30 euros, if the bank started plucking the fruits that it been promising for so long.

The analyst indicated that the managing board had missed out on some

10.9 million euros in bonuses over the period from 2004 to 2006. 'They will be more motivated to start delivering, especially given all the talk about mergers and takeovers and the growing pressure of hedge funds in the background. We do not believe in a Deutsche Börse scenario, but if things continue this way, active shareholders could get uneasy.'

Subtly, Graham then remarked that it would be a simple matter for any active shareholder to get controversial subjects onto the agenda of general shareholders meetings such as the one that would be taking place on 26 April. 'To do this, a shareholder would only need to own one per cent of the bank's shares. Remember that proposals for the agenda have to be tabled sixty days before the meeting.'

It was Tuesday 16 January. Michel Tilmant had brought in a caterer to serve a pleasant lunch at his home. The four key decision makers at ABN Amro and ING were finally together. This would be a decisive meeting. One of the largest banks in the world could be born here, and it would be Dutch.

Tilmant had decided not to talk much. This was the first meeting between the two heads of the supervisory boards, and they would need to find each other. Cor Herkströter also wanted it to be mainly a meeting between himself and Arthur Martinez. He was curious about what sort of man he was, and what he stood for. The suggestion that this American would be the first head of the supervisory board of the merged bank was on the table. Herkströter was concerned about this. That would mean that the biggest bank of the Netherlands would be led by a Belgian and an American. ING's supervisory board had agreed some time before that the head of the supervisory board should be a Dutchman, someone who would understand the context that head office operated in.

Martinez knew that Groenink had agreed that the first chairmanship would go to Tilmant. The ABN Amro chairman had told his president that Tilmant would do the job for a short while, and that he would take it over. Martinez assumed that the opposition had agreed to him being the first head of the supervisory board.

But Herkströter didn't react at all when Groenink raised these subjects. Martinez could hardly recognise Herkströter: they had had a pleasant conversation on the phone, but the man who was sitting here was distant and cold.

Herkströter was surprised too. Whenever he asked Martinez a question, it was answered by Rijkman Groenink. The American said nothing. Didn't he understand what his role here was?

Tilmant said that he thought two years would be too short, and that he wanted to be chairman for three years. Groenink agreed, but said that there was a limit for him; in three years he would be 60. Herkströter didn't respond to the questioning glances that he now got.

Groenink felt the resistance to him personally, and tried to settle things. He explained that it was simply a question whether he would in fact succeed Tilmant after three years. He would be older by then, and possibly not as motivated. What was important to him was the announcement they made now. It was vital for his authority at ABN Amro. He wanted to be able to settle some of his colleagues' concerns, and the deal would have to look like a genuine merger of equals.

Groenink wanted to resolve these issues now. But Herkströter made it clear that he wanted to look into the details, to have an idea what the merger would actually look like. The atmosphere didn't improve as the lunch proceeded; no one drank wine. Herkströter was irritated by Martinez's silence. It wasn't right, somehow. Why was he saying virtually nothing?

Tilmant also thought it a strange meeting. The two supervisory board heads didn't appear to understand each other at all. Tilmant also got the impression, again, that Groenink was doing all this on his own. That didn't make him feel good.

The four men sat together for one-and-a-half hours. As they took their leave, none of the senior managers felt that anything had been achieved. Worse, the feeling that they really wanted to get things going seemed further away than ever.

Speculation about the future of ABN Amro took on ever-wilder forms on the financial markets. Now rumours abounded that RBS and the Spanish bank Santander were interested, in addition to ING and Barclays. That something was going to happen was hardly in question. London's *Financial News* did the rounds of 40 bankers to ask where they expected to see a big deal. A large majority agreed: ABN Amro. The shareholders' patience was up, and they wanted to cash in the value of the bank. This would be a huge deal; tens of billions could be involved.

Any investment banker would have jumped at the news and seen an opportunity to earn a lot of money. It was clear that ABN Amro wouldn't survive, so they would have to get moving as soon possible. Any investment bank that missed out on such a big deal would have a problem later in the all-important league tables. ABN Amro, a big, broad and therefore inefficient bank, contained some real pearls. From their international networks the investment bankers heard that some banks were interested in various parts of ABN Amro. In London, teams of specialised investment bankers were rapidly put together to prepare a book, or game plan. Then they called possible buyers, explained the scenario they had worked out – and, of course, offered their services.

In the first week of February, Rijkman Groenink phoned Michel Tilmant to tell him that the takeover of the Brazilian bank Unibanco would not be going ahead. He told the ING chairman that he was now ready to do the deal they had been talking about, that he could sign a confidentiality agreement that day, if necessary. Groenink added that in his view the merger could be rounded off within a few weeks. Tilmant was irritated. He had worked for two months to get things moving with no result; they had got nowhere in all that time. But now that Groenink had dealt with his problems, he wanted everything to happen straight away.

Cor Herkströter had worked out why Martinez had hardly spoken during their meeting a few weeks before: the head of ABN Amro's supervisory board had been surprised by the things he had heard his chairman say. The American apparently didn't understand that he was in a sense Rijkman Groenink's boss, that he could make demands on the chairman. It was time someone explained this to him.

Herkströter hadn't liked Groenink's attitude during the entire process. After consulting with his governors, it was decided that Groenink would be unacceptable as a successor to Tilmant as chairman of the merged banks. It would mean that the chairmanship would be fixed for the next six years, which would discourage internal candidates. The board wanted Tilmant to become the first chairman; whoever succeeded him would be decided then.

Tilmant called Groenink to tell him this. The ABN Amro chairman realised that he would probably not get what he wanted and repeated his demand that ABN Amro would at least provide the first supervisory board chairman. This would give at least one of the seven points he had started out with, when he set out to achieve a merger of equals.

Sentiment on the ING supervisory board about a possible merger with ABN Amro had declined still further. Nearly three months before, they had asked for a confidentiality agreement, as proof that the two banks wanted to work together. This still hadn't materialised. Cor Herkströter had found it frustrating that they hadn't been able to start official talks. There had been no foundation for the talks that had taken place. ING's supervisory board also complained about the role played by Nout Wellink. Why was he not more sympathetic to ING?

On 14 February, ING's supervisory board told Tilmant that the decision as to who would lead the merged bank's supervisory board would have to be made by the supervisory board heads of two separate banks. This was clearly not Tilmant's responsibility.

Groenink called Tilmant a number of times to find out ING's position. But Tilmant said that his bank would need more time. Nout Wellink now began to worry. He knew there were problems, and that Cor Herkströter was not finding things easy, and there was still no deal on the table. He understood that the talks would require time. Groenink and Tilmant would have to carry the merger together, after all. But so far as he was concerned the timing was perfect. ABN Amro's considerably smaller size would compensate for ING's inferiority complex. And the position of Rijkman Groenink, who was not liked in ING circles for what many perceived as his arrogance, would be considerably weaker.

Wellink had understood that the head of ABN Amro's supervisory board stood at some distance from the bank – too great a distance. Wellink got in touch with Arthur Martinez and explained that he would have to be involved more closely in the negotiations. He noticed that Martinez was shocked by this; the American clearly had the idea that in the Dutch system the head of the supervisory board had little say. Wellink indicated to Martinez that he had obviously not understood the fact that he had final responsibility in the eyes of the law.

Martinez went into action. He called Cor Herkströter and suggested that they meet. There were clearly some serious wrinkles that needed ironing out. He asked Herkströter not to inform Groenink of the meeting. Herkströter was disturbed that Martinez wanted to keep the meeting secret from his own chairman.

Martinez suggested that they meet at a golf course just outside London. Herkströter said that he never played golf, and didn't like the sport. But Martinez explained that he knew the place well, and that they would be able to talk in peace there.

The men had some difficulty in finding a mutually acceptable time to meet. After the first chilly meeting a few weeks before, neither really wanted to speak to the other. Paging through his diary, Martinez told Herkströter that he had a lot of engagements coming up. Herkströter said that he would be going on holiday during the first two weeks of February in Switzerland. Finally they agreed to meet on 9 March in London.

Groenink felt uncomfortable. He hoped that the merger with ING would succeed, but was in the meanwhile talking to a second interested party. On 8 February he flew to the UK to speak with John Varley again. They had talked for a long time at the World Economic Forum, two weeks before. They were making progress. Groenink knew that he had no chance of becoming chief executive of this merged bank, but it had been more or less agreed that he would chair the Barclays board.

In London, the two bankers good-humouredly discussed the main points that would have to be satisfied to make a merger between ABN Amro and Barclays possible. They agreed to meet again on 27 February and take discussions further.

Meanwhile, Chris Hohn and Davide Serra were beginning to worry about ABN Amro's share price. Serra was a friend of Matteo Arpe, the chairman of Capitalia. Arpe was in a power struggle with the head of his supervisory board, Cesare Geronzi. The 71-year-old Geronzi had been suspended as president from mid-December to mid-January because he had been accused of involvement in a fraudulent bankruptcy. It was his second suspension in a year. During those weeks, the 42-year-old Arpe had tried to persuade Capitalia shareholders that it would be better if Geronzi didn't return.

ABN Amro had a 8.7 per cent stake in Capitalia and was therefore one of its largest shareholders; it had taken Geronzi's side in the conflict. Rijkman Groenink thought that he would be able to do business with Geronzi eventually. Geronzi had hinted in the past that a combination of Antonveneta and Capitalia would not be unthinkable.

With ABN Amro's help, Geronzi survived Arpe's attack. He wanted to strike back, and put Matteo Arpe's departure on the agenda of the shareholders meeting on 22 February. Arpe, Hohn and Serra were worried that Geronzi would invite the Dutch bank to take over Capitalia, out of thanks for ABN Amro's support. They didn't want to see that happen. They had, anyway, agreed with Groenink that there would be no takeovers. The shareholders decided to increase the pressure on ABN Amro and sent a letter to Rijkman Groenink and the head of his supervisory board.

On the evening of Tuesday 20 February, Rijkman Groenink invited members of his managing board, among them Joost Kuiper, to visit him at his home. His new house was finished at last, and could be shown off. During the dinner, he got a message that a letter was coming from TCI.

The following morning the ABN Amro chairman opened the letter, addressed to Mr Martinez and Mr Groenink. In the letter, the shareholders said that they thought it would be irresponsible for ABN Amro to throw itself into a takeover of Capitalia. 'This will have a negative impact on the share price and bring with it the risk that Capitalia's highly successful management team will leave.'

He noticed that the authors quoted from the report by the Merrill Lynch analyst, Stuart Graham. This was especially true of the passage that calculated that the separate parts of the bank were worth more than the bank as a whole. The shareholders mentioned an underlying share value of 30 euros per share.

Reading on, Groenink understood with rising anger that the shareholders were saying that it was in their interest to take ABN Amro apart. In their view, the management of the bank had been failing since 2000. Adopting the suggestion made by Graham, they said that, as shareholders of one per cent of the bank's shares, they wanted to place a number of motions on the agenda of the shareholders meeting on 26 April.

The points they were making were clear. They wanted to ask the shareholders to forbid management from doing takeovers. Specifically, they wanted to tell them to stay away from Capitalia. They also wanted all the shareholders to express themselves on proposals to sell the bank, or parts of it, or to merge with other banks and distribute the profit to the shareholders. TCI didn't think that ABN Amro had any further right to exist and believed that other shareholders would think so too.

Groenink cursed and realised immediately that he wouldn't be able to get around this. He had heard that the letter had found its way to the media. Within an hour, press agency Bloomberg reported that Chris Hohn had a new target in his sights. A short while later Rijkman Groenink called DNB, and reported the TCI letter. It could have serious consequences, he believed. Wellink and Groenink agreed to meet that Friday afternoon.

When Nout Wellink read the letter, he was shocked. He realised instantly that the merger between ABN Amro and ING was in danger. The shareholders would combine forces and start manipulating the media. Speculation on a quick cash-in of the added valued in ABN Amro would drive the share price up even faster. The old ING fears of a dominant ABN Amro began to resurface ... He had to do something. The ABN Amro share price would have to be put under pressure.

Something happened to the DNB president that had never happened before: he couldn't sleep at night. He was worrying about the cloud that hung over the country's most important bank. Wellink needed to find a way out, and he knew that he would have to push the limits of his responsibilities to do so.

Wellink, as head of the Dutch supervisory body, was under no illusion that he could directly influence the bank's share price. But he did feel that it was his responsibility as supervisor to call on politicians in The Hague to fight back. The most important bank in the country would be affected. Surely the country couldn't allow the bank to be pulled apart. Like TCI, Wellink decided to use the media to show that he didn't think it responsible to allow such an important bank to be cut to peices.

The DNB president knew that he would be in a much stronger position if he persuaded politicians to warn that any split of the bank would be unacceptable. As a prominent member of the Christian Democrat party (CDA), he had direct access to a fellow party member, prime minister Jan Peter Balkenende. But the man with whom he had direct contact officially was the finance minister. Wellink decided to call the finance ministry to arrange a meeting with the new finance minister as soon as possible.

Labour Party leader Wouter Bos was sworn in as finance minister in Balkenende's fourth successive cabinet that Thursday afternoon by Queen Beatrix. Nout Wellink was his first appointment on the Friday morning at nine o' clock; even before his first meeting with the new cabinet, which had been cobbled together with some difficulty by CDA and Christian Union.

Bos looked through his notes. On 19 February he had talked about ABN Amro with his predecessor, Liberal Party's Gerrit Zalm, during the handover of the finance minister's portfolio. There had not been a lot to say, as Zalm had not been particularly interested in the financial sector. His predecessor told him of the continuing talks between ING and ABN Amro and estimated that the merger would be realised in the short term, in March.

Zalm had remarked that the bank was also talking to Barclays. He had said that all contacts went through the president of the Central Bank and that Nout Wellink had done his best over the last weeks to get ABN Amro's supervisory board head more involved in the discussions.

Wellink expressed his concern that Friday morning and said that he would warn against a break-up of the bank. The new finance minister tried to put things into perspective. Bos said that he understood Wellink's concerns, but that he would have to guard against any Fazio-like fantasies. He reminded Wellink that he had gone to the barricades for ABN Amro with Gerrit Zalm one-and-a-half years before to plead for ABN Amro's takeover of Antonveneta and break the resistance of the president of the Italian Central Bank, Antonio Fazio.

Wellink got the impression that the minister didn't understand what he was saying, and explained that he wasn't worried about a possible takeover by a foreign bank. This was not about competition. Italy had been a friendly takeover; the management had supported the takeover by ABN Amro. No, what was at risk here was that the most important bank in the country might be broken up. Wellink was worried about prudence. Would it be sensible to let this happen – would it be good policy? If the bank were broken up and sold, as the hedge funds were demanding, then the bank could become unstable, and that would inflict considerable damage on the Dutch economy.

The minister insisted that he too had major questions concerning TCI's call. But he also wondered if he ought to be worried by the scenario. As it was, ABN Amro was talking with ING and Barclays about a merger. Wouter Bos said that he didn't want to find himself accused of protectionism on his first day as finance minister.

Bos warned Wellink that he might find himself accused of the same thing. He understood well enough that a successful ING merger would be in Wellink's interests, because he would then be the supervisor of one of the largest banks in the world. But he said that Wellink was a supervisor, and not a broker. Bos felt that it would not be sensible for Wellink to go public. The minister thought that in the end the DNB president had his own responsibility in the matter: he would have to do what he had to do.

In the NRC *Handelsblad* newsroom that morning, everyone was working hard to put the TCI letter into perspective. A staffer, Menno Tamminga, was the only journalist to call the Central Bank to ask for an interview with president Wellink and/or Arnold Schilder, the bank supervisor. On Friday afternoon at three o'clock he was called by a bank spokesman, who told him that he would be expected in one-and-a-half hours.

While Tamminga was waiting with a photographer in the DNB lobby, Rijkman Groenink came down the stairs. He had just been to see Wellink to update him on the situation. When the journalist asked him if DNB was worried, he said with a broad smile that he should ask them.

Wellink and his supervisor, Arnold Schilder, were more than worried. The Central Bank president said that TCI's suggestions went a bridge too far and added combatively, "You get the impression from the TCI letter that they themselves don't know what to do about ABN Amro. This is close to reckless. What they propose would be inconsistent with our responsibility. We can't let the solidity of the financial world be compromised. This isn't a country and this isn't a bank with a protectionist policy, but whatever happens must be done in the context of a healthy bank policy." Tamminga knew then the news that would be opening his paper the next day.

At the bank, the defence committee was hard at work. A broad collection of people had been called immediately after Groenink had read TCI's letter. Rijkman Groenink, Hugh Scott Barrett and Huibert Boumeester were there, as well as Jan de Ruiter, the bank's merger and takeover specialist and a number of staff. They wrestled through the forty-page manual that had been compiled by consultants from Morgan Stanley and the bank's lawyers. It described the steps that they would have to take in the event of a hostile threat. Lawyers from three different legal firms had been brought in to help.

The managers asked themselves how far they would have to satisfy TCI's demands. Should they put the five points on the agenda of the shareholders meeting? One lawyer fiddled with some of the formulation. Or would it be better to put some of the bank's own, rather different points on the agenda?

Some wondered if this was creating an atmosphere that might invite a hostile takeover of the bank. Groenink didn't see much chance of that. As he saw it, European supervisors wouldn't allow a hostile takeover of a big bank.

There was some reference to the way TCI had tackled the Deutsche Börse affair. The managers knew that they couldn't reckon on much support from the shareholders. The accusation that the bank was busy trying to take over Capitalia was not based on fact, but Capitalia had been on the list of banks being considered for takeover. TCI had not been entirely wrong. ABN Amro had wanted to take over Capitalia.

Jiskoot didn't believe that the bank could avoid placing the motions on the agenda. This wasn't only because of TCI. He knew that other, bigger shareholders shared TCI's opinion, and he thought that between 15 and 20 per cent of them would support the call. The bank would have to listen – whether it wanted to or not.

Groenink thought that it was all rather confrontational, but unavoidable. He concluded that the bank would have no legal leg to stand on if it decided not to table the motions.

They talked about other ways of stalling for time, so that they could stay in control and keep the initiative. De Ruiter suggested that they sell LaSalle immediately, pass the returns to the shareholders and announce that Groenink would resign. He was certain that they would gain some time that way.

Groenink looked at him sharply. He admired his directness, but said that he couldn't abandon the ship now, he felt responsible. There were nods of agreement. But it was evident that the bank's leaders didn't feel confident they could beat their hostile shareholder.

Arthur Martinez and André Olijslager, president and deputy president, held an emergency meeting about the TCI letter. They looked at each other and wondered what to do about the situation. What risks did they themselves run as governors in this process? TCI was an aggressive shareholder that wouldn't hesitate to take directors and governors to court.

They agreed that firing Rijkman Groenink immediately would be the easiest way to gain more time. The governors believed that they could gain six months in this way. But who would succeed Groenink? Kuiper didn't want the job, and the list of candidates that they had looked at six months before didn't offer any prospects. The two governors couldn't find a solution. Martinez didn't want to fire Groenink until they had a successor. That would only destabilise the bank.

The two governors then had a chat with Rijkman Groenink. They asked him what they had asked each other: What are we to do? How can we gain some time? Groenink rolled off the names of his managing directors and out-lined the possible effects on them if they lost their jobs. He didn't talk about himself.

The senior managers decided to shore up their defences with as many of the best consultants as they could get. The reasoning was simple: all that talent and intellectual ability wouldn't be working for the opposition. A range of in-vestment bankers were invited in to explain the services they could offer. Others offered their services.

Lawyers from Allen & Overy, Davis Polk & Wardwell and NautaDutilh were hired. The latter sent the bank a list of dos and don'ts regarding communica-tions with representatives of TCI. 'These limit TCI's room to claim that man-agement was not listening to them,' they explained, adding, 'Everything you say to them could be leaked to the press, or used against the bank at the share-holders meeting. It is advisable to listen, rather than talk. The content of the discussion is less important than the simple fact that it is occurring. Follow up on any promises you make, but try not to make any if you can. Remember, TCI will have been compiling a dossier since the beginning.'

In addition to the lawyers, an army of investment bankers was also hired. For corporate bankers, who are paid only if a transaction takes place, it is im-portant to be on the selling side of the deal, because that's where the money is made. A managing director is expected to earn between 15 and 20 million dol-lars a year for his bank. Between 10 and 15 per cent of that will usually be paid as bonuses. It was clear that something big was going to happen with ABN Amro, that is, the sell side, and that's where they wanted to be.

ABN Amro's managing board hired Morgan Stanley. This investment bank had been mapping competitors who might be interested in a hostile takeover of ABN Amro for some years. Morgan Stanley were assigned to look into the at-tractiveness of a merger with Barclays. Lehman Brothers – one of the big deal-ers in ABN Amro shares – were also hired, and now knew what the situation was with the shareholders. UBS got a role and Rothschild was hired to work out the bank's stand-alone scenario.

Talks were also held with the corporate bankers at Merrill Lynch. The large American investment bank had been all but forgotten at ABN Amro for some years. The last time they had played an active role had been during the unsuc-cessful bid for Generale Bank.

Joost Scholten was responsible for Merrill Lynch's contacts in Benelux. He had a large network. Huibert Boumeester was a good friend; they had shared a house as students in Leiden. Scholten was a member of the board of trustees of three charities that Huibert Boumeester had set up in 2005.

Scholten reported to ABN Amro with a proposal; the bank made a counter-proposal. Joost Scholten and his colleagues thought ABN Amro's offer was too thin, both as regards role and remuneration. ABN Amro and Merrill Lynch didn't arrive at an agreement.

Merrill Lynch would now be able to earn money on the deal only if they could find a convincing way to get in with the buying party.

When Boumeester told Wilco Jiskoot that Merrill Lynch would not be taking part, the seasoned corporate banker knew that Merrill Lynch would be certain to have another iron in the fire. Jiskoot knew that there were two banks with good relations with the American investment bank: Royal Bank of Scotland and the Spanish bank, Santander. He could not imagine, though, that they would be interested in the Dutch retail business.

16

Assault

23 February–21 April 2007

Lex Kloosterman was standing on a peak in the Swiss ski resort of Lenzerheide. Fortis's director of strategy had been trying to relax for a couple of days, but without much success. His mind was reeling. The TCI letter, the persistent rumours about discussions between ABN Amro and ING, not to mention Barclays. The suggestion that RBS and even Santander might be interested in purchasing parts of his former bank. The speed with which ABN Amro had recently engaged a large number of investment bankers. And then there were all the stories from former colleagues about the bank's internal problems. The fissure between board and senior management was complete. ABN Amro's management had thrown in the towel.

He felt badly about it. After all those years, his automatic reflex was to rush to the bank's defence. It would have been pointless, however. His job now was to define Fortis's standpoint and make sure it didn't miss a trick in the struggle for the bank that still bore the name ABN Amro.

Kloosterman wanted to see where he could get backing. Where was the available brainpower and which investment banker was still free? Standing on his skis, the Fortis director phoned Joost Scholten. The two bankers were brothers-in-law and knew each other inside out. The Merrill Lynch investment banker told Kloosterman that his bank had not been called in by ABN Amro, so there was no conflict of interests. There could be an opening here.

Kloosterman didn't want contact with the American investment bank to be muddied by family interests. The brothers-in-law decided he should contact Andrea Orcel. The 44-year-old Italian was the head of Merrill Lynch's investment banking department in Europe. Orcel confirmed that he was available and they agreed to meet a few days later.

Kloosterman told him what Fortis wanted. Obviously the strategy was to encourage growth, especially outside the Benelux countries; this, however, was the chance of a lifetime. Fortis wanted to take over ABN Amro's retail operations in Holland. The logic had been imperative for almost a quarter of a century now and it was also behind two earlier attempts to get the banks under one roof – in 1988 and 1989, between Amro and Generale Bank and in 1998, when ABN Amro tried to buy out Generale Bank. Their combined strength would make them the leading retail bank in Benelux, one with eleven million customers and a convincing story about size and synergy. Kloosterman knew ABN Amro inside-out – it would be a great move for Fortis.

Orcel told Kloosterman about the interest of Santander and Royal Bank of Scotland in parts of ABN Amro. He suggested that the three banks might form a consortium. Once each of the banks had control of the exact part they wanted a great deal of synergy could be achieved. In his report, entitled 'Now or Never', Merrill Lynch analyst Stuart Graham had already ascertained that 'the bank would make 2.1 billion euros more if every division of ABN Amro was able to achieve the cost efficiency of the peer group – a gain of 40 per cent'.

Kloosterman listened to Orcel, who was a great communicator; a consortium like that was unprecedented in the banking world. Three competitors who joined forces so they could all benefit from a takeover. He kept his cards close to his chest, however, because he knew that the chairman of Fortis, Maurice Lippens, still had another idea in mind. For the takeover of ABN Amro, Lippens had put all his bets on joining forces with Citigroup.

On 2 March, Cor Herkströter met up with Michel Tilmant. The head of the supervisory board wanted to know whether Tilmant and his managing board were still interested in the ABN Amro adventure and asked him to sound out his colleagues on the board.

On 6 March, the president of the Dutch Central Bank (DNB) had another meeting with the minister of finance. In recent days Nout Wellink had received a fair amount of criticism because of his warning in NRC Handelsblad that TCI's demands had gone too far. The European commissioner for the internal market, Charlie McCreevy, warned that DNB should not get involved in a struggle between TCI and ABN Amro. "Everyone has the right to operate freely within the lawful framework of capital markets." VEB, the Dutch retail investors' lobby, even lodged a complaint with the DNB board of governors that Wellink had no business making any public statements about individual questions. Furthermore, DNB should base its statements solely on facts and not on speculation. In *The Wall Street Journal* he was nicknamed Nout Fazio, a reference to Antonio Fazio, the head of the Italian Central Bank who had resigned after attempting to block the takeover of Antonveneta.

None of this gossip bothered Wellink, however. He was in The Hague to elicit political support for a merger between ABN Amro and ING. Both Tilmant and Groenink let him know they appreciated his help. He reminded the minister of the importance of this merger. If it didn't go through, ABN Amro could easily become a prey to speculative investors. Wellink thought he had the right within the limits of the European rules to point out what was best for Dutch interests. In his view, a merger of ABN Amro and ING fell into this category.

When Wouter Bos asked him exactly what he meant by political support, Wellink explained that it would be a good thing if the government told the two banks that they would not make an issue of the job losses resulting from such a merger. In this connection, he asked Bos for an appointment with the prime minister. His political approval would also be needed.

Wellink also discussed the possibility of starting talks straight away with the NMA, the Dutch competition authority. He wanted the minister to give the go-ahead for this aspect of the merger process. NMA would then have the information it needed and could quickly be brought on board when the merger was announced. He emphasised the urgency of the matter. His main concern was that all the obstacles should be cleared in advance.

The minister, however, understood something else. Bos was afraid that Wellink wanted to talk with the prime minister to discuss whether the ministers concerned could overrule any NMA objections. This was something that Bos was not prepared to inflict on Balkenende. He indicated that while Wellink could count on his support, he wondered why he wanted to talk with the prime minister. Bos and Wellink made an appointment to see each other again the next day. Wellink would bring Rijkman Groenink.

In the prime minister's diary, space had already been reserved for a meeting with Wellink. Bos, however, warned him. The ministers were still not used to their new roles. They realised that Wellink's statements about the TCI letter had provoked a lot of hostility in the European Commission and the VEB. Bos and Balkenende saw a parallel with the Antonveneta takeover. At that time Balkenende had urged the Italian prime minister to ensure that the European rules with regard to the internal market were respected by the Italians.

They also felt that with a merger the competition authorities should be free to do their work without any interference from the politicians. They would therefore not consider such a request. Balkenende confirmed that the finance minister was qualified to handle the matter. It also didn't help that Balkenende and Wellink were not on particularly good terms. Wellink was not a welcome visitor with his fellow Christian Democrat.

Next day at six, Wellink went to the ministry of finance with Groenink as arranged. He regretted that the talks between ING and ABN Amro didn't yet have any official status. Otherwise he could have invited Michel Tilmant as well.

Bos assured him that he was positively inclined towards the merger. He wanted to remove every worry that as leader of the Labour Party, the PvdA, his main concern would be about job losses. He saw the advantages of combining forces, but didn't see what he was supposed to do to encourage that.

Bos also wondered if ING wouldn't inevitably have to close down the entire banking division of ABN Amro. And if it did so, would the logic behind the merger still hold good? The discussion again turned to the competition issues that would rise when the merger was ready to sign. These might form an obstacle. One government adviser thought it a strange request, as if the two men wanted to bypass NMA. The ministry had already enquired whether a huge merger like this wouldn't land up in the in tray of the Brussels authorities. At the end of this somewhat informal meeting, Bos and Groenink swapped cell phone numbers.

Wellink was furious and he cancelled the date with Balkenende. He simply couldn't understand where either Bos or the prime minister were coming from. The minister of finance had no need to fear an informal conversation between two members of the CDA; he could simply have joined the meeting. In Wellink's entourage it was hinted that the rejection maybe had to do with the fact that a few months previously he had told Balkenende and Bos frankly that Gerrit Zalm was not welcome on the board of the Netherlands Central Bank. Bos and Balkenende had the notion that, having held the post of finance minister for twelve years, Zalm would be Wellink's ideal successor. After all, Wellink would be 65 in August 2008. Wellink put a stop to their gallop. He told them he loved his job, that his appointment only ended in 2011 and that he didn't care for the idea of having his intended successor sitting next to him on the board for three full years. Half-jokingly he remarked that maybe he'd stay on longer – he'd been on the board for 26 years already and had been president for eleven of them. Alan Greenspan had only started when he was 62 and had hung on till he was eighty. Maybe he'd do the same. Wellink gave Zalm the benefit of his thoughts too.

On 8 March, Fred Goodwin phoned Rijkman Groenink again, emphasising that RBS was not behind the rumours in the market that ABN Amro would be up for sale. He also repeated that he was interested in LaSalle. Four days later Groenink received a letter from him confirming what he'd said on the phone, but going a step further. Goodwin asked whether the two banks shouldn't cooperate in a broader sense in order to generate value. Groenink's antennae were immediately alerted; after all this sounded suspiciously like the earlier suggestion of the Tosca hedge fund.

On 9 March, the two heads of the supervisory boards of ABN Amro and ING met on a golf course near London. Cor Herkströter turned up with the Civil Code, thinking that his American colleague would know nothing about Dutch corporate law. He showed him the passages dealing with the functions and responsibilities of a supervisory board, a construction that didn't exist in the United States. He translated the texts into English and assured Martinez that his translation was reliable. He told him that the head of the supervisory board was legally bound to do everything in his power to further the interests of his company.

Arthur Martinez listened, bemused. He would have recalled Groenink's remark that the relation between Tilmant and Herkströter was not that great and that the former found Herkströter a difficult person to work with. He could picture it. He repeated that he genuinely hoped the merger with ING would go through. He added that he understood that Herkströter had a problem with Groenink and said he saw it as his task to tell Groenink that he wasn't the right person to succeed Tilmant.

He also argued that it was important that he became the head of the new supervisory board. The staff of ABN Amro needed a figure at the top whom they knew. Martinez proposed that he hold the post for two years and promised to move to Amsterdam. He said he'd already discussed it with his wife and they were excited at the idea of spending time in Europe. After two years someone like Jeroen van der Veer, the current chairman of Shell and an old colleague of Herkströter, could take over.

Herkströter must have given him an old-fashioned look. The notion that a man like Martinez would be his replacement was unimaginable, let alone now. In two months time his second term of office would end and he would turn seventy that year. It was assumed that he would resign then, but he was still worried about who would sit on the various committees. Especially the audit committee; the bank hadn't yet found the right people. It didn't sound sensible for him to leave his post right then. He was irritated that there was a fuss about this on his own supervisory board.

He told Martinez that he thought it didn't make sense for a merger of two Dutch banks to have an American as its president. After a conversation of some hours Herkströter said that he thought he would stay on a while. Martinez said that he understood what Herkströter meant and expressed the hope that they would keep in touch and think about matters further. He promised to phone.

That afternoon Herkströter met Michel Tilmant in London. The ING chairman understood from Herkströter that he wasn't comfortable about the merged bank being run by two foreigners. Tilmant emphasised once more that he had no problem with Martinez being appointed president. In fact Tilmant was beginning to lose interest in the whole business. He had returned to his calculations. The TCI letter and the resulting excitement had forced ABN Amro shares up to 28 euros. It was beginning to become too expensive. Furthermore his soundings of his fellow managing directors revealed little enthusiasm for continuing the talks.

On the ING managing board interest in the merger with ABN Amro had declined. While ABN Amro shares were rising, those of ING fell below 30 euros. During the talks ABN Amro shares rose by 30 per cent while those of ING fell by ten.

They had agreed that ING wouldn't pay more than 29 euros per ABN Amro share, including options. A maximum of 31 might be acceptable. The notion of an exchange of shares became virtually impossible; roughly 20 per cent of ABN Amro had to be financed in cash, and to finance this would require selling large pieces of the bank.

ABN Amro bank had become too expensive. It dawned on Tilmant that the merger should have taken place in January at the latest. He also understood that the discussions between ABN Amro and Barclays had meanwhile gathered momentum. And he had heard that Santander and RBS were also interested. The chairman of ING didn't hold out much hope of a merger any more.

A couple of days after their London meeting Martinez phoned Herkströter. He confirmed that it was all right for Tilmant to be chairman of the managing board of the new combination and that he had agreed with Groenink that he wouldn't succeed Tilmant. Martinez stated that the only condition was that he would be the head of the supervisory board. Herkströter replied by saying that he couldn't commit himself on paper to that as yet.

Martinez also said that the present ABN Amro supervisory board would have to have half the seats on the new board. Herkströter was annoyed by this sudden statement of new demands. He and his colleagues at ING had from time to time looked at the make-up of ABN Amro's supervisory board and asked out loud whether they were 'their sort of people'. He was no longer worried, however. The race was already run and nobody at ING was interested any more. At the meeting of his supervisory board on Friday 16 March, Tilmant presented the situation as he saw it. He felt that if they continued they would be painting themselves into a corner. He added that the market was deteriorating rapidly and that ING was in danger of paying a ridiculous price for the deal. Furthermore it wasn't beyond the bounds of possibility that Brussels would require that the retail activities of either ING or ABN Amro be sold. There was no synergy to be had there, nor was the business case attractive any longer. Herkströter underwrote Tilmant's argument. The whole business was too expensive and it was asking for trouble to pursue it further.

The motion was passed unanimously to terminate talks with ABN Amro. The chairman noticed that some of the directors were quite relieved, almost joyful, while others looked profoundly glum.

Late on Friday morning Tilmant phoned Rijkman Groenink, who happened to be standing in the huge glass central reception area of ABN Amro's offices in London. He told him that ING intended to discontinue the negotiations, that ABN Amro had simply become too expensive. Groenink was not exactly overjoyed by the news but easily appreciated that the ING merger was a thing of the past. Arthur Martinez, who was standing beside him, phoned Cor Herkströter immediately. He also got the message straight away and the conversation was a short one. Martinez laid the blame on Herkströter's slow response for the failure of the merger.

The two men were in London to see Chris Hohn. It was an arduous discussion. The active shareholder believed that the bank should be broken up. Over the past years the board of ABN Amro had had plenty of time to create synergy. They broke off their negotiations, agreeing to disagree.

With ING dropping out as potential suitor for the bank, the TCI scenario drew nigh and Groenink and Martinez were both aware of this. They decided forthwith to go for a new partner. Although only two days ago they were still hoping that the ING deal would be sealed, the supervisory board had given Groenink formal permission to engage in possible merger discussions with Barclays. That same Friday afternoon the chairman of ABN Amro got in touch with Barclays CEO, John Varley. ABN Amro was willing to be wooed but time was short.

Groenink asked Huibert Boumeester – it was his birthday – to start negotiations. On Sunday 18 March Boumeester and Barclays CFO, Naguib Kheraj, met to look at the conditions for a confidentiality agreement. On the same day there was a leak that the banks were in exclusive talks about a possible merger of equals.

On the basis of reports in the British Sunday papers, *Het Financieele Dagblad* reported a day later that Barclays had approached ABN Amro with a merger proposal. By engaging in negotiations, ABN Amro could fend off activist shareholders. With 47 million customers and 220,000 staff, the combined banks would become the second largest in Europe and the fifth in the world. The same day ABN Amro's share price rose 10 per cent to almost 30 euros, its highest quotation ever.

Two days later it was officially confirmed that the two parties were engaged in exclusive negotiations. It was agreed that Huibert Boumeester was to be the standard bearer for ABN Amro and would head the negotiations team, with Alexander Pietruska as second-in-command. The central figure for Barclays was Naguib Kheraj. It was agreed that John Varley would be appointed first CEO of the merged bank. Rijkman Groenink would be chairman of the one-tier board. In all probability the three young members of the supervisory board of ABN Amro would also get good jobs on the new board.

Hugh Scott Barrett too was enthusiastic about the combination with his fellow countrymen. His role wasn't clear yet but he reckoned on being appointed CFO in the new bank. One irritating feature was that Barclays had already announced in October that Kheraj would be succeeded on 1 April by Chris Lucas, originally of PricewaterhouseCoopers.

Even though they had given the go-ahead for talks, ABN Amro's supervisory board was surprised to see how detailed Rijkman Groenink's plans for Barclays were. Right up to the meeting of 14 March they had thought it would still work out with ING. And although they had never voted on it, Martinez's claim to be appointed president of this combination seemed a viable option. In recent weeks they were only scantily supplied with information about the discussions with ING.

Now that the plans with Barclays had suddenly landed on the table and in concrete form, they began to realise that the decision of July of the previous year would mean ABN Amro's takeover. The bank urgently needed a partner and the leverage for making their own demands had become precariously small.

They were relieved, however, that something was happening at last. For years they had listened to Groenink's summaries of all the failed talks with other banks. The best thing for this bank was to be brought under another roof as quickly as possible. What was more, Barclays promised most of them a good position on the board of the merged bank.

They realised they might have something of a roller-coaster ride during the weeks ahead. The papers were full of stories about conflicts between governors, directors and crusading shareholders. At the end of April there would be a meeting of the shareholders that promised to be a tense one for the bank. Until recently the governors could relax for hours in their well-padded chairs at these meetings. They sometimes played a game with each other by which they gave a mark to Groenink's answers to shareholders' questions. Trude Maas, for instance, would say that the chairman got a better mark from her if he'd also shown he'd understood the question.

There was no time for games now. Their legal advisers had warned the governors that the process in which the bank had now landed had to be pursued in orderly fashion. They could be held to account afterwards, if there were shareholders who felt that things hadn't been done properly; for instance if they hadn't gained the best possible offer for their parts of the bank.

To have more control over the detail it was decided to set up an ad hoc consultancy committee with members of the supervisory board. Arthur Martinez, André Olijslager and Rob van den Bergh would keep the board informed about decisions to be taken with regard to Barclays and TCI.

Various media sources stated that Barclays definitely was the ideal suitor for ABN Amro. There was almost no overlap in activities so that in the case of a merger or takeover, there would hardly be any need for slimming down. The entire Dutch organisation could remain intact. The analysts of the American investors bank, Keefe, Bruyette & Woods were, however, not enthusiastic for just that reason. In their view, the combination would just mean one huge bank that would generate little synergy. As far as they were concerned Barclays was at the bottom of the list of potential purchasers. There were parties for ABN Amro's shareholders that were much more interesting and could pay much more. Special mention was reserved for RBS.

Jean-Paul Votron, the financial manager of Fortis, Gilbert Mittler, and Lex Kloosterman were listening that week to Andrea Orcel. Orcel's story – the man was fluent in four languages – sounded rock solid. The corporate banker knew the financial sector well; he had good contacts with Santander and knew that the Spanish had been interested in Banco Real and in Antonveneta. Merrill Lynch had advised Santander three years previously in the takeover of Abbey National.

Orcel had been informed by his colleague Matthew Greenberg, the head of financial institutions, that RBS was interested in LaSalle and possibly also in large parts of the corporate banking activities of ABN Amro. Greenberg was one of Goodwin's most important advisers when the latter took over NatWest in 2000.

RBS and Santander had already sat round the same table a couple of times to discuss the fate of ABN Amro. They felt at ease with each other as they had regularly participated in different projects over the past eighteen years and had supported each other in expansion strategies. They did, however, have one problem, namely that neither of them was interested in the Dutch activities of ABN Amro. Neither the Scottish nor the Spanish bank had a high opinion of this small overcrowded market with its narrow margins.

Orcel and Greenberg had done a simple sum, by which they took on board the thinking of their colleague, financial analyst Stuart Graham. The fact that the different parts of ABN Amro were worth more separately than the sum of its parts gave more leverage for a high bid. If RBS, Santander and Fortis got precisely those parts of the bank they wanted, they could squeeze plenty of synergy out of them. If these three banks could arrive at a 'consortium offer' they would be virtually unstoppable. No bank separately could pay more than a consortium, let alone Barclays.

Kloosterman and Votron were enthusiastic, but pointed out to Orcel that Fortis was still planning a bid with Citigroup. They didn't know that Chuck Prince, CEO of Citigroup, had already phoned Arthur Martinez expressing interest. With a couple of large American banks Citigroup was engaged in a struggle for the largest share in the American retail market and was interested in taking over LaSalle. Martinez asked him to make a bid for the bank.

Martinez never got that far. Discussions between Fortis and the Americans didn't go smoothly. Chuck Prince was under great pressure from his shareholders who were increasingly frustrated by the bank's market value that had hardly budged for five years. Prince had even proclaimed 2007 as the year when there could no longer be any excuses for things not improving. Until now nothing had changed.

In the discussions with Citigroup, Lippens felt increasingly that he was like a sheep walking next to an elephant to catch another elephant, but with the sheep being expected to devour the largest part of this monstrous quarry. The Americans were in fact mainly interested in LaSalle and wanted to pass large portions of the firm's commercial banking activities on to Fortis. Lippens felt little enthusiasm, however.

Lippens felt uneasy and was relieved when Citigroup informed him that they had no desire to continue talks. Within twenty-four hours Lippens was on the phone to Andrea Orcel. Orcel proposed that they should discuss the possibility of making a joint offer with RBS and Santander for ABN Amro. They agreed to meet on 30 March. Assisted by the investment bankers of Merrill Lynch, Count Maurice Lippens and Sir Fred Goodwin met for the first time.

On 28 March, ABN Amro announced the agenda for the shareholders' meeting of 27 April. It was the first time that the bank replied officially to TCI's demands. All the matters requested by TCI would be on the agenda. Senior management realised now that the main task would be to persuade the shareholders that a merger with Barclays would be more profitable than TCI's suggestion that they should carve the bank into pieces.

In a letter to the shareholders Rijkman Groenink stated that, 'the purchase of extremely lucrative, rapidly growing parts of the company would lead to considerable superfluous costs and loss of profits.' He even proposed that a scenario for preserving their independence was preferable to carving up the bank. 'The results over 2007 and the future years would improve substantially. That makes the scenario of an independent future for the bank a persuasive alternative.'

Analysts pointed out that the chances were rapidly diminishing of an alternative purchaser emerging as ABN Amro and Barclays brought on board more and more advisers from different banks. Barclays had already covered itself with advice from Credit Suisse, Deutsche Bank, Lazard and JP Morgan Cazenove.

On 29 March, the British bank announced that they had also called in the services of Citigroup. The Americans made sure there was also something in it for them in case of the largest financial sector takeover ever. In the City the rumour spread like wildfire that the head of Citigroup, Chuck Prince had phoned John Varley to inform him that they were not interested in pursuing ABN Amro but that they would be happy to advise.

Goldman Sachs too was doing its best not to be left out. In the market it was already known that their adviser had cut loose from ING now it was clear that there was little to gain there.

On 30 March, Lippens fell immediately for the charm of Fred Goodwin. Preparatory to their meeting he had studied the Scotsman's impressive career. He was especially struck by the way Goodwin had put a relatively small bank on the map by taking over NatWest, twice its size. RBS was a couple of sizes larger than Fortis – in 2006 it had made a profit of 9.2 billion pounds. The 16 per cent growth in profits came largely from corporate activities.

When the subject turned to ABN Amro the two men soon found they had much in common. Fred Goodwin, who had travelled to Brussels, was clear that Fortis should have the retail bank, the private banking and asset management divisions. RBS would get the American subsidiary, global transaction services (GTS) and the corporate banking activities. Brazil and Antonveneta would of course go to Santander.

This sounded like a perfect arrangement. Lippens and Goodwin agreed to meet with Santander's representative. The calculations of Orcel and Greenberg looked extremely promising. It should be possible to go much higher than Barclays. Two days later the British Sunday paper, *The Business*, announced that Royal Bank of Scotland was sounding out its main shareholders about the idea of taking over ABN Amro.

Lippens was enthusiastic. He recalled his meetings with Groenink, his unbelievable arrogance when the bank tried to filch Generale Bank from him in 1998 like a thief in the night. But he kept his peace – no need to be spiteful when you've won.

He knew that Votron had good reason for wanting the deal to succeed – seven years earlier he had counted on being appointed to the ABN Amro board. Votron and Groenink were hardly friends. He was also confident that Votron would make a success of this moderately profitable retail bank. He knew ABN Amro inside out and had already made the Belgian retail sector of Fortis, which had just as narrow margins as the Dutch, a good deal more profitable.

Lippens had arranged with Votron to find out from the major shareholders as soon as possible whether they would support the takeover. Fortis's shareholders would put more than 10 billion euros on the table to make it possible.

On 3 April, Groenink and Varley paid a friendly call to DNB. Three days later at the presentation of the DNB annual report, Nout Wellink told the media that he would not stand in the way of a merger between the two banks. "I have meanwhile spoken to John Varley and it was more than just a preliminary conversation." Wellink also explained that he "would appreciate it if the main offices of ABN Amro would be housed in Holland, as had happened with Shell. That would also be positive for job opportunities."

Wellink took the opportunity to spell out why he was afraid of the scenario TCI had requested. *Het Financieele Dagblad* remarked, "A supervisor has the task of ensuring that savers are guaranteed their money. If anything in the system breaks down, you also get a chain reaction. Other banks are then affected and so are the tax payers." Wellink emphasised that from the standpoint of public interest there were clear limits to the maximising of shareholder value in financial institutions. According to him that made the situation with TCI quite different from the one where the Italian Central Bank attempted to block ABN Amro's takeover of the Banca Antonveneta. "This has nothing to do with preferential treatment for a Dutch bank," he said.

On 10 April, the Rothschild consultants presented the option of selling different parts of ABN Amro straight away, enabling it to continue as a smaller but still independent bank. Wilco Jiskoot in particular thought it important to make a thorough analysis of this stand-alone option. A number of his colleagues were attracted by this scenario that would preserve the bank's independence.

There was also another party eager to participate in discussions, namely ABP. Like Nout Wellink, Holland's largest pension fund with its invested potential of 220 billion euros, was worried about what would happen if ABN Amro disappeared. ABP knew that a crucial network would be lost if the 'purveyor of the best bankers in the Netherlands' ceased to exist. A number of directors of the pension fund wondered whether it wasn't their duty to prevent this happening.

In a series of relaxed talks the question arose of whether it would be helpful if ABP, which currently owned one per cent of the shares of ABN Amro, acquired a large stake in a stand-alone scenario, a strategy that was dubbed the third way.

Rothschild's investment bankers had calculated that, with the sale of the bank's American and Brazilian activities and Antonveneta, something between 31.5 and 36.4 billion euros could be raised. Some 13.9 billion for LaSalle, around 11.7 for Banco Real and 8.6 for Antonveneta. On paper the bank could pay shareholders roughly 23 euros per share. What would remain would be a small European rump.

From the start Groenink saw little in this scenario; Jiskoot also had his doubts after reading the report. Selling large portions of the concern under pressure would bring a variety of execution risks. With the sale of Brazil, for instance, a large sum would have to be paid to the Brazilian tax department. For the rest of the revenues it would take years for shareholders to get their money in a tax-friendly fashion.

ABP felt the chill wind of division and weariness in the managing board. Moreover it proved impossible to organise any broad popular support. ABP's connections with politicians in The Hague had become increasingly tenuous over recent years. Their support was necessary, because this investment of billions of euros with money from the pension fund was not exactly risk-free. There were also doubts about how long a reduced ABN Amro could stay autonomous. The third way never got off the ground and the scenario disappeared in the bin.

On 11 April, the bank published its seventeenth annual report, probably its last as an independent bank. It came to almost 300 pages and weighed 1.5 kg. The word Barclays only appeared once – as one of twenty banks in the peer group that ABN Amro compared itself with, in terms of total earnings to shareholders. ABN Amro was number sixteen, and Barclays was in the top ten.

Groenink promised the shareholders that 2007 would be the year the bank would finally reap the harvest of all that hard work. It was the first time that no photograph of the entire smiling managing board appeared in the annual report. There was, after all, little to smile about. On the board, enthusiasm for a merger with Barclays was at an all-time low.

John Varley was keen, however, as he explained in an interview with *Het Financieele Dagblad*. "Over the coming fifteen to twenty years we foresee an enormous growth in the financial industry and my task is to ensure that Barclays' activities are geared to this prospect as effectively as possible. The model of the universal bank is the one best equipped to take advantage of these developments." Barclays CEO emphasised that this universal bank would have to "aggressively" diversify and internationalise itself, especially in the United States and emerging markets. "We will do this on the one hand with our global activities, such as the credit card division and Barclays Capital investment bank. We will also do it with our private and corporate banks." In his view, ABN Amro, the bank where for seven years the concept of a universal bank had been taboo, would bring with it interesting markets in the United States, Brazil and Asia.

The directors of RBS, Santander and Fortis met for lunch in the Four Seasons Hotel des Bergues on the Lake Geneva on 12 April.

Prior to this meeting Lippens and Votron had often discussed the takeover. Lippens had given Votron a meaningful look as he asked his colleague whether they were going to jump. Could they in fact? They were the smallest of the troika. The takeover would cost Fortis more than 20 billion euros, over half of Fortis's total capital of 35 billion. They realised that not signing was no option.

Merrill Lynch's bankers were nervous. If it succeeded, they would earn a great deal of money; not only what they'd get for cooking up this deal but also for helping finance it. They might end up with half a billion dollars. Men like Orcel, Greenberg and Scholten knew they would each get millions for it.

First of all, however, the various players would have to click. The directors of the troika told Merrill Lynch's bankers in no uncertain terms that they would only go to sea together if they knew they would win. Losing face was out of the question. They felt no lack of confidence, however, and their first rough calculation suggested they could easily go 15 per cent higher than the offer they expected from Barclays.

Maurice Lippens had never met Santander's 73-year-old Emilio Botin. The latter was, however, ready for the encounter. Exactly what he would find in Italy was something he didn't yet know, but he felt good about being able to purchase Banco Real. ABN Amro had been too quick for him nine years ago. It was a great relief to hear that the deal with Unibanco hadn't gone through. His own bank hadn't had things easy in Brazil, but he could pounce now. He greeted the two Belgians warmly, gave them a tie with his bank's insignia and told them that they were in it together.

Lippens was impressed by Botin's bright and beady eyes, eyes that struck him as measuring him from top to toe. Lippens told him straight out that the Spanish and Scottish banks had better leave the Dutch part of the bank to Fortis – it wasn't their territory.

The Scot, the Spaniard and the Belgian came to terms and agreed to work together with the motto of the three musketeers in mind: all for one and one for all. They still had eight days to agree on a price and they had to lay their bid on the table before ABN Amro and Barclays clinched a deal.

The same day the three banks sent a two-sided letter to Arthur Martinez and Rijkman Groenink informing them that they 'were extremely interested in jointly taking over ABN Amro Bank. Furthermore they promised that their offer would be higher than Barclays. They requested access to the same information as Barclays and also to be given an opportunity to discuss the details. ABN Amro replied immediately, saying that their discussions with Barclays were exclusive and that while they were continued there was no way they could talk with any other parties.

Analysts responded enthusiastically to the news and predicted that ABN Amro's shares would reach 40 euros. The founder of TCI, Chris Hohn, was also delighted, stating that the initiative of the three banks should be viewed as "friendly with regard to his firm and shareholders".

Het Financieele Dagblad wrote on 16 April, 'ABN Amro was not prepared to give the consortium the same information as Barclays. The bank thought that the consortium's proposals were not sufficiently concrete. Bankers from Morgan Stanley were advising the ABN Amro board to ask the consortium to come up with a definite offer. And that they should also show in detail how it was to be financed.'

Rijkman Groenink was both surprised and angry. This was totally unacceptable. In his view, it was impossible to break the bank into three pieces without losing a great deal of value. It would destroy his 183-year old institution. He was livid with Fred Goodwin. He thought of the behaviour of the hedge funds at the end of the previous year, of the role of Mathewson and the latter's relation with the Scot. Groenink had always felt that Goodwin was leading him up the garden path and had never told him the truth.

He understood Santander's position, but was furious that Fortis was one of the consortium. While he could see the logic, he didn't think Fortis had the financial capacity for the deal. Groenink had respect for the investment bankers of Merrill Lynch whom Fortis had apparently bamboozled into intervening. He was sure that Votron was behind their success in selling this plan. He didn't understand, however, why Lippens had not put a stop to Votron's gallop. The chairman respected Lippens; saw him as a masterly and cunning manipulator. Count Lippens, however, had made a big mistake here and would live to regret it.

ABN Amro's chairman decided to do all he could to prevent his bank from being split in three. The idea was insufferable.

Many ABN Amro bankers agreed with Groenink. They were appalled by the idea that the bank that they'd worked for all those years should be torn apart. The thought that the heart of the bank, its domestic operation, would go to Fortis was something they found unbearable. Fortis for them was without any doubt the most pathetic bank in Holland. They hardly knew any of Fortis's people, nor did they want to. It never occurred to them to phone any of them or ask them if they would like to become involved in any project.

The feeling, however, wasn't so negative everywhere. In ABN Amro's domestic division the horror for Fortis was mixed with a certain optimism. The belief that the superior bankers were theirs, offered them the prospect of a reverse takeover, with ABN Amro bankers, in the Netherlands at any rate, dominating Fortis, which was a much smaller concern.

Some ABN Amro bankers couldn't resist doing a few calculations for themselves. The offer from the consortium would largely have to be paid in cash – otherwise it would be much too complex. With a bid of 40 euros per share they would get an average of 20 euros for each unpaid option. Most of the general managers and department managers would comfortably get a hundred thousand options and, in some cases, a great deal more. With 40 euros per share as the base line, a figure that was soon in circulation, they would earn millions.

Morgan Stanley's advisers were worried for that very reason, that such a large proportion was to be paid in cash. The evidence was still scanty, but if they were able to realise it, it could be a serious threat to Barclays' offer that would mainly be paid in shares. In situations like these, cash is usually king.

Like Rijkman Groenink, Nout Wellink was not happy with the consortium's offer. The Dutch Central Bank warned about the risks involved in a collective bid like this, "From the point of view of caution, the consortium's offer was a much more complex and risky factor, both in the preparations for the transaction as in its execution and implementation." DNB announced that it would 'judge any proposal with utmost care'. The members of the consortium had expected him to react like this. Nout Wellink had previously called TCI's suggestion a step too far. They knew that they could do nothing without the seal of approval of the Central Bank. They would have to approach this problem with tact. In a letter to Fortis, which was not made public, DNB warned that the complicated transaction 'puts a lot of weight on the solidity of the collaboration'. For the first time the stock market value of ABN Amro's shares began to fall. It now stood at 36.13 euros, a drop of one per cent. Investors knew that the supervisor might intervene in a case of conflicting offers.

Wellink was not amused by what happened next. First, there was the disappointment that the merger with ING hadn't gone ahead, then there was the problem with aggressive hedge funds and now there was a consortium that wanted to split the bank. He was responsible for supervising the solidity of the Dutch financial system, a system that had become the target of fortune hunters and adventurers. He cast his mind back with some nostalgia to his meeting with Wouter Bos at the end of February. If Bos had gone public with him then and had condemned TCI's demands, this consortium would never have emerged.

The creation of the consortium – three banks, none of which belonged to ABN Amro's peer group – was also a surprise for the supervisory board. They were convinced that no competitor for Barclays would appear on the scene. Things had become unbearably stressful. On 12 April the supervisory board engaged Goldman Sachs's advisers to help them with the necessary calculations.

For the time being the governors focused on Barclays. Over dinner at Duin & Kruidberg, John Varley and Naguib Kheraj explained the advantages of a merger with Barclays to ABN Amro's supervisory board. It was a positive meeting and the governors had hardly any questions. Considering how little was actually drunk, there were plenty of toasts. The meeting was chaired by Arthur Martinez.

For ABN Amro's managing board, the 51-year-old Varley had a less hopeful message. He told Groenink that on sounding out his main shareholders, he had discovered that Hugh Scott Barrett and Rijkman Groenink were not exactly popular. The former could therefore not become CFO and Groenink would not get the post of chairman. They discussed the possibility of him being appointed executive second-in-command beside Varley.

Furthermore Varley saw no room for the previously agreed-on three seats on the managing board for members of ABN Amro's managing board. Only one of them would get a seat as executive director.

A few days later John Varley contacted the seven managing directors of ABN Amro. He asked them for their views on the deal. Jiskoot had plenty of criticisms of its structure and proposed that if only one ABN Amro director were admitted to the executive board of the bank then it should not be an Englishman. He felt that this gave a bad signal to the rank and file of shareholders, who in his view got all too little out of the deal anyway. Groenink agreed with him and proposed Huibert Boumeester as the right person to sit on the managing board of the merged bank.

Martinez spoke to Marcus Agius, then chairman of Barclays, without consulting with Groenink first. The atmosphere was somewhat better than during the discussions with the chairman of ING's supervisory board, Cor Herkströter. They discussed the role assigned to Rijkman Groenink and went on to that of Martinez. The American offered to take over Agius's position for two years. He was still pursuing his dream of spending a few years in Europe with his wife.

Martinez pointed out that it was logical that ABN Amro would hold the post of head of the supervisory board if Barclays provided the CEO. He suggested that, as far as he was concerned, Agius could take the post back from him after two years. The two agreed that Rijkman Groenink would also sit on the board of the merged bank as an ordinary governor, a non-executive director.

Over dinner in Tante Koosje restaurant in Loenen, near Rijkman Groenink's home, Martinez told his chairman he would have to abandon the idea that he still had a leading role to play in the concern. He would be a governor and that was it. Rijkman Groenink was resigned to his fate. The writing was on the wall and he could do nothing about it.

During a joint meeting of the managing board and the supervisory board of ABN Amro on Tuesday 17 April, the day before the end of the period of exclusive negotiations with Barclays, it was suddenly noticed that there was still no agreement between the two banks. They needed more time and they decided to extend the period of exclusion by two days.

The decision was taken there and then to sell the American subsidiary company, LaSalle. It had been agreed the previous year that, if necessary, it would be sold in the context of a merger or takeover. The hour had come. Because ABN Amro was still under a cease and desist order, special permission had to be requested from the United States authorities to sell the firm. They agreed. Directors and governors were of one mind – this move would form a major stumbling block for the consortium. RBS in particular was interested in wresting LaSalle from ABN Amro, so that there was a good chance that it would back out of the deal. Martinez also thought that selling LaSalle would not come as a surprise for the board of Barclays.

ABN Amro knew there was plenty of interest in LaSalle. On Wednesday morning just after midnight, the advisers of UBS phoned Groenink to let him know that Bank of America was interested in LaSalle. They had in fact expressed interest a number of times over the past few years. They were now keen to act quickly and negotiations started straight away as the transaction had to be completed within a couple of days. Jiskoot chaired the proceedings and on Thursday Bank of America came up with a price – 20 to 21 billion dollars.

Joost Kuiper, responsible for United States activities, was not amused. He had just visited the US to reassure his American colleagues. He had told them about a meeting with John Varley, in which the latter had spoken warmly about the American activities of the bank. He booked a return flight immediately to inform his colleagues in person about the sale.

On the evening of Friday 20 April, Huibert Boumeester phoned Naguib Kheraj to tell him about the sale of LaSalle. The latter was furious. In his view this was not how banks worked together in good faith. He wondered out loud whether it was still meaningful to continue discussions. Boumeester could hear his anger. Obviously they needed to chill out a little at the other end of the line. Calmly he explained that the deal was nothing if not positive. It would create a distance between them and the consortium. Varley let Groenink persuade him that this move would only increase the chances of the merger.

Now that everyone knew what LaSalle was worth, Boumeester and Groenink believed that it would help them raise the price of ABN Amro. Barclays would in any case be able to pay more now. They had, after all, already arranged that the merged bank would sell LaSalle in the long run. Their opposite numbers at Barclays did indeed chill out and indicated that they were willing to continue talking.

That evening Rijkman Groenink got a call from Fred Goodwin. The consortium's spokesman told Groenink that RBS had a good reputation in takeovers of other firms and promised that in the event of a takeover everyone would be taken care of with regards to remunerations. Groenink and his colleagues had no need to worry. The chairman thanked Goodwin for his kindness.

Saturday passed like a weekday, with everyone working flat out. Teams of dozens of bankers and lawyers met to make sure everything was on paper and correct. They thought they were on course, but the sudden sale of LaSalle had sent them back to square one. They worked on all through Friday night and Saturday night as well. On Sunday morning a merger document of about eighty pages was ready for the two banks to agree on.

Barclays' advisers noticed that the Dutch bankers had great difficulty in accepting the fact that they were being taken over. They didn't always behave correctly. ABN Amro, for instance, insisted that the head office of the merged bank was to be in the Netherlands. The lawyers of the bank said that this was necessary to secure an AEX market quotation, something that turned out to be nonsense. The bank also struggled to get DNB nominated as supervisor. The British supervisor put a stop to that, however. He also insisted that the head office should be in the UK, so that it would be relatively simple to intervene where necessary. Nevertheless the Dutch got their way.

That evening ABN Amro director Piero Overmars dined out with a group of friends, to celebrate his forty-third birthday. From time to time his mind wandered to what the next morning would bring. He was planning to tell his colleagues on the managing board that he intended to vote against the merger with Barclays.

17

Despair

22 April–24 May 2007

Piero Overmars knew that Wilco Jiskoot would also vote the merger down. They both counted on the votes of Huibert Boumeester and Ron Teerlink. The four of them would form a majority on the managing board, a majority against the merger.

Overmars and Jiskoot regarded the result of the negotiations, achieved mainly through the efforts of Groenink and Boumeester, as unsatisfactory. They saw it as a pseudo-merger that would effectively mean a total takeover by Barclays. The UK bank would control all the bases. Overmars thought that if you wanted to sell ABN Amro, then you had to go for the highest price and get it, preferably in cash. The British were paying too little for their superb bank. He thought it quite unfair. The shareholders would not get what they were entitled to and the staff would have the wool pulled over their eyes. They would be offered an illusion of equality, while in fact they were being sold down the river.

Jiskoot was also against the merger. He felt that Barclays had poisoned the whole plan of a merger of equals, something that he hadn't believed in anyway. They would totally dominate the board of the new organisation. He was also convinced that Barclays Capital, the investment bank of Barclays, would swallow up most of ABN Amro's corporate activities. Jiskoot and Overmars thought they would get precious little say in them. They feared the dominance of the head of Barclays' corporate bank, the American, Bob Diamond. Diamond must have been the architect behind this *de facto* takeover of ABN Amro.

The idea of the consortium taking over the bank was more attractive to the two investment bankers. The ambitions of RBS seemed to fit in much better with those of ABN Amro's own investment banking activities. There seemed more room there for expanding their global markets and global client activities. Furthermore the consortium was prepared to pay the highest price and most of that would be in cash. They began to think that the consortium might well prove a success.

A takeover of the bank by the consortium would mean that the two parts of the bank – the investment and the retail bank – which had for years been entangled with each other would be separated.

In contrast with the extremely rational atmosphere in the meetings of the summer of the previous year – the meetings where it had been decided that the bank should allow for the fact that it might play a junior role – this meeting was charged with emotions. One after another, the board members raised their voices. The seven men could not agree on the best solution.

At an earlier stage Boumeester had already stated his doubts about the merger with Barclays. He felt that there were too few guarantees in the first agreements with the British bank for ABN Amro to make its voice properly heard. Boumeester had also frequently proclaimed that the bank should always try and determine its own destiny. He was by no means sure that this hadn't caused uncertainty with his colleagues. However he didn't agree with Overmars that the premium wasn't good enough. He didn't feel sorry at all for people who suddenly wanted to backtrack. They had agreed in July that they would go for a junior role if that were good for the bank. He explained that as far as he was concerned the merger with Barclays was the right move.

Jiskoot and Overmars turned out to be the only people who voted against the proposal. They hadn't agreed anything concrete with Teerlink and Boumeester beforehand, but they still felt let down that they had voted for the motion. They now represented a minority on the board, the target of Groenink's wrath. He saw it as disgraceful that the only thing they cared about was the consequences for their own club in the bank.

In the meeting with the supervisory board that Sunday afternoon Groenink announced that the managing board was not unanimously in favour of the merger with Barclays. A shock ran through the meeting – the supervisory board was after all unanimous. Overmars explained in highly charged terms why he was against it. He told the governors that he felt a responsibility towards his people. Olijslager and Van den Bergh understood his disappointment; without a seat on the new managing board it would be difficult to preserve your credibility towards your colleagues.

Arthur Martinez was furious – he didn't agree with the criticisms either. He thought the results of the negotiations were good. ABN Amro would occupy eight of the nineteen seats on the board and they would provide the chairman – seven governors and one chairman. Furthermore the head office would be located in Amsterdam. He thought it showed surprising naivety in the directors that they hadn't realised that Barclays would be the dominant partner; after all, it was the larger of the two banks. And of course it was a takeover.

The head of the supervisory board felt he had to restore discipline in the ranks. He made a short speech saying that for the merger with Barclays to be successful there had to be unanimity on the managing board. He proposed they should meet again to hammer out a unanimous proposal, with or without Overmars and Jiskoot.

When the issue of the sale of LaSalle came up, almost no one asked any questions. The actual yield was some billions of dollars lower than the 21 billion stated because ABN Amro had to convert a subordinated loan into their own capital. The good news was that, according to Groenink, the sale of LaSalle had ensured that Barclays' bid would end up roughly two billion euros higher. Apparently the governors realised that these two matters were inseparably linked. At the time, moreover, they didn't feel the chance of a successful bid by the consortium likely. They didn't even want to think it over. They were satisfied with the solution they had.

Olijslager considered it all extremely unsatisfactory; he was sick of the supervisory board always reacting after the fact. He had the idea that there was nowhere they could turn now. The conviction was growing that the supervisory board had failed at every stage. Trude Maas and Arthur Martinez also felt that the board hadn't functioned properly in the whole affair, particularly with regard to their failure to tackle the poor relations in the managing board. They should have insisted on clarity much earlier on.

Maas suspected that Groenink with his macho character had never been a good leader; he was too little of a unifying figure. Martinez saw how Groenink and Jiskoot had kept each other, and hence the whole bank, in a stalemate position for years.

Groenink could sense the board's weariness; he saw that the governors suddenly looked punch-drunk. All that stuff, first about ING, then Barclays, followed by the consortium and LaSalle ... and as a backdrop to it all the endless bickering in the managing board. The governors wanted to say goodbye to all that and they said as much – their attitude was that the deal with Barclays should be clinched, if need be without Overmars and Jiskoot.

The two dissidents saw that they would either have to resign or be fired if they didn't agree to the merger. They calculated their options. If they were fired, they would in a sense have let down their colleagues. They decided that to be fired now would only damage the bank's reputation further.

They remembered once more that the report of a merger, which would become public knowledge the next morning, could also create ripples in the consortium – a consortium that in any case could pay more than the British bank. Jiskoot and Overmars threw in the towel and voted for the merger with Barclays.

All that Sunday the echelons under the managing board eyed their Black-Berries and cell phones. Over the past weeks the general managers had been updated step by step about the secret discussions with Barclays. They knew that the exclusive negotiations had to have some result today and had been told to make themselves available the whole day. The meeting planned for one was postponed till four, however. And that for four was shifted to nine.

When the twenty-five top bankers finally sat down together in one of the large upstairs rooms at head office, there were vintage wines on the table. The bankers gazed enquiringly at Rijkman Groenink. The chairman was visibly nervous. He did his best to look poker-faced as he told his colleagues the news. "We have a deal with Barclays," he said. "We are going to go for it. We decided today to agree to a merger of equals. We will work as equal partners with the British bank." Groenink explained that he was also in a certain sense disappointed, that he would have preferred it to have turned out differently. Nonetheless he was convinced that the bank had reached a safe haven.

He was greeted by a deathly silence. The wine, however, flowed freely. No one believed his assurances about the two banks being equal partners. Alexandra Cook was unable to restrain herself and shouted out that Groenink had sold the bank. She was followed by other colleagues. When the chairman saw himself surrounded by this sea of emotion, he said that he felt like bursting into tears himself. None the less he managed a stiff upper lip, and said that as chairman he couldn't allow himself that luxury.

After this emotional interlude, various bankers also came up with questions about the consequences for their own situation. How would their shares and options be calculated? Would they be converted into cash or would they be given Barclays options? They all did their own calculations; if it was enough, they wouldn't have to join the new combination. They would be financially independent.

Maurice Lippens phoned Rijkman Groenink the same evening. He told him that he was looking forward to their meeting the following day. He emphasised that the future of ABN Amro was close to his heart and proposed that the members of the consortium and the directors of ABN Amro should meet for the first time about the potential takeover. In fatherly fashion Lippens urged Rijkman Groenink to treat his guests with care and not immediately go on the attack. He told him that the consortium's offer could also be advantageous for ABN Amro.

At about eleven at night Groenink and Martinez phoned Fred Goodwin. They asked the chairman of the consortium whether they would now come up with an offer for the bank without LaSalle or perhaps one for LaSalle separately. Goodwin was astonished by the offer and phoned back half an hour later informing him that they weren't interested. The consortium wanted to buy the whole bank.

Martinez had also had to work that Sunday night. Barclays requested clarity from ABN Amro about the possible claim by the American supervisor in the Iran-Libya affair. They would have to take this into account. Together with Carin Gorter, Martinez had succeeded in arriving at a provisional verbal agreement with the United States district attorney. The bank could escape prosecution by paying a fine of about 500 million dollars.

At 5.45 on Monday morning Huibert Boumeester walked from his house on Amsterdam's Singel canal to the offices of Clifford Chance, the lawyers engaged by Barclays to draw up the merger agreement. They had been busy the whole night getting everything shipshape. Naguib Kheraj and Boumeester were to sign the documents. The champagne was ready, but nobody opened it. Everyone was dead on their feet. Instead they ate bagels at a nearby cafe and went to bed.

Three hours later John Varley and Rijkman Groenink announced the merger between Barclays and ABN Amro. "This is the largest international merger in the banking world," Varley proclaimed. "We will be creating the fourth largest bank in the world both for retail and commerce," Groenink added. Varley went on, "This will be a good thing for our customers, good for our shareholders and good for our staff. The new company will attract talent like a magnet."

Barcleys would pay 3.225 shares for each share in ABN Amro. Against the latest quotes the British bank would thus pay some 66 billion euros for the Dutch icon, almost three times its book value. In the merger protocol the two banks agreed that they would be permitted to withdraw their reciprocal recommendation in the event of a better alternative bid.

Journalists could not fail to notice Groenink's enthusiasm. In an interview he stated, "I have always been a fervent advocate of consolidation in Europe. I have spoken to a number of my colleagues on the subject over the past years. This is the best opportunity for ABN Amro." Asked why the bank couldn't remain independent, he replied, "The question is not whether we could have remained independent. Of course we could. Our figures for the first quarter show that we are in a extremely good position. In the long term, however, banks in Europe will have to integrate. This step will be seen as a milestone in European banking history."

Reflecting on his own record, he said "Of the past seven years the first two were not easy. This transaction, however, shows that in recent years we have added substantial value for our shareholders. Barclays has been prepared to pay us for that. I leave this bank full of pride."

The news that LaSalle had been sold to Bank of America was interpreted in the media as a brilliant tactical move, aimed at stopping the consortium in its tracks. VEB took quite a different view and demanded that the bank should put the sale of LaSalle to their shareholders for approval. VEB director Peter Paul de Vries said, "This is a major transaction. If it is not put to the shareholders and the consortium pulls out, VEB will take the case to court."

ABN Amro thought this was nonsense, that it couldn't possibly be called a major transaction, because the sale value was less than a third of the total balance. De Vries disagreed. "That is one definition of the word major. There are others and the judge will agree with me that this is a major transaction."

Meanwhile Lippens, Votron, Goodwin and their entourage of about twenty staff were waiting in the Amstel Hotel for their appointment with ABN Amro's managing board. The appointment had been postponed twice already, to later that afternoon and then to early evening. They responded by cancelling the appointment and sending a letter to the board requesting clarity about the sudden sale of LaSalle.

The directors of the three banks were furious. Groenink had invited them to Amsterdam, only to regale them with the news that the bank was intending to merge with Barclays. ABN Amro's next move made them, if anything, even more angry. The bank proposed a meeting on Wednesday 25 April, knowing perfectly well that Goodwin had to be in Edinburgh then for his AGM. Groenink then excelled himself by saying that he had no wish to travel to Scotland and invited the bankers for a meeting on Friday 27 April, the day after his own crucial shareholders' meeting.

Goodwin must have laughed when he heard that ABN Amro and Barclays called it a merger of equals, something he didn't believe for a moment. When banks merge, one has to be top dog. There needs to be a dominating bank to see to the discipline needed to achieve the necessary savings and synergy in as short a time as possible.

To rub it in to ABN Amro's shareholders that they would lose money if they merged with Barclays, the consortium announced on Wednesday that they were prepared to pay 39 euros a share, roughly 10 per cent more than Barclays. The offer now amounted to 72 billion euros, with 70 per cent to be paid in cash and the remainder in RBS shares. In doing so the consortium stated that it was precisely by breaking ABN Amro up that the consortium was able 'to create solid companies with strong positions on the market and opportunities for growth in all the main ABN Amro markets'.

The quarterly figures of the bank initially appeared pretty good. In the discussion preparatory to the shareholders' meeting, however, Arthur Martinez presented the deal with the American district attorney; something that was a big surprise for Hugh Scott Barrett. Martinez announced that the bank had to set aside half a billion dollars, or 365 million euros.

Scott Barrett was livid. He was presented with a *fait accompli* and felt he had been made a fool of. The CFO had known nothing about this, nor did he know what he was supposed to do with it either. Was he supposed to slap this provision on the results now, or could he postpone it to the second quarter? In his fury, he phoned Rijkman Groenink, asking him why he hadn't been informed of this provision. Groenink said that he also hadn't known that this verbal provisional arrangement had been agreed on and told the British banker that he didn't care how he solved the problem as long as it was solved.

This was the limit for Scott Barrett. For a long time he had had the sense that he wasn't being taken seriously. Jokes about him were continually doing the rounds. He told Groenink that he couldn't carry on working like this and handed in his resignation.

Groenink was stunned. No one would understand a CFO choosing to quit at a moment like this. He tried to persuade him to go back on his decision. The latter, however, said that he no longer felt that he had the confidence of the chairman and that this was essential if he were to do his work. It was the last straw, because you couldn't operate as CFO if information was being withheld. His decision was one of principle.

Groenink and Martinez made a final desperate effort to keep him on board. He felt, however, that if he gave in now he would regret it the rest of his life. His wife supported him in his decision. Scott Barrett thought this was important, as his wife had a better knowledge of human behaviour than he did; her instincts were more developed. She also felt that Rijkman Groenink treated people with little respect and that her husband could no longer be happy working for the bank.

Groenink thought Scott Barrett had resigned out of pique that he wouldn't be CFO in the new combination with Barclays. He must have felt he would lose too much status. When Scott Barrett got wind of Groenink's opinion of him a week previously, he really hit the ceiling. The chairman was sickened by Scott Barrett's departure. As a responsible manager, how could he have thrown in the towel at such a moment? The bank had to be brought to a safe haven and Barrett had no business placing his personal feelings before his responsibility.

Groenink branded him a bad leaver. Martinez, however, who had spent a lot of time talking with Scott Barrett during this period, fully understood the CFO's view. He was concerned that at this moment of all times the bank was presenting a picture of being fundamentally flawed. Signalling that the managing board was divided could only do damage to its standing. He revised

Groenink's decision, altering Scott Barrett's status from bad leaver to good. The latter could redeem his shares and options in cash.

On the morning of Thursday 26 April, ABN Amro issued its quarterly figures. The announcement opened with the words, 'In view of the status of the United States Justice Department enquiry the result has been adjusted downwards with a figure of 365 million euros.' Now the deal with Barclays had been announced and the bank was to pass into other hands, ABN Amro hoped to put an end to the conflict with the United States authorities.

Ignoring this one-off imposition, the figures looked good. The operational result had increased by 25 per cent. Even cost discipline seemed suddenly to have improved. For the first time in the history of the bank, the efficiency ratio had dropped below 67 per cent.

The shareholders who met in The Hague's Congrescentrum that day were not, however, concerned about the results. The merger with Barclays wasn't on the agenda, as it had only come up a couple of days ago. What was on the agenda was the TCI wish-list. The hedge fund's requests conflicted with the plan for ABN Amro to fall into the arms of the British concern. Groenink had prepared himself for a highly-charged gathering; it was to be a head-on confrontation with his shareholders. His wife Irene came to give him moral support.

Groenink appealed to them to look beyond the higher indicative bid that RBS, Santander and Fortis were flaunting. "We are looking at every alternative bid. The price, however, was not the only thing that mattered. As human beings and responsible citizens, you will agree with me that we shouldn't only count the pennies." The shareholders applauded; here was something they couldn't disagree with their chairman about.

After that, however, they had to vote on TCI's demands. About 52 per cent of the total votes were present at the meeting. This was too much, even for the notary and he called for a recount. Four of the five TCI motions were supported by a large majority. So the meeting amounted to one big motion of no confidence in the managing board.

The bank's owners appealed to the managing board to do all they could to maximise shareholder value and if need be to proceed to splitting up the bank. Groenink was bitter, though not surprised, about the result. From a rational point of view, he could understand his shareholders' lack of confidence; emotionally he was appalled.

Peter Paul de Vries, VEB director, asked Groenink to let him know whether he intended to comply with the consortium's demand and revoke the sale of LaSalle. Groenink was exasperated, "What Royal Bank of Scotland wants is not my concern. Everyone is unhappy in their own way. If they want to propose conditions, that's their problem."

Immediately after the tumultuous meeting came to a close, De Vries announced emergency legal proceedings to block the sale of LaSalle. TCI announced straight away that it would support VEB's demand.

The consortium was in a hurry – 7 May was the deadline for an alternative offer for LaSalle. After the shareholders' meeting Goodwin spoke to Martinez. He complained about ABN Amro's demand that they should only be allowed to view their books if they promised not to make a hostile bid in the next twelve months. ABN Amro dropped its demand. They were given access for a limited audit and announced that they would make an offer.

In an email to the bank's staff that had read the press reports of the tumultuous shareholders' meeting with increasing concern, Groenink attempted to appease their worries. 'Up until now the consortium has given no reply to our questions about the way the bid will be financed, how they will divide the bank and how they will deal with the risks of execution.' He emphasised his conviction that in a merger with Barclays the bank would become 'one of the leading universal banks in the world … The result of the vote in the shareholders' meeting', he argued, 'didn't mean that the merger with Barclays wouldn't go ahead … although it did confirm the responsibility of the managing board to take other offers into consideration if these could potentially produce a higher yield for our shareholders and other stakeholders.'

On Saturday morning, VEB's case came to court in Amsterdam. At issue was the question of when the directors of a company were required to request shareholders' approval in advance of a decision. The law stated that when taking important decisions the board was required to put them before the shareholders. A numerical criterion was involved – in purchasing or disposing of holdings amounting to more than a third of the value of the assets of a company, the approval of the shareholders had to be sought. ABN Amro's lawyers had advised the managing board that the sale of LaSalle amounted to nothing like 33 per cent of the bank's assets (almost 1,000 billion euros) and that it could therefore take place without any problem.

VEB thought that in that case the bank should have borne the spirit as well as the letter of the law in mind. The pressure group thought that the sale of LaSalle was 'an important decision', as prescribed in the law, because 'the precipitate sale of LaSalle boiled down to a protection measure whereas the bank had publicly proclaimed that its structure was an open one and that it renounced all protective constructions'. VEB argued that the sudden sale of LaSalle was simply a poison pill concocted by the bank to prevent an alternative offer.

In the courtroom VEB received the support of the consortium of Fortis, RBS, and Santander. A chaotic situation arose. VEB, ABN Amro and the lawyers for the consortium and Barclays were all involved. ABN Amro denied there was any question of a poison pill involved in the sale of LaSalle. The bank's lawyers argued that Bank of America had approached ABN Amro and not the reverse. The bank had invited the consortium to make an offer for LaSalle separately, as well as for the rest of ABN Amro.

Bank of America's lawyers announced that their bank would make a considerable claim for reparations if the judge decided that the sale had to be revoked. The spokesmen of ABN Amro assessed that such a claim might easily amount to more than a billion dollars and they wondered out loud whether the judge would want to have a sum like that on his conscience.

Inside and outside the bank, opinions were deeply divided. On one point, however, everyone was agreed: namely that over the past fifteen years LaSalle had been of material interest for the bank. Its profits were formidable and it was one of the assets that had kept the bank afloat. Its importance should not be underestimated.

The chairman of the panel of five judges was Huub Willems. It wasn't the first time Willems and Groenink had met in a courtroom. On 3 October 1994, he had made a slip of the tongue, as president of the court, by addressing Groenink as the accused in the HCS affair in which he had sentenced Joep van den Nieuwenhuyzen to a spectacular six months in prison. As a witness Rijkman Groenink had been examined in minute detail by Willems; the judge had wanted to know how far the ABN Amro director had encouraged Van den Nieuwenhuyzen to carry out this transaction that in his view was illegal.

On this Saturday too it was obvious that the two men couldn't stand each other. In his final summing up Groenink stated resolutely that the bank and its shareholders might suffer serious losses if the judge blocked the sale of its American subsidiary, LaSalle, to Bank of America. "If this is your verdict, a chaotic situation will come about that will be ruinous for the bank and hence for its shareholders. LaSalle has been sold; that is a *fait accompli* and now I want to go home and mow my lawn. It's Saturday afternoon, after all."

As Groenink was mowing his lawn, Cees Maas had his farewell party as CFO at ING. Like Tilmant, Maas had been an advocate of the merger with ABN Amro. At one point in the negotiations it had even been agreed that the 60-year-old Maas would stay on as CFO and, like Rijkman Groenink, become a vice-chairman of the merged bank.

At the party, the speeches were all about Cees Maas and his impressive career, but over their drinks the guests were mainly discussing the future of ABN Amro. Cor Herkströter and Jan Kalff bumped into each other. They were good acquaintances, respected each other and in a sense they had the same concerns. They had both contributed to a book about entrepreneurship and the Dalai Lama, in which they attempted to reconcile capitalism and Buddhism.

Kalff had helped his friend, the author Laurens van den Muyzenberg with the final editing. In his piece Herkströter had written that, 'It was extremely important that the principles of a business should remain constant. Principles that change every year are worthless for the staff. Besides making clear what the goal of an organisation is, one of the most important tasks of a director is to define and defend the values of an organisation.'

Kalff and Herkströter talked about the failure of the talks between ING and ABN Amro. Herkströter said that Rijkman Groenink was the villain of the piece and told Kalff that he had constantly negotiated in tandem with Michel Tilmant but that for a long time Rijkman Groenink was the only negotiator for ABN Amro. Herkströter had found this extremely irritating. Groenink had admitted that he hadn't discussed the issues with the head of his supervisory board. Herkströter thought it perfectly obvious that negotiations conducted in this way could not be taken seriously.

Herkströter also told Kalff he had been worried throughout the proceedings about how the core ING values could be preserved in the case of a merger with ABN Amro. Kalff was stung by his words. What did he mean by saying that he questioned the way that ABN Amro did business? Ten years previously he had made great efforts to modernise the traditional values of the bank. That fact that ING questioned this and apparently thought its own values superior was something that the former chairman of ABN Amro's managing board found hard to take.

On Sunday morning a beaming Cees Maas appeared on the Dutch current affairs programme, *Buitenhof*. Maas spoke harshly about ABN Amro. Asked why the merger had failed, he said, "We didn't actually need it; ING is expanding considerably under its own steam and as long as you are growing independently, that's incremental for your own value. There was insufficient value in ABN Amro for us. The question was whether the costs and job losses that would come with the merger would not have outweighed any possible assets."

Maas explained that ING, which with 5.2 per cent was the largest shareholder in ABN Amro, was clearly in favour of splitting up the bank. At the shareholders' meeting his bank had voted for TCI's proposals. Maas explained this as follows, "I don't think that the break-up of ABN Amro is an ideal solution, but I also think that the interest of the shareholders is paramount. If the deal with Barclays goes through, then I'm landed with Barclays shares, and what am I supposed to do with them? I'd rather have cash."

Maas explained that the ABP, PGGM and Robeco investment trust had voted against TCI's motion, saying that they were relatively small shareholders.

The interviewer, Peter van Ingen, reminded Maas that he had been present at the founding of ABN Amro, and that seventeen years ago he had made his own contribution as auditor general. The journalist wondered whether the man, who was in favour of the break-up of ABN Amro today, didn't feel nervous about the future of the remaining Dutch banks. Maas replied somewhat stiffly, "You have to have a strategy that is accepted by the outside world and if that is not the case, you have a problem. You also have to deliver what you promise." He concluded by saying that, "It is a fact that Rijkman Groenink hasn't delivered what he promised. The managing board of ABN Amro has not done what it said it would."

On Tuesday 1 May, TCI appealed to the supervisory board in an open letter to dismiss Rijkman Groenink and take charge of the sale of the bank themselves. Chris Hohn thought Groenink should accept the consortium's indicative offer. "We consider that Mr Groenink is no longer credible as chairman of the managing board and that he has not acted in the best interest of the shareholders."

On the same day ABN Amro again appealed to the consortium to be more open about the financing of their offer. Morgan Stanley's advisers could not conceive that the American supervisors would allow Merrill Lynch to have committed such a large part of their available capital to this deal. ABN Amro also announced that if their questions weren't answered they would not consider a joint offer from the consortium for LaSalle and the rest of the bank. In doing so, the bank was alluding to the risks involved in splitting up the bank. Supposing, for instance, the Dutch Central Bank didn't give its approval, so that the consortium found itself in an impasse. What would that mean for ABN Amro's shareholders?

On 2 May, the representatives of Merrill Lynch met with Hugh Scott Barrett and Wilco Jiskoot, who had mentally already left the bank, to discuss the offer. Goodwin joined them. Merrill Lynch made it clear that they were prepared to stand as guarantors for the offer. ABN Amro had no cause for concern there and Merrill Lynch confirmed its willingness by letter the following day.

On behalf of Wouter Bos, a spokesman of the finance ministry told *Het Financieele Dagblad* that, "ABN Amro could have protected itself against a takeover, but that it had put itself up for sale." The ministry was responding to remarks by Bernard Wientjes, the chairman of VNO NCW, who had said that he found the possible break-up of the bank a worrying development and that he blamed the cabinet for making insufficient efforts to keep the main offices in Holland.

The next afternoon some 250 neatly dressed people gathered in front of the law courts on Prinsengracht in Amsterdam. They all wore T-shirts with the slogan, 'We are speaking for a staff of 100,000'. Some clasped green and yellow balloons, the bank's colours. 'People make the bank, the staff are also stakeholders.' The staff of ABN Amro felt angry and frustrated. On behalf of Sacha Scholten, who chaired the employees' council, a text was read out loud. 'These are confusing times and disturbing developments for us all. The decision will soon come. VEB has taken this summary action on behalf of the shareholders. But they are only one of the stakeholders. Unfortunately it is our perception that everything is focused one-sidedly on the interests of the shareholders.'

The staff members present cheered. They were fearful of the merger with Fortis. One employee stated their anxiety in a nutshell. 'It's as though Feyenoord had taken over Ajax.' They had hoped for a peaceful merger with Barclays without too many job losses. The senior executives in particular weren't so sure about that. Since the merger had been made public, the directors had formed so-called synergy study groups. Together with their prospective colleagues from Barclays they had studied where the joint bank would be able to realise economies. Many of the general managers and department managers were bitterly disappointed to find that Barclays would largely be calling the shots. There was a bad atmosphere in many of these groups. ABN Amro wouldn't be getting much of a look in.

Then the judge, Huub Willems announced his verdict. His criticisms of the behaviour of ABN Amro were devastating. 'The view that the consortium has given no evidence of being a serious bidder cannot be sustained.' Willems thought that the bank should first put the sale of LaSalle to the shareholders of the bank for approval because it was inseparably linked to the sale of the entire bank.

VEB director Peter Paul de Vries embraced his lawyer excitedly and spoke of a historical verdict, declaring that Groenink "had lost face incredibly. I can't imagine that he'll be able to hang on to his job." Rijkman Groenink was not present to hear the verdict.

Jan Kalff was there, however. The former chairman and former governor continued to feel concern for the staff. He was worried about the bank and about the increasing power of the shareholders. Looking depressed, he was one of the first to leave the court. The sale of LaSalle had been suspended. It was bad news for the bank in his view. He made a speedy getaway through the ranks of bankers and journalists.

Groenink couldn't believe his ears when he heard Willems's verdict. He was furious with his legal advisers, who had assured him a couple of weeks ago that the bank ran no risk whatsoever in this suit. One of them, Johan Kleyn, a specialist in the law of mergers and takeovers with the firm of Allen & Overy, was an old friend of Groenink. They had known each other since the second class of their secondary school and still played tennis together from time to time. Kleyn was also dismayed by the verdict.

On the evening of Friday 4 May, Fred Goodwin, Maurice Lippens, Jean-Paul Votron, Arthur Martinez and Rijkman Groenink met over dinner at the Amstel Hotel in Amsterdam. Emilio Botín didn't show up. It was the first attempt at this level to study whether the different parties could solve the matter in a friendly fashion. It didn't seem likely.

Maurice Lippens respected his enemy and warned his partners in advance not to underestimate Rijkman Groenink. He compared him to a kamikaze pilot. There was no stopping Groenink. He'd never surrender. He'd go on fighting, even if they shot off his arms and legs. He'd probably rise from his grave and chase after them.

As an attempt to humour the old crosspatch, Lippens told Groenink that the bank would have gone to the Dutch if he'd got the managing board behind his plans in 1998 to raise the offer on Generale Bank. Groenink didn't find this funny.

Arthur Martinez didn't expect much from this meeting. He knew that Groenink was adamantly against the consortium. In the talks he had spoken of it as the evil empire. The consortium would destroy his legacy and was to be shunned like the plague. Goldman Sachs's advisers had briefed him about the sensitive history between the different bankers at this table.

He knew the tales about Generale Bank and the bad feelings surrounding Votron's departure from ABN Amro. He was struck by the degree of mistrust between these men. It was obvious that Groenink and Goodwin disliked each other and the same was true of Votron and Groenink. The two proceeded to get bogged down in a tiresome discussion that Martinez felt would lead nowhere.

Groenink made a couple of caustic remarks. By now it was clear to them all that he would never consent to the break-up of his bank. The idea was anathema and he would do all he could to prevent this scenario from becoming reality.

The bankers were just sitting down to a glass of wine when bells began to toll. They looked at each other. Lippens realised that it was the signal to stand in memory of the fallen in the Second World War. He told Goodwin and Martinez that it was the tradition in Holland for everyone to stand for two minute's silence and he proposed that they should honour the custom. The Belgian banker stood and the American and the Scottish bankers, impressed by the solemnity of the occasion, did likewise. Votron and Groenink, despite being locked in bitter debate, sulkily followed suit. For a short while silence was observed. Martinez felt that these were the best moments of the meeting.

The next day Lippens, Votron, Goodwin and Botín wrote a letter to the managing and supervisory boards stating that they meant business. The consortium made a higher offer for LaSalle of 24.5 billion dollars, with the proviso that a friendly bid for the rest of the bank could also be made. The consortium was prepared to pay 38.40 euros a share and emphasised the great benefits it expected from the deal, especially as a result of reductions in expenditure. The bankers pointed out that ABN Amro's efficiency ratio for 2006 amounted to almost 70 per cent. Each of the three purchasers was a great deal more efficient. Fortis scored 61.2 per cent, Santander 48.5 and RBS 42.1.

ABN Amro replied by asking many new questions, particularly about what it saw as the vagueness of the conditions Merrill Lynch had attached to the guarantees underpinning the consortium's offer. The bank concluded that there were too many details that needed clarifying and that the bank therefore could not take up the offer. On the afternoon of 6 May, ABN Amro's advisers sent in a list of another thirty-one detailed questions.

For days hordes of lawyers and investment bankers had been phoning and meeting right up to the moment when the deadline passed in the night of 6 May. The parties didn't meet. It was an open secret among the bank staff that not everyone on the managing board was adamantly against the consortium's offer.

On Monday 7 May Rijkman Groenink phoned Peter Wakkie, a member of the managing board of Ahold, and asked him to come to the aid of his managing board. Groenink was worried about the progress of the verbal agreement that Martinez had negotiated with the United States district attorney. It needed to be more concrete as Barclays was insisting on clarity.

Wakkie had had a seat on the managing board of Ahold since 2004 and had had many civil and criminal proceedings, especially in the United States, settled without jeopardising the continuity of the battered grocery concern. He was surprised by the request but liked the challenge. However he hadn't yet got all he wanted for Ahold and it was difficult for him to leave right then. He couldn't start before September and the two of them realised that this would be too late.

As a lawyer, Wakkie had followed the whole affair with fascination. He was particularly concerned about the aggressive behaviour of the active shareholders. He wondered why on earth ABN Amro hadn't immediately shown them the door. A shareholder who had put his money in the bank so recently and then thought he could call the shots – you wouldn't allow someone like that to put you off course. Just let them dare start legal proceedings to get it on the agenda. It would cost them a lot of time, certainly too long for hedge funds like these who were only interested in making money quickly. Wakkie suspected that the board was apparently no longer united enough to take them on. The only thing that was clear to him was that either way ABN Amro would end up in other hands. It had lost control of the situation.

All was not lost, however. The managing board had in the meantime been persuaded by its own lawyers that it was in the right about the sale of LaSalle and it had appealed against the verdict. The hope was that the High Court would institute summary proceedings; a verdict in 2009 would be too late for everyone.

On 8 May, Wouter Bos invited a number of prominent governors and academics to discuss the bank's fate. It was a confidential gathering and the finance minister was expecting answers. What was he supposed to make of this situation? How had it happened that this Dutch bank now stood naked in the shop window of the world? They sat round the great oval table in the minister's office.

These former captains of industry and scholars were all agreed about one issue – that the failure was first and foremost that of the bank's own supervisory board. Their task was to supervise and they should have known what was going on. Despite the endless changes of strategy, the promised results had not been delivered ... They should have sacked Groenink a long time back and installed a new leadership.

After the meeting, it began to dawn on Bos that ABN Amro could no longer continue under its own steam. It was no longer viable.

On 10 May, the bank announced the resignation of Hugh Scott Barrett and that Huibert Boumeester was to replace him as CFO. In a press statement Scott Barrett explained, 'In view of the expected changes around ABN Amro this is a good moment for me to think about my future and to seek possible new career opportunities. Seeing that I have decided not to accept the post offered me in the new company that will emerge after the proposed merger with Barclays and ABN Amro, the only logical thing for me to do is to hand in my resignation.'

The same morning, *de Volkskrant* reported that ABP pension funds intended to vote against the appointment of Groenink as a new governor (non-executive director) of Shell at the shareholders' meeting on 15 May. One of the people involved told the paper that a heated debate had taken place among the institutional shareholders about the reasons for opposing Groenink's nomination. "One group said that he had no talent as a manager. The pragmatic wing preferred the argument that Groenink didn't have any time for such a responsible part-time post as that of governor."

Groenink, who had been officially proposed in March, had received warnings from various quarters. Robin Boon, the company's director of communications had advised him to think better of it. And earlier on governor André Olijslager had asked Groenink to show leadership by concentrating on the future of the bank and to abandon his ambitions for the post. Groenink, however, had informed him that he intended to hang on in there. ABN Amro's chairman was certain that he would not get any executive post in the new combination. His future needed anchoring with at any rate a couple of flagship governor's posts.

He was confident of the support of the departing governor, Aarnout Loudon. Loudon did all he could right up to the last to promote Rijkman Groenink as his replacement. His colleagues on the board told him, however, that ABN Amro's chairman was getting too much negative publicity. The managing board of Shell was unanimous that Groenink didn't belong in their midst. The non-executive chairman, Jorma Ollila, told Loudon bluntly that Groenink wasn't welcome.

The latter was bitterly disappointed. He withdrew his application, giving as his reason the pressure of the takeover battle. The headline in *de Volkskrant* read 'Groenink Unmasked'. The paper reported that 'On Monday the man whom Elsevier's weekly had proclaimed as its man of the year in 2005 after the takeover of Antonveneta, had to withdraw his application for the post of governor of the oil company. Groenink's image, already impaired by the reckless course ABN Amro has followed over the past years, is now in free fall.'

The takeover battle must have also rung a bell with Cesare Geronzi. Geronzi, who was head of Capitalia, had until recently not appeared ready to give up his independence, but was now all of a sudden desperately seeking shelter. Halfway through May it had become clear that Capitalia could make an alliance with Unicredito. The second leading Italian bank was also advised by Andrea Orcel. After summary negotiations it was announced that Unicredito would take over Capitalia for a sum of almost 22 billion euros. Together the stock exchange value of the two banks was a hundred billion. Geronzi got a seat on the managing board of the merged bank, while his rival Mateo Arpe had to quit.

Groenink suspected that he no longer needed to phone the Italians – after ING and Barclays, they were number three on his list. The Italian press reported that Unicredito had made handy use of the fact that at that moment they had little to fear from ABN Amro as a major shareholder in Capitalia.

At ABN Amro head office, the news was received with resignation. First the German HypoVereinsbank had been filched from ABN Amro and now this takeover had occurred. Unicredito, renamed Unicredit Group after the takeover, had carried out ABN Amro's dream strategy, thus becoming the largest bank in the entire Euro zone and, after HSBC, the largest in Europe. ABN Amro announced that it endorsed the Italian merger.

Meanwhile, Maurice Lippens was anxious about a potential nationalist backlash in Holland. He warned Goodwin and Botin about the problem of national pride and pointed out that fear was growing in the Netherlands of a Belgian scenario in which more and more head offices would go south. ABN Amro was a national institution and it wasn't at all certain the Dutch would be willing to let it go.

He phoned his Dutch network of chairmen of managing boards and governors, leading lights in the Dutch business world. He enquired about how much of a loss their number one bank would be. He was astonished by the response. Virtually no one felt any pride in ABN Amro any more. Many of his contacts thought the bank had messed things up for itself. Not only in the business community, but also in the political world, the message came back loud and clear – if the choice was between Barclays and the consortium, Fortis was perhaps the best option. Fortis was familiar with Holland and the staff spoke Flemish.

Lippens knew that Nout Wellink at least would be unhappy if the bank were broken up. He had been astonished by the statements the president of the Dutch Central Bank had made in response to TCI's letter. He felt that he had behaved tactlessly. In his view Wellink should never have gone off the handle like that.

It was decided that Jean-Paul Votron should be sent to talk to DNB to address its concerns about the consortium. He was, however, unsuccessful. The central bankers were irritated that he was so ill prepared for what in their view were relatively straightforward questions. The supervisor wanted to know in detail where the money for the takeover would come from and was shocked about the inconsistencies in his answers. The only effect of the meeting was to make DNB still more wary of the consortium.

In May Lippens spoke to Wellink in person twice and he also made frequent phone calls. Wellink warned him that he thought the dissolution of ABN Amro was a risky business. He added that he feared that it would be more than Fortis could digest.

Lippens defended himself and explained that Fortis was well able to cope. He noticed, however, that Wellink wasn't in a mood to listen. Instead he said that Lippens shouldn't be surprised if he didn't give a declaration of approval for the takeover. In that case, the minister of finance would have to comply with DNB's advice.

Lippens told Wellink that the consortium was busy preparing answers to all DNB's questions and that their efforts would probably come to around 1,400 pages. Wellink replied sardonically that the Dutch Central Bank might well retaliate with another three thousand questions. Both men were playing verbal hardball with each other. Lippens saw the clashes mainly as sharp words between friends, but he was still taken aback by Wellink's touchiness. He thought, however, that it was highly unlikely that he would forbid a takeover by the consortium *a priori* without the backing of the government.

Lippens had calculated the government's feelings and Wellink's role correctly. In The Hague almost no one supported Wellink. In discussions among the PvdA ministers, the feeling was that Wellink had spoken out of turn in his criticisms of TCI. It had been clumsy of him to comment on the statements of a hedge fund.

Wellink registered their disapproval and at the beginning of May he contacted the prime minister's office with the request to talk to him about the takeover. The officials there got in touch with their colleagues in the finance ministry. They decided that there were now two parties interested in taking over the bank and that there was also a law suit in progress. In all likelihood the minister of finance and the president of DNB would shortly have to consult about one or more requests for a declaration of no objection. Bos moreover was worried that Wellink would propose to Balkenende to phone the consortium informing them that they hadn't a hope of a declaration of no objection. It was decided not to make any appointment. Bos wanted to protect his prime minister against any such request from the Central Bank.

Once again then Nout Wellink didn't get to see the prime minister and had to lodge his concern and complaints with Ronald Gerritse, the general secretary at the finance ministry. He was baffled by the state of affairs. He wanted to update Balkenende on the developments concerning the country's largest financial institution. Why was his fellow party member so reluctant to grant him an audience? If he had been prime minister, he would have been on the phone to the DNB president straight away to ask him what on earth was going on.

There was little love left in The Hague any more for ABN Amro; not many people there had maintained friendly contacts with the bank either. Its bankers had not gone on trade missions with the politicians for many years now. And it was rare for the managing board to take part in network meetings, such as the annual lunch for the finance committee of the Dutch parliament. The idea prevailed that ABN Amro bankers thought themselves too big for Holland. At the same time, politicians and civil servants had observed that these arrogant bankers had made a bit of a mess of their product. No matter where they turned in the business world, support was hard to find.

Wouter Bos asked his fellow party member, the undersecretary for economic affairs, Frank Heemskerk, for his views. Heemskerk had worked at the bank for many years and had been Dolf van den Brink's assistant. He felt the impending loss of the bank personally, but he also knew that things couldn't continue like this.

The ministers were also concerned about the results of the disappearance of this institution. For instance, they recalled that a company like Ahold wouldn't have been saved if ABN Amro hadn't intervened and mobilised the appropriate ING and Rabobank bankers. Which other bank could possibly take over that role or dispose of such an extensive network?

They also recalled, however, that it was Groenink who had urged the European finance ministers in Scheveningen in 2004 not to rush to protect their banks any longer. The chorus of complaints from colleagues about the huge salaries and bonuses in the business world also didn't help.

The gulf between The Hague and the bank was profound. The *entente cordiale* between banking and political worlds that had prevailed in the days when people like Nelissen, Langman and Meys still worked for the bank had ceased to exist. Those bankers had known The Hague as well as their own living rooms.

In the political discussion the question arose whether the Barclays offer really was the better one for Holland, with various politicians and civil servants remaining unconvinced. With the British, they argued, you had to look not just at their words but at their deeds. The deal with Barclays was effectively a complete takeover. How solid would a promise made in a head office in Holland be when the supervisor was based in the UK? ABN Amro would end up as just a branch of Barclays. Bos thought he had to maintain a neutral position and he saw that the Fortis scenario had plenty of things going for it as well.

The politicians had also heard that there were advocates of the merger with Fortis in ABN Amro as well. In Holland the bank was much larger than Fortis and this would make it a takeover in reverse that would be dominated by ABN Amro bankers. In the national political arena, then, a consensus had begun to emerge. Of course Balkenende or Bos could say that a takeover by the consortium would be unstable, but they would have to make their case with concrete arguments. And except for Wellink and the managing board of the bank, nobody was coming up with these arguments.

Groenink knew that Wellink was on his side. He noticed that Arnold Schilder, the DNB supervisor, was considerably more cautious. Schilder thought it all both difficult and dicey.

Groenink also noticed that Wellink was conflicted. He had repeatedly told him that all he had to do was to phone Goodwin and tell him that for the sake of prudence he didn't intend to grant the consortium its formal approval. Wellink, however, told Groenink that he would have to have political backing if he were to do that.

Nout Wellink did his utmost to get that backing. He spoke to Wouter Bos on a number of occasions warning him that tearing apart the bank could endanger the continuity of its services. He also reminded the minister of the limited means of the three banks. The financial markets were already showing the signs of the impending storm. Would the consortium be able to take on this takeover if the markets started falling?

Bos informed Wellink that he didn't have any clearer view than he did on either of these matters. In his view it was precisely the task of the DNB president to assess such things. If he said that it was all too risky, the minister of finance would simply go along with him. The law stated that a declaration of no objection was the norm, but it was also clear that if DNB were to advise against, the minister couldn't just ignore him.

Wellink urged Bos to tell the consortium that the declaration of approval hadn't been issued; the latter, however, constantly returned the ball to Wellink's court, stating that these were three licensed European banks. What exactly then were the arguments against giving them a licence? He realised that Wellink was keen for the issue to be decided by the politicians. He appreciated that he was having trouble deciding.

Meanwhile Bos was almost regretting that he had given Rijkman Groenink his cell phone number. The chairman of ABN Amro was constantly on the line, warning him that it would be irresponsible of the government to allow the bank to be broken up by a consortium.

In one of these conversations Groenink told the minister that he should phone Fred Goodwin before the consortium had made a formal offer. He wanted Bos to tell Goodwin that they couldn't reckon on receiving the government's assent. Groenink knew that the minister didn't care for his aggressive tone, but he didn't let that stand in his way because what was involved was too important. Only the government could stop to the consortium's progress.

On 19 May, Arthur Martinez met Fred Goodwin, who headed the consortium. They discussed the progress of the three musketeers' offer. The head of ABN Amro's supervisory board began to believe that the consortium meant business.

On 23 May, ABN Amro and Barclays announced that they were making progress in their merger talks. A day later, VEB asked the EU commissioner Charles McCreevy to investigate 'whether the Dutch Central Bank had taken an impartial position in the current takeover battle regarding the bank and had treated the two candidates fairly and equally'.

The DNB president was displeased by this development. He was increasingly creating the impression of being opposed to the takeover of the bank and he seemed incapable of explaining that his concerns were quite specific ones to do with the possible consequences of the dissolution of ABN Amro.

Groenink and Boumeester observed that Wellink had probably run out of ammunition too early with his onslaught on the TCI letter three months previously. Groenink began to realise that he couldn't look to either the Central Bank or the cabinet for support in his battle to save the bank. He no longer knew where to turn. There were outspoken supporters of a takeover by the consortium even on his own managing board. *Het Financieele Dagblad* reported that 'the higher echelons of the Dutch banking firm ABN Amro were not *a priori* opposed to a possible merger with Fortis'. Fortis had announced that it had indeed received signals like this and that it was positive towards them.

Groenink thought this quite unacceptable. Jiskoot, the managing director responsible for domestic activities, phoned Schmittmann and asked him if he was involved in talks with the consortium and said that if that was the case he should take steps. He gave Schmittmann a couple of days to think it over. Schmittmann told him he didn't need any time. He swore that he hadn't been in touch with the consortium. The two men were good acquaintances; a long time ago they helped to put Laren hockey club on the map. Jiskoot warned Schmittmann to keep his cards close to his chest for the time being. The sensible thing was to keep his options open.

Schmittmann had already followed Jiskoot's advice. The head of the domestic operation felt responsible for its 25,000 employees, and it wasn't in their interest to state his preference. Schmittmann had also given a warning within the bank: it didn't seem likely that Barclays would invest much money in the country with the lowest yield. He told his colleagues that they should assume that in the years to come the Dutch operation would largely remain a cash cow.

Groenink felt irritated by this line of argument that he thought really stupid. How could his colleagues in the domestic division possibly imagine they would stay in charge of their affairs after a takeover by Fortis, just because ABN Amro in Holland was larger than the domestic division of Fortis and because they thought ABN Amro had better bankers? As though the Belgians would stand for that! He felt that this optimism was totally naive. He thought that the domestic division of ABN Amro would remain completely intact after a merger with Barclays and would get the opportunity to expand.

Schmittmann regularly sat in on DNB meetings to contribute to the discussions about the break-up of the bank. In various communications about his domestic division it was stated that this was definitely a possibility. To his astonishment and exasperation he saw that these conclusions were edited at group level before being sent on to the supervisor. Suddenly the statement read that there were great risks attached to splitting up the bank. Schmittmann was furious. He told the lawyer for the firm of Stibbe, Paul van den Hoek, legal adviser to the bank's supervisory board, that it was maybe a good idea to alert Arthur Martinez to his concerns.

When he spoke to the head of the supervisory board a couple of days later, Schmittmann confessed his worries. He asked Martinez whether he was being proactive enough. Wasn't it agreed after all that the talks with Barclays would be broken off, if a better offer for the bank came up? He pointed out to him that to his knowledge there had never been any proper calculation of the pros and cons of the two potential deals. He told him that in his view Groenink had shown inadequate leadership. Martinez thanked Schmittmann for his thoughts and told him he admired his courage.

Groenink didn't think his supervisory board had shown any courage; they clearly no longer had any stomach for this fight. The governors seemed mainly concerned about whether they might be faced with a claim. He began to feel completely isolated.

Meanwhile lawyers were assuring him that Willems had interpreted the law too loosely and that the High Court would decide in his favour that summer. The sale of LaSalle would not have to be revoked after all. For a while now, however, he had ceased to believe that this would mean the consortium would drop their offer.

The consortium had in fact already announced that it would shortly go public with a concrete offer. One last time, Groenink attempted to pressurise Wellink to announce publicly that he intended to give a declaration of approval to Barclays' offer and to say in the same breath that he thought the consortium's offer too risky. He suggested that Fred Goodwin might even be relieved by an announcement like that. It would give him a chance to withdraw and still save face.

Once again Wellink emphasised that he would only do this with the backing of the government. He was, however, beginning to realise that the politicians he was dealing with were not prepared to do what was necessary to stop the most important bank in the country from being broken up, as probably would have happened in countries such as France or Germany.

Martinez also no longer excluded the possibility that the consortium would keep its offer for ABN Amro on the table, even without LaSalle. From then on all that mattered was money. The shareholders had made it clear that they'd choose whoever offered them the most. He saw that the market value of Barclays was falling, with consequences for its offer for ABN Amro. He was also aware that nothing talked louder than cash. He decided that the consortium should be given a serious chance.

Arthur Martinez assumed that Groenink would drag his feet. He remembered Wellink's appeal, and Cor Herkströter's lecture, that as head of the supervisory board he had to be more proactive, that the Dutch system required this of him. The buck stopped with him. He had to act.

18

End

25 May–30 October 2007

Arthur Martinez knew the route from the bank to his house just outside New York like the back of his hand. He flew there and back, almost every other week. On the morning of Friday 25 May, he was in Schiphol again, but before getting into his plane the head of ABN Amro's supervisory board had one more call to make. He wasn't looking forward to it.

The day before, a closed meeting of the supervisory board had decided that things could not go on this way. In the space of a few weeks suspicion between the bank and the three members of the consortium had grown out of all proportion. Allard Metzelaar, a lawyer with the firm of Stibbe and Paul van den Hoek, legal adviser to the supervisory board, had already warned them that if any shareholders felt at the end of these negotiations that an interesting competitive offer had not been taken sufficiently seriously, they shouldn't hesitate to knock on the door of the supervisory board. The letter from TCI was also addressed to Arthur Martinez. It also seemed likely that the consortium would make a detailed bid soon.

The governors had decided that the consortium should be given a serious chance and wondered if that were possible with Rijkman Groenink in command. The chairman of the board was resisting the break-up of the bank tooth and nail. He found the notion of the consortium absolutely distasteful. The supervisory board had therefore asked Arthur Martinez to tell Groenink that Martinez, André Olijslager and Rob van den Bergh would take the sale negotiations over from him. His powers, as it were, had been curtailed.

Martinez had phoned DNB and explained the situation. He had asked the supervisor for permission to go ahead with this coup. The Central Bank had responded politely with a formula amounting roughly to saying that they could live with it. Martinez had been given the go-ahead. Wasn't that after all what they had been asking the supervisor for all along – to have a chairman who took responsibility?

Van den Bergh and Olijslager then discussed the matter with each other.

They both agreed with Martinez's analysis. Olijslager thought it high time something was done. He wasn't impressed with Groenink's qualities as a leader. The man never listened; all he did was tell other people what to do. He had done nothing to gain a following for himself within the bank. Van den Bergh too didn't think that Groenink should lead the proceedings. He experienced him as cold, lacking interest in other people and far too calculating.

The two relatively new governors had become increasingly disturbed by the tensions in the managing board and they held Groenink responsible. Like Martinez and some of the other governors, they were also conscious that he had been allowed far too much rope in recent years. Especially the past year, after the decision to start talks with ING, Barclays and Unicredit, they should have been much more hands-on.

The three, however, felt that it was better to move late than never – they had to act and that was that. They suspected that Groenink would probably not agree with them and might well throw in the towel. Martinez had asked Joost Kuiper to take over in that eventuality as Groenink's successor. Kuiper said he was prepared to do so, as long as it was temporary; they'd already agreed on that the previous year, and the measure was clearly a temporary one.

Arthur Martinez cleared his throat. He felt deeply unhappy doing what he had to do, and doing it by phone was still worse. He had arranged with his deputy on the supervisory board to visit Groenink with Rob van den Bergh that afternoon to inform him of the coup.

Martinez explained as calmly as possible to the chairman of the managing board that the supervisory board intended to take over the process of selling the bank. It was in the interest of the bank and everyone involved. The consortium had to be given a serious chance. Martinez did his best to make the news more palatable by assuring Groenink that there was some understanding within the supervisory board for his opposition to the consortium. He went on, however, to point out that these feelings no longer made any practical sense. Groenink would have to surrender the leadership to him, André Olijslager and Rob van den Bergh. Martinez told Groenink that he had already run this past the supervisor and that the latter had given him the go-ahead.

After the mutiny of the general managers and of his managing board, Groenink now had to deal with a supervisory board that was in full revolt. He replied angrily that he thought it a breathtakingly stupid proposal. He was convinced that a transfer of power at this stage would suggest that the bank was on the verge of collapse. And if there was anything that was disastrous for a bank, it was the fear that it couldn't fulfil its obligations. Customers would desert in droves and the damage would be enormous.

For a moment Groenink considered resigning. After all, this was a clear motion of no confidence. Could he continue to do his job under these circumstances? But he was aware that the people he was surrounded by were running around like headless chickens and that this was not good for the bank. He thought it a betrayal of trust to resign under such circumstances. He was made of sterner stuff than Hugh Scott Barrett. He prepared for battle.

A couple of hours after Martinez's phone call, Olijslager and Van den Bergh met Groenink in his office to inform him of the plan. They didn't get a chance, however. The chairman was in a towering rage and launched into a fifteen-minute tirade against the governors. He painted a doom scenario for them, which they as governors would be held responsible for. He told them that his colleagues on the managing board would rise in revolt. The two governors allowed Groenink to let off steam and arranged to meet again the following day.

Groenink phoned Nout Wellink immediately and asked how the Central Bank's supervisor could have been so stupid as to go along with the suggestion of his governors. By taking a step like this, the outside world would think ABN Amro was no longer stable, that it was effectively bankrupt.

Wellink in fact agreed with Groenink. He defended himself, however, by explaining that with a request like this the supervisor could do little more than ask the governors if they were fully aware of all the implications of their actions. It was their responsibility after all. Wellink admitted, however, that the supervisor had perhaps not thought things through properly. It was extremely dangerous for a bank to have a crisis of management.

Blushing, those at DNB who were responsible acknowledged that they had acted somewhat clumsily. Arthur Martinez was contacted to let him know of these concerns. They told him that the markets could misinterpret a signal like this. Martinez realised that he had to backtrack a bit and his proposal would have to be modified correspondingly.

Olijslager and Van den Bergh then sat round the table with Metzelaar, who was the head of the department of mergers and takeovers for Stibbe and who was responsible among other things for drafting the reports of the meetings of the supervisory board. They would have to find another approach and they drew up a single page of guidelines for the three governors henceforth known as the transaction committee. It had to be made clear that from now on the initiative no longer belonged to Groenink. They arranged for Wilco Jiskoot to take charge of negotiations with the consortium. Every day at six there would be a conference call in which, besides the three governors, Jiskoot, Groenink and Boumeester would also participate. The events of the day would be analysed and they would draw up a plan for the next day. Olijslager would show up at the bank every week.

When Arthur Martinez informed the rest of the supervisory board that this was the best possible result after his discussion with Groenink, he was greeted with astonishment. The board had been prepared to drop Groenink. Nonetheless they accepted Martinez's explanation. Above all, they didn't want to hear of any more surprises from Rijkman Groenink. On paper maybe he was still the boss, but in practice he was now completely hedged in.

Martinez then told Groenink that the governors no longer felt that he was the proper person to maintain contact with the consortium. He told his chairman that it was impossible for him to ignore his feelings and it therefore made no sense for him to be in charge of these negotiations. He also told him that he intended to ask Wilco Jiskoot to sell the bank.

Groenink didn't entirely disagree. He found it difficult to talk to a man like Fred Goodwin, who had promised him on various occasions that he wouldn't undertake any hostile action. He agreed with the formation of the transaction committee while positing the condition that the final responsibility should remain with him. That was something that he would on no account renounce. He was appalled by the idea of Jiskoot, who in his view had done everything he could over the past months to ensure the failure of the deal with Barclays, should hold final responsibility.

Wilco Jiskoot was pleased that the governors had asked him to head the negotiations with the consortium. He was confident that from now on he would be listened to more than the others. He also thought that their choice was a logical one; he was certain that ABN Amro would get a better deal if the consortium was approached in a positive and friendly fashion. They were the party with the money and it made no sense to alienate them.

Huibert Boumeester, CFO and second-in-command on the managing board, also thought it logical for Jiskoot to head the negotiations. For him to conduct them would have been completely implausible, as it was he who had pushed for the deal with Barclays. He was, however, irritated that Arthur Martinez, who had kept his distance all the time should suddenly be the one in charge.

On 29 May, the consortium announced the details of their offer for the bank. Per share, ABN Amro would get 30.40 euros in cash and 0.844 RBS share. The consortium proudly declared that the bid ended up as 38.40 euros, a total of 71.1 billion euros. The offer was 13.7 per cent higher than that of Barclays. Merrill Lynch's advisers had confidently informed their clients that it was a bid that Barclays couldn't possibly trump.

Goodwin announced that DNB's advice would be heeded, that one bank, RBS, would be given final responsibility for the whole process. The offer would be made by a Dutch corporation invented solely for this purpose, RFS Holdings. RBS would get 38.3 per cent of the shares, Fortis 33.8 and Santander 27.9.

The three banks would contribute proportionate amounts to the takeover.

Goodwin meanwhile emphasised that Jean-Paul Votron had had some fruitful meetings with Wellink and Schilder. The central bankers had promised that they would treat the consortium objectively and impartially. It had also been announced that Merrill Lynch would guarantee the issue of the various securities, in some cases with the support of other banks, such as ING and Rabobank.

The latter piece of news landed among ABN Amro bankers like a bomb. They couldn't believe that their Dutch competitors were helping to finance this offer. Wilco Jiskoot seized the phone at once and contacted his colleague at Rabobank, Hans ten Cate, who had formerly worked at ABN Amro. The two had known each other for thirty years. Jiskoot started swearing at the Rabobank director, asking him how he had the gall to do such a thing. Ten Cate replied drily that he had never heard Jiskoot say no when he was able to earn a few euros somewhere.

There were more reasons for being angry with Rabobank. The local branches in Berkel-IJssel, Zutphen and Zevenaar had sent ABN Amro customers a letter suggesting they jump ship and joined Rabobank. 'If you are concerned,' the letter said, 'about developments in the banking world, for instance about the ABN Amro takeover, perhaps Rabobank, which is a cooperative society, could be the solution'. Rabobank head office told *Het Financieele Dagblad* that it regretted these actions and had requested its 188 branches not to be too obviously proactive in recruiting new customers.

To show that the ABN Amro managing board also cared about its customers, Rijkman Groenink travelled to the office on Kneuterdijk in The Hague and talked personally to a dozen worried customers.

Meanwhile, inside the bank itself, opposition to the takeover by Barclays was growing. It was increasingly dawning on the staff that they had precious little say in the matter.

During a session with the business committee group (GBC), Piero Overmars had listed the pros and cons of the takeover by Barclays versus those of the consortium. In the absence of Groenink and Boumeester, a number of directors concluded that Barclays was totally unsuited to them. Of course there was plenty of opposition to the break-up of the bank, but for the separate parts it might well be a good thing.

At the end of June, a small group of six of ABN Amro's bankers, mainly investment bankers, called for a closer look at Rothschild's calculations, to see whether remaining independent was a possible option after all. They had a horror, however, of being labelled bad leavers and didn't dare go public with their findings. In the end, fear of being caught red-handed, more than the need to tell their grandchildren later that granddad had taken a heroic last stand to save the bank, meant that they did go public after all. In their plan Wilco Jiskoot and Piero Overmars were named as the only remaining directors.

Various politicians and trade union leaders were approached for support, but the response was minimal. As the plan had been announced in the media, however, the bank was forced to respond. The managing board replied by saying that the story had been investigated from every angle but it didn't hold water.

Barclays also began to realise that the ABN Amro takeover was no longer likely. The gap of 8.6 billion euros was too large. Furthermore ABN Amro had now moved the goalposts, giving the consortium a definite window of opportunity.

In the British media jokes were made about John Varley and Fred Goodwin – that what they were really interested in was giving each other a drubbing. It was also implied that Barclays' CEO would shortly come up with a substantially increased offer for ABN Amro, just to let people know it was still hanging in there. It was doubtful, however, whether Barclays' shareholders still felt for it.

The United States hedge fund Atticus, which had a one per cent stake in the British bank, thought Barclays should abandon its bid and called the goal of the takeover 'an inferior enterprise'. 'We share the concerns of the market that Barclays' hunger for an acquisition may lead to raising your already generous offer', the hedge fund wrote in its letter to chairman Marcus Agius. 'It is clear that you are not the best person to own ABN Amro. The RBS consortium has offered significantly better prospects for synergy.'

Barclays was cautious not to provide any job guarantees. If the unions were to make an offer like that public, Fortis would immediately launch a charm offensive. On 15 June the Belgians promised that there would be no forced redundancies in the Netherlands. After three years about 7,000 jobs would be scrapped, but these could all be cushioned through natural turnover. In an interview with *Het Financieele Dagblad* on 21 June, Lex Kloosterman made the story sound even more attractive. He warned his former colleagues that, "Under Barclays the bank would just be a branch of a UK bank. We can offer more than that. Our proposal means that we intend to give the bank continuity."

On 26 June, the solicitor general Levinus Timmerman recommended to the High Court that the court order regarding the sale of LaSalle be quashed. Timmerman stated that ABN Amro's managing board was within its rights to sell the bank. In about three quarters of cases the appellate court tends to comply with such recommendations.

VEB didn't wait for the High Court's verdict but went on the attack. It lodged a request with the court to sideline both the managing and supervisory boards and to appoint three independent governors to supervise the sale of the bank. VEB argued that the management of the bank was no longer credible and that it had up till then acted far too one-sidedly in favour of Barclays. It accused the supervisors that by failing to act decisively, they had allowed a crisis of confidence to arise with both shareholders and staff.

In a piece in *Het Financieele Dagblad*, VEB director Peter Paul de Vries asked why the governors had simultaneously approved of the sale of LaSalle and the merger with Barclays on the afternoon of Sunday 22 April, when they knew that a meeting had been arranged with the consortium for the following Monday. He answered his own question, 'I can only think of only one explanation. The supervisors had turned a blind eye to the attempt to force through the merger with Barclays by means of a poison pill.' De Vries pointed out that Martinez was to be rewarded by being appointed chairman of Barclays.

The trade unions voiced their agreement with VEB's criticisms. In *Het Financieele Dagblad* they were quoted as calling the merger decision 'irresponsible' and 'slipshod'. The union leaders labelled the sale of LaSalle 'reckless'.

Groenink was furious. He didn't understand the action; in his view none of the shareholders benefited from it and it would only lead to more delays and uncertainty. A day after the allegations he phoned Fred Goodwin, asking him if Goodwin supported the demands of VEB, something that Goodwin denied.

During a closed meeting of the confederation of Dutch industry VNO NCW, Rijkman Groenink was asked to state his case. Groenink emphasised the advantages of merging with Barclays.

In the hall, the former head of the supervisory board Aarnout Loudon was profoundly disappointed by the state of affairs. He felt that he had retired too early. In hindsight, he thought that appointing Martinez as his successor had not been such a sensible idea after all. An American probably couldn't appreciate the importance of this deal for the country and would tend to pay more attention to shareholders' interests. He felt that a Dutch president would have achieved a better result in the merger discussions between ABN Amro and ING.

Loudon regarded Cor Herkströter as most to blame for the failure of that merger. In February and March, the head of ING's supervisory board had made himself unavailable for too long. He was also angry with ING governor Godfried van der Lugt, who in his view had done all he could to block the merger. He also thought that Rijkman Groenink had not done anything like his best.

After Groenink had told his side of the story, Loudon raised his hand and suggested frankly that the failure of the merger with ING had been a missed opportunity and that Groenink hadn't done enough to make it happen.

Groenink felt this public criticism from the man with whom he had worked intensively for so many years as a stab in the back. He was, however, aware that he had to restrain himself; he couldn't afford to lose his temper here. Instead he was short with him, saying that while he could understand Loudon's feelings, he was obviously speaking with insufficient information.

Meanwhile, inside the bank ten thousand employees were trying to imagine how it would feel to work for managers from the UK, Spain, Scotland or Belgium. From one day to the next they oscillated between the alternative possibilities. Rijkman Groenink endeavoured to preserve the peace by writing little notes to his staff, complimenting them on continuing to do their work so well in such uncertain times.

Jan Peter Schmittmann sent all the Dutch customers a letter in which he promised that the provision of services would remain as good as ever. A huge advertising campaign in the national papers with the headline, 'ABN Amro is Still Here' explained to customers and staff alike that the 21,000 people who work for the bank will continue to provide the same services in the future. 'It is true that changes are going to happen, but they won't be at the expense of all these people with their skills and experience. On the contrary, that is precisely what attracts our future partners. Whatever happens in the near future, one thing is clear as daylight – the soul of ABN Amro will live on.'

On Friday 13 July, the High Court quashed the LaSalle verdict. A sigh of relief was heard in the board rooms of Holland. A spokesman of Bank of America even spoke of it as a victory for the whole country. "The Dutch business community can breathe again. A purchaser who is buying in good faith must be sure that he gets what he has paid for. If the Court of Appeal had decreed that LaSalle couldn't be sold without the shareholders' consent, no foreign firm would do business with Holland any more."

Rijkman Groenink was also relieved. He was again interpreted as having kept within the bounds of the law in selling LaSalle at such short notice. All he could do now was to see whether the consortium would throw in the towel. After all, Goodwin had been mainly interested in the bank's North American activities. Groenink warned his colleagues in a letter, however, that there was still a long way to go.

In the managing board Wilco Jiskoot had already calculated that the consortium could use the yield of LaSalle to increase the cash part of their offer. If the consortium hung on in there, they would win the battle with Barclays even more easily.

Shortly after the verdict Groenink phoned Fred Goodwin, wanting to know the consortium's position. Goodwin told him to be patient a bit longer.

Maurice Lippens, who at the request of Goodwin and Botin often went with his chairman Votron to the most important discussions, also felt unhappy. The Fortis chairman was not persuaded that Fred Goodwin would keep the offer on the table now that LaSalle had gone to Bank of America. Behind the scenes hard work had been done for quite some time to keep RBS on board, with Merrill Lynch's banker, Andrea Orcel, playing an important role.

Lippens was especially grateful for the support of Emilio Botin. The Spanish banker told Goodwin that Santander and Fortis would recover their losses from RBS if he were to break off now. Fred Goodwin changed his mind and decided that, even without LaSalle, the yield of which would go to RBS after the ABN Amro takeover, enough synergy would still be gained. While RBS calculated that the bank could realise 2.9 billion euros in synergy if LaSalle was included, Goodwin still expected to end up with 1.7 billion euros in synergy benefits on the basis of the takeover of the corporate banking activities and especially the bank's global transaction services.

Goodwin first phoned Martinez and then Groenink to tell them this. The battle for ABN Amro went on. He announced that the consortium would soon make a new offer that would again be higher than Barclays' and expressed the hope that ABN Amro's managing board would recommend the bid to the shareholders, even though it was still hostile.

When Groenink heard this he swore quietly. He realised he had lost and that this was the end of the bank. Only a miracle now could prevent the consortium from breaking up ABN Amro. It was curtains for his bank.

At ABN Amro they were now certain that the consortium would go on fighting even without a recommendation. Groenink again phoned Wouter Bos, asking him to tell the consortium they weren't welcome and that he would turn down their offer on grounds of prudence. The minister was astonished by Groenink's tone. It was a form of power play he wasn't used to, as though Groenink was talking to him like a schoolboy. He thought it weird, to put it mildly, that someone with a direct interest in the matter should ask a minister, who operated within certain legal parameters, to eliminate an opponent. It simply wasn't done to talk like that.

On Sunday 15 July, Goodwin again phoned Martinez and Groenink to inform them of the new offer. The consortium was still offering 38.40 euros per share, but 93 per cent of the total bid was now in cash. The three banks in the consortium were confident that their rival Barclays could not possibly trump it. The improvement was made possible by the sale of LaSalle – those billions of dollars would go to RBS. Martinez and Groenink promised Goodwin that the offer would be treated in the same way as that of Barclays.

At the last moment, VEB withdrew its suit against ABN Amro in which it called for the entire board to be replaced by three independent governors. The shareholders' club explained in a press release that, 'We are reassured by ABN Amro that the sales process will take place in an open and transparent manner.' A day earlier DNB had appealed to the president of the court to reject VEB's request, because it wasn't in the interest of any of the parties concerned, including the shareholders. According to the Dutch Central Bank, VEB's request 'was rashly jeopardising the stability of the bank'.

Over the past weeks, Wilco Jiskoot had had a number of talks with the consortium. It struck him that relatively little information had been asked of ABN Amro. The confidential due diligence audit was limited. He also noticed that the Scottish, Spanish and Belgian banks were keeping a close eye on each other. Clearly it was costing a lot of energy to keep the consortium on the road. Sometimes it looked as though they didn't want any new information about the fortunes of ABN Amro. Any information might upset the delicate balance in the troika.

Jiskoot, however, also understood that they couldn't request too much information either. The consortium was kept busy buying shares on the stock exchange and profiting from the fact that investors still had their doubts about the chance of success of the offer, which meant that the market value was relatively low. If they were to request confidential information, they risked being accused of insider trading.

There were more obstacles. With RBS and Fortis in particular there was some uncertainty about whether their own shareholders would back and finance the takeover bid. It was also not yet sure that DNB would give its declaration of approval. Doubts among investors meant that the bank's share price was still a good ten per cent lower than the consortium's offer.

On Friday 20 July, Rijkman Groenink announced publicly that he was throwing in the towel. In an interview with NRC Handelsblad he said that he was taking account of the fact that the consortium might win. He emphasised that he felt that a merger with Barclays was substantially better, but that the UK bank's offer was too low. The tone of the interview was somewhat grudging.

He said that he didn't have a seat at the negotiation table because he wasn't clever enough. Asked when he expected to join the negotiations he replied, "Never, I think. The consortium still wants to know some things about us and ABN Amro has still not had any answer to the questions we asked at the beginning of May. The consortium needn't lose any sleep about us, and so far it hasn't done so. We will have to talk with them." Later on in the interview he said, "We don't agree with the plans of the consortium and they haven't discussed them with us either ... They have made an offer that is substantially higher than that of Barclays. Let's not beat about the bush; the difference is too great for investors even to consider Barclays' offer."

He went on to say that, "Some people claim that I have a financial interest in Barclays' offer. But my financial interest in that of the consortium is of course much larger – it offers more money. That's a nonsensical argument, but then I don't agree with most of what has been said about me and the bank. Take the decision of the court forbidding us to sell LaSalle without the consent of the shareholders. One thing I do know is that there's no shortage of experts to tell us what to do ... what I really get angry about are those sneering remarks about the bank; they are so denigrating and so untrue. The bank hasn't underachieved at all; it's done excellently in comparison with similar European banks."

When the journalists asked why there had been so little protest in Holland against the splitting up of ABN Amro, they hit Groenink in a sore spot. "That's something that really makes me angry," he said. "The mentality that says it serves them right that they are being broken up, it's so Dutch. In every other country public opinion would have rallied behind this bank. But here, even the Socialist Party adopts free-market positions that in London you wouldn't find even in the City. Everyone here is quick to judge someone else, instead of coming to a carefully considered opinion. This is a country with half-baked opinions."

Three days later Barclays increased its bid, while also making it clear that they expected to lose this battle. The British bank announced that China Development Bank and the Singapore investment company, Temasek had bought an interest in the bank. For a total of five per cent they paid 3.6 billion euros. If the takeover were to go ahead, they would get an extra stake with a total that might rise to something more than 10 per cent. The yield enabled Barclays to raise its bid by 2.9 billion, with the cash part increasing to 37 per cent. Varley announced that this was their final bid. "We can't dollop any more cream on the cake," he said. The bank would now have to decide whether it would continue to recommend Barclays' offer to its investors. It hoped it would be just enough to make the difference.

That was the item on the agenda on Friday 27 July during the final strategy session of the managing and supervisory boards. The eighteen men and one woman knew that whatever happened, the bank would be broken up. It was an emotional occasion, but business was business and had to be done.

It was clear that the recommendation of the Barclays offer to their share-holders no longer held water. The consortium said that on the basis of their superior offer it now had the right to the managing board's recommendation. Without it the bid would remain hostile. A recommendation would diminish the risks of the offer, making financing it easier and therefore cheaper. Furthermore the shareholders of the three banks still had to agree to the takeover bid. They would be more easily persuaded if the offer was indicated as friendly by ABN Amro.

The head of the supervisory board had drawn up a balance sheet. ABN Amro in fact had had disappointing results since 2001. You had to earn the right to survive and to remain independent. The bank's underperformance had lasted too long. There were plenty of sharks in the sea and they had tasted blood. He also realised that the supervisory board should have been much more aggressive and that they should have replaced Rijkman Groenink earlier. If he had dismissed Groenink in the summer of 2006, it would have bought ABN Amro time to develop a new strategy. It was easy to be wise with hindsight, however. One thing Martinez was clear about was that, given the circumstances, the consortium's bid had much to recommend it.

There was plenty of resistance, however. Rijkman Groenink and Huibert Boumeester in particular were totally against it and refused to recommend the consortium's offer. They didn't believe in their strategy and thought it irresponsible to recommend it to their shareholders.

Martinez was irritated that Groenink and Boumeester had wanted the press release to state in more or less concrete terms that the consortium's offer was not good for the bank and that they still perceived it as hostile. He thought this was arrant nonsense. ABN Amro had no future if left intact. And the shareholders would be happy with this result.

The stalemate continued for four hours. Groenink and Boumeester won their colleagues in the managing board over with the argument that Barclays would immediately capitulate if the consortium's bid were recommended. If that happened, the consortium could then lower their offer and all would be lost. Once again the bankers expressed their anger with their short-sighted governors. Allard Metzelaar and Alexander Pietruska in particular took a long time to find the right, most neutral wording on paper.

On Monday 30 July, the managing and supervisory boards in their update on the offer for investors stated that 'the intended merger with Barclays was in accord with ABN Amro's earlier announced strategic standpoint ... but that, viewed from a financial viewpoint, we cannot recommend Barclays' offer to the shareholders, while we acknowledge the strategic advantages of a combination with this bank'.

About the consortium's offer, the directors wrote that, 'The present value of the offer is attractive for the shareholders of the bank but there are a number of significant risks attached. Although the acquisition risks are in broad lines comparable to those indicated for the Barclays bid, important questions concerning the intended break-up of ABN Amro and the way it should be done remain unanswered.'

The report then concluded, 'We do not yet find ourselves in a position to recommend either of the two offers to the shareholders of ABN Amro.' It was arranged with Barclays that the merger protocol, which contained a recommendation, should be altered.

At the presentation of the half-yearly figures on the same day, Groenink couldn't keep his mouth shut. He predicted that the three banks would have conflicts of interest as soon as they got their hands on ABN Amro. "The break-up will bring with it, not just one appalling risk, but a combination of a whole number of risks."

Three days later Het Financieele Dagblad reported that Rijkman Groenink had advised Fortis investors to vote against the takeover at their shareholders' meeting. "Fortis," he was quoted as saying, "is paying too much for ABN Amro. If the takeover goes ahead, the market value of Fortis will sink still lower."

A day later, Goodwin said he was dismayed by Rijkman Groenink's statements. Fortis also expressed its displeasure. 'The statements are in conflict with the neutral position that ABN Amro had adopted on Monday.'

A day later ABN Amro, RBS, Fortis and Santander issued their first joint press statement. It stated that the consortium accepted the explanation that the chairman was quoted incorrectly. Rijkman Groenink had had no intention of advising Fortis shareholders how to vote. In the same statement they announced that from now on the talks would take on a constructive character.

Despite another steep decline in its own share price, Barclays had not quite given up the fight. Barclays director Frits Seegers told Het Financieele Dagblad on 2 August, "When we announced the deal with China Development Bank our price was 7.50 pounds. Then the whole story of the United States mortgage loans undercut our figures. The result was a market correction." The price of a Barclays share was now 7.20 pounds and it would have to rise to 7.90 if it were to match the bid of the consortium. John Varley visited the bank's head office in Amsterdam for a final charm offensive. He dined with the managing board and the general managers. It was a weird meeting. No one believed that the love between ABN Amro and Barclays would ever be consummated; the engagement would shortly be broken off.

ABN Amro's directors asked Varley why he was still so persistent. Varley explained first of all in friendly terms that one who said A was obliged to say B as well. He then continued in a grimmer tone, saying that if the market were to collapse, he hoped it would happen so dramatically that no deal would take place at all. A number of the general managers suspected that John Varley was mainly unhappy at the thought of losing the battle for ABN Amro to his arch-rival Fred Goodwin.

On 3 August, the founder of TCI, Chris Hahn, phoned Charles McCreevy, the European commissioner for the internal market. The shareholder still had his worries that the Dutch supervisor would not judge both offers equally. He asked McCreevy to urge Nout Wellink to do so. TCI meanwhile was worth four per cent of the shares. If the deal was settled with the consortium, the hedge fund would soon gain 200 million euros.

On Monday 6 August, the Fortis board met twice with the shareholders, once in Brussels and once in Utrecht. Three-quarters of those present were for the merger. The bank would have to launch a new issue of stock amounting to 13 billion euros at least. Investors would welcome the move eagerly. The Fortis directors felt confident about the result of the vote. In July the bank had approached 130 of its major investors. These institutional shareholders were good for 80 per cent of Fortis's stock and they would have to agree to the merger. Financial director Gilbert Mittler told *Het Financieele Dagblad*, "Their conclusion is that what we are involved in makes an incredible amount of sense." He wasn't wrong. The Belgian part of the bank voted 95 per cent in favour of the merger.

A couple of hours later 519 shareholders arrived for the meeting in the Karel Appel Room at Fortis's head office in Utrecht. They represented 39 per cent of the votes. While U2's 'Where the Streets Have No Name' was booming dozens of times down the loudspeakers, Lippens, Votron, Mittler and Kloosterman climbed out of the helicopter and walked onto the platform a few minutes later.

Count Maurice Lippens was at his most charming. He spoke of the historic character of this meeting. He recalled the Dutch King Willem I who was present at the founding of three of the societies in the 1820s that later became known under the names, Generale Bank, AG 1824 and ABN Amro. These three societies would now probably be brought together once again by Fortis, assuming, that is, that the shareholders thought it was a good idea.

Lippens reminded his audience that up till now Fortis had succeeded with the takeovers of ASLK, MeesPierson, Generale Bank and the insurance firm, Stad Rotterdam Verzekeringen, doing better than the expected synergy on each occasion. "We have shown that we have the capacity to guide a major complex operation through to a good result. Of course 24 billion euros is a huge sum, but you have to pay a price for quality. The price is a correct one and there is work to be done. We must present a united front and that will require discipline and a high degree of professionalism." Lippens was full of praise for Jean-Paul Votron, whose efforts had shown "that we are capable of pulling this off."

Just before these meetings with the shareholders, Lippens had an urgent conversation with Votron. The two men discussed the increasingly negative reports about the financial markets. Confidence was waning. In Germany both the finance ministry and the German Central Bank had sounded the alarm. One German bank, IKB had to be hauled back from the brink of bankruptcy after it turned out that some 3.5 billion euros of United States subprime loans had not been paid. The United States housing market was plummeting. The same problem had caused two hedge funds of the renowned United States commercial bank Bear Stearns to keel over. On 2 August Jochen Sanio, the director of the German banking supervisory authority BaFin, warned of a systemic crisis, "This could lead to the greatest crisis since 1931."

Lippens had asked Votron whether he thought that Fortis was not heading into trouble. The Fortis chairman was afraid that he was steering his ship full speed ahead with too much ballast on board into a storm. The chairman and the CEO urged each other not to lose their nerve. They persuaded themselves that they were purchasing the least volatile piece of ABN Amro. It would all work out all right, they argued. It was too good a chance to miss. They could do it.

In Utrecht, Votron did what he did best and sold the deal. "It isn't every day that we get the chance to become the biggest bank in Benelux and number five in Europe." Votron showed how in 2010 Fortis would realise 1.3 billion euros in synergy, with 80 per cent coming from cutting costs. Adding that amount to the profitability of the part of ABN Amro that fell to Fortis, 1.2 billion euros, came to 2.5 billion euros. Votron argued that Fortis would actually be paying less than ten times the profit of this target. This, admittedly optimistic, calculation irritated some of his audience. After all, you can't base your calculations on results that you hope to book in the future. Fortis actually paid twenty times the profit.

Votron turned for a moment to the years he'd worked at ABN Amro. "I know what I'm talking about from personal experience. ABN Amro is one of the best banks in the world. If we buy into it we know exactly what system we'll be ending up with; there's an extremely detailed business transition plan already in place." Should any shareholder feel timid about the differences in banking culture, Votron assured them, "I see the difference in banking culture as an enrichment for us." Asked about the potentially strict Dutch tax laws, he said, "We have spoken with the Dutch tax authorities ... they also see that what we are planning has a historical value ... we can sleep easily." And when the issue of the Dutch Central Bank was raised, he said, "We are working full-time on it. We are confident that we can comply with the requirements."

In Utrecht too the victory was massive; 96 per cent of the shareholders supported the motion. As far as they were concerned, the takeover was on.

All eyes were turned now on the Dutch Central Bank. While Fortis shareholders were giving their blessing to the takeover, the board was holding a marathon meeting. On Monday 6 August, Nout Wellink, Arnold Schilder, their fellow directors and external advisers met from nine in the morning to nine at night. First on the agenda was the request by Barclays.

The DNB board was worried. For a while the barometer had been pointing towards bad weather. Back in April they had done a stress test to see what would happen to the markets if credit dried up and confidence disappeared. The supervisor didn't need to be told – they were in for a storm.

On 9 August, the European stock exchanges took a beating, with average losses of 2.5 per cent. The banks no longer trusted each other, and were unwilling to lend each other money. The direct cause was the news that BNP Paribas, the largest bank in France, had frozen the assets of three investment funds. It said that it was no longer able to fairly value their underlying assets as a result of exposure to United States subprime mortgage markets. Central banks in Europe and the United States pumped billions into the system. The European Central Bank offered commercial banks the possibility of taking out virtually unlimited amounts of money with a short maturation period. Some 95 billion euros was made available. They hoped in this way to prevent credit from freezing. The president of the Dutch Central Bank was now convinced that the problems in the financial markets could only grow worse.

On 13 August, the Dutch Central Bank issued a declaration of no objection to a merger with Barclays. Wouter Bos adopted the bank's advice. On 15 August, Chris Hohn upped the pressure on both parties to do the same for the consortium. In a letter addressed to Bos, Wellink and the European commissioner for competition, the shareholder said that, after the declaration of no objection for Barclays, it was of the utmost importance that the same declaration should be issued for the consortium.

Hohn pointed out that all the banks involved were entirely reputable and that they were supervised by 'extremely professional supervisors'. They had plans to integrate ABN Amro in their own business. 'Actually the two offers differ in only one regard – namely that that of the consortium is far and away superior to that of Barclays.'

He argued that as a result of the increasing stress in the financial markets ABN Amro could do with a strong partner. 'The consortium,' he stated, 'is financially stronger than Barclays, which risks biting off more than it can chew with the takeover of ABN Amro.' Hohn concluded by stating that, 'TCI will not accept it if the Dutch Central Bank or the ministry of finance refuse on unreasonable grounds to grant or to delay granting a declaration of no objection to the consortium. In that case we will not hesitate to resort to every legal means to recoup our damages. These damages could amount to 10 billion euros.'

Meanwhile, chaired by Wellink, meetings were continuing at fever pitch at the Dutch Central Bank about whether to grant the consortium a declaration of no objection. All possible scenarios were considered with pros and cons being scrutinised in detail. Sandwiches were brought to the table at noon. Sometimes the discussions continued into the night.

The proposals of the consortium, the financial capacity of the banks and the financial crisis were minutely analysed. The consortium cooperated by answering all the new questions to the best of its ability. The arrangement was that there could be no decision while discussions were still going on.

The most recent news of the financial crisis fed into the discussion. On 17 August Asian markets fell by the largest amount since the attack on the World Trade Center. On 24 August, ING predicted that borrowing money would become more costly not only for large firms but also for medium and small businesses.

The supervisor was constantly coming up against new uncertainties and questions. Special attention was often paid to Merrill Lynch's guarantees. The central bankers asked the United States investment bank to show them the contracts that supposedly guaranteed the financing of the takeover. Wellink felt unhappy about this issue. Was Merrill Lynch strong enough to take the strain itself and how resilient were the parties behind the guarantee? Merrill Lynch's bankers were asked to give an account of themselves.

On 28 August, VNO NCW and the finance ministry invited various captains of industry to meet them at the prime minister's residence, Catshuis, to talk about whether Holland was being sold down the river. It was a closed meeting. Rijkman Groenink was also invited.

The civil servants involved were struck by the lack of warmth with which the bank was discussed. No one said anything about whether ownership should be kept in Holland. Nor was any appeal made to the ministers present to save the bank.

Groenink saw that each party was entrenched in its position; this cabinet had decided that this wasn't a sell-out. Nonetheless he couldn't restrain himself from warning those present. He remarked that there was a dangerous trend operating in the country by which legislators, the Tabaksblat Code, public opinion and the judiciary had become overly anxious about the rights of shareholders. The result has been the loss of Stork and VNU and now ABN Amro was in similar dire straits. Groenink saw that he had angered the minister of finance. Bos told him drily that this wasn't his analysis of the situation.

On 3 September, Bos gave an interview to *Het Financieele Dagblad*. He guaranteed that Barclays and the consortium would receive equal treatment, adding, "In theory a declaration of no objection should be granted unless you can give good reasons why you don't intend to issue one. If you're not going to give a declaration you must have solid arguments." To the question why there was no room for a political discussion of the matter, he replied. "This situation is unprecedented. We learn through our mistakes whether the rules are adequate. Once the dust has settled, there will surely be some matters that will need adjusting."

The minister made it clear that he felt no need to keep the bank in Dutch hands. "It would be a great pity if the activities of the bank depart from our borders, but who owns the bank is a secondary matter. I have no intention of artificially struggling to keep Dutch companies Dutch. Sentimental patriotism can lead you up the garden path. It often results in old, traditional, large-scale firms being protected instead of encouraging young innovative ones."

A few days later both Wouter Bos and Rijkman Groenink addressed the first congress of the Holland Financial Centre in the Spiegelzaal of the Concertgebouw in Amsterdam. The Holland Financial Centre was a pressure group set up a couple of months previously by the banks, the supervisors and the government. Groenink warned of the sombre situation that prevailed in the Netherlands. He complained about the lack of funding for education and the limited support for innovation. He said that the country didn't exactly provide fertile soil for international businesses. With a smile he added, however, that Barclays were happy to have Amsterdam as the location for their head office in the case of a merger. Bos said that Holland had to become one of the leading financial centres in the world, after London, New York and Tokyo. "Our ambitions," he said, "are not modest; our aim is to create an innovative and competitive international financial services sector."

As the credit crisis spread, the fears of ABN Amro's directors grew. By now they were exhausted and they were in a race against the clock. Arthur Martinez, who had flown back and forth to Amsterdam almost twenty times in 2007, suspected that the crisis might thwart their plans. The head of the supervisory board feared that the consortium would lower their offer, reducing it to 32 euros per share. Or, worse still, that the consortium would fall apart, which would be a real nightmare. Now that the bank had retracted its recommendation for the Barclays offer, it was by no means certain whether ABN Amro could return to it later.

Discontent among RBS and Fortis shareholders was increasing as the markets declined. Compared with 12 April when the consortium announced its intention to make an offer for ABN Amro, Fortis had lost 23 per cent of its value and RBS had fallen by 20 per cent. Only Santander remained steady. On 10 September the British press reported that 10 per cent of RBS shareholders were bitterly opposed to the takeover. They complained that the part of ABN Amro RBS was planning to purchase was the most vulnerable. ABN Amro's shareholders were shocked by this news and the shares of the bank fell by 2 per cent to 33.10 euros.

It was only three weeks before the deal was to be signed and all the obstacles seemed to have been removed. And yet the reigning emotion was doubt. This was demonstrated in the decline in the bank's share price. The consortium had promised to pay 38.40 euros per share, while ABN Amro's market value was 14 per cent below that. The staff of the bank didn't have any faith in the takeover either. In an enquiry organised by the trade union, De Unie, 55 per cent of the 6,000 members of staff who had filled in a questionnaire supported a 'stand alone' scenario and 39 were for a takeover by Barclays. Only six per cent supported the break-up of the bank.

Nout Wellink paid one more visit to Bos to inform him of his doubts about the break-up of the bank and to warn him of the worldwide decline of the markets. He wondered what this would mean for the banks involved in the takeover. Would they have the capacity to absorb ABN Amro?

The minister assured him that what was involved was three healthy European banks, all of which had their shareholders' approval for the takeover. There was no reason to suppose they would back down. He asked Wellink whether the banks had done their best to get their documentation in order and Wellink said that they had.

Bos told him that he would not query his judgment if he felt a takeover by the consortium was not advisable, for instance, because of the pending credit crisis. If the president of the Dutch Central Bank decided not to grant a declaration of no objection to the consortium, he would go along with that.

Bos thought that Wellink would not dare give negative advice on his own initiative. He had received a great deal of criticism over his remarks about the

TCI letter. Furthermore negative advice could be contested in the courts. The law is drawn up in such a way that a declaration of no objection is granted unless there are good reasons for not doing so.

On 14 September, Nout Wellink was at the meeting of European finance ministers in Oporto. He said that in a worst case scenario the financial crisis might cost 1,200 billion euros, nine per cent of the total amount of all the balance sheets in the banking system. "If all the banks were to evaluate their credit portfolios it was completely unclear how much they would have to write off," Wellink told *Het Financieele Dagblad*. "The question is, what would you get back on the balance sheet, 50 or 55 per cent? No one can say for certain."

Wellink called the problems on the money market "a process of adaptation that could last months and which is extremely troublesome. Accidents on the way cannot be excluded. The financial system, however, should be able to take it. There are sufficient reserves of cash. It is, however, uncertain at what moment the banks with surpluses will dare to lend money to other banks. Trust is the key." Next day the British mortgage bank, Northern Rock, sent out an emergency signal and issued a profit warning. In the media there were photos of long queues of customers waiting to withdraw their savings. The Bank of England had to come to the rescue.

On Sunday 16 September, the supervisors of the Dutch Central Bank met again to talk about the declaration of no objection. The shareholders' meeting would take place in four days; the central bankers would have to decide now.

It could have gone either way. The spokesmen of the Dutch Central Bank had had instructions to draft two communiqués, one with an affirmative answer and another in case the answer was negative.

During these final marathon sessions the question on the table was whether a postponement of the declaration of no objection would have to be requested. After another heated discussion, it was decided that this could only add to the uncertainty about ABN Amro's future. It was also evident by now that all kinds of legal proceedings would begin. TCI's announcement was clear on this point.

Prompted by recent developments on the markets, all the risks were run through one more time. The issue was what could and what couldn't be done from the viewpoint of the supervisor. The conditions that it was thought he could go along with were fine-tuned. It was agreed that the declaration would be valid only if the offer had been agreed to before 31 December 2007. Moreover, a detailed plan should be made available within two months of the takeover to be presented to the Dutch Central Bank for approval. Furthermore, the troika of banks would be required to ask permission again at every stage in the break-up and assimilation of ABN Amro.

At the end of that Sunday Nout Wellink finally reached his conclusion, namely that the consortium would be granted a conditional declaration. In any case ABN Amro would acquire new shareholders; what they could do with the bank would be decided on stage by stage.

On Monday 17 September Wouter Bos adopted the advice of the Dutch Central Bank. He said that he had never thought of not granting the declaration. "But then the financial crisis broke out," he said, "and we have followed its progress with some concern." The break-up of ABN Amro had become inevitable.

The consortium responded that they had no problem in complying with the conditions. "The conditions come as no surprise," said a Fortis spokesman. "We have the utmost confidence that we can comply with them."

At the end of Monday afternoon the Fortis directors met in a restaurant on the A10 in Belgium. Their relief was great and about twenty men raised their glasses in a toast. The meeting was, however, a little subdued.

On the evening of Thursday 20 September, Henk van der Kolk, the chairman of the FNV, the largest trade union, was standing with a bullhorn in his hand in front of the Doelen conference centre in Rotterdam. As the shareholders of ABN Amro trickled into the hall for this informational meeting, a handful of them stopped to listen. Van der Kolk said that he thought it a disgrace that a firm with so much history should have become a plaything in the hands of the financial world. "The shareholders have too much power; everything today revolves around money. And the employees suffer the fallout. We won't let this pass!"

Traditionally poorly organised in the banking world, the trade unions seemed not to know what role they could play in this battle: especially because ABN Amro had already resigned itself to the takeover. Van der Kolk therefore argued that the ordinary bank employees should be given job security and the right to a takeover bonus, the same as the directors.

As at the previous meeting, Irene Groenink also attended this one to lend her husband moral support. In his account of recent developments, the chairman concentrated mainly on the analysis, explaining in a lacklustre tone why the bank had to be sold. He told the shareholders that "the choice to renounce our independence had been carefully prepared in 2006." He went on to explain how in April of this year the shareholders had sent a clear message to the managing board by voting overwhelmingly for TCI's motions. He gazed sternly into the auditorium, "And then the consortium developed its offer. As a board we had to return to TCI's motion that you backed as shareholders."

He continued with barely concealed emotion, "Should we let go of this bank? Can we allow this identity to be lost? These are existential questions that the managing board has asked many times. We have come to the conclusion that merging with another bank is better in the medium term." He explained that it was impossible for his board to recommend the offer of the consortium, "We never wanted it. The bid by Barclays, however, no matter how well it suits us strategically is not large enough, so we cannot recommend that either. We cannot ask you to bridge the 14 per cent gap with the offer of the consortium out of your own pockets."

Groenink returned to the demands that the shareholders had put to him and the board back in April. "You wanted us to split up the bank should that be necessary to obtain the maximum yield ... ladies and gentlemen, we have complied with the demands."

Two days later he was admitted to hospital with a burst appendix. To his profound regret, he had to take it easy for two weeks.

Jan Kalff didn't agree with Groenink. Appearing on RTL Z TV he vented his criticism. "This is the worst possible scenario," he said. "With a merger much of the bank would have remained intact. This is no longer the case. I am extremely distressed and disappointed. I don't blame TCI or any of the shareholders for stating their views. That has to be allowed. What upsets me is that this letter landed in such fruitful soil. The problem should have be been solved in the eighteen months prior."

Kalff was also angry with the politicians. "It really astonished me," he said, "that no action was taken either by the cabinet or by VNO NCW. Where was the finance ministry that was so keen to promote the Netherlands as a country to set up businesses in? How are you supposed to encourage foreign businessmen to settle in Holland, if you don't intervene? This would never have happened in France, Germany, Italy or Spain."

Fortis meanwhile had been given the go-ahead by Brussels. The European Commission required that there should be a fourth competitor in the Netherlands and Fortis therefore was expected to put about 10 per cent of the Dutch part of the bank up for sale. Fortis decided that it would hive off Hollandsche Bank Unie, thirteen consultancy offices and two corporate client units. This would cost money, however. Fortis would pay about twenty times their profit and the compulsory sale meant they would get a much smaller return. The items for sale, moreover, were still located in the heartlands of the Dutch bank (in Amsterdam and Eindhoven, for instance). It wouldn't be easy just to get rid of them. Lippens wasn't put off, however; Brussels could have made many more demands. He had the idea that the European Commissioner, Neelie

Kroes, who was Dutch, would have liked to be more obliging to Fortis, but that the people in her department didn't let her.

Within ABN Amro this report was viewed with horror. The new owner would be slicing off pieces that were close to their heart, something that was technically almost impossible. After anger, however, came resignation. Fortis was the boss.

On Friday 5 October, Barclays announced that only 0.2 per cent of the ordinary shares had been tendered and they withdrew their offer. John Varley sent a letter to the roughly 400 advisers who had supported Barclays over the past months. In it he said that the Barclays team had fought the good fight and that 'we should have won, because we played the better game', only to conclude by saying that 'the definition of winning has changed.'

On Wednesday 10 October, the consortium announced that their offer was unconditional. Votron, Botin and Goodwin paid a visit to ABN Amro's head of-fice. At the same time the bank issued a statement announcing Rijkman Groenink's resignation. Arthur Martinez explained, 'Rijkman Groenink de-serves a great deal of praise for the services he had rendered the bank in a ca-reer of more than thirty years. Under his chairmanship ABN Amro has been transformed into a tightly knit organisation with a distinct focus on the mid-dle market sector of commercial and private customers. The offers ABN Amro has received are a good reflection of our solid results, the increased profits and value that have been generated over the past years. During the takeover process this year Rijkman Groenink has given the bank imperturbable leader-ship under great pressure, with the result that we have stayed on course under difficult market circumstances. On behalf of the entire staff of ABN Amro I would like to offer heartfelt thanks to Rijkman and wish him a splendid future in both his work and his life.'

In his final letter to the staff Groenink, who was just convalescing from his appendectomy, said, 'Mergers and takeovers are always accompanied by diffi-cult and sometimes painful decisions and this one was no exception. The con-sortium had always made it quite clear that ABN Amro could not continue in its present form. I have had the honour to be the chairman of the managing board over the past seven years. It has been a weighty, sometimes difficult po-sition and a genuine privilege. I am confident that the power of ABN Amro that has such deep roots in the culture and history of the bank will be transferred to our three purchasers. Our culture, values and standards and our way of working will be reflected in Royal Bank of Scotland, Santander and Fortis.'

Next morning the roughly 108,000 employees received another letter, this time from the new owners. 'Dear colleagues', it read, 'this is an important mo-ment for all of us. The combination of our businesses will unleash formidable competitive forces in every market. The scale of what is possible is exciting. The challenge now is to realise this together. We will begin today.'

On the evening of Tuesday 16 October, some seventy directors of ABN Amro belonging to Rijkman Groenink's circle dined together at Duin & Kruidberg's restaurant. Confusion reigned – were they there to honour Groenink's departure or was this more a kind of evaluation of the process they had all gone through over the past months? Surely the real farewell to the chairman of the bank would take place somewhere like the Concertgebouw with at least 1,500 people attending. The rumour spread like wildfire that the consortium was not willing to give Groenink his golden handshake moment.

Groenink had in fact chosen this small-scale occasion himself. In two weeks' time he would formally have lost all control over the bank. He had no desire to organise any big public event now his bank was under new ownership. It was this or nothing.

There was a strange atmosphere in the restaurant. The intention was for Wilco Jiskoot to speak, something that some colleagues felt unhappy about. They knew that Jiskoot was angry with Groenink – angry because of his failure to communicate adequately over the past period and also because of his arrogance towards his colleagues. Right to the end Jiskoot and Groenink were polar opposites.

This split between the two leading players, endlessly debated by the senior staff of the bank, made those present curious as to what Jiskoot would say. A few of them had observed that Wilco Jiskoot could also gaze at Groenink fondly. The investment banker was aware that in all these years, Groenink simply hadn't known what he was supposed to do with ABN Amro. Groenink was a leader who at heart lacked confidence and who had increasingly painted himself into a corner.

Jiskoot, however, didn't show up. He had cancelled at the last moment due to family problems. Joost Kuiper was asked to toast the departing chairman instead. He got up to speak without having had any time to prepare, and everyone could see that he wasn't enjoying himself. He struggled to find the right words and made a joke that nobody thought funny, about how lazy the chairman was. He also paid his former boss some compliments. He spoke of his courage and his great perseverance.

Kuiper felt hopelessly uncomfortable. He remembered that it was important in speeches like this to exaggerate a bit. He told Groenink that he had been a splendid leader. On sitting down he was greeted by lukewarm applause.

At the end of the evening it was Groenink's turn to make a speech. He repeated what everyone knew already, that the decision for the bank to give up its independence had been taken with great care and in consultation with the governors. He said that he was exceptionally proud of the fact that they had built a bank together that had had so great a value and for which so much was being paid. He emphasised that he had gone to work with great pleasure every day over the past thirty-three years. He told his audience that he greatly regretted that many of them would lose their jobs and that he wouldn't be there for them any longer. In conclusion he tried to cheer them up by saying that if they'd been able to put up with him for so many years, they'd be capable of taking anyone on in the future.

When he had finished speaking, he was greeted with silence. There was no response. Jeroen Drost couldn't bear it and stood up to applaud. Robin Boon followed his example and, after a little hesitation, the rest followed. It was all over.

Next morning the Dutch parliament reviewed Rijkman Groenink's retirement bonus. By cashing in his shares and options he had made some 20 million euros. He also received a bonus of twenty-two monthly salaries – another 4.3 million euros. The name Groenink kept on turning up and the politicians spoke as one about their distaste for this "scandalous example of self-enrichment." It was a rare phenomenon, as parliament does not normally discuss individual cases.

Wouter Bos spoke of it as "an absurdly high sum of money", but the managing board defended Groenink against these accusations. 'There isn't a scrap of evidence that they hadn't acted correctly. The directors of ABN Amro consistently made the case for a takeover by Barclays, even though they were better off with one by the consortium.'

A majority of the members of parliament asked the minister to take action against what it called perverse incentives and to ensure that in future company directors should not profit personally from a takeover of any of their firms that were listed on the stock exchange.

There was also plenty of criticism of what many of the members saw as the passive attitude of the ABN Amro supervisory board. They appealed that the governors should ensure that rewards like this were no longer permitted. None of the politicians expressed any concern about a potential fallout from the break-up of the country's most important bank.

Many ABN Amro bankers took stock of the situation with mixed feelings. Rijkman Groenink was not the only member of the staff who had earned a great deal of money from the break-up of the bank. In exchange for their options and shares, a total of roughly 1.4 billion euros was paid to the staff. About one billion of this went to senior executives. A rumour circulated in the bank that general managers had received an average 7.5 million euros.

Many of the general managers and department managers thought it only right that they were finally given a generous bonus. They had worked hard for years without their bank ever becoming one of the top ten banks in their peer group, let alone the top five. After seven years they had achieved that status all at once but in the cruellest way. Furthermore the shareholders had also been generously rewarded. On the other hand they felt distressed and humiliated. They had worked for years for their bank and now it had suddenly ceased to exist. Many of them would have given up the money if it meant they would get their bank back – the bank they had worked for half their life and to which they owed so much.

On 30 October, another farewell dinner was held with the supervisory board. Arthur Martinez had arranged for all the governors and managing directors to be given a handsome souvenir in the form of a gold Baume & Mercier watch. On the back was engraved: ABN Amro 1824-2007.

The chairman thought it was in poor taste. You give someone a watch when he retires. He also felt the inscription was offensive. On the penultimate day of his chairmanship, Groenink had no desire whatsoever to celebrate when what was involved was the downfall of the bank. Any feeling of pride was conspicuous by its absence.

Groenink didn't have it easy. The entire national trauma and the related whirlwind of negative publicity seemed to have landed on his plate. All the accusations stuck to him and him alone and he was spared none of the anger. He told colleagues that it didn't affect him and that he was used to it. The media didn't like him and never had. For years he had thought that his surroundings in the bank were too dull to attract their attention. It was obviously his personality that they found interesting. He noticed that it suited the people around him that all the shots were aimed at him. So be it.

He also didn't feel the need to defend himself. Of course he was hurt. He would have infinitely preferred to have had the Barclays shares instead of the almost 25 million euros he now received. He couldn't accept the fact that the bank had been broken up. Where had everything gone wrong?

It didn't take long for him to make his analysis. He concluded that he had made a few major mistakes. On taking up his post in 2000 he had been far too euphoric about Arrow. He would have done better to have waited calmly for the figures and then taken a decision about the bank's strategy; then that ignominious volte-face would not have been necessary. Above all, he thought that he had taken too long dissolving the wholesale sector of the bank. He had also listened too much to Wilco Jiskoot.

At the end of 2004 he shouldn't have allowed himself to be talked round by

Aarnout Loudon. He should have largely closed the corporate banking division and forced Jiskoot's resignation by saying it was either him or me. He hadn't done so because he had thought there was enough time, and that he would succeed in calling the corporate banking division to heel.

He also regretted the takeover of Antonveneta. The temptation of finally having a successful takeover after all the misfortunes and malaise had been too strong. Strategically it had made sense, but tactically it was a mistake. Investors didn't understand it; they only saw that the profit-share ratio had deteriorated. The last remnants of confidence among the shareholders faded away then.

When the former chairman of ABN Amro looked back on his own functioning as chairman of the managing board, he saw himself as someone who had been too trusting. He had been too ready to believe the people around him when they promised that they would book certain results. He thought that the criticism of his colleagues that he had been too much of a loner was nonsense. It would have been better if he had been. As chairman of the board he had tried too hard to find a compromise, always out of a need to avoid disastrous splits. That he hadn't succeeded in this was a disgrace. The break-up of the bank had never been inevitable.

He realised that he had won every battle in his career, except this last and most important one. The bank had disappeared and he felt responsible. He would have to learn to live with that, but he had no doubt that he would succeed. The pain he felt was similar to that of the hunting accident of twenty years ago. He had had to learn to live with that too. Groenink recalled the doctors who had warned him then that nine out of the ten victims of an accident like that would have had to retire from active life. He hadn't accepted that scenario then, nor would he do so now. He felt grateful that it wasn't in his character to be like that. It made no sense to sit and ponder after that sort of setback. He also had far too much energy to do any such thing.

He looked forward to being in the thick of things once again. He had a splendid post on the supervisory board of SHV (a company where Antony Burgmans had also just become a governor). The seat on Shell's supervisory board had also not yet been filled; perhaps they would ask him after all.

For the time being he had plenty to do at home. There was a lot of wood that needed chopping. He liked his domestic duties and enjoyed being with his children. Not all that long ago he had told himself that it was important for his sons to defeat him now and then.

Epilogue

6 October 2008

Jan Kalff turned his mobile off with a sigh of relief and focused on enjoying the rest of his holiday. For the past few days the retired banker had been standing around the Aya Sofia and Topkapi Palace in Istanbul on the phone, discussing the future of ABN Amro. Three major firms, institutional investors and a private equity house had asked him to advise them about possibly taking over Fortis's ABN Amro subsidiary. Five to ten buyers were considering laying out between 7 and 10 billion euros.

Kalff was trying to ensure a future for the remaining 22,000 ABN Amro employees and had already offered his services to the Dutch Central Bank (DNB). They didn't need his help yet, though. The bank's domestic retail operation was already back in Dutch hands.

The Dutch prime minister, the minister of finance and the president of the Central Bank had negotiated deep into the night of 2 and 3 October to temporarily nationalise Fortis's activities in the Netherlands, including ABN Amro. They had no choice. Less than a year after the takeover, Fortis was on the verge of bankruptcy. Last year's predator had itself become a prey. And so all at once, its 45,000 bankers and insurers were civil servants.

The three men who had failed so miserably to understand each other last year, when ABN Amro's future lay in the balance, stood firm and united at the microphone that Friday, 3 October. Their message was clear: what went wrong in 2007 would now go right. "We have ensured that the Netherlands will retain key financial activities," finance minister Wouter Bos explained.

Bos emphasised that many of the problems really lay under the surface in the Belgian half of Fortis. "We have cordoned off the healthy parts of the Dutch bank from a possible infection. The cash that this generates on the Belgian side will enable them to resolve their problems."

Fortis needed that money. It was one of the high-profile victims of the credit crisis that had now reached hurricane strength. It had all gone wrong from the moment the Belgian bank-insurer had transferred 24 billion euros to ABN Amro's shareholders in October 2007. While the division of the bank had made ABN Amro's shareholders rich, it had made Fortis's shareholders poor. Many investors lost between 80 and 90 per cent of their outlay.

Nothing the Belgians did could persuade the world to see the potential in their acquisition of ABN Amro. The credit crisis had forced Fortis to write off huge amounts of debt; billions of euros were needed to shore up its balance and enable it to integrate ABN Amro. As the share price sank, they began to re-alise at Fortis that they would have to ask for another huge injection of cash from their investors.

In September the president of the Dutch Central Bank, Nout Wellink, had become increasingly concerned. Especially since he would have to give the go-ahead in the first week of October for the actual integration of ABN Amro by Fortis. There would be no going back.

In October 2007, Wellink had agreed to the takeover and the new share-holding, but a condition had been attached: the new owners would have to put their own house in order before they could integrate ABN Amro. In the months that followed, the DNB president had seen the very events unfold that he had most feared. At 24 billion euros, 19 billion of which was pure goodwill, Fortis had paid far too much for ABN Amro. Investors no longer believed in it. While the poor communications skills of the people who ran Fortis annoyed Wellink, growing numbers of major clients lost faith entirely and turned their backs on Fortis.

In late September, the DNB president had warned Bos: it would be irrespon-sible to let Fortis absorb ABN Amro Nederland. The finance minister agreed. At last the two men were talking the same language; they decided to take swift action to secure the Dutch bank.

On Friday afternoon, 26 September, the vulnerability of Fortis was laid bare for all to see when a visibly stressed CEO Herman Verwilst, who had succeed-ed the sacked Jean-Paul Votron in June, announced that the bank had lost at least 3 per cent of its clients. Verwilst hammered home the message that the bank was solid and solemnly promised the assembled journalists that Fortis would not go bankrupt. That same evening, Verwilst was replaced by Filip Dierckx. The third CEO in three months.

Fortis was on the verge of collapse. Its imminent liquidity crisis could only be resolved by pumping in billions of fresh capital. The president of the Euro-pean Central Bank, Jean-Claude Trichet, travelled to Brussels to beg the gov-ernments to intervene. Wellink and Bos were already there.

Fortis chairman Maurice Lippens put all his effort into getting his bank in its entirety under the French umbrella of BNP Paribas. In response, Bos and Wellink asked ING to take over Fortis as a whole.

But BNP Paribas and ING's corporate bankers were staggered by what they found, especially in the Fortis's Belgian operation. They were astonished at the lack and poor quality of the available information. But above all, they were shocked by the scale of a problem that many other banks had also been wrestling with since the start of the crisis: the so-called collateralised debt obligations (CDOS). Fortis had over 40 billion euros of obligations covered by collateral whose value had become ephemeral as a result of the credit crisis. Because of the absence of trust between financial institutions, there was no market, so there was no price, and so it was impossible to establish value. Moreover, the collateral was extremely complex; it was one debt financed by another, and that by yet another. The true underlying value was almost impossible to trace.

ING and BNP Paribas bankers feared that the takeover would leave them with billions of euros of debt that they would simply have to write off. So they proposed in the negotiations to place these bad debts in a bad bank and to cut them loose from the rest of the bank. But when it became apparent that the governments weren't willing to guarantee all or even part of this, the French and Dutch bankers ran a mile.

It was clear to the governments and the Belgian supervisor CBFA that Fortis would need a lot of money to survive and that this would have to be supplied by the state. Fortis could not be allowed to fail; it would leave millions of account holders in Benelux penniless.

The Belgian and Luxembourg governments were the first to fork up around 7 billion euros in all. The Dutch waited. Only after the Belgians had agreed to the sale of ABN Amro (its domestic business and private clients units) by Fortis, did Bos okay a capital injection of 4.1 billion euros, in exchange for a 49.9 per cent stake in the Dutch half of Fortis.

That Sunday night, pressure was brought to bear on ING to at least take over ABN Amro's Dutch operation from Fortis. Since the European Commission had made it clear that strict conditions would be attached with regard to market dominance (just as when Fortis had taken over the bank), a major, and costly reorganisation would be inevitable. ING proposed to pay a maximum 5 to 7 billion euros for the proffered parts of the bank.

That offer was rejected. With 22,000 employees and a profit of 1.3 billion euros, the bank would be worth at least twice that: about eight times profit. ING chairman Michel Tilmant felt he couldn't ask that of his shareholders. At that moment, they were paying no more than five times profit per ING share.

Liberation Day, was how Dutch bankers described 29 September, the day they heard that Fortis would have to sell ABN Amro. In one branch, the ABN Amro flag was carried in triumphantly. The relief was enormous: there had been little love in this marriage.

Jan Peter Schmittmann, chairman of ABN Amro Nederland and responsible for integrating with Fortis, was also happy to be rid of the Belgians. For a year he had sat in on countless tortuous meetings with them. Time and again the Dutch had seen how the people at this Mickey Mouse bank had no idea what to do with ABN Amro's state-of-the-art expertise. Meanwhile, the Dutch arrogance had made the Belgians furious. The conflicts were endless.

That ABN Amro managers, many of whom had done rather well out of the takeover, were being told what to do by Fortis managers who had been informed that due to the current malaise there would be no more bonuses for a the present, didn't help matters either.

Yet the relief was accompanied by doubt. What Fortis was divesting was a purely Dutch bank. It was too small to give major clients the services and products they needed. Many managers were convinced that the bank would be unable to survive on its own. They were pleased when they heard that DNB would for the time being not okay the sale of 10 per cent of ABN Amro Nederland (around 1,000 staff) to Deutsche Bank, as demanded by Brussels.

There was little time for planning. The calm that the three governments had hoped to buy with their capital injection was still a distant prospect. On 29 and 30 September, another huge wave of cash withdrawals hit Fortis. New liquidity problems brought the parties back to the negotiation table on Tuesday evening.

By now the Dutch government knew it would have to go all the way. Even Balkenende, the prime minister, had concluded that the state could no longer leave the problem to private initiative, given the risks and the continuing crisis. To quell the alarming fear that was gripping savers and especially large corporate clients, the government would have to nationalise Fortis Nederland (both bank and insurer) and ABN Amro Nederland.

The government's opening offer was around 12 billion euros. In the tough discussions – Balkenende's description – that followed the Belgians eventually dropped their demand to 16.8 billion euros. A price that conformed with market levels, according to Bos. Fortis advisors disagreed, and pointed out that the whole of Fortis was only valued at 14 billion euros on the stock exchange. Apparently, the Dutch operation was worth more than the whole bank with the Belgian and Luxembourg sections combined.

Nout Wellink was relieved. Even though he realised that his treasured ABN Amro had been dismantled and that it was never coming back, it would still be possible to rebuild the bank in the Netherlands, a bank that would continue the ABN Amro name.

For many overwhelmingly conservative ABN Amro bankers the shame was now complete: first the management failed, then the bank was partially taken over by a buyer they had never taken seriously and now it was state-owned. Surely only the weak get nationalised?!

Schmittmann had foreseen the possibility. He was happy that it would bring a period of rest. This was the time to build. For Schmittmann it was clear that the integration with Fortis would now proceed with ABN Amro in the driving seat. Although he found Wellink's suggestion that the integration should be fast-tracked and might produce synergy benefits of 1 billion euros annually, optimistic.

Schmittmann felt that the new ABN Amro should try to move out from under its government umbrella as soon as possible. It was in essence a commercial organisation. Moreover, state ownership distorted its competitive position. He estimated that this would be realised at the earliest in late 2009 or early 2010. He was also 90 per cent sure that the bank would then have to look for a new partner. A partner with a network and state-of-the-art expertise in global markets and global products. Perhaps Deutsche Bank, or maybe RBS. It might be possible to enable the new bank to stand on its own feet in a strategic alliance with the Scots. This could be explored now. The two banks knew each other intimately by now: in the course of 2009 the bank could start outsourcing the Scots.

Schmittmann believed that the taxpayer wouldn't need to worry. He estimated that the new banks would make a profit of around 2.5 to 3 billion euros a year. Once the market entered calmer waters, the bank-insurer would easily be worth 20 to 25 billion euros.

For Wilco Jiskoot, nationalisation was the best solution in the short term. Of course he hoped that the bank would soon be back on its feet; a strategic alliance with RBS was certainly not unrealistic. But he warned the new-style ABN Amro: look for more than just one partner, spread the risks, otherwise this would turn into a truck system.

In sharp contrast to the relief among ABN Amro's bankers was the anger and frustration at Fortis. Little remained of the Fortis brand. Less than a year ago they had marched into ABN Amro with raised heads to teach the arrogant ABN Amro bankers a lesson. They felt humiliated and furious with their directors. Especially Maurice Lippens.

Hans Bartelds, who had set up Fortis over eighteen years before together with Lippens, understood their anger. He felt sympathy for his former colleagues. What had happened to the bank was terrible; he hoped for a period of calm and reflection, for space to examine what had gone wrong. He had emailed Maurice Lippens and had given him some personal encouragement, expressing the hope that the time would come when the Belgian count would come to terms with his loss.

That wouldn't be soon though. By the time the negotiations drew to a close on Sunday 28 September, Lippens was no longer present. He was too tired. Anyway, there was no need for him to be there. He was being deposed. That day, the Dutchman Jan Michiel Hessels took over as chairman of the board.

Maurice Lippens was suffering. In many ways. As shareholder, the adventure had cost him around 30 million euros. A lot, but he could absorb that. What really hurt was the loss of trust which people had placed in him. It had evaporated. A walk in the street, a bicycle trip was out of the question: accusing looks from his fellow Belgians spoke volumes. The disgraced count had been branded in the press as a model of hubris and megalomania. Belgians were deeply disappointed in their colossus, the man who had promised them the biggest Benelux bank.

Above all, the suggestion that he had been driven by pride to take over ABN Amro was particularly hurtful. He hoped that his tombstone would one day read that here lay a man who was not weighed down by hubris. Because the gods never forgave hubris. Rijkman Groenink had been proud, not he. Genuinely not. Maurice Lippens assumed that now he had left Fortis, everyone would have forgotten about him within three months. He could see his own position in perspective. A sense of humour was essential to carry on.

Lippens had also learned that history constantly repeats itself. He had decorated his office at the Fortis building, opposite King Albert's palace, with pictures of historic events. He had used one, a print by Jean-Pierre Le Roy entitled *Triumphal Entry of Willem 1 of Orange-Nassau into Brussels in 1815*, in December 2007 on a card to business contacts, to wish them a happy new year. He had added a text to the print: King Willem 1 of Orange-Nassau had contributed to the establishment in the 1820s, of three companies that would subsequently become known as AG 1824, Generale Bank and ABN Amro. Those three institutions were now in 2007 all part of Fortis.

He only got to enjoy that for a short while. Lippens hoped that he would some day get the opportunity to show that he had only wanted one thing: to build something good for the country, for Benelux. Something that was right. And that the taking over part of ABN Amro had been right strategically, he was still convinced of it. After Amro's attempt to merge with Generale (1989) and then ABN Amro's attempt to take over Generale (1998), third time had to be lucky. It should have placed Fortis in the first division of European banks. But his Fortis had collapsed. It was small comfort that his choice of rescuer, France's BNP Paribas, would become Belgium's biggest employer on 5 October for the price of 14.5 billion euros.

Most of the banks involved in the dismantling of ABN Amro were in trouble. Fortis's partner, Royal Bank of Scotland, had been brought to its knees. The Scots had already written off almost 16 billion pounds. Compared to a year before, RBS's share price had plunged 80 per cent. Rumours that the problems at RBS (and Barclays) were far from over continued to circulate.

Faith in Goodwin was also beginning to crumble. Here too, people were asking whether the takeover of ABN Amro hadn't been driven by pride. The head of RBS's supervisory board, Tom McKillop, had already declared that they had paid too high a price. Goodwin termed it a purging experience. But the Scot still insisted that the takeover had been a strategically sound move. He informed his investors that the integration was going well and would produce results even sooner than expected. Analysts surmised that Fred the Shred wouldn't have to fear for his position if he really did manage to produce synergy benefits faster than anticipated.

How quickly the Scots would manage that was still unclear. Goodwin said little to the media. In February 2008, he had commented, almost with relief, that ABN Amro had run an extremely old-fashioned operation. He had been surprised by the lack of coordination. In an interview with Dutch journalists he had said that, "When I walk into a room, I can pick out the ABN Amro people just like that. All I need to do is ask how business is. An ABN Amro banker invariably starts talking about earnings, an RBS banker starts with profit." Goodwin believed that there was enormous room for cuts.

Merrill Lynch, architects of the takeover, didn't survive the credit crisis. In late 2007, the investment bank was still crowing about the ABN Amro deal. 'Our commitment to complete this high-profile transaction demonstrated a new level of partnership in investment banking.' The bank itself earned around 500 million dollars on the deal and ensured that none of the main players did badly. It was reported that Andrea Orcel and Matthew Greenberg both took home 25 million dollars. Joost Scholten, who had drawn up the figures with Huibert Boumeester the previous December while enjoying a pleasant glass of wine, received around 10 million dollars.

Not many of their colleagues were as lucky. In the year following the ABN Amro deal, Merrill Lynch had to write off at least 50 billion dollars' worth of bad debt, sack thousands of staff and watch as the share price tumbled. On 14 September, Bank of America took over the world's biggest equity house in a share trade worth 50 billion dollars that was done and dusted in the blink of an eye.

That same Black Sunday, the 158-year-old firm of Lehman Brothers filed for bankruptcy. A couple of months earlier, JP Morgan, supported by a Fed loan of 30 billion, had taken over the ailing Bear Stearns.

And a few days after the collapse of Merrill Lynch and Lehman Brothers, Goldman Sachs and Morgan Stanley asked to be allowed to become regular banks. The money they needed for their deals had become too expensive. Only regular banks are allowed to accept savings, something investment bankers had eschewed for decades. The price for this new status was that all the major corporate banks would now come under Fed scrutiny. Deal makers and traders would have far less space to organise risky transactions.

'End of investment bank era', *Het Financieele Dagblad* headlined. All five bulge bracket investment banks, for years the inspiration for ABN Amro bankers such as Wilco Jiskoot and Rijnhard van Tets, were finished. Two old-school ABN bankers found it hard to suppress a smile as the news sank in. Former ABN Amro chairman Rob Hazelhoff enjoyed the irony that even Merrill Lynch had been taken over. He considered corporate banking the icing on the cake in a universal bank. And you have to be careful with icing, it can go off.

For his successor Jan Kalff, the epitome of the universal bank ideal, this was the proof that this much-derided concept of a large retail bank combined with an investment bank had been rehabilitated. He believed that it was now obvious to all that investment bankers should be kept on a tight rein. They shouldn't be allowed to call the shots.

Wilco Jiskoot believed that large banks would always need the ability to advise clients on mergers and acquisitions and to launch shares on the market. This would never change. He hoped that banking would be better regulated in future and expected that some of the extremes would disappear. There should in any case be a greater focus on organising downside risk: corporate bankers and traders would have to feel it in their pocket if they created and offered products and services that resulted in large losses.

The corporate bankers were not the only ones to feel the pinch. JPMorgan Chase's analysts calculated that European banks had written off 116 billion euros, globally the figure stood at around 520 billion. Many believed that this was just the beginning of a massive purge.

In recent months across the world, governments had been nationalising and providing capital and guarantees. In the United States the government had acted vigorously. Freddie Mac and Fannie Mae, together holding half the country's mortgages, were rescued with 200 billion dollars of taxpayers' money. In return for a capital injection of 85 billion dollars, insurance giant AIG handed the country a 79.9 per cent stake. American treasury secretary Henry Paulson received the green light to buy up 700 billion dollars' worth of bad loans.

Europe's governments followed suit. Some set up a similar emergency fund, others guaranteed their citizens' savings.

The world no longer trusted bankers and the awareness had grown that something fundamental had to change in the way banks did their work. They had to start putting clients first again.

In the last twenty years the focus had shifted at almost all major banks from winning the trust of clients in the long term to winning the short-term trust of shareholders. Growth and quarterly figures and the accompanying bonuses had become sacrosanct. The attention and energy of many bankers had shifted from the relatively simply equation of risk and profit, to increasingly risky activities. Activities that very few understood or trusted.

The Fortis ABN Amro debacle had unleashed a discussion in The Hague about how to restore trust in banks and bankers. On the day of the state opening of parliament, 16 September, finance minister Bos wrote in NRC *Handelsblad*, 'Government is not powerless. Supervisors are being given new authority. New regulations for financial institutions and caps on top incomes are being put in place by governors, unions, shareholders and parliament.'

Nout Wellink was pleased. For years he had been ridiculed for saying that banks shouldn't aim to maximise shareholder value because it was account holders who had the most money in the bank. He had tried to convince The Hague that banks weren't like ordinary companies, they provided a public service and politicians had to get involved. The future of banks couldn't be left to market forces. The people who ran the big banks knew full well that the state would have no choice in the end but to rescue account holders.

The DNB president knew also that it was his job as supervisor to prevent bankers from acting irresponsibly and taking unreasonable risks. He accepted some of the blame himself too. If Wellink had known in 2003/2004 that ABN Amro was planning to scrap its protective construction to woo its shareholders, he would at least have complained. He was sorry that he hadn't been sufficiently aware at the time of what was happening.

That's why Wellink wanted to focus more on raising standards on supervisory boards. In the ten years that Aarnout Loudon had led ABN Amro's governors, Wellink had never once spoken to him about the state of affairs at the bank. This had to change. Wellink had told the finance minister that in future, the DNB supervisor would be screening bank governors not just for reliability but also for expertise. It was crucial that governors knew how a bank worked.

DNB got started immediately. The new bank needed a new supervisory board that would maintain a balance between the demands of its sole shareholder and the requirement from Brussels that temporary nationalisation shouldn't unduly influence the Dutch market. European commissioner Neelie Kroes had made it clear: the board had to be independent.

Rob Hazelhoff knew just what the new governors had to do: they had to ensure that the bank would be led by people with both feet on the ground. Bankers who provided simple products and above all realised that they were ordinary working people. Employees earning a reasonable salary. Salaried managers who worked for the bank as a whole, not just for themselves.

Hazelhoff was delighted when he read in the press of growing doubts about the CEO model. ABN Amro's growing acceptance of the CEO mentality and the disappearance of a sense of collective managerial responsibility had been, in Hazelhoff's view, one of the bank's biggest mistakes. That was what had started ABN Amro's senior executives working to their own agenda and had allowed division to hamstring the board.

ABN Amro's first chairman, Roelof Nelissen, was convinced that it was the excessive bonuses which bankers had received that had really caused the trouble. As the greed increased, a climate emerged in which bankers took ever greater risks. Risks that they were able to take because, as he saw it, there had been far too little control. The coming period would be one of sobriety.

For Kalff, perhaps the main lesson of the whole credit crisis was that the management of a bank had to devote personal attention to the managing the risks that the bank was taking. He couldn't emphasise it enough: each week the bank's managing board had to examine the risks, collectively, in detail. And that meant the principal credits too.

Dull, reliable bank managers; transparency and comprehensible services. That's what parliament wanted too. In the debate on the rescue of ABN Amro and Fortis, minister Bos was asked how it was possible that the go-ahead had been given in September 2007 to an institution whose solidity had apparently not been properly investigated. The minister explained that the whole world was trying to figure out that problem and emphasised repeatedly that there were many lessons left to learn.

Bos had already wondered at a far earlier stage whether the government shouldn't have played a more active role in the merger talks between ABN Amro and ING in late 2006 and early 2007. He had set up an inquiry to assess if the ministry had been too passive, just after he had become minister. Based on conversations with the main players, his staff had concluded that after February, Wellink and Groenink had been living in fantasy land. Whether or not the ministry should have contacted ING, it was clear that there was not much the minister could have done.

At ING, the failure of the merger with ABN Amro still left mixed emotions. They had their hands full with the crisis: many were actually relieved. Yet some had their doubts: an ING ABN Amro combination, formed in a friendly merger, would have stood strong in this storm. Perhaps ING should have been less timid?

Some ING managers wondered why, if the merger had been more or less on equal terms, Rijkman Groenink couldn't have been allowed to chair the combined bank until 1 January 2009. A gesture like that would have won considerable time in the negotiations. In the knowledge that Michel Tilmant would succeed him, and that the leadership would *de facto* revert to ING. Then the Netherlands would have had one of the world's biggest banks on home territory.

ING chairman Michel Tilmant had learned lessons from the affair. He had been astonished by the weakness of ABN Amro's supervisory board and its consequences. Tilmant would be requiring better quality and greater involvement from his own governors. A new president had already been named in the person of former Philips director Jan Hommen.

Cor Herkströter hadn't waited for the shareholders meeting; on 1 January 2008 he called it a day. Not least because his wife had pointed out to him that since his retirement they hadn't been on holiday together for longer than three weeks. Herkströter believed that ING bankers had plenty to thank for the caution with which they had handled the proposed ABN Amro merger.

That if nothing else, at least ABN Amro Nederland would survive, breathed new life into the club of former managing directors. They needed it. The 45 men (and one woman), three-quarters of them once with ABN, had been devoting considerable thought to whether the members of the last managing board should be allowed into their club. A questionnaire had revealed that almost half the former directors, among them Hazelhoff, would resign if Rijkman Groenink and his fellow board members were admitted. They still held their former colleagues to blame for the collapse of the bank.

Groenink was disappointed when he heard that he wasn't wanted. However, Groenink, Jiskoot and Kuiper were welcome at the informal club of former Amro directors. That Amro directors had kept contact all those years came as a big surprise to their former ABN colleagues, some were shocked. There had never been a separate ABN directors club.

It dawned on the ABN set: that disdainful Amro cowboy culture had apparently been stronger after all. Some former ABN bankers felt bitterly that their former Amro colleagues had gambled away the bank, that they had had no respect for the 183 years of heritage which had been left in their care.

To their former Amro colleagues, this was nothing but nostalgic sentiment. It wasn't nice that ABN Amro had been sliced apart, but they were more concerned with analysing the causes. It had simply not been possible to turn ABN Amro into an efficient, well-run bank, to convince the shareholders and investors that the bank really had potential. It was logical: in the absence of performance and trust, the bank would inevitably fall.

The men who had turned off the lights at the bank in October 2007 had also been picking up the pieces in their own way. Of all the former managing board members, only Ron Teerlink had survived the dismemberment. He now sat on the group executive management committee of the Scottish bank and was responsible for RBS's entire back office.

Hugh Scott Barrett joined Capital & Regional, a London property investor, as a director in April 2008. Scott Barrett had sworn never to visit Holland again. Piero Overmars had set up a pleasant office near home. From there he worked as a consultant for companies and charities. After those brief, hectic years, Overmars had promised to devote more time to his family. Huibert Boumeester had also had enough of working full-time in bankland. He planned to work as an investor, in the background. Joost Kuiper had retired and was enjoying his family and sailing. He had also started studying history.

Wilco Jiskoot felt that the people around him had suffered more from the collapse of the bank than he had. What's done was done, he preferred not to dwell on the past, he wanted to focus on tomorrow. Jiskoot had no wish to serve as a governor in industry, that much was certain. If he had learned one lesson it was that governors were far too distant from their companies. Jiskoot wanted to be involved and work as an investment consultant. He had been in touch with Marcel Boekhoorn, one of the country's most successful informal investors. Jiskoot knew Boekhoorn well: over five years ago, he had advised him to take the former Ahold chairman Cees van der Hoeven on board.

Wilco Jiskoot had no desire to talk to Groenink about what had happened. They had never had that conversation in all those last seven years. He didn't particularly care how his former boss was doing.

Rijkman Groenink's attitude to Jiskoot was equally indifferent. Less than a year after his departure from the bank he still had little contact with his former colleagues on the board. He occasionally spoke to Joost Kuiper and Huibert Boumeester. He saw Jan Kalff a couple of times a year; they were both on the board of ABN Amro's historical archive foundation.

At 59, Groenink saw no chance of a return to banking. He hoped he might find a few interesting positions as governor, but realised that after all the bad publicity, that might have to wait a while. He had joined with investor Marcel van Poecke to set up an investment company to promote alternative energy.

Groenink had been deluged by emails, text messages and voicemails towards the end of September, all with the same message: you were right! The news that their interminable problems had more or less forced Fortis to sell ABN Amro, proved what he had said all along. After all, it had been his expertise in special credit and solutions for problem cases that had propelled his career in the bank. He had never believed that Fortis could carry ABN Amro. He had warned the politicians in The Hague and Fortis's shareholders time and again.

Groenink felt that his former opponents, Fortis directors Maurice Lippens and Jean-Paul Votron, should have started counting their cents when the credit crisis erupted in August 2007. Then they would have realised that a hostile takeover of ABN Amro was too heavy a load for Fortis. He believed that it had been a combination of ego, ambition and frustration that had driven the takeover and so the carve-up of ABN Amro.

In fact Groenink was surprised how long Fortis had held on. The former ABN Amro chairman felt that, apart from the bankers, the supervisors and politicians had persuaded each other that everything was fine far too long. They had been blind. They had nurtured an illusion for the public that had been cruelly unmasked when Fortis was revealed to be on the verge of bankruptcy and had come cap in hand to the state. From then on, public trust had evaporated.

For a moment, a year after his fall as the last chairman of ABN Amro, he reflected blithely. The hunter who had bagged him was now the prey. Perhaps a small plaster on a big wound: the awareness that it was under his command that the great ABN Amro had been lost.

References

Besides interviews with people directly involved, key sources include annual reports, SEC filings, press releases and ABN Amro statements of the last seventeen years.

Other sources include files half a metre thick of confidential internal presentations to the managing board and supervisory board, as well as the neatly arranged issues of all manner of internal publications kept at ABN Amro's historical archive.

Apart from printed editions, extensive use was made of online archives of *Het Financieele Dagblad, NRC Handelsblad, de Volkskrant, De Telegraaf, Elsevier, FEM Business, The Wall Street Journal* and *Financial Times*. Occasional use was also made of the media archive of NOVA and Radio 1.

Also consulted were piles of reports by analysts from Merrill Lynch, JP Morgan, Morgan Stanley, SocGen, Deutsche Bank, Barclays, ABN Amro and various other institutions.

Bibliography

Associatie van Business Coaches, *Hofnar en Schatbewaarder. Tien leiders over Executive Coaching*
Philip Augar, *The Greed Merchants. How the Investment Banks Played the Free Market*
William D. Cohan, *The Last Tycoons. The Secret History of Lazard Frères & Co*
Dalai Lama and Laurens van den Muyzenberg, *The Leader's Way*
Dominic Dodd and Ken Favaro, *The Three Tensions van Marakon consultants*
Mariëlle Hageman, Stefanie van Odenhoven and Ludger Smit (eds), *De Bazel, Tempel aan de Vijzelstraat in Amsterdam*
Manfred Kets de Vries, *Wat leiders drijft*
Jonathan A. Knee, *The Accidental Investment Banker*

Niccolò Machiavelli, *The Prince*

Marcel Metze, *De geur van geld*

Stefaan Michielsen and Béatrice Delvaux, *Zes huwelijken en een begrafenis, grote en kleine geheimen van de Belgische haute finance*

Mike E. Nawas, *Management van fusie en integratie. De vorming van ABN Amro*

Emilie van Outeren, *Tussen bank en schip*

M. Simon, *De strategische functie typologie*

Joh. de Vries, Wim Vroom and Ton de Graaf (eds), *Wereldwijd bankieren ABN Amro 1824-1999*

Index